CLASS DIVIDE

8/22/15

To Bob Byron —

with best wishes

Howard Gillette

CLASS DIVIDE

YALE '64
AND THE
CONFLICTED LEGACY
OF THE SIXTIES

HOWARD GILLETTE JR.

CORNELL UNIVERSITY PRESS
ITHACA AND LONDON

First published 2015 by Cornell University Press
Printed in the United States of America

Library of Congress Cataloging-in-Publication Data

Gillette, Howard, Jr., 1942– author.
  Class divide : Yale '64 and the conflicted legacy of the sixties / Howard Gillette Jr.
      pages cm
  Includes bibliographical references and index.
  ISBN 978-0-8014-5365-6 (cloth : alk. paper)
  1. Yale College (1887–). Class of 1964. 2. Yale University—History—20th century. 3. Yale University—Alumni and alumnae—Biography. 4. Social change—United States—History—20th century. 5. United States—Social conditions—1960–1980. I. Title.
   LD6329 1964c
   378.746'746809046—dc23   2014042247

Cornell University Press strives to use environmentally responsible suppliers and materials to the fullest extent possible in the publishing of its books. Such materials include vegetable-based, low-VOC inks and acid-free papers that are recycled, totally chlorine-free, or partly composed of nonwood fibers. For further information, visit our website at www.cornellpress.cornell.edu.

Cloth printing   10 9 8 7 6 5 4 3 2 1

For
Ellery, Raffaella, and Raphael
Felix, Jenny, Hugo, and Dexter

Contents

Preface

Sometime in the fall of 2003 I received a phone call from the deputy director of Joe Lieberman's presidential campaign. Had I traveled to Mississippi with Lieberman in October 1963, he asked? I knew immediately what was at stake: the need to counter media doubts that Lieberman had participated in the campaign to draw national attention to the blatant exclusion of African Americans from the right to vote. Forty years after the fact, Lieberman's editorial, "Why I Go to Mississippi," issued when he was chairman of the *Yale Daily News* during his senior year in college, still resonated. Although he had been publicly silent about that experience for years, it resurfaced as a point of pride in 2000 when Al Gore selected Lieberman as his Democratic vice presidential running mate. Three years later, several news organizations were challenging Lieberman's claim, and the candidate, not remembering whom he was with the week he spent rallying support for Mississippi Freedom Party candidates, was hoping I might have been one of them and thus able to verify his account.

At Yale, I was a fellow member of the class of 1964 and managing editor of the *Yale Daily News*, so Lieberman and I had worked closely together. A good half dozen of our *News* colleagues did travel to Mississippi that fall, and it was reasonable enough to suppose I might have been among them. But I was not alone in finding the challenge to leave college for a week, to enter into a largely unspecified and inherently dangerous role, beyond me, and I did not go. All the more credit to Lieberman, and to our fellow *News* officer and classmate Stephen Bingham, who was among the first to join the effort. Arrested and jailed on a false charge during his campaign effort in Mississippi, Bingham

spent the remaining months of his college career building on the experience
to expand voter registration in the state in what became a landmark of the
modern civil rights movement, Freedom Summer, 1964.

The broad details of that highly significant period are easy enough to recall
today, but it should not be surprising that Lieberman could not recall who
accompanied him to Mississippi. Memory is like that. The particulars of any
event can be lost unless they are reinforced, and it was the core experience in
Mississippi, not all the details, that resonated over time. Viewed historically,
the role Lieberman and Bingham played in Mississippi just a month before
the assassination of John F. Kennedy can be seen as reflecting both the hope
and the disillusion with Kennedy's presidency. Deeply resistant to bringing
to bear the power of the federal government to do even so much as protect
civil rights workers in the South early in his term, Kennedy had finally put a
bold civil rights proposal before Congress. But in October 1963 its prospects
for enactment were dim. Thus those who felt a moral imperative to press for
action believed they had to do so on their own. Their example, they reasoned
correctly, would compel others to follow. As Lieberman said in his *News* editorial, "I am going to Mississippi because there is much work to be done there
and few men doing it. . . . I see countless Negro Mississippians who are too
terrorized to act. It all becomes a personal matter to me, I am challenged
personally."

Lieberman's Mississippi experience might well have escaped widespread
attention had he not become a public figure. Surely Stephen Bingham's commitment to the civil rights struggle also would have remained obscure had he
not himself become the object of public attention in the early 1970s. Charged
with murder in the aftermath of an alleged escape attempt of a client, Black
Panther George Jackson, from San Quentin prison, Bingham spent thirteen years in obscurity and exile abroad before finally being acquitted of the
charges against him. His path through life could not have been more different
from the one his colleague Lieberman laid out in the years following their
graduation from Yale.

Naturally news about Lieberman and Bingham interested me over the
years, as did reports about other prominent members of the class. Char Miller's 1982 book, *Fathers and Sons*, suggested a provocative hypothesis about
Bingham: that he was carrying out a missionary tradition that went back generations in his family. While Miller's thesis stirred my interest in getting at
the larger meanings of Bingham's life, his explanation seemed insufficient.
My own memories of Bingham and the world he emerged from in maturity
demanded a more complete interpretation. It was about that time that I first
entertained the idea of testing my understanding of events affecting my own
life against that of peers with whom I had studied at Yale.

Like many of the classmates I write about in this book, I was deeply touched by the events that helped define "the 1960s," both as an undergraduate and in the years immediately after. That I owed Yale that sensibility was uncontestable. Raised in the sheltered Chicago suburb of Lake Forest, Illinois, I was only indirectly aware of the emerging national and international forces of the post–World War II era. My family had what they called "colored" help. What did I know of the lives they lived in Waukegan, some miles away from my exclusive community? When President Harry Truman fired General Douglas MacArthur for insubordination in Korea, I did not question the decision either way but joined throngs of spectators as MacArthur made his way from Chicago through our town in what appeared to be a triumphal procession defying the president's action. It wasn't until I reached Yale that my worldview expanded. Only weeks after I arrived in New Haven, I broke my leg during soccer practice, gave up sports, and changed course to seek a position with the *Yale Daily News*. This new vantage led to an eye- and conscience-opening immersion in the most compelling social and educational issues of the day. Thanks to the *News*, I came to know extraordinary classmates like Joe Lieberman and top members of the Yale administration, including university chaplain William Sloane Coffin Jr. and presidents A. Whitney Griswold and Kingman Brewster Jr.

The summer after I graduated, I readily volunteered to serve as a tutor in the university's first summer high school, established to prepare promising minority youth for college. The work naturally extended from earlier summers, when I had worked as a counselor at a summer camp in New Hampshire serving inner-city children from the Boston area. I might well have maintained further continuity by following my father into the navy, a choice a number of my classmates were making through officer training before the Vietnam War heated up. Instead, when the opportunity arrived to pursue American Studies in graduate school, I seized it, ultimately maintaining a military deferment that kept me from the draft.

Everything on university campuses was changing in the mid-1960s. To the stable of old-line Yale faculty were added new figures, among them C. Vann Woodward, whose landmark book on Jim Crow segregation had helped revolutionize southern history, and Staughton Lynd, a veteran of Freedom Summer himself, who helped spark opposition on campus to the Vietnam War. As a member of Lynd's course on the radical origins of the American Revolution, I happened to be included in a 1966 Associated Press photograph greeting him as he returned to campus from a highly controversial trip to Hanoi. By that time, the imperative to become politically active was as pervasive as starring in classroom discussion once had been. While many students turned sharply left, my own foray into politics was more traditional, grounded in my family's Republicanism, even as it was informed by the mounting challenges to traditional practices so pervasive among my peers.

After a short stint as a volunteer in Republican John Lindsay's campaign for mayor of New York and an improbable role as manager of a Yale student's campaign for a seat in Connecticut's state legislature, I found allies in the New Haven chapter of the liberal Republican research and policy organization, the Ripon Society. Locally, that took me into opposing the displacement of African Americans by urban renewal programs touted by New Haven Democrats. Nationally, I joined colleagues pressing for a negative income tax (which ultimately morphed into Richard Nixon's unsuccessful family assistance proposal), even as we challenged Nixon's effort to build a majority coalition, which counted on his attracting the support of whites put off by advances associated with the civil rights movement. Through Ripon, I assumed the position of cochair of Project Pursestrings, an organization formed shortly after President Nixon caused a national furor in the spring of 1970 by sending American troops into Cambodia. Our intent was to lobby Congress on behalf of the McGovern-Hatfield Amendment to the selective service bill that would terminate funding for the war. Bill Clinton was one member of our hastily organized effort in the months before he attended Yale Law School. Gregory Craig, who served as Clinton's special counsel during his 1999 Senate impeachment trial, served as cochair. Ripon's subsequent criticism of Nixon's conduct of the war, while I was president of the society, prompted the president to describe our leadership in an internal memo as "juvenile jerks." After one last and unsuccessful try to contest the rightward turn of the Republican Party through John Anderson's 1980 presidential campaign, I joined a number of my Ripon colleagues leaving the GOP and redirected my energies to teaching and research.

Struck, as so many of my academic peers were in the 1960s, with shortcomings in American democratic practice, much of my teaching focused on those forces that continued to impede realization of the full promise of American life. If the civil rights movement of the 1950s and 1960s could be seen as a "second reconstruction" helping rectify the failure to secure those rights after the Civil War, then much still remained to be done in the latter part of the twentieth century. If we could see in retrospect how Eleanor Roosevelt advanced progressive causes that Franklin as president could not embrace because of obstacles in Congress, we could still see decades later the continuing relevance of many of those issues. At the heart of the continuing contradictions in American life was a culture outwardly united on core values but internally riven on how best to achieve them. The titles of my books struck the connection: *Divided Metropolis; Between Justice and Beauty; Camden after the Fall;* and now *Class Divide*. As my account of Harvard humanities professor and classmate Stephen Greenblatt in this volume affirms, serious scholarship requires subjects of ultimate personal concern. Now I have reversed the usual formula of historical analysis, foregrounding the personal stories of my fellow classmates, but showing in their lives the effect of lasting social change. Doing so has offered me the opportunity to help make sense of major issues that challenge me and others who continue to hope that the idealism of our early college years will not be buried in the new century.

The sample of men's lives I draw upon here is undoubtedly select; yet I contend that their stories, when set in the context of the larger structural changes at home and abroad that have marked the past half century, reveal much about the nature of the enduring cultural shift in America that originated in the 1960s. Unlike other critical assessments that use the form of group biography, this sample is defined not by ideology or cause, but is necessarily limited to those whom a group of admissions officers sitting in New Haven deemed worthy to become Yale's first class to matriculate in the 1960s. Recovering their stories, like any historical exercise, has involved considerable sifting of evidence, from university archives, standard printed sources, numerous evocative reunion reports, and oral interviews.

Of course not every experience adds to our understanding of underlying change. So rather than attempting to make these life histories add up to generalities about their times, I have focused on the illumination that comes from select experiences. Stephen Bingham's life after his acquittal, for instance, necessarily attracts less attention than experiences that led to the tragedy at San Quentin and his exile abroad. Joe Lieberman's long political career is not recounted except as it relates to issues central to his classmates' lives. Relating these experiences to the central issues that animated the 1960s and afterward, I necessarily draw selectively on different individuals. It is the collective tapestry of these experiences, bound by a common point of reference to Yale and cross-connected in time, that adds up to a picture of not just a class but of a nation divided.

Bill Coffin was a powerful presence in the lives of these men when they were undergraduates. Not everyone embraced the intensity he brought to the position of Yale chaplain when he joined the Freedom Rides in 1961 or when he helped persuade Lieberman and Bingham to join the Mississippi Freedom Party campaign in 1963. Yet, as I conducted interviews for this book, I found that the charge to challenge prevailing practices that Bill Coffin frequently made to us as undergraduates still retains a hold on many of my classmates in our later years. In that light it is worth recalling the prayer he offered at the time of the Yale senior dinner in 1964. In the spirit of his frequent call to think "beyond knowledge and power, pride and certainty," he asked God to "grant them grace to develop the habits of heroism, lest, looking back on their springtime fifty years gone, they say, 'Those were the days,' and be right."

Introduction

What a Hinge Generation Can Tell Us

"I'm not satisfied with Yale as a magnificent factory on democratic business lines; I dream of something else, something visionary, a great institution not of boys, clean, lovable and honest, but of men of brains, of courage, of leadership, a great center of thought, to stir the country and bring it back to the understanding of what man creates with his imagination, and dares with his will. It's visionary—it will come."[1]

So speaks Brockhurst, the student-philosopher in the 1912 classic *Stover at Yale*, a book of fiction everyone had heard of and no one had actually read when I was at Yale in the early 1960s. But as I look back from the perspective of some fifty years, this inflated picture of what a Yale education might do for a young man seems just as pertinent in 1960 as it was at the onset of the twentieth century. The stolid Yale was still there in 1960—its Gothic architecture but one manifestation of encrusted tradition that said to one and all, "Enter here, and you shall become a Yale man." But so too was the reformist spirit captured by Brockhurst. As the hazy glow of the affluent Eisenhower years receded, cracks appeared in the educational edifice that had served so well and so long as a crucible for national leadership. The election of John F. Kennedy proved but one of a host of changes in the early 1960s that raised fundamental questions of exactly what vision for Yale might triumph in a new age.

I entered this world, molded by tradition yet increasingly open to winds of change, in September 1960. So, too, did an impressive number of men who, by design or by chance, would fulfill the mission of leadership entrusted to them. Future United States senator Joseph Lieberman arrived as I did. Two years behind us was future senator, presidential candidate, and secretary of state John Kerry, and arriving the year we graduated was future governor and president George W. Bush. Bush's vice president, Dick Cheney, was in and out of Yale twice, briefly associating with the class of 1964, before leaving to finish his degree at the University of Wyoming. Did they aspire, like Brockhurst, to stir the country? Well before he graduated, Lieberman was being fondly referred to as "Senator," and Kerry's ambition was no less manifest, as he worked campus politics to the hilt. That George Bush's low-key campus profile did not immediately presage his rise to power did not entirely exempt him from absorbing the Yale ethos. More than one commentator pointed out, when he and Kerry squared off for the presidency in 2004, that both men had been members of Skull and Bones, Yale's oldest and most exclusive secret society. Add Howard Dean, Yale 1970, into the political fray of 2004 and you get comedian Jay Leno's crack: "John Kerry's victory over Howard Dean has completely changed the presidential race. Now, instead of a rich, white guy from, you know, from Yale who lives in the White House facing off a rich white guy from Yale who lives in Vermont, he might have to face off against a rich white guy from Yale who lives in Massachusetts."[2]

Clearly men of such similarly privileged backgrounds as Kerry and Bush might be expected to succeed. A Yale degree was but one of a number of credentials that made such expectations reasonable. In an earlier era, one might even have expected such men to have become rivals, perhaps a Teddy Roosevelt to a William Howard Taft, arguing about the details of Progressivism in their 1912 presidential campaigns, rather than its basic premises. Not so in the twenty-first century. As much as Kerry and Bush shared in social background, they could not have been further apart politically. Their differences owed much to the 1960s. If Kerry did not always choose to emphasize his own anti-war position with Vietnam Veterans Against the War, his stance remained throughout his career a prominent part of his identity. Bush, on the other hand, not only distanced himself from the era's popular causes among American youth; he made them the object of social derision. "Even today," Nicholas Kristof reported in a profile of Bush as a presidential candidate, "Mr. Bush thunders in his stump speeches against boomer-style self-indulgence and appeals for a 'responsibility era' that in some respects sounds like the 1950s."[3]

Rather than a passing phenomenon, the changes that washed over Yale and the nation in the 1960s remain very much in place in contemporary America. The specific upheavals of the era ultimately dissipated, but underlying shifts in social structure, cultural values, and ideology continue to define American life. The cultural divide that emerged remains a potent determinant of public as well as private lives. Conservative politicians berate the cultural divide, popular culture eulogizes it, contemporary citizens struggle with its lasting effects, whether understood or appreciated.

* * *

There is no lack of material dissecting the 1960s. Memoirs abound, and scholars have depicted a wide range of the era's features. Almost daily, the media remind us of this turbulent era, and yet as political scientist Edward P. Morgan makes clear, the overall effect is to confirm stereotypes that mask rather than illuminate the nature of changes that had such lasting effect. The media, he insists, do the public a disservice, distracting public attention from persistent problems addressed frontally in the 1960s—of rights for women and minorities, poverty, national security, and protection of the environment, among others—by reviving latent conflicts from the era. "We need a reckoning with this past that we can learn from, not a discourse that keeps a distorted past alive while simultaneously trying to bury it," he asserts.[4]

Decades are arbitrary yet useful shorthand devices for depicting distinct periods of time. As the era receded, references to "the sixties" assumed less the character of a particular set of years than a set of connotations associated with the latter part of the decade into the early 1970s, carrying at least through the resignation of Richard Nixon in 1974. These "long 1960s," or "bad 1960s," as at least one scholar has chosen to identify the period 1963–1974,[5] were marked by social, cultural, and political excesses. They are the primary object of commentary and criticism. The hopes, expectations, and even preliminary accomplishments of the first years of the 1960s are all too often treated as though they belong to a separate era, yet the first years of the decade clearly set the stage for what followed.

In this collective portrait of the Yale class of 1964, I have detailed the experiences of an elite group of men as they entered college and experienced society's upheavals, then lived through the unforeseen drama of their later years, in order to widen the picture of the 1960s and illuminate the full range of changes associated with the era. In their collective experiences, my classmates reveal not the dramatic elements that fuel the stereotypes that Morgan complains of, but the rich tapestry of selective adaptation and reorientation to a universe of experience that was markedly different from what they had been socialized to expect as they grew up in the 1950s.

Situated socially and temporally at a critical juncture in the nation's modern history, Yale 1964 straddled the great divide that came to characterize the nation. While most did not join the countercultural revolution that materialized shortly after they graduated, these men nonetheless broke from the expectations and norms of earlier graduates. Joseph Hinkle described the class position succinctly if wryly in his contribution to his twenty-fifth class reunion book. Protesting the request to complete a questionnaire that included references to his sex life, Hinkle responded,

> For reasons I cannot recall, I started with the poll. I began okay, choosing to answer some questions and ignore others until I arrived at the question of my sleeping habits. Did I sleep with my wife: Answer, yes (thinking it a little curious that you should be interested in whether we employed a double or single bedded arrangement, but I pressed on). How often? Answer, every night (wondering why we would sleep in one place one night elsewhere another night). Then IT dawned on me, just what this question was about. . . . Who in the 1980s talked about sex as sleeping or even gave a holy hoot about the subject? Then I saw our class more clearly. A strange crossing point between the gentlemanly, fraternal Yale of the fifties and the confrontational, issue-dominated Yale of the sixties and seventies. We were a class too old to be new and too new to be old. Our roots were in a prior era, but we still wanted to face those new issues.[6]

Not so distinctive as to constitute a generation in themselves, the members of Yale '64 nonetheless were bound, as sociologist Karl Mannheim has defined generations, as people in the same age group sharing a historical location in the same way that people of the same class share a social location, thus exposing them to "a specific range of potential experience, [which] redispose[s] them for a certain characteristic mode of thought and experience, and a characteristic type of historically relevant action."[7] The years of youth and early adulthood are a critical period for learning about the larger society, religious historian Wade Clark Roof adds: "Memories arising out of the intersection of personal and national history during these years live on in our lives. Thus because they have quite differing pasts, the generations see and act toward the world differently."[8] Positioned just ahead of the baby boom generation that has drawn so much attention over the years, these men shared much, though certainly not all, with that generational cohort. Certainly the members of this group, like those who followed them over the next fifteen years, were significantly boosted as well as affected by a vibrant postwar consumer economy as they matured. They had the advantage over those who followed, however, of starting their careers before the economy soured in the 1970s and competition for desirable graduate placement and jobs intensified as a result of the postwar population bulge. Many of the professional profiles of these men, then, looked very much like those of graduates of select universities who immediately preceded them. And yet, something was different. For a good number, wherever their career path took them, the "silent revolution in social values," as Leonard Steinhorn describes the cultural revolution associated with the baby boom generation, proved irresistible.[9] In matters both public and private, their lives took turns that could not have been anticipated when they undertook their undergraduate education. In this way, as Joseph Hinkle suggested, they were in the new generation, but not entirely of it.

The four years that marked the college education of the great majority of these men brought the election of John F. Kennedy and his assassination, the rise of Goldwater conservatism, the first student lunch counter sit-ins to protest segregation, the Cuban missile crisis, and the construction of the Berlin Wall, to say nothing of the introduction of the pill and rock 'n' roll. No doubt the class of 1964 shared much besides their admission to an elite institution. If Yale has not been traditionally identified as a hotbed of change in this period, it is hard to deny how thoroughly these men were exposed to the shift in outlook and experience that set the 1960s apart from earlier years. It was not just Yale's Rev. William Sloane Coffin who pressed students into dangerous service in Mississippi; it was William F. Buckley Jr. and Barry Goldwater calling students to arms against communist tyranny abroad and creeping collectivism at home. The lawsuit that established the right of privacy that formed the basis for the *Roe v. Wade* Supreme Court decision legalizing abortion had its origin in New Haven in these years. Both the northern counterpart to the Student Nonviolent Coordinating Committee and the conservative Young Americans for Freedom formed at Yale or in close association with the university within months of '64's matriculation. Malcolm X and the governor of Mississippi both singled out Yale students for criticism for their involvement in voter registration efforts in the South. It would have been hard to bury oneself in the stacks or the fraternity house to such a degree as to have missed such challenges to prevailing experience in those years.

Located at the hinge of social upheaval, this group of men divided themselves. As common as their background and education may have seemed, they acted very differently over time. The full range of those disparities is manifestly displayed in the lives of this group's most public figures: environmentalist Gus Speth, social reformer turned radical activist Stephen Bingham, literary scholar Stephen Greenblatt, and conservative icons and heroes John Ashcroft and William Bradford Reynolds. Joseph Lieberman's conscious effort to bridge the divide only served to place him uncomfortably on both sides. In that divide, which extended well beyond these public figures to the lives of their classmates, we can begin to identify larger meanings. If the goal of securing individual liberties for all people could be understood as fundamental in the early 1960s, how were the means for securing those rights recast in later years? If American power had once been perceived as essential to the defense of those liberties, how were agents of authority to be treated in light of perceived violations of trust, whether at home or abroad? Once sexual mores subscribed to in practice and supported by law for generations were challenged by new definitions of liberty, what would be the new basis for acceptable behavior, inside or outside of marriage? How would matters of faith and social responsibility fare as fundamental challenges to traditional outlooks and practices came under fire?

* * *

It might be possible to examine any elite university from the mid-1960s to pursue the questions addressed in this book. Certainly Yale was but one of a number of educational institutions especially responsible for honing the social as well as intellectual skills of the nation's future leaders. Still, there is considerable utility in selecting out Yale—where the weight of tradition was manifest in so many ways—as a testing ground for change. If the old saying held that you can always tell a Harvard man, but you cannot tell him very much, the Yale man was less likely to have resisted, either in college or afterward, university efforts to mold exemplary graduates. No unit of the university garnered greater attention or resources than Yale College, especially under the presidency of A. Whitney Griswold, who considered professional schools something of a diversion from the university's larger mission. Through a host of institutional arrangements, extracurricular as well as curricular, the university sought not just to inform but to inspire its charges, a goal that did not cease at graduation, as alumni publications and events continued to reinforce the sense of belonging to a special community. As Griswold put it, a Yale education was not intended simply to advance "self-expression" but to prepare its charges for "responsible membership in society after graduation." Joseph Lieberman, citing Griswold, revealed how completely that message had been received when he declared in a 1963 open letter to Yale alumni addressing the civil rights movement, "We envision Yale as a training ground for a democratic elite."[10]

The goal of advancing not just individual but the larger public welfare remains very much in place at Yale College today. What has changed is the means to achieve that goal and who is selected to pursue it by taking advantage of the education the university offers. In a shift that was evident even as the members of the class of 1964 were graduating—the selection of Kingman Brewster as Griswold's successor in 1963 and the subsequent reorientation of undergraduate admissions policy—Yale turned more explicitly toward advancing an intellectual meritocracy. Much to the consternation of defenders of established traditions, Yale College no longer confined admission to men exclusively, but opened its doors both to women and increasingly to those not already privileged by birth or social connections. Although that shift occurred too late to fully shape the class of 1964, the foundations for selecting a more diverse student body were already manifest in the early 1960s, in ways that contributed to the disparate paths these men took upon graduation.[11]

While there is considerable disagreement about when exactly the social and cultural upheaval so closely associated with "the sixties" began, there is some agreement on 1964–1965 as a hinge moment in the seismic shift that has given the period its reputation. In *The Last Innocent Year: America in 1964—the Beginning of the "Sixties,"* Jon Margolis writes, "There was never an innocent year. . . . But there was a time when the delusion of innocence was easy to believe, when the myth was at least as useful as it was deceiving. That time ended when 1964 did." Historian James Patterson agrees, pointing to escalation of the war in Vietnam, civil disorders in Watts, the splintering of the civil rights movement, and mounting cultural change and polarization in 1965 as "the time when America's social cohesion began to unravel and when the turbulent phenomenon that would be called the 'Sixties' broke into view."[12] However the period is defined, Yale's class of 1964 rode the crest of this wave of social change, and the lessons they took away from that experience tell us much about the era's lasting effect.

If there is a companion story to this volume, it could well be found in Miriam Horn's *Rebels in White Gloves*, an assessment of Hillary Rodham Clinton's Wellesley College class of 1969.[13] What 1964 was for men, 1969 was for women: a period that marked a major generational shift. For women, the shift was most often greater, involving challenges not just to redefine their lives in public, but also their traditional roles as wives and mothers. As the stories of Yale '64 reveal, men too had to adjust to shifting mores related to sex, marriage, and the family, but because they dominated the public arena—in work, politics, and civic enterprise—the challenges to traditional expectations for their lives, if profound, were in some ways more subtle. Changes in their private lives were nonetheless central to their life experiences as well.

Our story starts in the fall of 1960. Even as members of the class of 1964 made their way onto the Yale campus, many for the first time, the *New Yorker* issued an extended essay about the admissions process that brought these men together. Reporter at large Katharine Kincaid choose to give dean of admissions Arthur Howe the last word on their selection: "If you want to know how difficult it is, come up here in September and sit on the fence out on the Old Campus and watch these kids arriving, with all their parents' hopes and fears right behind them—not to mention ours. Then ask yourself which ones will make good and which ones won't."[14] Fifty some years later, Howe's implied question could be answered, at least in part, in the considerable list of accomplishments that Howe would find familiar and comforting. But much more compelling than their credentials is the array of social experiences behind these men's lives. It is that story that *Class Divide* now addresses.

CLASS
DIVIDE

1

Bright College Years, 1960–1964

Many commentators point to the Free Speech Movement that roiled the University of California campus at Berkeley in the fall of 1964 as the event that marked the outset of the upheaval that permanently rocked American culture. No doubt, there were many premonitions of these changes, and at Berkeley, mid-1960s activism built on years of student protest, aimed first at the excesses of anticommunism and subsequently at obstacles to achieving civil rights in the North.[1] Few universities matched Berkeley's fervor, and there is considerable evidence that California's premier academic institution was attracting activists from other parts of the country intent on joining the growing protest movement there. Still, just as at Berkeley, the signs of change were appearing widely on college campuses. As pollster Daniel Yankelovich puts it, "The campus upheavals of the sixties gave us the first premonitory sign that the plates of American culture, after decades of stability, had begun to shift."[2] That they never exploded in quite the dramatic fashion of Berkeley, or Harvard, Cornell, or Columbia in the East, makes the changes at Yale no less significant. The upheavals of the 1960s ultimately died down, but underlying shifts in social structure, cultural determinants, and ideology remained to redefine American life. Their origins can be found even in the intuitively unlikely locus of a group of Ivy League students entering the 1960s with the reasonable expectation that their ascent to the privileged condition of Yale men assured them of an uncomplicated path to future happiness and success.[3] As much as their expectations were formed by past tradition, Yale as well as the nation was changing in ways that proved inescapable. Like it or not, this class was going to be part of a major transition.

To a modern eye, the one thousand freshmen who descended on the Yale campus in September 1960 were a strikingly homogeneous group. Predominantly Protestant, virtually all white, and all male, they hailed from many parts of the United States and abroad. Still, the greatest number came from the Northeast, and, in a pattern that went back generations, more than half—56 percent—had attended private preparatory schools.[4] This group included no fewer than thirty-six and thirty-one students respectively from Andover and Exeter academies.[5] A majority of these students had been offered the equivalent of preadmission, an A rating that relied as much on a headmaster's evaluation of a student's character as his demonstrated academic performance. By contrast, only two students arrived from the heavily Jewish Bronx High School of Science, one of New York City's highest-rated public high schools. The class included eleven students from New Trier High School in Winnetka, Illinois, another outstanding public school, though one that was regularly approached by enthusiastic Yale alumni seeking recruits to the football team.

A few names stood out among those newly arrived at Yale. Among these were Timothy Mellon, the son of banking heir and philanthropist Paul Mellon; George Humphrey II, the grandson of the secretary of the treasury under Dwight Eisenhower; Peter Wallace, son of newscaster Mike Wallace; and Maynard Mack Jr. and Peter Woodward, sons of prominent Yale faculty. Joe DiMaggio Jr. spent a year with the class, trying to avoid the attentions of local New Haven girls drawn to the fame associated with his name, before dropping out.[6]

According to the extended report on Yale's admissions process that appeared in the New Yorker even as the freshmen arrived, this was Yale's brightest class ever, albeit similar claims had been made for earlier classes in the preceding decade. Academic strength, as measured by standardized test scores and high school performance, mattered, of course, but just as important was "personal promise." Yale, admissions director Arthur Howe Jr. recounted, was interested both in "brains and character." As fellow admissions officer Waldo Johnston, whose own son was joining this class, explained, the goal was to identify outstanding scholarly capacity while at the same time searching out what he called the spirit of each prospective student, "the selflessness, integrity, and honesty that are so badly needed in this day of false ideals."[7]

Continuity marked the rituals launching the new academic year. Traditions in place for years were cheerfully embraced by students and administrators alike, including the all-day outing at nearby Hammonasset Beach State Park, featuring plenty of physical activity and food, and President A. Whitney Griswold's freshman address, laced with praise for a liberal education and capped with his oft-repeated call to service. Years later, '64's Thomas Barton still recalled that message, paraphrasing what he remembered: "We will give you the best education in the world. We do not do this for your personal enjoyment or enrichment. We do it as a part of Yale's sacred mission to educate the future generations of the leaders of this nation and the world. . . . Work hard and be worthy of the trust we have placed in you because the future of our nation and the world will be what you make it."[8]

Submission to posture pictures that required photographs of each new student in the nude were more grudgingly accepted, even if many freshmen must have concluded that such practice was consistent with the emphasis on their physical well-being that had always been a part of their education. Some years later a national news story revealed a darker set of intentions from anthropologists determined to test their theories of eugenics at elite colleges.[9] The practice ended at Yale in 1968, but for this class the hold over administrators of desirable physical attributes remained. As Jerome Karabel reports, admissions officers at Yale viewed signs of manliness especially favorably, going so far as to provide alumni interviewers with a checklist of physical characteristics for review, a practice that continued until 1965. Each year, as part of the posture exams, the height of each freshman was recorded, prompting the university to report with pride what proportion of the class was six feet or more. Yale '64 stood at 24.8 percent.[10]

Whatever manly traits it sought in its candidates for admission, Yale, starting with President Griswold at the top, still considered its freshmen to be boys and treated them accordingly. The Yale handbook on regulations spelled out the university's position, warning, "Students are held fully responsible for any breach of generally recognized rules of gentlemanly conduct whether or not covered by the printed rules. Any student whose character or conduct does not meet Yale standards is subject to dismissal at any time . . . whatever his scholarship record may be."[11] Determined to assert its position as *in loco parentis*, the university maintained an Office for Freshman Year, with its own dean, Harold Whiteman, who made it clear to the incoming freshmen that rules would be enforced, especially, he told the *Yale Daily News*, those related to neatness, including wearing neckties to meals. Whiteman must have been serious. Years later, William Roth recounted how, because he suffered from the neurological movement disorder dystonia, which caused involuntary muscle contractions, he substituted a scarf for the required necktie. This apparent act of rebellion prompted a rebuke from the dean, with the postscript adding, "Remember, disorder is contagious." Undaunted, Roth recalled, "Strangely pleased with the reprimand, I stuck to my scarves, and thus began my career in institutional reform and social protest."[12]

No fewer than fifty-nine counselors, one for every seventeen students, were housed on the Old Campus in order to oversee the daily activities of the freshmen. On weekends, female visitors were welcome in dorm rooms, but only until 6 p.m. on Friday and 10 p.m. on Saturday, a practice that was soon modified only slightly under prodding from the *Yale Daily News* by extending Saturday night visitation by an hour. An unsigned article that appeared in the *Yale Daily News* the following year, intended to help freshmen interpret the rules, appeared to be gently tweaking university administrators when it stated, "Freshmen are forbidden to use their rooms to house live animals and women. The ladies, however, are allowed to visit within clearly defined and rigidly enforced limits—no sex after seven on Fridays and Sundays nor after eleven on Saturdays."[13] When students violated these rules, the consequences could be severe, including suspension from school, a position the university stressed particularly in the aftermath of unwanted national publicity in the first part of 1960 to the effect that a young woman from New Haven had been readily providing oral sex to undergraduates.[14] Years later, '64's Thomas Trowbridge commemorated his roommate Ned Evans's sexual indiscretion in verse:

> I roomed with Ned until early November
> 'Til a football weekend he's sure to remember.
> Ned's date seemed quite friendly, the prospects were rosy.
> "Come to my room" he said, "You'll find it quite cozy."
> A noisy one, she made a bit of a ruckus
> That led to Lux et Veritas interruptus.
> Through holes in the door made by Ned's mallet for polo
> Campus cops saw that he wasn't totally solo.
> Yale's response, we think, was a bit to the radical:
> "Take," young man, "an undergraduate sabbatical."[15]

All freshmen were required to meet with security director John Powell their first week on campus to assure that they were aware of their rights as well as their responsibilities in the city of New Haven. Such information, Whiteman reported, was intended to prevent students from allowing what was becoming an annual ritual, the freshman riot, from spilling over into the city. Powell was perhaps more immediately on target when he warned students of the bad consequences of using faked identification to buy liquor.[16] No doubt many new arrivals had anticipated the problem. As Larry Pratt later reminisced in his review of freshman year for the 1964 graduation yearbook, "I mentioned earlier that I did not feel very well prepared for Yale. This is not entirely true, for I had packed two fifths of Scotch among my underdrawers, where it was far from Mater's prying eyes. This, I expected, would see me through Freshman Week and probably beyond."[17]

Room inspection.

Although Yale virtually abandoned such rules in the mid-1960s, restrictions on women's visiting hours in men's rooms were not well received in the first part of the decade. A fair representation of campus attitudes toward such rules was captured in Kenneth deF. Solstad's illustration for 1964's graduation yearbook under the title "Room inspection."

If the status quo appeared in place, it did not go without challenge, especially from the faculty, which itself was evolving from a clubby group of mostly Yale graduates to a more diverse and intellectually engaged community. Concerned that Yale was losing too many of its most academically gifted candidates to Harvard, the faculty issued a report in 1960 calling for greater emphasis on academic performance in admissions decisions. Bowing to faculty pressure, President Griswold appointed a committee on the freshman year. Psychology professor Leonard Doob led the group of distinguished faculty, which included law professor Eugene Rostow, who as early as 1945 had protested Yale's restrictive admission of Jews. Issued in April 1961, the report extended well beyond a greater emphasis on academic performance for admission and the treatment of new applicants in their first year to urge greater scholarly demands on students in the curriculum. "More of the graduates of Yale College, we think, must become professional scholars and teachers," it concluded.[18]

The immediate effects of the Doob report were decisions to integrate freshmen more fully into the life of the university by relieving them of special activities and rules and allying them upon admission with the university's residential colleges, whose functions extended well beyond dormitory space to include the presence of faculty fellows, seminars, intramural sports, and a host of social activities. Not incidentally, a series of faculty lectures soon replaced the outing to Hammonasset. As groundbreaking as the report and the implications for the future of Yale College were, the culture of the place did not change immediately. What dean of admissions Arthur Howe said of the Yale he entered in 1939 could just as well be reiterated in the early 1960s: "The dominant element of undergraduate life was not formal intellectual activity." As much as students might enjoy their classes, "much time and energy went elsewhere, into social, aesthetic, and a great variety of other extra-curricular activities."[19] The Yale definition of success remained for the moment only secondarily attached to academic excellence.

Over many years, outsiders to Yale's preferred pedigree bridled under the college ethos. The city builder Robert Moses, class of 1909, for instance, famously set about establishing his own alternative standards for achievement when his Jewish heritage barred him from desirable social affiliations.[20] Others, while recognizing their outsider status, learned to navigate the expectations of the place. Calvin Trillin, 1957, expressed the difficulty outliers from the provinces faced on entering this environment: "Yale could strike a high school boy from the provinces as something like a foreign country—a rather intimidating foreign country." A Jewish public school graduate from Kansas City, Trillin drew his quote from the classic 1912 novel *Stover at Yale*. Improbably, Trillin's father—an immigrant grocery store owner—had not only read *Stover*, but the book inspired him to make it possible for his son to follow in Stover's steps. "I think his notion was this," said Trillin: "he would send me to Yale, I would have an even start with the sons of the country's most powerful industrialists . . . and after that it was up to me." The reason for Yale's existence, Trillin thought his father believed, was "to turn the likes of us into the likes of them. I don't mean he wanted us to be like them in accent or dress or social connections; he had no interest in that sort of thing. He wanted us to have the same opportunities." The Yale Trillin found when he arrived "didn't have much resemblance on the surface to the place my father had read about in *Stover at Yale*," he reported, "but the more I think about it, the more I think that we were closer to the world inhabited by Dink and Tough than we were to the world of today's Yale undergraduates."[21] The same could be said for the class of 1964. Yale remained a place where "the likes of us" were pressed to make the effort to turn into "the likes of them."

Of classmates from private preparatory schools, Trillin observed, "Yale seemed very much *their place*."[22] Protest as one might, the dominant tone established for acceptance and social success was set by them. Various institutional mechanisms helped maintain their hold, starting with fraternities, which survived despite a lack of support from the university; membership in Mory's, an eating club whose walls were covered with pictures of Yale athletes posing for posterity; and the rambunctious Haunt Club, whose only function was to serve drinks to Yale men and their dates before home football games.[23] Try as he might in his freshman address to arouse his charges to break out of pressures to be "shoe"—a term referring to the trend among campus leaders to wear the requisite scuffed-up white shoes associated with a good prep school education—university chaplain William Sloane Coffin could not disguise the break between those who easily stepped into the right presentation of self and those poor outliers who retained the habit of wearing black or brown shoes.[24]

Whatever the shoe color, adapting to Yale for those who failed to fit the mold could be difficult. As Robert Lamson noted of his transition from Mercer Island High School outside Seattle, "I felt like the western hick actually. I showed up with clothes that were typical western style, plaid shirts and jeans and stuff, and at the time it was more jackets and khakis." Compared to the prevailing sense of friendliness he had experienced in the West, a number of Yale students seemed surprisingly standoffish.[25] George Sheckleton of Worcester, Massachusetts, was the first of his family to attend college. His mother took in laundry and did housework, while his father made wooden parts for looms in a Worcester factory that Sheckleton described as being "straight out of Dickens." Sheckleton threw himself into the study of biochemistry because its intensive demands provided an escape from social interactions that he did not enjoy.[26] Frank Franklin, of West Orange, New Jersey, entered Yale from Pingry Country Day School in nearby Bernards, New Jersey after attending Catholic school through fifth grade. Despite his experience in private school, as a member of an extended Italian American family (whose name had been changed from Franchino), Franklin never felt entirely comfortable at Yale. He was appalled to realize that he had been paired as a roommate freshman year with Andover graduate Anthony Lee, who had grown up in the exclusive New Jersey suburb of Short Hills. Years later, the two become friendly, but they parted after freshman year, never quite able to overcome the social divide between them.[27]

Gary Saxonhouse had a similarly disorienting experience on arriving at Yale. Growing up in the Forest Hills section of Queens, in New York City, the son of Jewish immigrants who spoke German at home, Saxonhouse attended an all-Jewish high school. As part of a strongly countercultural clique in high school that took its cues from the emerging folk music revival, he later remarked, "You can't imagine how different this place was from where I went to high school. It was a real shock coming here."[28] The head of Wayne Minami's private school in Honolulu, formerly a campus minister at Yale, encouraged the National Merit Scholarship semifinalist to enroll. But whatever advantages that connection provided, Minami's background as the son of a Japanese immigrant to Hawaii who ran a pig farm until he died in 1952 ill prepared him for either the social or physical climate in New Haven. For his first two years, Minami joined Fred Sakamoto, the only other member of the class from Hawaii, for dinner every night. Minami eventually excelled academically but struggled his first year to keep up, while marveling how easily the work seemed to come to his roommate, Charles Pulaski, who had prepared at the Taft School in Watertown, Connecticut.[29]

Such observations underscored the importance of the "prep" in prep school. Although Richard Berk entered Yale from the Hill School, his background was not that of a typical prep school student. He was the first in his family to attend college. His father was a labor activist in the men's outerwear business in the Bronx and a supporter of Henry Wallace's maverick presidential campaign in 1948. Berk found himself at the Hill School only after he acted up in a public junior high school and Hill School headmaster Edward Hall was willing to take a chance on him. It did not hurt his chances for admission to Yale that Berk proved an outstanding football player who arrived with two other Hill School teammates.[30]

No doubt Patrick Caviness also benefited from a transition from public school to Yale through a year at Taft. His father, the son of an Arkansas farmer, managed to work his way through the University of Arkansas and George Washington University Law School before taking a position with the U.S. Treasury in Little Rock. Patrick considered his youth idyllic. An outstanding football player, he played for Little Rock's Hall High School, newly opened in 1957 even as Central High admitted nine black students after President Eisenhower assured their safety by bringing in the army's 101st Airborne Division. To overcome Governor Orval Faubus's obstruction, Eisenhower also federalized the Arkansas National Guard and posted troops at both schools. Caviness thought integration proceeded smoothly enough, but on the day school was scheduled to open the following year, Faubus closed all the city's public schools, claiming there had been death threats and violence associated with integration. Despite the shutdown, the two high school football teams incongruously played a full schedule, culminating with a contest to determine the state championship. Although his play helped Hall win the state championship, Caviness remained without a degree despite having attended classes at Arkansas Polytechnic Institute for a semester. Fortunately, a group of local businessmen persuaded his family to send him to the Taft School, where he was awarded a full scholarship. Only then did Caviness receive his high school degree, even as he continued to play football. Recovering nicely from the disruption of the previous year, he entered Yale, where he quickly adjusted to new academic challenges and stood out on the freshman football team.[31]

Prep school, however, was not an absolute credential required for success at Yale. The eldest of five children, James Rogers was born and raised in Demopolis, Alabama, where his father and his uncle ran a factory. Finishing at the top of his class in Demopolis, Rogers was nonetheless terrified about the prospect of attending Yale. "How would I ever compete with students from fancy Northeastern prep schools?" he asked. Yet compete he did, and after being named a ranking scholar and serving as coxswain on the Yale crew, he won a scholarship to Balliol College, Oxford, where he studied politics, philosophy, and economics and continued to excel as a coxswain. After a stint in the army, he became George Soros's junior partner in an offshore hedge fund, making enough money to retire at thirty-seven.[32] Joseph Wishcamper was similarly concerned about his prospects on arriving at Yale from Fort Worth, wondering who he was and how he could possibly fit in. The grandson of migrant farmworkers, he spent his early years on a farm in the Texas panhandle, where his parents regularly hosted passing hoboes in their barn until one attempted to attack his mother, which prompted the family to move to Fort Worth. After a period of adjustment academically as well as socially at Yale, Wishcamper did well enough to join dozens of classmates entering Harvard Law at the time of his graduation.[33]

While success came to him too, Joseph Lieberman's transition from Stamford High School in Connecticut was also difficult initially. The grandson of immigrants on both sides of his family and the first to attend college, Lieberman recalled, "I arrived at Yale as an outsider, a public school kid among the preppies from Andover and Exeter. I had a rocky time with my classes the first semester, terrifying enough that I imagined I might be told to leave."[34] By his second year, he was on solid ground, ultimately climbing the ladder to the prestigious position of chairman of the *Yale Daily News* and selection to write a senior honors thesis as Scholar of the House. John Ashcroft was another outsider, as the class's only student from Springfield, Missouri, where his father, an evangelical preacher, located to be near the Pentecostal Assemblies of God headquarters. Because it revolved around alcohol and sex, Ashcroft assiduously boycotted Yale's dominant social scene. Yet he joined his classmates on the football field freshman year and earned selection to the first class entering the St. Elmo's senior society after it had closed as a fraternity.[35]

The struggle to make it could be social as well as academic. Gus Speth was one of only four classmates from South Carolina. He still remembered some fifty years later the roar of laughter that greeted him when he responded to one of the few female instructors in any classroom by saying "Yes, ma'am." Clearly, southern manners did not hold much sway with his classmates.[36] As a fellow southerner, Jim Rogers had a similar experience. Finding he was having trouble understanding the concepts in his economics class, he approached the professor, who had, Rogers thought, a thick Northeast accent. "I'm afraid I can't understand you most of the time," he reported, to which the professor replied, "I'm afraid I can't understand *you* most of the time." With nothing to be done about his own accent, much less the professor's, Rogers turned to a tutor to help him through the course.[37]

Although Yale's admission process was already becoming more inclusive before it took a sharp turn toward academic meritocracy in the mid-1960s,[38] it was narrow enough to make true pluralism difficult. Admissions director Author Howe was proud of his family's historic commitment to civil rights and social justice. Not only had his grandfather, Samuel Chapman Armstrong, been a founder of the historically black college, Hampton Institute, he had grown up there while his father, Arthur Howe Sr., served as president. High on Howe's list of priorities for broadening the range of students entering Yale was the inclusion of more African Americans, whose numbers for years had remained in single digits. Howe personally visited a number of schools never previously contacted by Yale, including a number of black schools in the South.[39] Among his African American recruits to the class of 1964 were James Lomax, who had attended Escambia County Training School, in Almore, Alabama, before completing his preparatory studies at Classical High School in Springfield, Massachusetts, and Stanley Thomas, a Harlem resident who attended the high-powered Horace Mann School in the Bronx. Still, of the nine black students entering the class of 1964, four were born outside the United States: Akintola Aboderin and Samuel Adetunji in Nigeria, Wendell Mottley in Trinidad, and Edouard Benjamin in Guinea. Mottley and Benjamin proved outstanding athletes, who managed the college's social as well as academic challenges effectively.[40]

Not everything was easy for at least one American-born black student, Arthur Reagin. His coming of age coincided with the 1954 desegregation of the Washington, D.C., school system. After attending the all-black Bruce Elementary School—named for Blanche K. Bruce, the African American elected U.S. senator from Mississippi during Reconstruction—Reagin joined some twenty black children assigned to the previously all-white McFarland Middle School. Over the course of the first few days at McFarland, he was greeted by adult pickets and jeering classmates. It was a jarring experience for the young Reagin, and he was not sure after his first day he would be able to stand the pressure. On his second day, a white youngster, a tough kid who had had his own problems with bad health and brushes with the law, stepped in. As he greeted Reagin, whom he knew from the neighborhood playground, he motioned the angry pickets to back off. When the black students gathered together in a corner of the lunchroom, the same student intervened, insisting that they join whites at other tables. The remaining two years in middle school were not without insults or difficulty, but Reagin mastered the storm, even as he excelled academically. Moving on to Roosevelt High School, he finished fourth in his class, high enough to receive offers of admission to both West Point and Yale. Encouraged by his talented parents—his father a history professor at Morgan State, his mother an accomplished teacher and administrator in the District school system—to attend a better school than they had, he selected Yale. His decision was encouraged by his cousin, George Bundy Smith, who had attended Yale and was currently in the university's law school class of 1962, along with his twin sister, Inez.[41]

Reagin's transition to Yale proved academically challenging, despite his strong SAT scores and outstanding academic record. As an outlet, he played pickup basketball during the fall semester, joining an especially strong freshman team as a substitute over the winter. During his warm-ups at a game against Brown in Providence, a local fan tried to unsettle him by calling him out as "Yale's brown man." The intended provocation prompted Yale's star recruit Rick Kaminsky to challenge the fan physically, but Reagin was not especially bothered, having heard much worse insults as a youngster playing basketball in Washington. What did bother him was an effort to shepherd him and his two African classmates off to a separate room to meet black Vassar girls at his first social mixer. Even more humiliating was being rejected for a fraternity because of his race. "I wondered, still do, if I had been a name athlete like [Stan] Thomas or Mottley, rather than a bench-sitter, whether things might have turned out differently," he wrote twenty-five years later.[42]

Reagin was right that his classmate Stanley Thomas thrived as an athlete, but that did not make Thomas any less immune to the sting of racial discrimination. A story passed down through his son and confirmed by his football teammate Patrick Caviness harked back to freshman year. Caviness was in the habit of joining Thomas for dinner along with the other freshmen at the Yale Commons. One night he was joined in the walk over by another student from his dormitory, a fellow southerner. After they had selected their meals from the cafeteria line, Caviness motioned to Thomas, who was finishing up his scholarship job cleaning tables, to join them. As Thomas sat down, a look came on the third student's face that Caviness described as a mix between shock and disgust, as he said, "I can't continue eating. I just can't sit at the same table as a Negro." Caviness was stunned and moved immediately to apologize for his classmate, whom he didn't know very well in any regard. Thomas shrugged it off, saying "Don't worry. These guys, you've just got to let them die out." Apparently Thomas did not encounter other such incidents in college. Still, the story survived within the family fifty years later.[43]

Jews were a much larger presence on campus than African Americans, and yet there was still a widespread consciousness of their minority status and its maintenance by quota, which appeared to have remained at 10 percent of each class for years. A film prepared for the class of 1961's fiftieth reunion in 2011 recounted the bizarre story from one member of the class, Peter Bergman, who believed he had been "traded" to Yale by Harvard's admissions office in return for a strong prospect for the crew team, the assumption being that Harvard could afford to give up a smart Jew and Yale could use another one. Turning the tables, one of the primary characters in Erich Segal's fictional account of Harvard's class of 1958, Jason Gilbert, turns up at Harvard because he has been a victim of Yale's Jewish quota. The realization complete, Gilbert blurts out, "Look, Dad, I don't want to go to a school that doesn't want me. As far as I'm concerned, Yale can go to Hell." He is assured, however, by his headmaster, who responds, "Now, let's think positively. After all, your second choice is a very good school. Some people even think Harvard is the best school in the country."[44]

Hillel offered Jews an alternative to mainstream social activity by providing speakers in conjunction with Friday services and, as the decade progressed, opportunities to engage in social service by tutoring youngsters after school at the predominantly black Winchester Community School in New Haven. While some Jews could not recall hostility directed toward them while undergraduates, such was not the case for Stephen Greenblatt, who along with Joseph Lieberman was one of several members of Yale's class of 1964 wait-listed or denied admission at Harvard, most likely because Harvard had its own Jewish quota. An outstanding student at Newton High School outside Boston, Greenblatt, as a Yale freshman, showed talent that quickly brought him to the attention of his English teacher, who suggested that he assume the position of his research assistant. In an effort to fulfill the offer, Greenblatt proceeded to the financial aid office. There, he reported some years later, he was greeted by a graduate of the college—confirmed by the class ring on his finger—who after the briefest of formal introductions remarked, "You're Jewish, aren't you, Mr. Greenblatt?" Hearing the affirmative, the Yale administrator retorted, "Well, frankly, we're sick and tired of the number of Jews who are coming into this office after they're admitted and trying to wheedle money out of Yale University." Greenblatt questioned the generalization, only to be further assailed by the claim that "it's all in the statistics. . . . We could people this whole school with graduates of the Bronx High School of Science." Stunned and close to tears, Greenblatt could have been excused for missing the immediate implication, confirmed years later by Jerome Karabel, that the Yale admissions office purposely avoided recruiting at high-powered New York City high schools with high proportions of Jewish students.[45]

Catholics appeared to be arriving under a similar 10 percent quota. To combat the relative isolation that they also experienced as part of a religious minority, many found a socially supportive environment through the Saint Thomas More House under the direction of Yale's Roman Catholic chaplain, Father James Healey. Traditional activities revolving around formal religious services expanded in the 1960s, with the institution of a speaker series in 1961 and a program that sent students to Mexico during summer breaks to conduct secular service projects like those instituted in the early 1960s by the Peace Corps and private programs such as Crossroads Africa. Seeking strength in numbers, '64's Charles Mokriski recalled, "We reached out to all students imprudent enough to check 'Catholic' on the religious identification cards. . . . We worked to make More House not only Catholic but catholic."[46]

Yale is now known as a very gay-friendly university, but such was not the case in the early 1960s and previous years. Much of the speculation Calvin Trillen directs at the cause for classmate Denny Hensen's suicide in 1991 revolves around Hensen's conflicted homosexuality. David Finkle, 1962, writing in his fortieth class reunion book, reported that his greatest triumph in life had been his coming out after living for fifty years with sexual shame.[47] At his fortieth reunion, '64's Robert Ball also spoke movingly about the humiliation he felt hiding his sexual preference as an undergraduate. While other gay members of the class might have revealed their orientation in confidence, there was virtually no alternative culture to masculine heterosexuality on campus. Ball was stunned when classmate Stephen Wolfe, without apology, revealed his intention to enter the ministry despite being gay. Finding that assertion astounding, Ball recalled feeling doubly burdened, not just by his conflicted feelings about his sexuality but also by his alienation from Yale's social culture dominated by prep school graduates whose prime interests, he believed, were to get drunk and get laid. Only when the opportunity to further his own musical talent introduced him to members of the graduate school's faculty and students did he find a supportive social circle.[48]

Ball was not alone struggling with being in the closet in those years. Paul Monette, a gay activist who died of AIDS in 1995, entered Yale the fall of Ball's senior year, determined to disguise his sexuality at all costs. To his roommate's "knee-jerk loathing of queers," Monette admitted, he was "the first to go along, frantic to hide my own fellow-traveling. Eagerly I learned how to mock my brothers behind their backs—anything to make Jake laugh."[49] So too, '64's Kenneth Demario struggled with his sexuality at Yale. Writing for his fiftieth class reunion book, Demario revealed that while he appreciated the intellectual openness he found in college, he could never reveal his sexual feelings, choosing instead to present a heterosexual façade. "Dating was an ordeal," he confessed. "I felt compelled to have a date for big weekends—to pass as straight at all costs, subjecting myself to miserable experiences and using unsuspecting young women to further my self-protective needs." It was not until 1970 that he could bring himself tentatively to share his sexual orientation with another closeted gay classmate, Nathan Marinuzzi. After seeing *Boys in the Band*, he reported, "we finally dropped pretense, reveling in our nascent self-acceptance and regretting our inability to have connected back at Yale. We remained good friends until his death from AIDS in 1989."[50]

Nor was the campus prepared to deal with anyone with a serious disability. William Roth's outstanding record at New Haven's Hopkins Grammar School garnered his admission to Yale. He was nonetheless deeply distressed to overhear a telephone conversation between his father, a respected New Haven physician and a Holocaust survivor, and the head of the Yale health clinic. "Out of kindness," Roth reports, "Yale had decided that, though I had been admitted, I would be better off not going. Clearly, being a Yale man would be too demanding for a boy with a disability, although I was fully capable otherwise." Appalled as the younger Roth was by what he had overheard, he was gratified that his father persuaded the Yale clinician to drop opposition. "I have seen courage," Roth's father declared. "I have seen courageous soldiers fight against the Germans. I have never seen anyone as courageous as Bill." Still, that conversation continued to haunt and confound Roth, prompting him to recall his introduction to the campus "with great horror." Looking forward to living in a dormitory and meeting new friends, he found himself instead assigned a single room, prompting him to conclude, "Yale had ordained me a hermit."[51] Once the university relented, Roth made his own way without much further help, ultimately joining Joseph Lieberman, among others, as a suite-mate and becoming a prestigious Division IV Honors major and ranking scholar.

Under pressure from chaplain William Sloane Coffin and Rabbi Richard Israel, both of whom arrived in the late 1950s, President Griswold in 1962 issued new admissions guidelines that committed Yale to removing economic, social, and religious barriers to equal opportunity. With this virtual elimination of quotas, the share of Jewish students arriving that year rose to 16 percent and continued to climb until it reached a level of between a quarter and a third of each class.[52] Yale's shift in policy clearly related in part to the recommendations of the Doob report to consider more highly qualified academic candidates. The report's recommendation to admit women

When a few *Yale Daily News* editors conspired to give the impression that Yale was finally prepared to admit women, they staged a rally in support of the cause. *News* chairman Joe Lieberman led the boisterous rally shortly before he left to join other supporters of the Mississippi Freedom Party's mock election for governor. The author is to the far left in the photograph. Copyright Yale Daily News Publishing Company Inc. All rights reserved. Reprinted with permission.

as undergraduates, perhaps in recognition of the opposition generated when a rumor circulated in 1956 that Yale would soon follow such a course, got nowhere within the administration, however.[53] Even the modest decision in 1963 to open to women the Linonia and Brothers reading room, established as a gentlemen's lounge and the only place smoking was allowed in Sterling Library, drew opposition, including from the facility's director, who feared the change could be a step toward admitting women as undergraduates.[54]

Several weeks after the *Yale Daily News* reported this small step, it ran a banner headline reporting that women across the country, responding to rumors that policy was changing, had flooded the admissions office with requests for applications. An editorial supporting admission of women and a boisterous rally headed by *News* chairman Joseph Lieberman, his fist raised to spur the crowd, made the case for action.[55] In fact, the stir was created by *News* officers who organized the letter-writing campaign themselves to draw attention to the lack of action on the Doob report's recommendation. Yale College remained all male until university administrators, perceiving a loss of competitiveness as long as it remained a male bastion for undergraduates, finally opened the door to coeducation in 1969.[56] In the annals of Yale history, then, the first part of the 1960s represented more a stirring than anything revolutionary. Still, significant changes were there, even if their implications were not fully understood or appreciated at the time. Nowhere was this clearer than in the realm of politics.

* * *

Long considered a proving ground for future public figures, the Yale Political Union drew attention to its speakers and sparked heated electoral contests between its members. In the early 1960s a new Progressive Party, inspired by the historically identified Progressive campaigns of Teddy Roosevelt and Robert La Follette, joined established Conservative and Liberal caucuses as well as a Party of the Right. Additionally, a number of entirely new political organizations sprang up in the early 1960s, including an active chapter of Young Americans for Freedom, the Yale Student Peace Union, Yale Socialists, and Alternative, a peace organization seeking to replace the prevailing policy of mutual nuclear deterrence with the goal of disarmament. Even as these relatively adventurous organizations appeared, other organizations on the outer limits of the traditional political spectrum flexed their muscles, bringing prominent speakers to campus and drawing crowds to their presentations. On the right, the libertarian Calliopean Society argued strenuously against any restrictions on personal freedom, including imposition of income taxes. On the left, the George Orwell Society brought committed Marxist socialists to campus. Daniel Berman, who remembered being recruited to the group simply because it needed a freshman member to retain its charter, thought they were a group of ex-Trotskyites. Indeed, a featured speaker in the spring of 1961 was Raya Dunayevskaya, Trotsky's former secretary, now in exile and an ardent anticommunist.[57]

Political opinion on campus was clearly divided. The Kennedy-Nixon presidential contest that dominated headlines in the fall of 1960 drew mixed responses from undergraduates, with neither candidate fully capturing campus loyalty. The Calliopean Society's Michael Uhlmann, 1962, one of eight Yale students who attended the inaugural meeting of the Young Americans for Freedom at the Sharon, Connecticut, estate of *National Review* editor and Yale 1950 graduate William F. Buckley Jr., in early September, was sharply critical of Kennedy. Following Kennedy's generally admired performance in debate with Nixon, Uhlmann wrote, "Kennedy showed himself entrenched in the collectivist illusions and contradictions of Mr. [John Kenneth] Galbraith, dedicated to an unlimited expansion of Federal power. The old saying of Harry Hopkins has sunk into his brain, and whether he realizes it or not, his entire remarks of the evening could be summarized up in that . . . saying, 'Spend, spend, tax, tax, elect, elect.' "[58]

As a group, the founders of Young Americans for Freedom were cool to Nixon, giving their hearts instead to Barry Goldwater, whose 1960 book *Conscience of a Conservative*, ghostwritten by Buckley's brother-in-law and former Yale debating partner Brent Bozell, repudiated the Eisenhower legacy of coexistence and compromise. Seeking a more activist role in politics, YAF members, with Buckley's visible support at Yale and elsewhere, promoted a hard-line conservative agenda of defeating communists abroad and lifting government restrictions on individual liberty at home. The Sharon Statement behind the organization, so named for its origins at Buckley's Connecticut estate, in the spirit of Buckley's 1951 book, *God and Man at Yale*, urged conservative youth to affirm eternal truths, foremost among them "the individual's use of his God-given free will," and to reject the "relativistic empiricisms and pragmatisms of secular modernism."[59] As for students, Richard Cowan, a member of YAF's board of directors and a member of Yale's class of 1962, considered the Sharon Statement a "declaration of war against the forces of campus collectivism who would impose upon us fascism in the name of Liberalism, and a national purpose as a substitute for Freedom."[60]

As adamant as many students were in upholding Cold War tenets, the first cracks appeared in the fervid anticommunism that pervaded most political circles, liberal as well as conservative. At a campus talk by a critic of the House Un-American Activities Committee in the fall of 1960, conservative students paraded through the lecture hall bearing signs charging the speaker with having been involved in thirty-nine communist front organizations. Several months later, in response to a debate over the future of HUAC, members of the Connecticut Anti-Communist League charged that there were more than two hundred communists living in New Haven, some of them working at Yale. Massachusetts Republican representative Joseph Martin subsequently defended HUAC before the Yale Political Union. Shortly afterward, however, in early March, two members of the class of 1964, Mark Hein and John Friedberg, formed a committee devoted to abolishing the controversial anticommunist committee. Their effort, which followed publicized efforts at Cornell and Berkeley to challenge the committee, was spurred in part by a *Yale Daily News* editorial calling for HUAC's reform.[61]

The following semester the newly formed Yale Peace Union hosted Joan Baez and Bradford Little, coordinator of a San Francisco–to–Moscow "walk for peace," in a "Folksong for Peace" concert. Baez generously donated the proceeds of the concert to the organization, improving its financial status greatly, according to one of its founders, '64's Wallace Winter.[62] Members of the organization, including Bob Ball and Winter, subsequently joined a national rally in Washington against atmospheric testing of nuclear weapons, a practice that was banned the following year.

Conservative students, headed by '64's William Johnson, chairman of the Connecticut chapter of Young Americans for Freedom, countered with a "Victory Walk" from New Haven to Groton, Connecticut, in support of the Polaris missile program, which had also attracted peace protests. "We should like to show the political leaders of the Communist and so-called neutralist countries that the young people of America firmly support a strong defense establishment for our country and are not afraid to say so," Johnson declared. Union workers welcomed the student support, noting that it was the first demonstration of its kind on behalf of the program. New London metal trades leader John Wymer responded, "We don't like the pacifists. Let's buck these communists and pacifists and fight for America because that's what we believe in."[63]

Barry Goldwater spoke twice on campus in the spring of 1962, using his second appearance to blast tendencies toward pacifism and "appeasement thinking" in a speech to the Yale Political Union.[64] A series of articles authored by Joseph Lieberman pronounced conservatism at Yale "alive and well," and a subsequent article greeting incoming freshman to the fall 1962 semester described the Young Americans for Freedom as "perhaps the most vigorous political group at Yale." Lieberman identified one lonely dissenter, classmate Stephan Klingelhofer, who quit in objection to the organization's restrictive ideology. Years later, Klingelhofer recalled how, when he questioned the featured speaker at a YAF meeting, his fellow members called him a communist. Hurt and disillusioned, he continued to move left while at Yale and afterward, away from a conservative heritage that had included family visits from Richard Nixon through their neighbor, William Rogers, who later served as Nixon's secretary of state.[65]

Reports in the fall of 1962 that the Political Union would issue an invitation to Communist Party chairman Gus Hall to speak on campus prompted a barrage of criticism from Bill Buckley, who agreed to speak to the union himself, only on condition that the entire membership vote on a proposition to rescind the invitation to Hall. Buckley's position carried the day, though narrowly. By that time, however, the campus was caught up in the terrible uncertainties generated by the Cuban missile crisis. President Kennedy's blockade of Fidel Castro's communist regime drew a modest number of protesters from various peace organizations, generating taunts of "commies" and "chicken" from passing cars. Some student counterdemonstrators carried their own hammer-and-sickle signs. However dire the circumstances, not all Yale students paid attention. Keith Huffman remembers vividly the scene at Zeta Psi fraternity the evening President Kennedy declared on national television that any missile fired at the United States would result in massive retaliation against the Soviet Union. "Not a second passed after his speech ended," Huffman recalled, "until the room was back on the real important subject before us—the Zeta rush."[66]

A *Yale Daily News* editorial authored by Jonathan Rose, 1963, a moderate midwestern Republican, commended Kennedy's "firm, but carefully limited initiatives aimed at ending the Cuban offensive buildup. . . . Although a small minority of Yale students have deemed the crisis serious enough to take to the hills of Vermont, we are optimistic that the administration's determined but restrained offensive will ultimately produce a Soviet retreat." That Rose's hopes were realized did not quiet debate over Yale's preparation for nuclear war. Following reports of how little had been done to identify proper shelters, a *News* essay in December stated, "As a result of the recent speed-up of the University's civil defense plans caused by the Cuban crisis, the colleges have now begun to implement plans for converting their basements into shelters in time of atomic warfare to avoid fallout." Following the objection of some members of the Yale Peace Union that a bit of food and water put away in such locations might provide a false sense of security without tangible benefit, Provost Kingman Brewster decided not to pursue the idea any further.[67]

* * *

Although a good deal of campus debate focused on Cold War issues, such concerns were overshadowed by interest in the civil rights movement, which had remained high ever since college-based activism burst into national attention in February 1960 when students from North Carolina A&T College began a series of sit-ins at a Greensboro Woolworth's lunch counter to demand the end to segregation in public accommodations. Malcolm X spoke before a standing-room-only crowd in the law school on October 17, 1960, ironically the same day Nixon spoke to a relatively modest crowd on the New Haven Green. Paired in debate with the NAACP's national youth secretary, Herbert Wright, Malcolm rejected the central premises of integrationist civil rights activism he had embraced only months earlier, calling instead for the complete separation of the races. Among those he made an indelible impression on was Lewis Lehrman, 1960, who as a teaching fellow instructing a freshman history class recorded Malcolm's chilling effect and warned his students of Malcolm's potential influence.[68] In January 1961, South Carolina senator

Strom Thurmond described himself to the Yale Political Union as "a regular old-line Democrat of the states-rights, free-enterprise, and individual liberty school, who feels that the New Deal–Fair Deal element pirated the party name and perverted it with socialism and communism." Weeks later Ralph McGill, publisher of the *Atlanta Constitution*, also speaking before the Political Union, challenged everything the Dixiecrat Thurmond stood for by urging immediate government legislation to implement desegregation of southern schools. A conservative student coalition defeated the ensuing Political Union resolution that the federal government had a duty to intervene.[69]

Prompted by the growing debate on as well as off campus, Augustus Kinsolving, 1962, announced plans to investigate racial conditions in the South over the coming spring break. If enough students were interested, he suggested, the group would buy a truck to take participants into the Deep South to meet with members of the NAACP, the American Legion, and other groups involved in the civil rights controversy. Responding to criticism in the *Yale Daily News* that "twenty Yalies traveling en masse through Mississippi might well harm the Negro cause by stirring up resentment and animosity," the group shifted focus of "Project Truck" to traveling by car. Ultimately fourteen fellow members of Saint Anthony Hall made the trip the first week of April. They met not just with students at North Carolina A&T, including student president Jesse Jackson, and at LeMoyne College in Memphis, but also with fraternity mates at the University of Mississippi and members of the white citizens councils that had vigorously opposed integration in Mississippi and throughout the South. Taking advantage of their Yale connections, they stayed with Saint Anthony member Gus Speth's family in South Carolina and in otherwise genteel quarters in major cities, including the home of Daniel Huger in South Carolina, where they were given a guided tour of the former plantation, including outbuildings that had once housed sharecroppers. One carload followed up *Atlanta Constitution* editor Ralph McGill's speech at Yale by meeting with him in Atlanta, while another carload stayed over in Greenville, Mississippi, to meet with the progressive editor of the *Democratic-Times*, Hodding Carter. In an unsigned report in the *Yale Daily News*, a Greenville native reported that the group had intended to join a sit-in there but left before it took place, thereby averting certain arrest.[70]

Even as Project Truck formed, differences were aired on campus. After new officers of the Yale NAACP announced their intention to spur efforts to attract more black students to Yale, Edgar Leon Newman, 1962, responded in a letter to the *News*, "By limiting its sphere of activities to Negro-Americans, the NAACP plays into the hands of those who divide their fellow-countrymen into separate, ethnic blocks. There can be no hyphen before the word 'American,' and any group that puts one there hurts America." Members of the Young Americans for Freedom generally adhered to Barry Goldwater's contention, confirmed in the debate before the Political Union, that civil rights should remain a state issue.[71]

Project Truck doubtless was modest in result as well as intent, but at Yale, students were not excused from confronting racial injustice, at least if given the chance by the university's young and dynamic chaplain, William Sloane Coffin. Every bit a quintessential Yale man, a graduate of the class of 1949 after interrupting his studies to join the army, Coffin completed a divinity degree at Yale after working three years for the Central Intelligence Agency. The generally conservative Griswold appointed the thirty-four-year-old Presbyterian cleric chaplain in 1958 after Coffin had served one-year positions each as chaplain at Andover Academy and Williams College. The sense of urgency Coffin communicated in multiple speaking engagements around the country was well summarized in his Easter Sunday sermon delivered at Yale's Battell Chapel in 1961 when he commended "not education of the mind but a total transformation of one's whole being. . . . Enough of these less than halfway measures! There is something pathetic about people running around lighting lights when what we need is to have the whole bloody night come to an end."[72] Coffin put his own principles to work when he joined black and white Freedom Riders traveling on buses through the segregated South to test the Supreme Court's 1960 ruling that declared segregation in interstate bus and rail stations unconstitutional.

Although Coffin was not one of the seven blacks and six whites on two buses who left Washington, D.C., for Birmingham on May 4, 1961, the violence that greeted those passengers bothered him deeply. Joining a rally of Yale students on the New Haven Green supporting the effort, he declared that the Freedom Ride movement was "not a case of the North interfering with the South but the South interfering with the nation." Setting aside his own concerns and those of Kennedy administration officials who urged him not to join in, citing among other factors his appointment to head a training program for the first group of Peace Corps volunteers that summer, Coffin decided to lead a third group of Freedom Riders in late May.[73] Joining Coffin were Yale professor of religion Gaylord Noyce, who was white; Arthur Reagin's cousin George Bundy Smith, a Yale law student who as an undergraduate deacon at Battell Chapel had gotten to know Coffin; and four others, two of whom were black. Another black student, Marian Wright, 1964 Law, also wanted to participate, but Coffin objected, explaining, "She was only twenty then, and something in me, probably male chauvinism, wanted to protect a woman from physical harm. So I withstood her entreaties, even when they turned into tears."[74]

Coffin drove to Atlanta, where his party boarded a bus for Montgomery, Alabama. There, to President Kennedy's implied criticism of "curiosity seekers,

Yale chaplain William Sloane Coffin arrives in Montgomery, Alabama, May 24, 1961, along with other Freedom Riders, determined to challenge segregated public facilities. Coffin's arrest the following day for disorderly conduct for seeking service along with his racially mixed delegation prompted the ire not just of local whites but also of a number of university alumni and some students. Others, including Yale president A. Whitney Griswold, however, rallied to his defense. AP Photo/Perry Aycock. Courtesy of AP/Wide World Photos.

publicity seekers, and others who are seeking to serve their own causes," Coffin issued a statement replying, "We can't drag the name of the United States in the mud. The name of the United States is already in the mud." Arrested for disorderly conduct the next day after seeking service at a segregated lunch counter, the racially mixed group drew taunts from a crowd of 150. Released the following day after posting $1,000 cash bail, Coffin generated feature coverage in the *New York Times* as well as *Life*, which ran an article with his byline under the title, "Why the Chaplain Rides." Joined by the Reverend Dr. Martin Luther King Jr. and other leaders of the movement at the Montgomery home of Ralph Abernathy, the group sought guidance in prayer for their next steps. Despite the considerable pressures to turn back, which now included charges from Mississippi senator James Eastland that the rides were communist inspired, Coffin's party voted unanimously to press on.[75]

Coffin's identification with Yale provoked an outpouring of criticism and hate mail from alumni, including letters threatening not to contribute to the university if such actions continued. But many students rallied to his support, providing bail money and crowding Battell Chapel for Coffin's first sermon after he returned. There, Coffin questioned Attorney General Robert

Kennedy's call for a cooling-off period in tests of segregation in the South. Any return to normalcy "means a return to injustice—any cooling-off period must have some promise, some hope of later adjustment," he asserted. "Why should the Negroes be asked for a return to normalcy? Why shouldn't Governor [John] Patterson be asked? Why should the Negroes have to be the ones to make the concessions?"[76]

Four undergraduates who challenged Coffin's actions, including David Boren, 1963, a leading campus conservative bound for a political career, went to the extent of taking out a paid advertisement in the *News* charging the chaplain with inappropriate political behavior. "All Christians," they claimed, "abhor racial discrimination, but it is not the duty of the church or its spokesmen to dwell on questionable methods of eliminating these." Charging that "the Christian church at Yale has become an institution dedicated to the propagandizing of political liberalism under the label of Christianity," they urged Coffin to give up his outside activities and called for an investigation of his suitability to hold the position of chaplain.[77] When a *News* editorial defended Coffin, the foursome's complaints continued in letters published over several days. Notwithstanding the protests, President Griswold backed Coffin's freedom to act and shared with him the form letter he had prepared himself to respond to angry alumni. For his part, Coffin invited his student critics for an evening of "Bible study" at his home. A primary issue they raised was the feeling that protesters had injured property rights. To what must have been a rather extensive sermon concluding that there was nothing sacred about private property itself, the chaplain met the reaction, "That smacks of socialism." Coffin chose to remember that evening charitably, believing that by night's end he had made his point, even if his charges had not embraced it. In subsequent years, three of his four critics asked him to officiate at their weddings.[78]

Dissent against civil rights tactics surfaced repeatedly over the next three years, but it never matched the intensity or extent of pro–civil rights activism. By the start of the 1961–62 academic year, such efforts were in full swing, galvanized in part by the creation, with Coffin's support, of a Civil Rights Coordinating Committee to seek improvements in race relations in the North. The committee was headed by Charles Jacobson, 1962, and included leadership from Marian Wright and Freedom Rider George Bundy Smith, who warned a Yale audience, "Angry young people of today will not accept the status quo any longer."[79] Students rallied in September to raise $700 toward the $10,000 in bail set for five students jailed in McComb, Mississippi, following a sit-in at the local Woolworth's. Speakers, including Students for a Democratic Society founder Tom Hayden, flooded the campus to recount gruesome stories of resistance to civil rights actions in the South.[80]

Simultaneously, the reasons for Arthur Reagin's concern about his own admission to a fraternity became manifest when Saint Anthony Hall elected its first black member, his classmate Wendell Mottley. Although serving as a three-year version of Yale's senior societies, Saint Anthony was also part of the national Delta Psi fraternity, with chapters in North Carolina and Mississippi as well as in Virginia, whose members of the Upsilon chapter immediately objected. The Yale membership politely but firmly told a delegation of fraternity brothers who flew to New Haven from Virginia that they were not backing down, a position that was quietly insisted on by Yale administrators and commended by the *Yale Daily News*.[81]

Another new organization, the Northern Student Movement, modeled after the Student Nonviolent Coordinating Committee (SNCC) and headed by Peter Countryman, who dropped out of Yale to launch the effort following the 1961 Freedom Rides, led a series of protests. They started with a demonstration against local housing discrimination in cooperation with New Haven's newly formed chapter of the Congress of Racial Equality (CORE). Further demonstrations followed in Baltimore in December and continued on Maryland's Eastern Shore in the spring, where students were met by a hostile mob armed with broken bottles. By the spring of 1963, the effort had grown sufficiently to merit an article in *Time*, which reported the involvement of some twenty-seven hundred students on fifty campuses. Not insignificantly, the magazine coupled its report with another article chronicling high jinks at various campuses, including Yale's still annual freshman riot.[82]

The growing civil rights activism persisted through 1962 into 1963 as special attention was directed to the South, where student demonstrations extended over the summer. James Meredith's effort to integrate the University of Mississippi drew particular attention. The *News* dispatched columnist John Lehr, 1963, to the campus for daily reports during the early part of October 1962. While a number of Yale students donned white armbands in solidarity with Meredith, others countered with black armbands. Yale '64's Michael Van Horn explained the countermeasure, writing, "I am neither a Southerner nor a segregationist, but the ideas which come from groups such as Northern Student Movement are usually so ludicrous that I feel we should show these groups that they are usually ignored and ridiculed." David Boren extended his assault on integrationists by writing, "In this age in which centralized government devours more and more of our individual freedom, the threat of a power hungry judiciary becomes a haunting nightmare. . . . While the hate and violence are deplorable, some Mississippians have made great sacrifices to raise a valid constitutional question."[83]

Despite such criticism, civil rights interest continued to grow, spurred additionally by Martin Luther King's January 1962 sermon delivered in Yale's

Battell Chapel at Coffin's invitation. Presented in an erudite manner to his largely academic audience, King's discourse on "A Complete Life" lacked the passion of his civil rights organizing, but his declaration that students sitting in at lunch counters represented "the best in the American dream" drew positive response. Writing to thank his speaker, Coffin noted, "I am really heartened by the movement in the right direction I sense at Yale. Of course we are always too slow."[84] Additional groups of students prepared throughout the spring of 1963 for summer travel to Mississippi to assist civil rights campaigns. Directing them, together with Marian Wright, was Bob Moses, a native of Harlem and a graduate of Hamilton College who had taken a central role in organizing voter registration efforts in Mississippi in the early 1960s. It was his appeal for help at the Yale Law School that launched the effort.[85] Among those most receptive to the message was '64's Stephen Bingham.

Bingham was the most recent Yale student in a long family tradition that included his grandfather Hiram Bingham III, former U.S. senator and governor of Connecticut, and his father, Alfred, a liberal activist and founder during the Great Depression of the leftist journal *Common Sense*. Despite his private school preparation for Yale, Bingham did not associate with the prep school crowd. Instead, he threw himself into an array of student activities, including the Yale Political Union, the Yale Young Democratic Club, and the National Student Association, where he fought unsuccessfully to establish a Yale chapter. Also a member of the Northern Student Movement headed by Peter Countryman, he considered civil rights "an ideal which is seen as far more important than merely helping the Negro toward a better life" because it was organizing around the broader "problem of changing society."[86] A prolific contributor to the *Yale Daily News*, he was elected to the paper's leadership as executive editor in the spring of 1963.

In his coverage of civil rights activism, Bingham was especially impressed with Bob Moses, and it was no surprise he was one of the first volunteers to embrace Moses's idea of running a parallel "freedom vote" campaign for governor of Mississippi in the fall of 1963, a mock election that "would demonstrate . . . that the Negro people of Mississippi would vote if they were allowed to register free from intimidation and discrimination." Getting black residents to vote, even if the results would not be officially counted, was dangerous work. When liberal activist and 1954 Yale Law School graduate Allard Lowenstein pressed SNCC to bring white northern college students into the effort, Moses and the SNCC organizers initially debated the utility of the idea. Ultimately convinced of the need for more workers to get out the vote and the publicity value their presence would bring, Moses agreed to Lowenstein's plan to recruit at Stanford and Yale, where, through an invitation from Bill Coffin, Lowenstein had lectured on the evils of apartheid in Africa and discussed his 1962 book on the subject, *Brutal Mandate*.[87] On October 6, 1963, Mississippi civil rights leaders "nominated" for governor Aaron Henry, a black Clarksdale pharmacist and president of the Council of Federated Organizations, a civil rights coalition formed in the state in 1962. Edwin King, the white chaplain at Tougaloo College and a civil rights worker who bore disfiguring scars from the beatings he received in his efforts, joined the freedom slate as lieutenant governor.

On the evening of October 16, with the short Mississippi campaign just under way, Lowenstein appealed to Yale students gathered in Dwight Hall, the central location for coordinating student volunteers. "Mississippi is a sick place," he declared. "It's so sick that to go to Mississippi is to leave America in the way that we think of America and to see America in a grotesque mirror in which all the warts are magnified. But it is our warts. It is us. It is our racial sickness." Reminding those in attendance that they were "of the most privileged part of America and the most privileged products of the greatness of our society," he urged them to donate money, or better, sign up to help the Mississippi campaign. At a subsequent meeting at Coffin's home, where Lowenstein called for volunteers, Steve Bingham made his formal commitment.[88] Together with classmates and fellow members of the *News* staff Gary Saxonhouse and Jon Van Dyke, he joined the first convoy of Yale students driving south the following morning. An editorial penned by *News* chairman Joseph Lieberman, an accompanying column by William Torbert, 1965, and a direct appeal to Yale students from Aaron Henry, published as an exclusive interview in the *News*, added a sense of urgency to the effort.[89]

Publicity surrounding their departure prompted Mississippi governor Ross Barnett to lash out specifically at Yale students for intruding, a position that found some support on campus. South Carolina native Gus Speth described the mock election as useless, comparing giving the vote to blacks to imposing a sophisticated political system on an underdeveloped country. Speth's complaint generated support from history professor Howard Lamar, but prompted sharp retorts from classmates Wendell Mottley, who accused him of misunderstanding the Negro plight, and Thomas Roderick, cochair of the Yale Human Relations Council, who asserted that the struggle for civil rights was everybody's struggle: "If it goes badly it is less the fault of those in the front line than it is the fault of those who stand by silently. . . . At some time we will have to go into the South and into the slums of our Northern cities and work and sweat in the guts of the problem."[90] But it was Joseph Lieberman who set the tone for the extensive coverage of the effort in the *News* in his October 28 editorial, "Why I Go to Mississippi."

From the moment he took the position of *News* chairman in January 1963, Lieberman wrote eloquently about the realization of the dream of equal rights

and opportunities for all Americans. As an intern with Senator Abraham Rib-
icoff that summer, he joined the March on Washington, later writing, "For
me, this was America at its best, America as my upbringing with family and
friends in Stamford had encouraged me to believe it could be. Hundreds
of thousands of us, of all religions, races and nationalities, joined together
peacefully but powerfully to petition our government to right the wrong of
racial bigotry."[91] In the first part of October 1963 he used the paper's front
page to address an open letter to all Yale alumni, urging them to use their
influence to advance civil rights. "If Yale graduates do not act from their positions of importance in the North and South, who will act?" he asked. Now, as
he prepared to join other students in Mississippi, he pointedly announced he
was writing for himself, not for the paper, stating,

> I am going to Mississippi because there is much work to be done there
> and few men doing it. I look to the facts of the history of this State's
> treatment of its Negro citizens and I see very little but hatred and
> painful dehumanization. . . . I see countless Negro Mississippians who
> are too terrorized to act. It all becomes a personal matter to me, I am
> challenged personally. As the Talmudic fathers have written with such
> sagacity, "If I am not for myself, who will be? If I am for myself (alone)
> what am I? And if not now, when then?"

Refusing to consider himself an outsider, Lieberman declared, "I am an American. This is one nation or it will be nothing. . . . As one fights against hatred
and illegality in New Haven, so too does one have the right, and indeed, the
duty to oppose malice and injustice in Indianola." Citing the Reverend Coffin,
Lieberman concluded that the presence of Yale men in Mississippi would make
it clear to black Mississippians that this struggle is "not one which puts white
men against black men; rather, it is a struggle which puts white and black men
against injustice."[92]

Lieberman made his commitment to travel south at the meeting held in
Coffin's house on October 16 with Allard Lowenstein, who was there on the
premise that if he could recruit the "best and brightest" from the American
establishment, he would be able to show that the system could work. For his
part, Lieberman recalled, "We talked a lot about religious values, and you've
got to do this to be consistent, and if you do it others will follow. I found it to
be an irresistible argument." Publicly, Lieberman described his own experience, working out of Jackson, Mississippi, as relatively uneventful: drafting
press releases, calling reporters, circulating brochures in black neighborhoods
encouraging people to vote in the mock election. In an interview in the early
1990s for Jodi Lynne Wilgoren's senior essay at Yale, he was less guarded,

commenting, "We would look for black diners and restaurants to eat in because we were more comfortable there than in white establishments. It was the first time in my life that I felt racial division so seriously, and I was in this unusual and sort of perspective-changing position of feeling that my own race was a threat to me and those who were black were not, were protective." [93]

Coffin considered Lieberman's leadership from the bully pulpit of the *News*, and his own commitment to the cause, essential. Among those Lieberman recruited directly for the effort were two fellow members of the senior society Elihu, Jonathan Greene and Thomas Powers. Both found the experience highly unsettling. Greene recalled that initially he thought he would find less acceptance from blacks, some of whom were clearly uncomfortable with his presence, than from whites. By the time he got to Meridian, Mississippi, however, he felt the force of white resistance and admitted he was really scared.[94] For Powers, the lesson came quickly as he entered the Mississippi Delta. There he and fellow students were stopped by a sheriff's deputy, his gun drawn and issuing the sinister message, "Our Niggers are content the way things are run. Nothing is ever going to change here." Days later, after being informed while at the Freedom Vote headquarters in Jackson that Yale graduate student Bruce Payne had been shot and wounded, Powers prodded his partners to leave early the next morning. As they departed, however, a truck across the street pulled in behind them and followed at high speed for miles. Fortunately the students' car was faster, and they finally pulled away, but there was no doubt of the threat to their well-being. Had they hit an obstacle in the road, Powers reflected, they would have been lost.[95]

Not every experience was quite so confrontational. Chip Nielsen and Frank Basler, whose service as Battell Chapel deacons their senior year put them in close touch with Coffin, joined the trek south with his encouragement. During his first day in Greenwood, where Bob Moses had launched the Mississippi registration campaign several years earlier, all Nielsen's companions were arrested for distributing literature supporting Aaron Henry's campaign for governor. Whether or not he was spared because of his formidable height at six foot five, Nielsen felt obliged to inquire after the safety of his companions. Instead of being arrested himself when he reached the jail, he found himself engaged by a member of the prison staff who offered him a tour to see how the people of Mississippi really lived in peace. While he did not accept the invitation, Nielsen was sufficiently impressed to arrange an exchange of newspapers between Greenwood and his hometown in California, in the naïve belief, as he later recounted, that a bit of education would help over time.[96]

Frank Basler was arrested in a separate incident involving leafleting in Indianola. As he was released, he too was encouraged to get to know the place better through southern eyes, this time by a member of the local white citizens council. The sales approach was consistent with public actions of the council, which attempted to set itself apart from the Ku Klux Klan through a commitment to nonviolence. Shortly after taking an outwardly cordial tour of the town, Basler received a call from his father, who after becoming aware of his son's trip to Mississippi for the first time when he heard the news of his arrest, insisted he return to Yale.[97] As part of his reporting for the *News*, Jon Van Dyke interviewed Mississippi governor Ross Barnett. Sharply critical of outside interference in his state, Barnett made inflated claims for his black constituents, 90 percent of whom, he asserted, stayed in the state after graduating from high school. Van Dyke concluded his interview by quoting the governor: "Stay around for a while and we will doctrinate you. Mississippi's way of life is the best in the world."[98]

Bingham found himself traveling directly with Lowenstein from a rally in Greenwood to Clarksdale, where they sought shelter for the night. Once they reached the city limits, a car began following them. Soon police pulled them over and ticketed them for going through a stop sign that did not exist. As they walked from their car to enter the Alcazar Hotel across the street, police stopped them again and arrested them for loitering and violating the curfew. Yale students rallied to news of the arrests of Bingham and others by raising hundreds of dollars in bail money. Further demonstrations of goodwill prompted one Yale professor to proclaim that the university was "on the moral map as it never has been before."[99] Meanwhile, Bingham was spared the worst when Lowenstein, given the chance to make one phone call, addressed his remarks to Franklin Roosevelt III in a sufficiently loud voice to make sure they would be heard by his jailers: "No, don't call President Kennedy tonight; wait until tomorrow." From that point on, Lowenstein's biographer reports, "the prisoners were treated in a model fashion." Released after paying a fine the next day, both men returned to their cause.[100]

Nothing he experienced in Mississippi struck Bingham as model, a position he made clear in a letter to the *Washington Post* after his release and return to the university. "I write as a Yale student who has in recent days experienced the horrors of police harassment, arrest and jailing for no other reason than that of campaigning for a Negro candidate for Governor of Mississippi," he declared. Urging the Justice Department to finally take action to secure equal rights, he asked, "How long must we wait for justice? By we, I do not mean the Negroes, for I am not a Negro. I do not mean the whites either. I mean all self-respecting men. It is indeed difficult for anyone who has not tasted the dust of the cotton fields, who has not canvassed the dirt streets of Jackson, who has not seen the total segregation of all facilities to imagine that a large part of this great country exists without justice, with law harassment instead of law protection."[101] At Yale, he led a rally along with other returned students and urged further financial contributions to support civil rights workers. He reiterated his plea in a subsequent *News* column, asserting that "until the black people of Mississippi and the rest of the South—and North—are free, we shall not be free." The same day, the *News* reported that Malcolm X, holding a news conference in New Haven, disparaged the Yale effort in Mississippi, saying that blacks did not need the vote so much as self-sufficiency. "I've never met an intelligent white man yet who could whole-heartedly accept the Negro as equal," Malcolm was recorded as saying in a story that ran below the front-page lead, "Four Yale Students Beaten in Mississippi Freedom Vote."[102]

* * *

President Kennedy's assassination on November 22 shocked the Yale campus and the world. Students gathered around television monitors in disbelief. Activities associated with the Harvard-Yale weekend came to a screeching halt. Most Americans who lived through that moment can recall where they were and what they were doing. Many look back on that moment as the shattering of liberal dreams for a new era. Under the headline, "A Void," Joseph Lieberman, after declaring that Kennedy gave new meaning to the American dream, concluded, "his actions spoke with unmistakable clarity to us—the young, the dreamers whose dreams rest in the political system. He renewed our faith; he extended our vision of what was possible." Others echoed that sentiment years later, even after Kennedy's personal and political limitations had been widely exposed and dissected. For the moment, however, '64's Martin Padley reported, "you and I went on after that November afternoon and so did our senior year."[103] Several weeks later, conservatives swept the Political Union elections, retaining '64's Charles Garland as speaker. Three days later five students who were caught with dates in their rooms at 1 a.m. were denied social and visiting privileges until the beginning of Christmas vacation.[104]

If these were signs of a return to normalcy, they did not affect the whole campus. On December 12 the *News* printed a special supplement on civil rights activities in New Haven. The issue was dedicated to the memory of '64's Vincent Taus, who had been killed in an automobile accident the previous week. Taus had founded a tutoring program at Community Baptist Church. His work was being carried on by others, including classmate Thomas Roderick, cochair of Yale's Human Relations council, who reiterated the importance of involving students in projects aimed at improving the social conditions of minority groups.[105]

For Steve Bingham, there could be no return to normalcy. Seeking to build on wide publicity and sympathy that the mock election in Mississippi had generated outside the South, Allard Lowenstein argued for recruiting even more northern students to register voters. Once again SNCC workers debated the value of involving white students in southern registration campaigns. Once again, Bob Moses prevailed, determining to recruit as many as one thousand volunteers to form the backbone of support for Freedom Summer 1964. Bingham devoted the remainder of his school year to building the Mississippi voting rights campaign. As he recalled, "I don't remember going to school for the rest of the year. The thing so traumatized me in a positive sense, that everything at Yale just suddenly seemed irrelevant, and this summer project became the only thing worth spending time on." Yale was designated one of twenty Freedom Centers around the nation charged with providing information and helping screen potential summer volunteers. As head of the Yale center, Bingham spoke on college campuses throughout the Northeast and helped review thousands of applications that came in through a little office he set up on the Old Campus. Lowenstein visited the campus repeatedly to help recruitment, a process that accelerated when Martin Luther King's endorsement of the project was broadcast in the law school auditorium.[106]

Bingham later wondered how he ever got through the semester. In fact, he failed a course and had to make it up at the end of his Freedom Summer commitment. With the advice of C. Vann Woodward, Yale's newly arrived distinguished southern historian, he arranged with University of Mississippi historian James Wesley Silver to write an independent research paper in order to complete his degree. Ironically, on the same day that the *Washington Post* had printed Bingham's letter about the mock election, an editorial praised Silver for his landmark book, *Mississippi: The Closed Society*.[107]

Yale's 263rd graduation ceremony held on June 15 marked a fitting transition for the class of 1964. In a year filled with news of the turmoil stemming from civil rights activism, it was especially apt to see Martin Luther King presented an honorary degree. His presence had been very much in doubt because he had been arrested and jailed in St. Petersburg, Florida. At the last minute, King was released and able to receive the honor in person. King's recognition acknowledged, "As your eloquence has kindled the nation's sense of outrage, so your steadfast refusal to countenance violence in resistance to injustice has heightened our sense of national shame." To further make the point, Kingman Brewster, in his first address to graduates since becoming Yale's president, urged them to avoid the kind of "moral timidity" that excuses either racial oppression "because it is socially conditioned" or mob violence because "you can't blame the victims of oppression."[108] Looking to the graduates' next steps, it seemed equally fitting that President Kennedy's brother-in-law Sargent Shriver was also honored that day, as both founder of the Peace Corps and director of President Johnson's emerging War on Poverty.

Among those attending the celebration were the families of Art Reagin and Jim Rogers, suite-mates and close friends, despite the difference in their backgrounds. Reagin's father had grown up in Selma, Alabama, just miles away from the Rogers home in Demopolis. In the charged era of civil rights activism, the two young men were concerned about how their families would get along. They need not have worried. As their parents exchanged pleasantries about the area of Alabama they knew so well, Reagin and Rogers could enjoy the occasion, assured that divisions in social origin, race, religion, and ethnicity that had once marked their classmates were, for now, bridged, even as the country continued to undergo considerable change.[109] Every outsider had, as Calvin Trillin put it, become the likes of them as a Yale man. The day was beautiful and full of promise. What might have seemed like a shaky world in recent years appeared predicable enough. That, of course, was wishful thinking.

2

Into the "Long Sixties," 1964–1974

Peter Harding's Yale experience left him a changed man.
A native of Ohio, where he grew up imbued with the legacy of his great-uncle, former president Warren Harding, he quickly shed his Republican affiliation after witnessing the dynamic John F. Kennedy's campaign stop in New Haven in 1960. Following his graduation in 1964, Harding also forsook a long family tradition of attending medical school and entered law school at the University of Michigan, then recanted and trained at UCLA's medical school. The college experience often caused such shifts in direction, but classmates must have been startled to hear the rest of his declarations of independence. Years later he took pride in recounting the full range of countercultural experiences he embraced once he relocated to the West Coast: literally, drugs, sex, and rock 'n' roll. As he put it, "I tried everything I could, every drug, many kinds of sex, and listened to a lot of music on acid, all the while getting through medical school, albeit dropping from a good student to just getting by. When I was an intern, I purchased raw oceanfront land in Big Sur and headed there every weekend for eighteen months to drop acid. That was an important aspect of my training, especially as a psychiatrist. Once you've been through something like that, a lot of fear goes away, and I could appreciate first-hand the concepts of catharsis and abreaction. It's a perfect kind of training if you can survive it."[1]

While Harding's post-college embrace of the countercultural trends, so widely associated with the sixties, was not unique, his experience hardly qualified as typical for his classmates. One could argue, as '64's John Meigs did in his tenth reunion report, that his own immediate age group was "trying for a success in terms astonishingly similar to that to which their parents may have wished" and that it was people a few years younger who "seem to me to have been liberated, not us."[2] A survey for '64's tenth reunion report confirmed the impression that this group of men had sailed through the era. Fully one-third were working as doctors or lawyers, with business and academic professionals taking up a major portion of the other listed occupations. Although more than half of those surveyed anticipated changing jobs in the future, fully 59 percent reported that they were doing what they said they would be doing on graduation. "Things going along nicely as the 'American dream' unfolds," Robert Jacobs, then a senior attorney for the Bendix Corporation in Michigan, commented. "After Yale graduation my most important goal was to be a success in the materialistic business world so that I could continue to have and to give to my family the advantages I had been fortunate enough to have," John Mettler reported, after parlaying a business degree from Columbia into ownership of his own company in Connecticut.[3]

They were not alone in charting the kind of career successes that had marked generations of Yale graduates before them, and yet a close look at their classmates suggest quite another set of experiences and outlooks. In the decade extending beyond their graduation, a period culminating in Richard Nixon's resignation and often referred to as the "long sixties," these men's lives changed significantly. Ten years out, this class that once looked so homogeneous was already divided in ways that only the 1960s could explain.

In time-honored fashion, some 1964 graduates proceeded immediately to employment, many of them drawn to the rich opportunities located only seventy miles away in New York City. To a striking degree, the world they entered remained that of their fathers. Even as Guild Copeland landed a job with the advertising firm of Lennon and Newel, he encountered a culture every bit as excessive by contemporary standards as that portrayed in the popular television show *Mad Men*. One of the first bits of advice he received was not to drink vodka at lunch. The intended moral was not that drinking was bad but that if a copywriter were to make any mistakes with a client, he wanted the blame to be attributed to the liquor on his breath (presumably, vodka was odorless) rather than to any lack of native intelligence. To make the point of how insulated he was from the changes that emerged over the next few years, Copeland recounted his experience in an advertising seminar some years into his career. The subject was the use of musical presentations, and the instructor hoped to elicit a response when he asked whether anyone in the group had been at the iconic Woodstock music festival in 1969. Copeland was the only one in the room to raise his hand. But before the team leader could call on him for inspiration, Copeland dashed his hopes by reporting, "I was there for the National Guard."[4]

However great the continuity with previous alumni of elite colleges, a significant number of Yale's latest graduates were entering new territory, prompted most notably by the challenges associated with their years in college. The most striking departure from the past was the decision of more than thirty class members to enter the Peace Corps. One other class member, Terry Holcombe, chose a parallel opportunity offered by ACCION, a privately funded community development organization founded in 1961 and based in Venezuela.[5] Many who chose to serve abroad cited John F. Kennedy's challenge to their generation. Others found avenues at home to achieve similar social goals, as the Northern Student Movement extended its tutoring efforts to cities across the Northeast and Midwest, and Yale launched a summer high school using its own students and a group from Hampton Institute as tutors to inner city youth chosen from around the country to prepare for college.[6] Most immediately visible for the class of 1964 was the Freedom Summer effort Stephen Bingham had worked so hard to bring to fruition the last part of his senior year. The perceived success of introducing white northern college students to SNCC's voter registration campaign in Mississippi in the fall of 1963 now expanded to include some one thousand students from across the country, including, in addition to Bingham, classmates Tom Rowe, Dan Berman, and Nick Allis.

Even as volunteers gathered in central Ohio to train for their summer commitment to register African Americans in Mississippi, it became clear that the high stakes of the previous fall's mock election campaign had risen even higher. Tom Rowe's arrival was delayed a bit, and he remembers entering his first orientation session just as Mickey Schwerner's wife delivered the chilling news that her husband and two other civil rights workers were missing after their release from a Philadelphia, Mississippi, jail. No one missed the implication. "We began to see ourselves as possible sacrifices, horrible but perhaps necessary," Stephen Bingham recalled. "There was, sad to say, a strong feeling that only by the death of white northerners would the nation ever wake up to the horrors of Mississippi."[7] Fellow trainees feared the worst, their concern vindicated with the discovery of the civil rights workers' bodies two months later. Further reports of violence prompted some trainees to drop out, but the vast majority, the Yale contingent included, pressed on.

Neither Rowe, whose assignment was in Gulfport, a military town where 27 percent of eligible black voters were already registered, nor Allis, who worked out of Hattiesburg, where the largest number of volunteers were concentrated, faced any immediate danger. Daniel Berman received a number of threatening calls while on duty at SNCC headquarters in Meridian, the home of James Chaney, one of the three civil rights workers murdered in nearby Philadelphia. An elderly deacon was shot in the calf at the church where he and other volunteers congregated, but Berman considered his time in the state safe enough. By summer's end, he felt confirmed in the belief that he was making a positive difference.[8]

Bingham's assignment was in Mileston, Holmes County, where he lived for six weeks with some dozen colleagues, facing incessant hostility, including the torching of a SNCC car and an attempted bombing. In Bingham's words, it was all "fighting off the heat, the dust, the discouragement, the fear." As he had been as a *Yale Daily News* writer, Bingham proved a thoughtful observer of the landmark civil rights effort, coming to believe that Mississippi's black residents needed better wages in addition to the vote in order to break the hold of the region's paternalistic society. He also recognized growing tensions between black and white workers, noting, "Not a lot was articulated, but it was just an undercurrent of everything that was going on, that this was a ticking bomb and somehow we have to get a handle on this."[9]

Having completed his stay in Mississippi, Bingham made his way to Berkeley's Boalt Hall School of Law in the fall of 1964. There he encountered the first major student rebellion of the new era, the Free Speech Movement, a challenge to university authority catalyzed in large part by the equally impassioned civil rights advocate with whom he had roomed in Mississippi, Mario Savio. The protests that escalated from growing objections to university restrictions on student political activity to include the occupation of university buildings and violent clashes with police stemmed precisely from the kind of activities that had drawn Bingham's attention at Yale. Yet as he started law school that fall, he found the work daunting, and the most he felt he could do under the circumstances was to take a lunch break at times when demonstrations were building so he could observe what was going on.[10] Indeed, with only a year of law school behind him Bingham married and determined to leave Berkeley together with his wife, Gretchen Spreckels, to join the Peace Corps.

The opportunity to serve abroad provided a natural complement to Bingham's civil rights activism in college, and that background was just what Peace Corps staff looked for in stressing the importance of community development skills among volunteers. The assignment to apply the organizing principles of Saul Alinsky to the village of Njama via Tabe in central Sierra Leone appealed immensely to the young couple. But they soon found their training at Hampton Institute inadequate and became more frustrated when their assignment changed to an area that spoke a different language from the one they had learned. Bingham later insisted that he gained a lot from the two-year experience, but he found it difficult to put theory into practice abroad.[11] By the end of his assignment, he was eager to return to law school. What he felt back in the United States was culture shock.

Mario Savio, in residence, Holmes County, Mississippi, Freedom Summer, 1964. To the rear is his fellow civil rights volunteer Stephen Bingham. Both men returned to Berkeley for the new academic year, where Savio helped ignite and direct the Free Speech Movement that ushered campus protest fully into public view. Copyright 1978 Matt Herron/Take Stock.

The mood on the Berkeley campus had darkened considerably by the fall of 1967. Escalation of the war in Vietnam, and the draft calls that came with it, heightened antiwar activity and brought increased civil disorder on and off the campus. Everything was in incredible ferment, Bingham recalled. He had not been exposed to drugs his first year in law school. Now they were everywhere. At demonstrations police were beating young people right and left. An ardent opponent of the war himself, Bingham felt his best contribution lay in helping to provide legal assistance to protesters, and he threw himself into that effort through the Boalt Hall Community Assistance Program. As activism consumed more and more of his attention, he drew apart from his wife, separating during his first year back in law school and divorcing the following year. That break coincided with a growing immersion in Marxist doctrine, which further honed his now fierce opposition to the liberal orthodoxy of the Johnson administration.[12]

When the primary challenge to Johnson's presidency came in the spring of 1968, Bingham campaigned for Bobby Kennedy. After Kennedy's assassination, Bingham received funding from a small foundation that allowed him to turn from electoral politics to organizing a team of law and medical students to serve poor communities in the San Joaquin Valley in central California.

They directed their effort at farmworkers, many of whom were being organized by the United Farm Workers headed by Cesar Chavez. The experience
reminded Bingham of Mississippi because he found injustices everywhere,
including government programs he felt were propping up farm growers
at workers' expense. As summer drew to a close, he arranged for Eldridge
Cleaver, author of the searing and controversial indictment of American racism, *Soul on Ice*, to speak at a wrap-up event in Santa Barbara.

Ever more determined to bring resources closer to the people he was to
serve, Bingham vowed on his return to Berkeley not to be a "suit-and-tie lawyer who sanctimoniously receives the client in his well-appointed office," and
to avoid "the traditional liberal's self-satisfying, but irrelevant band-aid dis-
pensing." When news broke that the university was buying up grapes and
offering them as the only available fruit in campus dining halls in defiance
of the national boycott called by Chavez, Bingham and three other Anglos
joined seven Chicanos to blockade Berkeley president Charles Hitch's office.
Bingham ended up being arrested together with three other white supporters of the group, including Dan Siegel, who the following year led a student
protest that turned violent at Berkeley's People's Park. Quickly tabbed the
"Chicano 11," despite their mixed racial identity, the group spent five days in
jail. Far in time and space from the experience of his first arrest with Allard
Lowenstein in Mississippi, Bingham, while incarcerated, joined his colleagues
in a hunger strike in solidarity with the grape boycott.[13]

Another cause, shared by other self-described radical law students, was to
revitalize the nearly moribund National Lawyers Guild. The guild had been
founded in 1937 as an alternative to the American Bar Association and its
exclusionary membership practices and conservative political orientation.
During Freedom Summer, guild lawyers had played an active role in defending civil rights workers, despite objections to their participation from the
NAACP because the guild had previously defended communists. Although
never officially listed as a communist front organization, the guild had a
leftist reputation that prompted many young lawyers in the 1950s and early
1960s to avoid it. Bingham, however, participated in a series of roundtable
discussions the guild sponsored his first year in law school. By the time he
had returned to a radically altered political climate, the guild struck him and
many of his associates as dated, locked into an old-left ideology that was out
of touch with the issues that were currently roiling college campuses.[14]

Together with other Bay Area activists, and supported in the guild's
national office by its director, Bernardine Dohrn, Bingham worked first to
secure student membership and then to shift the direction of its leadership.
Locally Bingham joined other guild members in securing defense lawyers for
some seven hundred San Francisco State students arrested at a 1968 strike

to demand an ethnic studies program and to protest the war. At the guild's insistence, Bingham reported, defendants stuck together and resisted making individual plea bargains that might have resulted in modest fines and community service. When activist lawyers succeeded in getting the charges dismissed entirely, the decision evoked the ire not just of Acting President S. I. Hayakawa, but also of Governor Ronald Reagan and most of the California political establishment.[15] Having completed his degree and passed the California bar exam in the summer of 1969, Bingham accepted a community services fellowship funded by the federal Office of Economic Opportunity and joined Berkeley Neighborhood Legal Services. There he worked on tenants' rights and redevelopment issues in West Berkeley. Together with a group of seasoned activists from various Bay Area protests, he moved to a house in Oakland just beyond the Berkeley city line. In Oakland, he lived a communal and spartan existence, supported by friends who shared the determination to resist the misuses of power they witnessed in their lives and in their work. Through his legal assistance work, he came to know the Black Panther Party's attorney, Charles Geary, whom he described as "an amazing lawyer." When police threatened to raid the Panther headquarters in Oakland, he was among a group of volunteer attorneys from the National Lawyers Guild who agreed to stay there overnight to defend residents from any misuse of search warrant procedures by local police. Looking back, he felt the effort and the publicity that came with it may have saved lives by preventing the kind of violent confrontation that took place in other Panther facilities around the country, such as the killing by police in Chicago of Panther leader Fred Hampton while he was asleep in his house.[16]

* * *

Bingham's Berkeley experience typified the shift among early activists to more radical causes, as lines hardened over how far the civil rights effort should go as it assumed greater militancy and as establishment claims for the extension of American ideals in Vietnam withered under intense scrutiny. By the late 1960s, a number of the members of the class of 1964 besides Bingham had refashioned their early idealist views in strikingly new forms. One of these was Michael Price, like Bingham a prep school graduate and returning Peace Corps volunteer.

Struck by the mass migration to cities he encountered while serving in Ethiopia, Price enrolled in Harvard's program in regional planning upon his return to the United States. Initially he thought he would direct his training toward Africa's needs. Once he realized, however, that American cities were going up in flames, he decided instead to address urban issues closer to home.

By the time he started classes in the fall of 1966, after narrowly avoiding a military physical that would most likely have led to his induction, Price found the university already in turmoil. Students for a Democratic Society was building to oppose the war, and in the process was questioning university authority, including rules in place as late as the fall of 1965 that prohibited women, even mothers, in student rooms during the week. Price had never encountered marijuana at Yale. It was everywhere he went while he served in the Peace Corps, and as a consequence he was hardly put off by the omnipresence of drugs in Cambridge nor the activism that was building on campus. Much of his time as a graduate student at Harvard was taken up in endless meetings that culminated in the strike that resulted in the occupation of College Hall and the ejection of university administrators there in the fall of 1968.[17]

Harvard's urban planning program concentrated on conveying technical skills, an approach that Price found unsatisfactory. As a result, he transferred to MIT's planning program, where he came under the influence of Gar Alperovitz, an early critic of U.S. Cold War policies and a pioneer in advocacy planning. While still at MIT, Price moved to a cheap apartment in East Cambridge, where he undertook a community organizing effort among the city's poorest residents. The following year, he took his first job, as a community organizer devoted to stopping an extension of Interstate 95 through low-income areas of Roxbury, Dorchester, and Jamaica Plain. As a result of the opposition, Governor Francis Sargent ultimately halted the highway's construction.[18]

Among Price's activities on his return to the United States was membership in the Committee of Returned Volunteers (CRV), which was composed largely of former Peace Corps participants, as well as other U.S. citizens who had served in a volunteer capacity abroad. Price became the head of the Boston chapter, which was composed largely of graduate students like him. As a central project, they undertook a study of Cuba, which Price considered at the time a possible third alternative to the gray socialism of the Soviet Union and capitalism in the United States. Through a contact at *Ramparts*, the national organization received an invitation to visit Cuba in the summer of 1969. Price joined a group of several dozen members of CRV who traveled through Mexico to Cuba for a stay of close to three months. As part of a national effort to break the embargo on Cuba and to highlight its effect on poor farmers, members of the delegation spent some time cutting sugarcane. But the bulk of their time was spent visiting institutions such as schools, mental health centers, and a model farm where they heard from Cuban representatives about the island's presumed virtues.

A freighter had been designated to take the delegation back home at the end of its stay. Price remembers watching from the upper deck as another group of a dozen or so people marching in lockstep and chanting revolutionary slogans ascended the gangplank to join his colleagues on board. There, at the head of a recognizable delegation of radical activists, was Bernardine Dohrn. Subsequent accounts revealed that the group had received monetary as well as moral support during their Cuban visit for the "days of rage" that soon followed their determination to break from SDS in favor of more revolutionary tactics as the new Weathermen faction.[19] For the most part, Dohrn's group had nothing to do with the CRV delegation, but Price did note her striking looks as she led fellow militants in exercises while clad in a bikini.

When they were about to leave Havana harbor, Price engaged two attractive blond women who were part of Dohrn's group. They were standing at the rail watching the sun set in what seemed like a beautiful night in Havana. By way of breaking the ice, he asked, "I wonder when we'll be back in Havana again?" One of the women turned to him and said, "Never." Had she had such a terrible experience? he asked. "I'll be dead in a year," was the reply. At the time Price cringed at such revolutionary pretensions, but the person speaking was most likely Diana Oughton, whose death in fact was widely reported in March 1970, when she and two other members of the Weathermen accidentally were blown up in a New York City brownstone by explosives they were preparing to direct at civilian targets. It was Oughton's death, as part of a radicalizing process that had its origins in the 1968 student strike that convulsed Columbia University, that drew the attention of '64's Thomas Powers. His reporting for United Press International won the Pulitzer Prize and culminated in a subsequent book, *Diana: The Making of a Terrorist*.[20] Caught up in the Columbia strike was another member of the class of 1964, Tyler Smith.

As an undergraduate, Smith had had his social conscience awakened by the emerging civil rights movement and experience tutoring New Haven's inner-city children. Thinking he might want to become a journalist, Smith took a job the summer before his senior year with the *Hartford Courant*. Assigned to the mid-afternoon shift, he used the first part of his day tutoring children in Hartford's North End. Through his reporting, he encountered an energetic community-oriented architect and determined he would rather build structures than write about them. It was too late to shift his English major, but he was accepted his senior year at Columbia's School of Architecture nonetheless. There, in his fourth year, as Students for a Democratic Society called for a general strike, he found himself in the middle of considerable controversy.

Being contrarians by nature, as Smith put it, Columbia's architecture students refused to join the strike, offering instead to keep their quarters in Avery Hall open as a "safe house" for dialogue. For Smith, this position between the strikers and university authority represented part of a straddling experience that characterized the next few years. He found himself ambivalent about aspects of the strike and especially its ambitious leader, Mark Rudd. According to an account of the strike published by his Yale classmate Richard Rosenkranz, Smith responded viscerally to Rudd's posturing, turning to his fiancée Sissy Williams at one point to ask, "Who is this asshole?" As Rudd's rant continued, Rosenkranz recorded Smith's musing: "I had no time to stay longer. I had to finish my thesis so I could leave this miserable school and start figuring out what to do with my life. And for the time being, all I wanted was a long hedonistic honeymoon on some small island in the Mediterranean. I even said to Sissy, 'Fuck the Revolution.' But she just told me to shut up. She wanted to listen."[21]

Smith's realization that he was only a month shy of graduation and his disdain for the strike leadership, which he ridiculed as "little Guevaras" and "the vanguard of the revolution," helped maintain his ambivalence about joining in—until police swept the architecture school and he narrowly escaped arrest. "Before the bust, I simply didn't believe them, but after the bust, that was it," he reported. "No more thought of my thesis; no more thought of schoolwork or graduation. Finally, and a little belatedly, I joined the strike." Together with some two dozen other students, he walked out of the architecture program in order to set up an independent organization devoted to providing architectural services to those who otherwise could not afford them. Over the next two years, with some foundation assistance, the group poured its effort into building sixteen storefront "street academies" for high school dropouts. "Our group, Urban Deadline," he recalled, "was set up as a kind of extension of the strike with lots of the premises of the strike: that people should be in a position to determine their own lives, that no one should find himself in a situation where an institution—just by having accumulated wealth and power and associations—has the right to override and manipulate those people who don't have such power."[22]

The work of Urban Deadline was sufficiently impressive to receive an award from the Citizens Union in 1969 as the architectural firm that had contributed the most to the city of New York that year. Drawing on members who had joined the nonprofit organization from Columbia's historic preservation program, Urban Deadline also managed to save a number of buildings from demolition in what is now the Great Falls National Park in Paterson, New Jersey. Pivotal for Smith was his fateful decision to move, with his new bride, into the Firehouse Commune on New York's Lower East Side. He and an Urban Deadline colleague were drawn to the challenge of renovating this abandoned and dilapidated former city firehouse and also building a neighborhood park on a nearby vacant parcel. Near completion of the firehouse renovation, Smith invited his father, then chairman of the Aetna Life and Casualty Company in Hartford, to stop by and see the product of their efforts on the way to an uptown board meeting at Morgan Guaranty. After a five-minute walk-through, the elder Smith glanced at his watch and with a pat on the shoulder said, "Well, son, if you're going to be a revolutionary, be a good one! I have to get to my meeting." Smith's mother's concern about her son's life took a different track. She sent the commune a washing machine for her son's birthday. No doubt the gift was welcome, but Smith's design of the communal living quarters proved to have personal and painful consequences. His new wife found the communal sexual openness much to her liking, and for Smith that ended any illusions of maintaining his marriage.

Leaving the Firehouse Commune marked the beginning of Smith's gradual exodus from New York City. Life and work had become increasingly chaotic and fragmented. He found that many of his "clients," blacks and Puerto Ricans, "didn't want my help, didn't even trust me, and wanted to go it alone." The final blow came, when working diligently to install a new floor in a day care center, Smith was jolted by an explosion across the street where a self-professed radical had accidently detonated a bomb he was making. According to Smith, "It had all gotten too crazy." He left New York early in 1970, but not without receiving his architecture degree. After a year out of school, he and several other students submitted the drawings they had done in Urban Deadline, arguing that they were sufficient to qualify them for graduation. Apparently the university did not object. Soon thereafter Smith was awarded the degree. From New York, he moved to Martha's Vineyard, where he designed and built a small house for his father. In 1971, he returned to Hartford, where he founded a preservation organization called the Hartford Architecture Conservancy, before establishing his own architecture firm in 1977.[23]

For his part Richard Rosenkranz, who as an undergraduate had participated in a direct action campaign against substandard housing in the predominantly black Dixwell Avenue area of New Haven,[24] sought to explain the Columbia strike out of frustration with elders who refused to consider the cause even worthy of consideration. Writing in his early memoir, *Across the Barricades*, he cited his mother's charge that he had become a communist dupe when she learned he had joined strikers in Avery Hall, and a reporter's analogy that the effort was the generational equivalent of a panty raid, as reasons enough to dispel "pat stereotypes to be used on the cocktail party circuit." Disclaiming any intent at subversion or even membership in SDS, he presented his account as a means of necessary communication between generations, writing, "The Kerner Commission on riots, along with many other commissions, has reported that the nation is fragmenting into separate pieces, each shouting and hating and not understanding the others. With this book, I hope to build a few bridges."[25] As part of Urban Deadline, he could list a number of accomplishments. Still, his frustration bubbled up as he admitted that even as he expected to continue working "in a vaguely positive direction," he might not escape the ultimate fate of taking "a nice respectable job within the dirty old establishment."[26]

If Rosenkranz sounded defensive about his embrace of student protest, such was not the case with his classmate William Roth. Determined to make up for the social as well as physical deprivations of the lifelong disability that made it difficult to control his physical movements, Roth moved to Berkeley right after he graduated from Yale. There he joined CORE, experimented with drugs, and quickly became, in his words, "a part of the nascent hippie culture." One of the first students to storm university administrative offices in Sproul Hall to protest restrictions on political activity on campus in the fall of 1964, he was quickly convinced that "conventional social structure lay in shreds. . . . There was no going back." Roth managed to complete his PhD in political science despite the distractions, but he would never be the same. "It is easy to look back at the '60's with condescension," he later wrote. "I find that inappropriate. This country changed at a time when I changed."[27]

* * *

Change America and the class of 1964 did, but not with the same effect and often in unanticipated ways. At relatively staid Johns Hopkins University, Yale '64's Richard Berk became active in the New University Conference, an organization of graduate students and faculty loosely associated with SDS. Never an outstanding student as an undergraduate, Berk sought admission from a number of graduate programs in psychology, offering his services as an assistant football coach in return for tuition and board. Shortly after his arrival in Baltimore, he shifted his field to sociology, an interest that was reinforced through a part-time job he secured working with youth gangs in the city and the mentorship of Peter Rossi, whom Berk described as "rough cut" and one of the few faculty "whose shoulders were wider than his hips." Through Rossi, with whom he later coauthored several books and scholarly papers, Berk was enlisted to do research for the landmark Kerner Commission report on civil disorders. In the meantime, exposure to conditions in Baltimore's ghetto, in addition to his rising anger at the Vietnam War, drew Berk into the New University Conference. In the fall of 1970 he joined several dozen other students in storming a university trustees meeting and refusing to leave. The meeting immediately adjourned, and demonstrators were barred from further access to the campus. Berk sidestepped the exile when Rossi arranged work space for him off campus so he could finish his dissertation. What Rossi could not fix, though, was the cancellation of Berk's speech at graduation. Since it was too late to remove his name from the printed program, the university simply whited it out.[28]

Yale was scarcely a hotbed of radicalism in the mid-1960s either, but even there protest proved irresistible to many. Willard "Ward" Cates, according to one of his classmates, was the first person he thought of when Old Yale traditions came up. His grandfathers on both sides of the family were in the same Yale class of 1907, and both had been deeply invested in athletics. J. M. Cates was a runner, who ultimately became athletic director at Yale. M. B. Sands, on Cates's maternal side, was the track coach. Ward Cates, as a history honors major, a member of the class council, the class gift committee, and the senior society Book and Snake, might have had a predicable future in law or business. After two postgraduate years of study at King's College in England, however, he found his interests had shifted enough to cause him to return to New Haven to take the classes he needed to enter medical school. So much had changed in his absence, he later reflected, that he thought he might as well have entered another planet.

A social libertarian in college who cast his first presidential vote for Barry Goldwater, Cates now embraced the new tenor of the times. As president of a radicalizing Yale Medical Student Association, he threw himself into antiwar activities, marched in black power parades, and volunteered in free clinics for low-income residents. Both he and his wife, Joan, knocked on doors for the McCarthy presidential campaign in New Haven. As a student at Yale Medical School he took electives in public health, ultimately attaining a master's degree in public health, even though the university had yet to formalize the field. A member of ROTC as an undergraduate, he chose as an alternative to active military service in 1974 to join the Center for Disease Control, where he was assigned to the Abortion Surveillance branch in the Family Planning Evaluation division. There he joined colleagues evaluating the effect the *Roe v. Wade* decision legalizing abortion was having on women's health.[29]

Social turmoil and growing opposition to the Vietnam War in particular had a lasting effect well beyond university campuses, sending many '64 graduates searching for excuses not to serve, when several years earlier they would have accepted military duty without question. At least one member of the class, David Elliot, moved to Canada, where he took a university teaching position, never to return to the United States. Another class member, Andrew Harris, met his military obligation, but at considerable personal cost. Finding his way to an internship in Madison, Wisconsin, following completion of his medical degree at the relatively placid University of Virginia, Harris threw himself into antiwar demonstrations, which were frequently countered by National Guard troops lining the rooftops of university buildings, their weapons and tear gas canisters at the ready. Fearing an assignment to Vietnam at the end of his residency if he were drafted, Harris instead gambled on joining the National Guard, with its promise of domestic service. The decision proved harder than he imagined, in part because of his unwillingness to turn his back on his own politics. Following participation in Friday night antiwar demonstrations, Harris recalled, he would put on what he called "the hated uniform of the Guard" on Saturday to train at the armory. The conflict between his military obligation and his opposition to the war was so great that he found himself sobbing throughout the drive to his assignment.[30] Others who lacked the deferments granted to graduate students and men with families clung to the flimsiest of excuses not to serve.[31] There was a positive and lasting effect, however, as a number of these men, in addition to Ward Cates, used the availability of alternative service to affirm commitments to improving social conditions at home while avoiding what they had come to see as questionable extensions of those American ideals abroad.

Robert Hilgendorf reported that he was never one to express his social conscience by marching in protest. Still, as he contemplated his prospects after attending Harvard Law School, he asked himself why not go somewhere he might be needed? Although he greatly enjoyed his time in Cambridge, he was put off by the careerism that dominated the atmosphere at Harvard. A summer internship on Wall Street was enough to persuade him to explore alternative paths. When it came time to make his decision, he considered joining a program being established to help educate prisoners at Walpole State Prison in Massachusetts. Instead, he opted for an entirely new federal program to bring lawyers to Indian reservations. Together with his new wife, Hilgendorf set off for an assignment with the Navajo in Arizona, which he thought might last several years. He stayed for nearly eight, in what proved to be a life-changing experience. Although he ended up in private practice following a stint in the office of the attorney general's office in New Mexico, he continued to maintain clients from the Navajo nation and assist Anglos through a bankruptcy practice. Today, he maintains the same satisfaction helping people fix legal problems when they are in trouble, whatever their ability to pay, as he did first in Arizona, when he aided an Indian whose livelihood was threatened after his tools were confiscated along with the truck he was driving when it was repossessed.[32]

No fewer than a half dozen members of the class of 1964 entered service on Indian reservations, some as lawyers and others as doctors. Such experiences could prove deeply disappointing, as service in the Peace Corps was for some. Richard Reichbart reported, for instance, that in order to avoid the draft, he opted to work on a Navajo reservation. He soon discovered that such work proved to be a misguided attempt on his part "to appropriate (in an impossible fashion) the often times superior attributes of a very foreign culture." His reaction was to turn inward, writing in the 1974 class reunion book, "Since then, I have embraced the interior journey of psychoanalysis, and find myself fascinated by the worlds of psychology and parapsychology for what they have taught me."[33]

Not all such efforts to bypass the draft ended badly. David Plimpton chose to join VISTA (Volunteers in Service to America) for two years as an alternative to military service. Building on his own commitments to social justice as an undergraduate over two summers in Africa through the auspices of Crossroads Africa, he provided writing tutorials to youngsters in East Harlem, working with a number of them to find placement in private schools that were seeking to build minority enrollment. Ultimately trained in psychiatry, he spent his career meeting the needs of underserved clients, largely out of an office in Coney Island.[34] John Clark O'Brien, after serving in VISTA in West Virginia for a year, chose not to return to the government work he had done in Washington for a year before the draft threatened to take him. Instead, he worked for legal services in Washington, before leaving to train law students to do clinical work at St. Louis University. Wallace Winter, after a stint in Brazil in the Peace Corps, acted on his Quaker faith and record of social service as an undergraduate to complete a distinguished career at the Legal Assistance Foundation of Chicago.[35]

For doctors who joined the U.S. Public Health Service, assignments could be remote, beyond Indian reservations to places as isolated as parts of Alaska and the Arctic north. Such assignments could have lasting effects. Jack Rodnick, according to his college suite-mate Angus Gillespie, was a brilliant scientist destined for an equally brilliant career in research. After completing medical school magna cum laude at UCLA in 1968, he chose as an alternative to military service a two-year commitment to the Public Health Service. Reflecting on the purpose he served as the sole physician taking care of one thousand Aleuts on the Pribilof Islands in the middle of the Bering Sea, he decided, in his words, "to become a generalist in a specialist world, an environmentalist in a lumberyard." While he established a national and international reputation in family medicine through a highly successful career at San Francisco State University, his life course turned out to be very different from the one he had envisioned at Yale as a research scientist.[36]

Such choices blended with a broader array of decisions that pointed members of this group of men away from established career paths to work that did not just provide a living but also accommodated some of their deepest aspirations for social change, generated during and immediately after college. Angus Macdonald represents a case in point. Following completion of his graduate degree in architecture at Yale, he took a position with a large firm in New York, Harrison and Abramovitz, architects for Rockefeller Plaza. Perceiving that some of his colleagues resented favoritism directed at him for his Yale credentials, he left after a year, using a contact through a former roommate to join a small firm in Jamaica. Glowing in the aftermath of independence granted in 1962 and in Cold War competition with Cuba in the Caribbean, Jamaica proved a wonderful laboratory for a young architect. As part of a small firm, Macdonald gained many interesting assignments, but it was in the slums of Kingston that he discovered a compelling goal, what he later called his holy grail. As he drove the filthy streets, the abject poverty made him cry. Wastewater and blocks of structures made of burlap were everywhere. He realized then how fortunate he had been in life and vowed to make something affordable to meet pressing needs for shelter.

Macdonald's revelation was not entirely new. His master's thesis, born from extensive fieldwork in West Harlem, sought a solution to the need for low-cost housing in depressed neighborhoods. "My treatment was to unite these spaces by creating sustainable communities featuring self-reliance and self-respect, missing elements in slum society," he reported. His social conscience was further pricked when, during a trip to Washington, D.C., he witnessed the effects of the civil disturbances that followed Martin Luther King's death in 1968. None of his prior encounters was as formative as Jamaica, however, and it was here in the early 1970s that he set a goal of being able to produce attractive but affordable housing for those in need. "In a remarkable way the dreams of helping humanity through the practice of architecture have possibilities of fulfillment but in a less egotistical way than I imagined during school years," he reported in his tenth reunion book. "My research into indigenous systems of low-cost construction using local materials available in tropical countries seems to have special relevance now, and it is this sense of urgency which was one of the factors prompting me to stake my personal future on my ideas." The task proved formidable. He experimented first in Jamaica, then after relocating to Virginia he developed pioneering techniques of combining concrete and galvanized steel. After building test panels for several prototype buildings, he formed a company, am-cor inc., to market and distribute a unified steel and cement system. With targeted construction not just in Jamaica but also in other underdeveloped countries, he sought to reach a goal of producing structures at $20 a square foot while substantially reducing their carbon footprints at the same time.[37]

Edward Ranney turned away from a possible business career by choosing not to follow in the steps of his father, George, a prominent Yale graduate and long-serving general counsel at Inland Steel Corporation. Determined not to enter the military, Ranney, after a year's Fulbright fellowship to study in Peru, sought a teaching job. Instead of pursuing a possible position at the Hotchkiss School, where his former history teacher had just become headmaster, Ranney took a job at a new experimental school in Vermont. Devoted to serving youngsters whose behavior, because of drugs or mental illness, kept them out of the regular public schools, East Hill School instilled confidence through a number of activities, including completion of chores on the facility's farmland, as well as academic exercises. Ranney stayed in the position for four years, until he was no longer draft eligible. Married to a fellow teacher, he headed to New Mexico to take up photography professionally. Despite his father's insistence that he would never be able to support a family, Ranney bought a ranch in Santa Fe for $10,000, fixed it up, and with the addition of his wife's teaching salary and some money from a trust established by his grandfather, launched what turned out to be a distinguished career, as he had hoped, as a photographer.[38]

A number of entries in the 1964 tenth reunion book, completed even as Richard Nixon faced impeachment, expressed disillusionment with government service. In the mid-1960s, however, the hopes vested in the Great Society and associated activist programs remained high. Among those seizing the opportunities to engage compelling social issues was '64's only American Indian, Philip "Sam" Deloria. The son of an Episcopal priest and a native of the Pine Ridge reservation in South Dakota who came to Yale after a year at St. Albans School in Washington, D.C., Deloria considered himself an outsider to the campus and, after a semester on the dean's list, an indifferent student at best. Lacking the grades to attend Yale Law School, he returned to South Dakota. He worked on mental health issues for a year on a federal grant to the state health department before an influx of money from the Office of Economic Opportunity opened the door to antipoverty work. From 1965 to 1967, he worked out of an office at the University of South Dakota to get technical financial assistance to Indian tribes in several midwestern states. As he later wrote, the War on Poverty provided an essential boost to young Indian leaders, even as it moved Indians closer to the goal of self-sufficiency and legitimized Indian tribes as governments.[39]

Deloria's work brought him to the attention of Robert Kennedy, who offered him a position with the Senate Committee on Indian Education. After Kennedy's death, Deloria made his way finally into Yale Law School. But finding his studies no more compelling than his undergraduate work, he seized the opportunity in 1971 to join the new American Indian Law Center being established at the University of New Mexico. The next year he was named director. Except for a brief appointment in President Jimmy Carter's Bureau of Indian Affairs, he served continuously in the position until 2003. Through the center's pre-law programs, he was responsible for helping vastly increase the number of Indians attending law school. He also established a research and policy center devoted to providing legal assistance to tribes throughout the United States.[40]

Others took up government work as well. Stanley Thomas and Russell Byers joined the Department of Health, Education, and Welfare in the Nixon administration, and Brian Rapp assumed the position of city manager in the beleaguered city of Flint, Michigan. George Sheckleton, a Yale-trained medical doctor who extended his public health commitment beyond an initial assignment to New Orleans, traveled west to work with two other physicians serving Paiute and Shoshone Indians on the Walker River reservation in Nevada. After sending Sheckleton to Hawaii to complete an additional degree in public health, the Public Health Service assigned him to Montana, where he worked in the Indian Health Service area office. When Yellowstone County and the city of Billings decided to open the first City/County Health Department, Sheckleton won the contract as health officer, continuing to work for the Health Service. In subsequent years, he launched a number of initiatives, including the city's first urban Indian clinic, a health care for the homeless clinic, a community health center, and many other cooperative programs. While he believed government suffered from a number of inefficiencies, he nonetheless felt satisfied that he could make his own public service programs work effectively.[41]

* * *

When I mentioned that I intended to write a book about our class and the 1960s to Rick Kaminsky over dinner in 2009, he responded curtly about our years at Yale, "We missed the sixties. We didn't smoke dope and all that stuff." No doubt, Kaminsky identified "the 1960s" with traits associated with the counterculture that emerged after 1964. Those elements, including drugs, were hardly present during this group's undergraduate years. That does not mean, however, that members of this class did not ultimately embrace some portion of the range of features that set a culture of opposition apart from established habits and norms. One who did was William Duesing.

Determined to study architecture at Yale following his graduation, Duesing soon gave up his intent and instead joined a group of fellow graduate students experimenting with computer-based programs of light and sound as the basis for public art installations. Known as Pulsa, the group formed officially in 1967 with about a dozen members, including painters, musicians, sculptors, and engineers working at Yale. Drawing donations, such as strobe lighting and other technical equipment, from corporate entities, Pulsa broke new ground with installations at Boston's Public Garden and in the New York Museum of Modern Art's outdoor sculpture garden, marking the first time that part of the museum was open to the public without fee.

Members of Pulsa combined the use of new technologies with countercultural values to make their mark on a rapidly changing artistic arena. Here 1964's Bill Duesing, second from left, joins fellow Pulsa members David MacIver Rumsey, Michael Cain, Patrick Clancy Pratt, and Peter Kindlemann at the Wadsworth Atheneum in Hartford in November 1969. Courtesy of Bill Duesing.

Despite appearing to work in collaboration with the existing establishment, Pulsa operated on countercultural principles. In 1969 the all-male group moved to a farm outside New Haven, in Oxford, Connecticut, where they formed a commune. By day, during the academic year, the seven lead members commuted into New Haven to Yale's School of Art and Architecture, where they taught seminars and led discussions on art, technology, and city planning. A large property and barn in Oxford allowed for production of expansive installations like the one Pulsa introduced to the Yale golf course in 1968. The farm provided a base for members to take assignments throughout the country. At home, however, the group acted communally, sharing responsibilities not just for housekeeping but growing their own food. A Pulsa statement published in 1970 explained both the practical value of feeding themselves and bartering with neighbors. In addition, Pulsa noted, "Agriculture provides information about long-term growth rhythms and is comparable in scale and as energy to Pulsa's other art works. . . . We have also experimented with the effect of sound on plant growth and have used some of this information in other installations."[42] One of the members of the group had migrated from Harvard, where he had had plenty of contact with Timothy Leary. He introduced other Pulsa members to LSD, which Duesing credited as an important source of the group's creativity.[43]

Pulsa's understanding of how to reenvision cities provided the most clearly stated declaration of principles behind its work. At a time when New Haven was rocked by turmoil, including riots that greeted ambitious efforts to remake the downtown and adjacent neighborhoods, Pulsa joined other activists in insisting on the devolution of power, declaring, "Corporation engineers and governmental agencies should not control the reorganization of artifact systems; this would better be determined by the people of various neighborhoods who can decide for themselves how they want to relate to their systems." Going beyond the criticism of liberal organizations, however, Pulsa asserted that it was artists, not architects or engineers, who would unlock that potential. Describing the city as "an art object" needing only systems capable of revealing "the living gestalt," Pulsa offered its "public sensoriums" as means for facilitating "an abstract aesthetic awareness" of the city and its life-supporting infrastructures on the part of the human organisms populating it.[44]

Pulsa's work was intense, ambitious, and dramatic, but it did not last. Corporate donations dried up in the early 1970s. Members began to marry and move on. The property where the commune had located had been available cheaply while its owners awaited a propitious time to build an industrial park, so its future was uncertain. With that in mind, Bill Duesing looked all over the Northeast for a new farm to settle, finally selecting another property in Oxford. By the tenth anniversary of his graduation, he could report that he had been growing food and was looking forward to being a full-time farmer, "the balanced diversified organic farm being perhaps the best environmental art/work life/work and one of the few sane options in today's world."[45]

Like Duesing, Peaslee DuMont found the lure of an alternative mode of living immensely appealing, though he found it more difficult to reconcile his early education and socialization with his new aspirations. A three-year graduate of a top high school in California's Bay Area, DuMont spent a post-Yale year in India before entering Stanford Medical School in 1965, at the same time Mitt Romney matriculated there as a freshman. As Romney found to his dismay, the winds of protest from nearby Berkeley reached Stanford that year,[46] and DuMont, at least, found himself for the first time questioning his drive to achieve in the standard academic fashion. Through a newly instituted Free University that offered courses on any subject of interest not included in the university curriculum, he found his way to a weekend experience at a commune north of San Francisco. He was so impressed with the "marvelous mountain men" who constituted the permanent residents that he secured a year off to join the group. Part of his plan was to write an ethnography of the place for an associated degree in anthropology, which he did as a participant-observer. At the same time, he threw off the guise of objectivity to fully take part in the communal life. Having thwarted the prospect of being drafted by declaring his intent to return to medical school in a year's time, he was strongly tempted to risk that protection by extending his stay another two years. Talked into returning to Stanford instead, he found it virtually impossible to reconcile his newly acquired views stressing a life of health with the medical education he was receiving, as it dealt primarily with disease. Yet he persisted. It was only years after he received his medical degree, when he was drawn to a conference of practitioners of holistic medicine, that he found his personal values could be reconciled within the profession, as he altered his practice to provide patients "integrative medicine for body, mind, heart and soul."[47]

What was suggestive in DuMont's professional life was even more manifest in Peter Harding's work. Building on the personal experimentation that marked his medical training at UCLA, Harding embraced a trend that historian Edward Shorter has called "antipsychiatry." Influenced by the French theorist Michel Foucault, this approach was popularized in America in the early 1960s through Thomas Szasz, who argued in his 1960 book, *The Myth of Mental Illness*, that mental disturbance was not so much medically induced as socially constructed. In addition to resisting the institutionalization of patients, Szasz and his adherents sought to treat their clients as whole beings rather than isolating a singular source of the "disease."[48] Harding reflected his attachment to this emerging trend of what came to be called holistic medicine by challenging a questionnaire circulated for his tenth reunion. "I refuse to accept the mind-body split implicit in the question," he wrote. "For a while I actively turned off my thinking in order to make contact with non-verbal feelings and have allowed myself to grow out of this dichotomy, a significant change from the heavy intellectualization that is rewarded at most universities."[49] Deepening his commitment, Harding studied the principles of Gestalt therapy with his wife, Peggy, who had herself been introduced to the field by James S. Simkin, one of its American pioneers. Simkin brought his practice to Southern California from New Jersey in the early 1960s. In the hands of Fritz Pearls, who trained Simkin and subsequently followed him to California, where he introduced the practice to the emerging hotbed of 1960s experimentation, the Esalen Institute, Gestalt stressed the value of therapy to the whole person. Although Pearls had departed before Harding moved permanently to Big Sur as Esalen's physician on call, Pearls's influence and that of Gestalt remained. Harding went on to study a number of exotic disciplines there.[50]

Trained in psychology at the University of Pennsylvania, Brooks Carder took a similarly distinctive direction. A native of Kansas City, where he received an exceptional education, Carder was initially terrified by Yale. Once he made a strong showing on his first hour test, however, he decided to compete without pushing himself too hard. He spent much of his freshman year playing bridge and coasting through his courses without much effort. Originally determined to apply to medical school, Carder turned to psychology as a major after being dissatisfied with the courses he took in chemistry and biology. He did know he wanted to be a scientist, and at the suggestion of a Yale mentor he matriculated in the PhD program in psychology at the University of Pennsylvania in the fall of 1964.

During the summer following his graduation from Yale, Carder was exposed to LSD, thanks to a graduate student, but he did not take to drugs. In his second year of graduate study, marijuana arrived with a vengeance. Now, Carder discovered, social events were dominated by groups forming a circle, each one facing outward, absorbed in his or her own trip. Drugs bothered Carder enough to lead him to study their behavioral effects, and that became his specialty when he took a faculty position at UCLA in 1968. Carder's career was advancing well enough in the early 1970s, but he did not like either Los Angeles or the university, feeling that neither one fostered any sense of community. After six years at the university he quit his job and moved to Tomales Bay, north of San Francisco, to join Synanon, a pioneer drug-treatment program formed in the late 1950s that had evolved into a commune and social movement. His university colleagues were shocked.

In his last year at UCLA, Carder had been teaching a pioneer course of his own on drug treatment, so the connection with Synanon was not outside his research interests. He considered his own motivation to be personal rather than professional, however. Introduced to the organization through his wife, who had attended the wedding of a friend there and become an immediate enthusiast, Carder began his association a full year before his university resignation, in 1972, by regularly playing the "Synanon game" that served as the core experience for the organization. This intense truth-telling exercise had originally been designed to force drug addicts to confront their own self-destructive behavior. As information about the game circulated, though, it attracted others, drawn in part by the therapeutic release promised by promotional brochures that declared, "The Game, the seed of Synanon . . . is a sport—an enjoyable, often demanding pastime pitting a person against opponents. . . . Synanon Games are fast-paced and exciting, with frequent wild accusations, screams of rage, and peals of laughter." Among those participating was Werner Erhard, who later adapted the game to create the Erhard Seminars Training (est).[51]

Drug programs necessarily required residency for participants, to assure total control of the recovery process. Outsiders like Carder, who were drawn to the game, decided they would get more from the experience if they too became part of the resident community. Admitted as "squares," so-called because they lacked drug addiction background, these newcomers accepted rigid rules for communal living under the tight direction of a nonprofit foundation. As brutal as the encounters might be within the Synanon game, relations outside the exercise were friendly and pleasant. Thus offered the chance to direct the organization's school in Tomales Bay, where his wife would teach, Carder seized the opportunity and continued over time to consider it the best possible option for himself. "As I look back over my life," he recalled, "I had a very high intellectual intelligence and very low emotional intelligence." By receiving so much powerful feedback over the years, "I ended up a very different person, and I think I'm a much better person for the experience."[52]

Carder realized that the life change he had accepted had its risks. The school he directed was highly experimental—"hip," as he described it—combining elements of Montessori training with open classroom structure. All children, starting at the stage of toddlers, were boarded away from their parents, in order to receive comprehensive life training, even as their parents were freed to devote more of their time to the community. Children were taught to value hard work, honesty, and self-reliance, and their schooling made a conscious effort not to separate vocational from traditional learning.[53] Carder's own children, who were four and six when the family relocated, lived outside the household, and while the older child relished the experience, the same was not the case for the younger child or a number of other children. Still, Carder loved the work. Accepting the stipend of some sixty dollars a month and the basic services that other members of the commune received, he lived modestly but happily enough in a setting whose shared values represented everything he had missed in Los Angeles. Shortly after he arrived, the organization shifted its status to that of a church, which he considered largely a ploy to keep a growing number of critics of the organization at bay. What seemed to be a personal Garden of Eden for Carder was not perfect, however. The chief problem, the snake in the garden, was Synanon founder Charles Dederich, whom he and many others considered "out of his mind." Carder rationalized his decision to stay, however, by reflecting, "If he lives long enough this place will fall apart. If he doesn't, it will survive and be great. Unfortunately, he lived long enough to destroy it."[54]

Synanon fit closely the profile of a number of unorthodox organizations that proliferated in the 1970s, especially on the West Coast. As sociologist Paul Heelas suggests, these disparate approaches to comprehension and belief, often described as "New Age," rested on agreement that "it is essential to shift from our contaminated mode of being—what we are by virtue of socialization—to that realm which constitutes our authentic nature."[55] Synanon's emphasis on self-actualization through a number of exercises beyond the game owed much to humanistic psychology, especially as promoted by Abraham Maslow, who paid a visit to the organization and wrote favorably about it early in its history. Despite his satisfaction with the experience, Carder was not an enthusiast for humanistic psychology himself, considering it largely a political movement rooted in the societal changes as they affected academic practice in the 1960s.[56] For him, the organization's emerging business enterprises, established to sustain the community, offered alternative opportunities to directing the school, at which he proved very adept. Thus, in a way that might not have been clear even to himself, he managed to be successful in a time-honored entrepreneurial fashion, even as he adopted a tightly prescribed lifestyle that could not have been imagined at the time he entered college.[57]

Beyond his business activities, Carder's administrative skills brought him new positions in the organization, first as treasurer, then as controller, and finally as chairman. The balance between social and professional success faltered, however, as the organization came increasingly under scrutiny and attack. Synanon spent eighteen months defending itself in a dispute over how much taxes it owed on its business activities. The court's decision in 1991 overruling Synanon's appeal forced the organization to liquidate its assets in order to meet the Internal Revenue Service's payment demands. Carder bore the burden of this effort, spending four days in court unsuccessfully challenging the government case. His report in his twenty-fifth reunion class book that he was fighting to save "an embattled organization" scarcely suggested the trials of the organization's last years.[58]

* * *

The unexpected turns represented in Harding's and Carder's stories in particular suggest an uneasy melding of past aspirations with contemporary movements and a distancing process away from the particular forms of idealism prevalent in the early 1960s. Drawing directly on what he perceived to be the experience of senior societies at Yale, most notably the oldest of these, Skull and Bones, the popular writer and critic Tom Wolfe postulated that the proliferation of encounter groups and unusual spiritual beliefs—what he called a Third Great Awakening—had the effect of turning idealists inward and away from the external objects of earlier reform efforts. The communally oriented mid-1960s had in effect become by the mid-1970s a "Me Decade."[59] If such a characterization does not apply neatly to Harding or Carder, nor to the bulk of their classmates, it nonetheless was reflected in a number of assessments these men made as they marked their first decade out of college.

Noting in his 1974 reunion entry the lack of leadership in the United States, Lawrence Pratt, who had become an investment adviser after serving in Malawi in the Peace Corps the first two years after his graduation, announced his departure for the countryside "to cultivate my garden and contemplate the disintegration of society." Nathaniel Childs left his position as an electrical engineer at MIT's Lincoln Laboratory, as he said, "to get out of the rat race," and moved to Vermont, where he occupied himself renovating a farm. After completing a degree in law at Cornell in 1969, Peter Avery Anderson left private practice in Groton, Connecticut, and moved to Maine, where he made a transition working for legal services. There, he later wrote, "I tried living close to the land. I built a house, grew huge amounts of vegetables, gathered fiddleheads, brewed beer, made maple syrup, and socialized with all the others who were doing many of the same things in Waldo County, Maine." A Peace Corps volunteer in Cameroon, West Africa, before entering law school, he remained actively engaged in social causes, representing opponents of nuclear power and volunteering for George McGovern's 1972 campaign for president. "But I gladly came back to the homestead in the evening to the dogs, cats, children, gardens, fields, spouse, and the beautiful, scary wilderness of rural Maine," he reported. "Wood smoke from the stove curled acridly from the chimney; Simon and Garfunkel crooned from the stereo; and lots of friends came and went in the crackling cold winter nights and the humid, buggy summer dusk."[60]

If there was a "victim" to the inward trend associated with the early 1970s, '64's Bill Stage probably qualified. With his good looks, easy manner, and social credentials honed in the exclusive Cleveland suburb of Shaker Heights where he grew up, Stage cruised through Yale. In the words of roommate Bill Drennen, "His study habits appeared non-existent, just enough for the low B and nothing below" and he never missed "the opportunity for a pick-up game at the gym or on the street." Having managed a degree in law, largely to stay out of the draft, he headed to California, where he took on odd jobs, including marrying friends under the authority of a certificate from the Universal Life Church. There, a friend remembered, he spent his time "hanging out with hippie doctors and lawyers . . . playing hoops, watching sports on TV, smoking pot, dropping acid, and going to rock concerts." His contribution to the tenth reunion book revealed his state of mind: "A wondrous journey to the beautiful shores of the Pacific. Ridge behind beach dotted with Eucalyptus and Pine. To get here my consciousness finally slid into flow. I live in silence giving none of my energy to the coming apocalypse which threatens the world. Fortunately we all know that this hologram we've agreed to materialize isn't real so we may not worry, remain happy."[61]

No doubt, the shift from grand to diminished expectations for self and country was part of a greater disillusionment that attended the culmination of nearly a decade of polarizing politics and policy, climaxing with the Nixon resignation. One anonymous contribution to '64's tenth reunion book described the mood most succinctly: "America is screwed up and Nixon is a sign of the times we should expect. I'm the same person I was ten years ago, but much the wiser for my observations. I personally am overwhelmed by the 'job' that needs to be done—have 'copped out' and chosen to live my own life—honestly, simply, with a few close friends, doing what little I can to improve this world for my kids." "Stay high and stay crazy," William Fink declared, adding his determination to "be responsible to myself before all other real and imagined gods." That attitude had plenty of support, but it was far from unanimous. Richard Berk's sentiment, "From liberalism to radicalism to cynicism (but still trying)," echoed in other submissions. "I hope the next ten years will not see an ostrich mentality, a 1950's approach," wrote Dennis DeSilvey, then fulfilling his medical service as chief of cardiology at Walson Army Hospital in Castleton, Vermont. "We have the potential to work

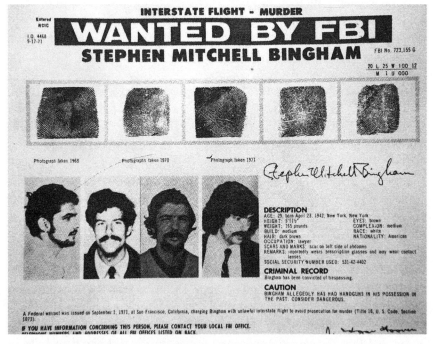

Wanted: Bingham in flight. Reproduced from the Yale '64 tenth reunion class book.

for a good future for ourselves, our children and our families." Thomas Powers also chose to be positive, writing, "It's clear we should not just ignore them and try, when the smoke has cleared, to fluff up our national innocence again, as if Vietnam, Watergate and all the rest had never happened. That would be stupid and perverse. But at the same time it would be wrong to conclude that we are the enemy, and to start slipping military secrets to the Albanians. . . . Perhaps the best response is simply to conclude that our innocence is well lost, and to proceed from there."[62]

Innocence lost was certainly the case. Ideals that had crystallized in these men's years in college had been tested to the full. If some gave in to disillusionment, most adapted. Even those who seemed to follow the new era's cultural imperatives to an extreme maintained some measure of continuity with the mainstream, including Peter Harding, as he helped spur the preservation of Big Sur's fragile ecology and bring hospice care to California. Few could say they had not been touched by the 1960s, but as befitted a transitional generation, the effects of cultural change differed greatly.

Neither Joseph Lieberman nor John Ashcroft found either his personal or professional life sharply altered in the decade after graduation. Trained in law right out of college, married with children and thus not subject to the draft, each man moved decidedly toward a political career. Neither chose to comment in the tenth reunion book, but biographical information listed there confirmed Lieberman's election in 1972 as Connecticut state senator representing New Haven and Ashcroft's position as state auditor of Missouri. One person whose biographical information was missing entirely was Stephen Bingham. The only reference to him appeared as the last selection in a collection of photographs of his classmates. His image, captured from three different angles, appeared in the reproduction of a FBI most-wanted poster under the title "Interstate Flight—Murder."[63] Caught up in the boiling controversies that have since skewed the memory of the 1960s as a whole, Bingham, as he remained in isolation and exile abroad, was thwarted for more than a decade in his effort to realize the causes he cherished in the early 1960s. In his story, as in others, we find the test of values as they solidified over the first decade following graduation. Neither a Me Decade nor a We Decade for this group as a whole, the long 1960s nonetheless sent these class members in divergent directions, leaving them, like the country they expected to thrive in, divided enough to last a lifetime.

3

Civil Rights

Shortly after he arrived at Yale, '64's Arthur Reagin was pulled aside by his cousin Inez Smith and given a thorough lecture about what was expected of him in college. Pointing to her brother, George, who as a Yale Law student had become a Freedom Rider along with Bill Coffin in 1961, the message was clear: Reagin had to get involved in the civil rights movement. Despite the difficulties he had had with his own transition to integrated schools in Washington, D.C., Reagin did not take up the challenge. He was going to chart his own path in life. Civil rights activism in fact did not become part of his résumé, and he later looked back critically on African Americans who joined Yale classes in the latter part of the 1960s for trying to emulate black power advocates like Stokely Carmichael. Still, he could not escape the reach of the civil rights movement entirely. During a summer break in his own studies at Yale Law School, Reagin held an internship at the U.S. Office of Education. There he handled the difficult assignment of personally serving notice to southern school districts that had failed to comply with desegregation orders. His travels took him to Strong, Arkansas, not far from where three civil rights workers had been murdered in Mississippi in 1964. There, ominously, he and his companions were trailed by armed opponents of integration. Although he did not march in his father's hometown of Selma, Alabama, he did return some years later to visit the Pettus Bridge, where the most violent confrontations took place on March 7, 1965.[1]

As a lawyer at IBM, Reagin enjoyed a career that looked a good deal like that of a typical Yale man. Joining a civil rights organization was not any more important to his success than it was to other classmates. But advocacy was not the point. Few of his classmates, white or black, were untouched by the civil rights movement. How they perceived and acted upon the ideals of equal justice under the law and a color-blind society said much about the contested view of civil rights that emerged out of the latter part of the 1960s and continued to haunt this generation.

* * *

For a few, commitments made as undergraduates extended seamlessly in the years after graduation. That was largely Thomas Roderick's experience. He arrived at Yale in the fall of 1960 from the elite suburb of Silver Lake outside Akron, Ohio, where his father was a prominent attorney known for defending corporate clients. Always uncomfortable with the homogeneity of his neighbors, Roderick was initially no more comfortable with Yale's social tenor. Being naturally shy, he maintained a low profile his first years on campus. A family crisis led him to read Camus—also a favorite of civil rights activist Bob Moses—and at about the same time he came under the influence of the Reverend William Sloane Coffin, whom he found "bold, clear, and inspiring." He attended Martin Luther King's lecture in Battell Chapel in January 1962, discovering over time that religious language could help him describe his own experience, despite arriving at Yale as an agnostic. Through Coffin and subsequently Peter Countryman, he became involved in the Northern Student Movement, tutoring black children in New Haven public schools. When his father, joining him for a visit in New York, made disparaging remarks about African Americans over dinner, Roderick's determination to extend his civil rights commitment strengthened. The summer before his senior year, he returned to Akron to start a tutoring program fashioned after the one he was involved with in New Haven. Despite the theft of the family car while he was working in Akron, Roderick's family accepted his efforts enough to host a graduation ceremony at their home in Silver Lake. He believed it was the first time blacks had been welcomed in the community in any capacity other than household help.

In his senior year Roderick's commitment deepened as he assumed the chair of the Yale Human Relations Council. Then, as graduation loomed, tragedy struck. Three college classmates who had been celebrating a twenty-first birthday in New York City were killed in a car crash on the trip back to New Haven. Roderick had been part of the party and would have been in the car himself had he not left early. The dead were friends from Timothy Dwight College, including Vincent Taus, who had also played a major role in crafting the New Haven tutoring program. Stunned, Roderick did his best to get through the year, receiving solace and support from Reverend Coffin as well as drawing closer to a small circle of friends in his residential college, including Stephen Bingham and J. Walton Senterfitt, another activist and member of the class of 1965, who had joined Coffin in civil rights demonstrations in St. Augustine, Florida, that spring.

Together with Senterfitt, Roderick took a position the summer following graduation with the Philadelphia Tutorial Project, the most significant of four programs Peter Countryman had established to create the Northern Student Movement. Based at Temple University, by 1964 the project had 175 tutors in nineteen centers, mostly in North Philadelphia.[2] Roderick thrived on the work, but as tensions built between him and the African American director of the program, he was forced to quit. Starting anew in New York and determined to get the professional training he knew he needed to make a career in education, he entered Bank Street College. His teacher placement took him into Harlem and ultimately to a position teaching third grade at Public School 92. The school was already famous, thanks to journalist Nat Hentoff's *Our Children Are Dying*, a moving portrait of the school and its dedicated principal, Elliot Shapiro, who battled City Hall to get the resources the children deserved. Making his commitment complete, Roderick moved into a brownstone on 137th Street, three blocks from the school. After Martin Luther King was assassinated, he represented the school at demonstrations in Memphis.[3]

Through his civil rights efforts Roderick was finding a deep sense of purpose and enjoying the diversity that had been missing in his youth. But despite his growing competence as a teacher and the strong bonds he was making with his students, he was in turmoil. The Vietnam War and the assassinations of Robert Kennedy and Dr. King in 1968 tested his idealism. He began to see that despite his best efforts and the work of a dedicated faculty, PS 92 was not able to deliver what its children needed to thrive. Through a fellow teacher and Radcliffe 1964 graduate, Dorothy Stoneman, he met Leroy Looper, an African American activist known for his work with the poor in San Francisco and New York.[4] Looper introduced him to encounter sessions, one of which he participated in soon after King's death. In this "marathon," in which he stayed up through an entire weekend, Roderick was moved to deep and sustained sobbing. The experience marked a turning point. "Although I hadn't slept for 40 hours," he recalled, "I left feeling lighter, as though I'd shed a heavy burden. I was finally able to grieve the loneliness of my years at Yale, the tragic deaths of my friends, the disappointment of Philadelphia, and the terrible shocks of 1968. Also, I realized that to sustain my work for the long haul, I needed to take better care of myself."

To address the isolation he had been feeling, living alone on 137th Street, Roderick persuaded Dorothy Stoneman and half a dozen other friends to move in and create a communal house. At the same time he decided to leave PS 92 to take a position with the East Harlem Block Schools. Founded by a group of Puerto Rican mothers in 1965 with funds from President Johnson's War on Poverty, the Block Schools comprised two nursery schools and a fledgling elementary school with a first and second grade. As teacher-director of the elementary school, Roderick spent the next seven years building this "independent public school" into a full eight-grade elementary facility that eventually became part of the public system. "At the Block Schools," Roderick recounted, "I found my New York City home. Classes were small, and each class had two teachers, a professional, and a parent. Parents governed the schools, and I worked closely with them. I saw lives transformed, as children got the attention they needed. Parents went on to get high school diplomas and college degrees, and some became professional teachers."[5]

Roderick maintained and deepened his passion for social justice through-out the turmoil of the "long 1960s." Buffeted by the deaths both of close friends and public figures he deeply admired, he found solidarity among like-minded idealists even as he tested his personal capacities through one of the cathartic encounter organizations that proliferated in the period. Although the toll of his work forced him to step back for a time in 1975 before redirecting his efforts, his devotion during and after college to advancing goals informed by the civil rights movement proved a solid foundation for the rest of his career.[6]

Roderick's classmate Joseph Rich similarly navigated a tumultuous period to act on convictions formed as a youngster and deepened as he reached maturity. Alerted to the nature of racial prejudice when a very talented black grade school classmate was rejected at the private academy he and other white classmates attended in Buffalo, Rich was drawn to civil rights primarily for the challenges it posed for a young lawyer's career. Following completion of a law degree at the University of Michigan, he joined the Department of Justice's Civil Rights Division in 1968, just as the Supreme Court's decision in *Green v. County School Board of New Kent County* sped up the desegregation of southern schools. When Richard Nixon attempted to slow the process in 1969 as he tried to court southern supporters, a number of lawyers in the Civil Rights Division protested, and some were fired for insubordination. The Nixon administration lost the case in October 1969 anyway, when the Supreme Court, in *Alexander v. Holmes*, insisted there be no further delays in implementing desegregation plans. As the pace of desegregation accelerated in the South, Rich found the department an especially exciting place to work. In a career that extended until 2005, he played a role in every major civil rights challenge, moving first from school desegregation to the Fair Housing Division and ending his service as head of the Voting Rights Division. Look-ing back over the course of the 1970s and 1980s, he reflected, "Confronting these problems on a day-to-day basis often leaves a certain sense of frustration and even outrage at the degree to which a person's race continues to play on all-too-important and debilitating role in our society. Yet, from a broader perspective of comparing where we are now to twenty-four years ago when the first major civil rights legislation was passed, I cannot help being struck by the rather remarkable and in some ways revolutionary change (particularly in the South) that has transpired in this country's race relations."[7] Other classmates found the turn in civil rights in the mid-1960s more personally and professionally challenging.

As the glow of accomplishment faded from the landmark civil rights acts of 1964 and 1965 in particular, as black nationalists contested integrationist strategies, as cities across the country erupted in violence, and as racial polarization became a part of national politics, white commitments to civil rights goals became more complicated. Even the best-intended reforms appeared inadequate to the task after legislative successes proved only partly effective against society's deep intransigence. For Stephen Bingham, whose growing radicalism had long since replaced the liberal optimism of his college years, the path he sought to justice was perilous.

* * *

On August 21, 1971, a dramatic news alert went out from San Quentin prison in San Rafael, California. Black Panther George Jackson, twenty-nine years old and author of the acclaimed 1970 book of letters *Soledad Brother*, who a year previously had been charged with murdering a prison guard, lay dead in the prison yard after an alleged attempt to escape. Three guards, their throats slashed, and two other prisoners were also dead. Within hours, police issued alerts seeking to question Stephen Bingham, the last outsider to see Jackson before the prison melee. With no sign of him anywhere, authorities charged Bingham with five counts of murder as accessory to the shooting. "I have reached the conclusion that there is no other way Jackson could have obtained the death gun except during his visit with Attorney Stephen Bingham just before the killings started," District Attorney Bruce Bales declared. "The fact of Bingham's sudden and complete disappearance directly following the terrible and tragic events that he triggered at San Quentin Prison is not insignificant, especially in view of my repeated public request to talk to him."[8]

Jackson's death occurred at a moment when the social and political climate had reached a boiling point, not just in Berkeley but across the nation. Locally, self-professed radical lawyers in the Bay Area had been calling attention to what they described as untenable conditions in California's prison system. Jackson's 1970 book detailing the gruesome facts of life under maximum security protection caused a sensation, lending weight to charges that California's modern prison system, born in the spirit of reform, had become racially oppressive. The book owed its publication to Fay Stender, Jackson's primary defense lawyer and, with Bingham, an active member of the National Lawyers Guild. "The horror of prison isn't even absorbable," Stender charged. "Words don't even begin to get at it. Working with the prisoners as I do is like being present at Dachau. . . . In the prisons, convicts are literally at the mercy of an arbitrary system which is almost completely above and beyond the law."[9] These conditions, Bingham later reported, had "festered like mushrooms that grow best in the dark, and concerted efforts by activists to change them were driving state and county officials crazy."[10] It was not entirely surprising then that the man immediately in charge of San Quentin at the time of Jackson's death, associate warden Jim Park, blamed "dilettante revolutionaries" for the carnage, telling reporters in an emotional statement the night of August 21, "We've been running scared in the face of shyster lawyers and bleeding-heart motherfuckers for too long. This is going to stop. It's a direct outcome of all this violent talk, kill the pigs and all this crap, but it's still murder. This revolutionary bullshit is getting people killed who didn't want to buy into it in the first place. The revolutionaries aren't lying here in a pool of blood." Governor Ronald Reagan weighed in days later, blaming "revolutionary elements in our society intent on extending their religion of violence, hate, and murder within the walls of our prisons."[11]

The message was not lost on Bingham, who, fearing for his life, chose to flee rather than leave his fate in the hands of vengeful prison guards. He might just as well have feared retaliation from the Panthers, some of whom apparently concluded that Jackson had been set up to be murdered. In his decision to flee, Bingham was aided by allies gained through years of activism. They shielded him the night of Jackson's death, and a former colleague, Karen Jo Koonan, reportedly provided him with false papers to allow his exit from the country.[12] Bingham's sudden disappearance lent some credibility to claims of his culpability, but his father stoutly defended him, as did others who knew him. Still, as Bingham remained silent, theories emerged that he had fled either to Cuba or to Canada. News accounts, which invariably identified him as a Yale graduate and a member of a prominent family, implied, if they did not state it, that this might be yet another member of the country's elite blinded by revolutionary fervor.[13]

Bingham may have been considered the logical culprit, but authorities had some serious contradictions to address in making their case. Conflicting official accounts of the events leading up to the shootings, including what weapon had been used, raised considerable doubt about the credibility of the charges against Bingham. Although subsequent information emerged that Jackson most likely had planned an escape attempt, it was very unlikely he would have chosen August 21 to do so. More probably, he intended to flee days later when he was scheduled to be taken to trial in San Francisco.[14] Officials speculated that Bingham had smuggled a gun to Jackson, who had been strip-searched before their meeting that day. But claims that such a weapon escaped notice while concealed in a tape recorder that Bingham had not himself brought to prison and in which he could hardly have concealed a gun, let alone the one in question, a large 9-mm Astra automatic, undercut authority charges. The day he visited Jackson, Bingham was accompanied by Vanita Anderson, a member of the Berkeley wing of the Black Panthers, which was at the time in a difficult relationship with the Oakland leadership headed by Huey Newton. She was the one who brought the tape recorder to the prison. Although denied permission to see Jackson, she remained in the visitors' area during Bingham's entire time in the prison and left when he did. Logic suggested she should have been every bit the object of legal interest that Bingham was, not the least when it was discovered that the gun Jackson used had belonged to one of her housemates and fellow Black Panther, Landon Robert Williams, who was then being held on trial in conjunction with the murder of a Panther informer in New Haven.[15] Yet authorities never even questioned Anderson. Reporters who tracked her down in Texas years later found her unwilling to talk about the incident.[16]

Bingham had not been a central player in George Jackson's defense. After Jackson reportedly asked Fay Stender to channel royalties from his book to the Panthers, she resigned as his lawyer in February 1971. John Thorne took over Jackson's defense, and through the Lawyers Guild he recruited Bingham to gather information on the conditions in the infamous Adjustment Center where Jackson was held, with the thought that a civil rights suit might ultimately be brought against the state's corrections department. Replacing Stender on Jackson's authorized visitors list, Bingham began a series of six meetings with his client that ended August 21. His goal was to gather information. His legal training did not prepare him to join Thorne's defense of Jackson against charges he had killed a guard in Soledad Prison in 1969.[17] Bingham himself believed that prison authorities had set up Jackson. "I'm certain George was targeted," he stated in a 2006 interview in the *Socialist Worker*. "It's clear to me that his responsibility in bringing international attention to prison conditions in California brought on him the wrath of the California Department of Corrections. This, together with his designation as field marshal of the Black Panther Party, certainly put him in their crosshairs." It also sent a "very scary message to political lawyers," not the least in the charges brought against him, not to get involved.[18] Bingham's claim appeared to be supported by members of the Marin County grand jury. Despite voting for the indictment, one of several dissatisfied jurors remarked, "It was not justice, but vengeance." Another juror resigned because, as he said, the grand jury was unwilling "to seek impartial legal advice during indicting sessions and makes impossible a fair and just procedure which can mete out genuine justice."[19]

For thirteen years, Bingham's status remained a mystery, his only public communication coming in 1974 through a *New York Times* string reporter who had been a law school classmate at Berkeley. Issued in a front-page story from an undisclosed location in Canada, the *Times* report revealed that Bingham was alive and holding to his revolutionary ideals.[20] It was another ten years before he returned to the United States to face trail. Citing Watergate and the exposure of other government abuses, including COINTELPRO, the secret counterintelligence program the FBI had directed against antiwar protesters as well as the Black Panthers, which he believed undermined charges against him, Bingham told reporters he believed it was finally safe to return and possible to receive a fair trial.[21]

Bingham's defense was a long and difficult process, involving hundreds of thousands of dollars in legal costs, some of which Yale classmates helped raise. His defense committee was studded with 1960s luminaries, including Noam Chomsky, Julian Bond, and former attorney general Ramsey Clark, whose testimonial on a promotional brochure read, "Stephen Bingham has devoted his life to freedom and equality for all." Bingham himself pointed to his own history, asserting that "everything I've done in my life has had a nonviolent premise to it. And it just defies imagination that I would become part of that."[22] With the tangible evidence against him highly circumstantial, Bingham's lawyers had to attack the prosecution's primary case against him, his flight. To do that they had to put their client's situation into the context of a repressive political climate, explosive militancy among minorities inside and outside of prison, and what Bingham considered the real possibility of being killed by guards furious at the grisly murder of several of their colleagues. "To understand the case," his lawyer asserted, "you have to understand 1971, . . . We're talking about a time when students were murdered at Kent State and Jackson State."[23]

Bingham's acquittal in 1986 drew national attention. His own view was that his lawyers had succeeded in addressing a difficult part of the past. No doubt the prosecution continued to see Bingham through the lens of 1960s excesses, exemplified in investigator Fred Castillo's view, "You were either on one team or the other in the sixties. Bingham was on the other team."[24] That view had its effect, Bingham noted in 1989: "Most of the prospective jurors for my trial associated the sixties with violence—a distorted view that the media are largely responsible for. But people can be educated. Through the questioning of my attorneys, most of the prospective jurors became receptive to another side of the story of the sixties. My acquittal demonstrated that in 1986 an American jury could listen to the government's case and not be irrationally inflamed and find me guilty because I was active in the movement for social change in the sixties."[25] At the time of the verdict, he was tearful and vastly relieved. He was also defiant, asserting that "in 1986 the values of the 1960s endure." As evidence, he pointed to opposition to aid for Nicaraguan counterrevolutionaries and efforts to fight South Africa's apartheid laws, a cause he had been familiar with since he had been introduced to the subject by Allard Lowenstein's talks on the Yale campus during his undergraduate years.[26]

* * *

While Bingham may well have seen ratification of 1960s values in his acquittal, what was most striking at the time was the shift in national politics to cast those same values as pernicious. Ronald Reagan was now president. Black power and the Panthers in particular had been publicly discredited, and Jackson's revolt, if not made central to the critique, did not escape notice.[27] More fundamentally, the approach to civil rights and the reaction to it had changed. Although judgments differ as to what direction civil rights should have taken in the post-1960s era, accounts generally agree that the movement took a new turn as early as 1965 with passage of the Voting Rights Act and certainly by 1971 in the landmark *Griggs v. Duke Power Company* affirmative action case in the U.S. Supreme Court. No doubt civil rights laws, backed by their most ardent supporters, sought to ban forever intentional discrimination, whether it involved access to public education, the voting booth, employment, housing, or public accommodations. Assuring opponents of landmark civil rights legislation that new government powers would not be employed for preferential treatment of any group, liberal stalwarts such as Hubert Humphrey wrote such testimonials into law.[28] By the mid-1960s, a liberal consensus reigned that the goal should be, in marked contrast to differences institutionalized under Jim Crow legislation, a color-blind society. This ideal was embraced by Bill Coffin, Allard Lowenstein, Stephen Bingham, and practically everyone active in the civil rights movement.

Removing bars to equal opportunity was not the same as assuring results, however, as sustained resistance to *Brown v. Board of Education* had demonstrated so clearly. Given the expectation that barring discrimination would yield results consistent with a color-blind society, both administrative agencies established under the Civil Rights Act of 1964 and the courts felt obliged to demonstrate results. The pace of school integration did not pick up significantly in the South until the Supreme Court ruled in *Green v. County School Board of New Kent County* in 1968 that "freedom of choice" plans were not acceptable in meeting the goals established under *Brown*. As for voting rights, the cause that so animated the efforts of Yale undergraduates who made their way to Mississippi in the early 1960s, there could be a number of institutional arrangements that, while possibly not intentionally discriminatory, had such an effect. In the years leading up to 1980, the courts came to accept a rule of "totality of effect" in determining prejudice, thus providing a standard by which the Justice Department could require revisions in electoral law in the South.[29] In matters of employment, the landmark *Griggs v. Duke Power Company* case of 1971 shifted even more dramatically the burden from proving discriminatory intent to discriminatory effect. In that case, the Supreme Court ruled against any employment practice having a disparate or disproportionate impact that would leave women or minorities underrepresented in the workforce.[30]

A number of factors conspired to advance this new race-conscious approach to civil rights. Dating back to President Kennedy's 1961 Executive Order 10925 requiring special efforts to include minorities in companies seeking government contracts, the term "affirmative action," according to historian Hugh Davis Graham, initially had a "soft," inclusionary side, while later programs assumed a "hard," equal-results approach requiring the selection of minorities over other qualified candidates in what appeared to be a zero-sum game perpetrated at white expense. One of the ironies of the history of affirmative action, Graham and others point out, was the way Richard Nixon enabled the Department of Labor to make such actions national policy. Despite his effort to court southerners, Nixon embraced Secretary of Labor George Shultz's plan to require trade unions to hire African Americans in a revived "Philadelphia plan," so named for its initial policy target. As Graham points out, Nixon embraced the program, both as a way of combating inflation in a tight labor market and of dividing civil rights groups from their traditional allies in labor as retaliation for their successful opposition to his choice of the southern conservative Clement Haynsworth for the Supreme Court.[31]

No doubt Nixon's actions were important, but sociologist John David Skrentny suggests that the logic for more proactive policies was there, whatever actions Nixon took himself. Under the rule of administrative pragmatism, as he coins the term, agencies established under the Civil Rights Act of 1964 began to seek "affirmative" means for achieving results, including in the field of employment, by means of the introduction of numerical goals and timetables. Such efforts were coupled with what Skrentny labels crisis management, as government responded to civil disorders with liberal interpretations of existing regulations to speed up the goal of achieving demonstrable

results. The courts embraced such a view, going beyond the narrowest construction of the legislative record to devise new means of assuring results.
Most famously, Justice Harry Blackmun, defending some weight for racial
preference in graduate medical admissions, asserted in the 1978 *University of
California v. Bakke* Supreme Court decision, "In order to get beyond racism,
we must first take account of race."[32]

Neither Graham nor Skrentny denies that civil rights groups seized the
opportunities offered by affirmative action. While Graham emphasizes the
way rights activists managed, for their own, race-conscious purposes, to "capture" agencies designated to exercise affirmative action, Skrentny describes
the process more benignly, writing, "The point is, that a race-conscious society and a reification of difference were not the ideological goals of the mainstream civil rights movement. Race-conscious justice was a tool that emerged
when the classical liberal litigation tools failed to achieve the classical liberal goal of nondiscrimination."[33] Jimmy Carter's assistant attorney general
for civil rights, Drew Days, agreed with that appraisal, writing, "Courts and
administrative agencies essentially looked beyond the text of the Constitution
and modern civil rights statutes and held that such arrangements were justified by the underlying purpose of those provisions. They argued that both
constitutional and statutory structures against discrimination originally were
designed to address the plight of blacks. Consequently, the explicit use of race
in fashioning a remedy to ameliorate the plight of blacks could not be reason-
ably viewed as raising any problems of discrimination."[34]

The very concept of preferential treatment did not sit well with many liberals, to say nothing of conservatives, who ultimately turned public dissatisfac-
tion with affirmative action to political advantage. During the 1970s, a group
that historian Dennis Deslippe identifies as "color blind liberals" struggled to
justify "soft" measures aimed at targets that critics claimed looked a lot like
quotas. Most prominent in this group were Jews, who, like Joseph Lieberman,
were especially wary of preferential treatment at select universities where until
recently their own admission had been restrained by quotas. Such actions
struck them as a direct blow to merit and a dismissal of the right formula
for success in America: hard work plus brains.[35] Their own uneasy relationship with affirmative action was reflected in the court's split decision in the
Bakke case, most notably in Justice Lewis Powell's contested argument that
race could remain among the multiple factors affecting admissions decisions
among otherwise equally qualified candidates. "Color-blind conservatives,"
many of them academics themselves, challenged preferential treatment, both
by organizing at universities and by supporting legal challenges to affirmative
action. Their lack of success with either a sitting president, Gerald Ford, or
the courts, left them, however, without tangible victories in 1980.[36] It was not

surprising, then, that so many of these critics put their hopes for eliminating affirmative action in Ronald Reagan's election as president.

As early as 1977, Reagan had seen the potential attraction of appealing to white voters by opposing policies that might constitute reverse discrimination, a position brought into contention by the Carter administration's defense of affirmative action in the *Bakke* case. Following a pattern established as early as 1972, the GOP platform in 1980 denounced quotas, even as Reagan criticized Carter for favoring both busing to achieve racial balance and racial preferences in employment and university admissions. "We must not allow the noble concept of equal opportunity to be distorted into federal guidelines or quotas which require race, ethnicity, or sex—rather than ability and qualifications—to be the principal factor in hiring or education," he declared. Prompted in part by a Heritage Foundation report calling for a color-blind approach to civil rights policy,[37] the Reagan administration as it came into office was ready to challenge political orthodoxy by treating civil rights organizations simply as special interest groups attempting to use the legal structures that emerged in the 1960s and early 1970s to seek special privilege. And who had been named Ronald Reagan's assistant attorney general for civil rights with the greatest authority to determine the way government would act on new readings of the law? Stephen Bingham's Yale classmate William Bradford Reynolds.

* * *

No less than Bingham, Reynolds came from a distinguished family, carrying into his Yale undergraduate days all the privileges associated with wealth and social prestige. He was able to trace his lineage all the way back to his namesake, Massachusetts Bay Colony governor William Bradford. His mother was a Du Pont, his father the head patent and trademark lawyer at the DuPont Company. Accepted to Harvard, Princeton, and Vanderbilt, where his father had attended both college and law school, Reynolds chose to stay with a contingent of close Andover friends who elected to attend Yale. A member of Delta Kappa Epsilon fraternity and a varsity tennis player at Yale, Reynolds, like Bingham, came to know Allard Lowenstein. With the encouragement of Yale administrator Joel Fleishman, he joined the March on Washington in 1963, noting in retrospect, however, that he saw himself more as an interested observer than an active participant in the civil rights movement. That experience, unlike Joe Lieberman's trip to Mississippi, never became a part of the public record.

In fact, nothing further conspired to involve Reynolds in civil rights activity in the immediate years after he left Yale, as he followed his father's path to study law at Vanderbilt. There his high academic performance earned him the position of editor in chief of the university's law journal. In those years marriage and a child maintained his military exemption, thus eliminating any need to decide whether to serve as controversy mounted around the Vietnam War. Following graduation, he joined the prominent New York law firm of Sullivan and Cromwell, a position of the kind embraced by a good number of his undergraduate classmates. Three years later, after being recommended for the position by Supreme Court justice Byron White, with whom he had interviewed for a clerkship on completing law school, Reynolds became an assistant attorney to U.S. Solicitor General Erwin Griswold. While in that position over the next three and a half years he became close to William Rehnquist, then heading the Department of Justice's Office of Legal Counsel and whose office was literally through a shared door. Even as he learned from Rehnquist, he argued eleven cases before the Supreme Court. Given primary responsibility for prosecuting draft evaders, he lost his most prominent case, against Muhammad Ali, when Justice John Marshall Harlan changed his vote at the last minute.[38] Following government service, Reynolds joined the Washington firm of Shaw, Pittman, Potts and Trowbridge in 1973, where he was named partner with a salary in excess of $200,000 a year. Among his cases was the defense of the Metropolitan Edison Company following the nuclear power accident at Three Mile Island.[39]

Reynolds's path to wealth and prestige, like that followed by many of his classmates who had entered law or medicine, seemed uncomplicated and secure, when, in 1981, he again returned to government, this time to head the Department of Justice's Civil Rights Division in the Reagan administration. He was recommended by former solicitor general Griswold and selected for the position when the two ranking members of the Senate Judiciary Committee, Ted Kennedy and Orin Hatch, deadlocked over each other's preferred candidate for the position. Reynolds's supporters considered his lack of a civil rights record positively in anticipating possibly difficult confirmation hearings. In fact, no one stepped forward to oppose his confirmation.[40] During his term in office, however, the term "zealot" was widely applied to him, even as his consistent, articulate, and often charged arguments for achieving color-blind justice without the government interventions that had proved so controversial in the late 1960s made him a genuine hero to the conservative movement. Nominated in 1985 to become associate attorney general, the third-ranking officer in the Department of Justice, he faced a barrage of criticism from Democrats and liberal elements of the media. Following the Senate's rejection of his nomination, he wrote a pessimistic assessment of national politics for his reunion classbook, noting for himself, "I have learned first-hand the meaning of controversy. Some people thrive on it; I am not among that set."[41]

That Reynolds proved such a galvanizing figure was not predicable. In preparing for the position, he publicly promised to take a "hard, fresh look at the issue of remedies in the civil rights arena" and vowed to seek specific remedies to specific problems rather than "trying, in one quantum leap, to cure all the social ills that have been in the works for generations."[42] In his first months at the Civil Rights Division, however, he threw his energies into upholding the Voting Rights Act of 1965 by assuring that southern electoral districts did not discriminate against African Americans. By all accounts, he held petitioners to a high standard, and he could claim at the end of his first year that he had required more revisions to electoral districts than the Carter administration had in a full four years.[43]

Although Reynolds indicated publicly that he was reviewing the Justice Department's past positions on school busing and affirmative action, he assured reporters attending his first press conference, in August 1981, that he did not intend a wholesale attack on existing court decrees. Only a month later, however, he announced that the government would reverse the Carter administration's support of a voluntary busing plan to maintain racial balance by three Seattle-area school boards. Reynolds felt the lack of judicial finding of discrimination merited a challenge to the busing plans. Because the challenge from his division was unprecedented, however, it prompted the *Washington Post* to charge that the action represented "a bold turn away from the department's previous opinion that the state prohibition [of busing for desegregation purposes] is unconstitutional."[44] Given the inevitable questioning that followed, Reynolds nonetheless received respectful attention a month later from the *Post* in response to his announcement that the Civil Rights Division would no longer impose hiring quotas for organizations convicted of employment discrimination. Despite opposition from the civil rights establishment challenging any such change, an editorial under the simple title "Affirmative Action" agreed with Reynolds, both that determining proportional hiring numbers was an inexact science and that their use demeaned those hired because of their race or sex. "For this reason, the Justice Department's new policy is an improvement," the *Post* declared, adding the important caveat, "if it can, by force of leadership and diligence of pursuit, be made to produce real job gains for the victims of discrimination."[45] In essence, the paper was giving Reynolds a chance to put his agenda into effect. Not so the *New York Times*, which remarked editorially that breaking away from affirmative action marked "a sad and historic shift in policy. The work of a decade is being reversed—with the job far from done."[46]

Even the *Post*'s patience was tested early the following year, when the Reagan administration moved to block the Internal Revenue Service's effort to revoke tax exemptions for private schools that discriminated against African

Americans. In charging that such IRS actions were improper instances of "administrative fiat," President Reagan ignored a 1971 judicial injunction when he suggested inaccurately that it applied only to schools guilty of racial discrimination in Mississippi.[47] Reagan's position, forcefully advanced by Reynolds, prompted a storm of protest, not the least among career lawyers under Reynolds's command, 150 of whom signed an open letter of protest. When one proclaimed that Reynolds was in danger of becoming a general without an army over the issue, Reynolds retorted, "If that happens, so be it. I'll get another army."[48]

Reynolds used criticisms from the Lawyers' Committee for Civil Rights Under Law and the Leadership Conference of Civil Rights as an opportunity to issue a fifty-five-page defense of Justice Department policies on civil rights. Charging that the Leadership Conference report issued in February represented an effort "to revive support for discredited civil rights remedies and to manipulate emotions through selective citation of fact, mischaracterization and irresponsible rhetoric," the report defended the department's "color-blind" approach, asserting that the real complaint was "with the Reagan administration's efforts to develop more realistic and responsive civil rights remedies to replace such discredited and extremely unpopular relief as mandatory busing and racial quotas."[49]

The debate escalated several days later when a number of members of Congress used the occasion of oversight hearings to launch their own rebukes. Reynolds, Representative Harold Williams charged, had signaled to racists that "they can return to business as usual without fear of government retribution." Representative Don Edwards, chairman of the judiciary subcommittee on civil and constitutional rights, added, "The steps you are taking may prove to be disastrous to the people whose rights you are charged with protecting. . . . On the basis of . . . limited experience, you are prepared to do away with remedies that were achieved by civil rights groups only after great sacrifice and suffering, remedies that have been enacted by Congress, approved by the courts and that have brought about the progress that has been achieved in this country in the past 15 years. You promise new, more effective remedies, but you do not tell us what they are."[50]

The emerging controversy over civil rights coincided with debate over renewing the Voting Rights Act of 1965, which had been extended without controversy in 1970 and 1975. With the law scheduled for review again in 1982, civil rights proponents sought amendments to counter the Supreme Court's high standard for determining prejudicial intent in the 1980 ruling *Mobile v. Bolden*. In a campaign led by Senators Ted Kennedy and Charles Mathias[51] and Representative Peter Rodino, critics of the ruling sought both to block Republican congressman Henry Hyde's effort to end the practice of requiring pre-clearance of new statutes by the Justice Department and to prohibit any practice "which results in a denial or abridgement of the right to vote." President Reagan asked Attorney General William French Smith and Reynolds to review the proposed legislation. Reynolds wanted to oppose proposed changes in the law to shift the weight of review from determining discriminatory intent to discriminatory effect. This was Reagan's position as well, but given wide support for the Voting Rights Act, the president was prepared to accept the changes. Reynolds objected and made his case publicly, urging that the act be extended as it stood. To uphold his position against what he called a "proportional representation scheme," he denounced a bill that he claimed would authorize "quotas in the electoral process." His critics shot back that he was using "scare tactics" as part of an "ideological crusade" against the Voting Rights Act.[52]

As part of his lobbying campaign, Reynolds sought especially the support of Republican Robert Dole, one of two members of the Senate Judiciary Committee considered undecided. Falling short of the votes needed for a negative recommendation from the committee, Reynolds and the White House agreed to what Dole described as a compromise, accepting the results provision while at the same time disavowing any right to proportional representation. The changes passed overwhelmingly and became law in June 1982.[53] In 1986, the Supreme Court, in *Thornburg v. Gingles*, upheld the race-conscious effort to assure black representation in North Carolina. The ruling was a setback for Reynolds as the Justice Department, for the first time, sided with a southern state in a voting rights case. The ruling boosted black representation following reapportionment on the basis of the 1990 census but also generated charges, following Reynolds's lead, that such actions represented "racial gerrymandering."[54]

Reynolds's active role questioning race-conscious policy in any form assured the hostility of those who had traditionally expected the Civil Rights Division to defend and promote the interests of African Americans. His declaration that quotas were "morally wrong" provoked angry retorts from black columnists Dorothy Gilliam and Carl Rowan, who assured readers that affirmative action programs were intended to make amends not only for slavery but for "today's entrenched racism—with racism that is practiced in corporate board rooms, union halls, newspaper city desks, and offices of senators and congressmen this very day." Their criticism was joined by an especially pointed letter published in the *Washington Post* accusing Reynolds of benefiting from a "white racial spoils system." Peggy Anne Hansen of Bethesda, Maryland, claimed that Reynolds, "as a product of a family from the right side of the tracks and educated in the right schools, was automatically connected with the old-boy network. Unless he behaved in a hopelessly lazy, stupid, or criminal manner, the personal and institutional support systems and power structures guaranteed a place for him." Arguing that it would take more than nineteen years from passage of the 1964 Civil Rights Act "to overcome centuries of being excluded from the competition," Hansen urged Reynolds to give affirmative action a chance.[55]

As Reynolds continued to engender criticism from the liberal press and from civil rights activists, it was not surprising that his nomination in June 1985 to be associate attorney general, while warmly supported by the *Wall Street Journal*, generated opposition from the *Washington Post* and a Democratic Congress. Congressman Don Edwards could not resist criticizing Reynolds for including whites among those whose interests he was obliged to defend. Reflecting Peggy Anne Hansen's criticism two years earlier, Edwards told Reynolds: "You and I are white male attorneys. We come from families with some money and were educated in the right schools. Unless we behaved very stupidly, the family and institutional support systems guaranteed places for us. We benefited from a racial spoils system." Writing for the *New York Times*, Anthony Lewis, a frequent Reynolds critic, was equally harsh about what he perceived as a bias for white privilege, declaring, "Mr. Reynolds is an important figure, more important than his title. For he demonstrates how different the new right is from the old American conservatism: how ready to use the law for narrow instrumental ends, how impervious to the sufferings of history. In short, how lawless, how heartless." A *Times* editorial was also critical, accusing Reynolds of "trying to reverse past progress." In opposing the nomination, the paper asserted that "he calls his actions color-blind law enforcement. We call them misuses of power: civil rights wrongs. They assume a color-blind society that has already cleared its discriminatory past. All Americans of good will seek that society; it takes a peculiar, narrow vision to believe, like Mr. Reynolds, that it has already arrived."[56] Such criticisms stung, especially as Reynolds construed them to be directed at him personally as a man of privilege. Noting the effect on his family, Reynolds recalled, "Nobody likes their dad to be called a racist and then have to defend it." At the same time, he admitted, "I'd have to say it was a very invigorating and energizing experience. It was wonderful in a lot of respects."[57]

Persistent grilling challenged Reynolds and prompted him to escalate his own rhetoric as attacks on his position became shriller. Writing at the close of the Reagan administration and the twenty-fifth anniversary of the 1964 Civil Rights Act, he blamed civil rights leaders for breaking the momentum toward a color-blind society as they "advanced well-intentioned, but poorly conceived policies with the all-too-familiar consequence of dividing people along color lines. In [the 1970s], the bright future of race relations began to dim as discriminatory techniques—mislabeled as 'benign' or 'affirmative'—re-emerged to work their destruction on the hopes of a public anxious to find harmonious, goodwilled solutions to the problems of the past." Challenging "liberal orthodoxy" and its "sinister quota system," he claimed that the Reagan administration had aimed to counter "paternalistic whites who knew best when and where to slam shut the doors of opportunity when the preordained racial limit was 'reached.'" Charging civil rights activists with embracing a "frightening tilt" back toward "separate but equal" through policies that pitted race against race, he denounced the liberal establishment for rushing "to hand out society's limited resources under a racial spoils system."[58]

By 1989, Reynolds's position had become the orthodoxy of the right. Introducing a 1991 book on the Reagan record on civil rights, Robert Hawkins, president of the conservative Institute for Contemporary Studies, wrote, "The 'legislation' of civil rights law by an elite group of judges, lawyers, and administrators has estranged an entire generation of Americans from questions of racial justice. In the end this book questions whether it is still possible for Americans to create, through democratic and self-governing institutions, a just society, one in which we will be judged by the content of our character and not by the color of our skin." The book's author, Robert Detlefsen, extended the critique, warning darkly that the influence of liberal elites on the courts was great enough to pose the threat that representative self-government would gradually be supplanted by oligarchic rule. Conservative polemicist Peter Collier, insisting that equality of opportunity had been superseded by an "enforced equality of outcome" at the insistence of the civil rights establishment, also doubted that it was possible to achieve a color-blind society: "Not while 'racism' is asserted as a catch-all explanation for every difficulty black people face. Not while we have Leftists—black and white together—cynically manipulating the race issue and using it to indict America rather than bring all black people fully into a system which promises them their last best hope. We had a phrase for people like this in the Sixties: they are part of the problem, not part of the solution."[59]

* * *

One element illuminating the contention of civil rights policy lies in conservative reaction to what political scientist Steven Teles has identified as a liberal legal culture that permeated the courts and associated legal institutions in the latter part of the 1960s. As law schools hired young liberal faculty at top institutions such as Yale, and as many of their students launched public interest law firms in the spirit of a period of activism, conservatives felt their voices were being marginalized. Absorbing the lessons both of liberal success and early conservative failures, a number of well-funded moves followed to counter the liberal turn in the law, including the creation of the Federalist Society on university campuses and the promotion of the conservative brand of legal interpretation, known as the "law and economics" movement, pioneered at the University of Chicago and extended to Yale and other elite schools with the support especially of the Olin Foundation. These initiatives were too late to affect the large number of law graduates among Yale's class of 1964, a number of whom entered public service law, at least temporarily. By the time of Reagan's election, however, conservatives in legal circles had been energized, and William Bradford Reynolds counted a number of them among his top staff, not the least being Charles Cooper, a former clerk for Chief Justice William Rehnquist. Following service in the Reagan administration, Cooper joined with the new conservative public interest law firm, the Center for Individual Rights.[60] In choosing to contest affirmative action admissions policies at the University of Michigan, the center challenged the policies of another member of the Yale class of 1964, James Duderstadt.

One of the last Yale graduates to receive a bachelor of engineering degree before the university eliminated the program, Duderstadt took a broad course of undergraduate studies before roaring through a graduate degree in engineering science and physics at the California Institute of Technology and a fellowship with the Atomic Energy Commission. He joined the University of Michigan as a professor of nuclear engineering in 1968. His ascension to leadership there was as rapid, as he was named dean of the school of engineering, then provost, and finally president in 1988. In that position he accelerated and deepened Michigan's research funding, thereby decreasing the university's dependence on state support, a process started by his predecessor and mentor, Harold Shapiro, who had left Michigan for the presidency of Princeton. The author of a number of books and important papers in addition to his multiple leadership positions, Duderstadt was not pulled into the activist roles a number of his classmates had adopted. He was, however, deeply affected by the high aspirations of the civil rights movement. Recognizing how woefully underrepresented African Americans were in the university at all levels, he deepened and expanded Michigan's own form of affirmative action.

Since the 1960s, Michigan had been pressed, by a number of activist organizations, to increase black enrollment, without enduring effect. To be successful, Duderstadt believed, the push had to come from within the university and extend to all reaches, including the faculty. Under the "Michigan Mandate" instituted in 1987 on the basis of two years' worth of intense discussion and planning, the university added considerably to the seventy-six minority faculty already in its ranks. As president, Duderstadt required each department to report statistics on its racial, ethnic, and gender makeup. Seeking to provide a model for society as well as higher education, he explained his objectives as addressing both the underrepresentation of racial and ethnic groups and the imperative for enriching university life. "The insights and erudition of hitherto excluded groups can enrich our scholarly enterprise; indeed, it seems apparent that we cannot sustain the distinction of our university in the pluralistic world that is our future without the diversity that sustains excellence," he asserted.[61]

Michigan's affirmative action program attracted the attention first of one of its own faculty, Carl Cohen, who said he was shocked by the negative effect such policies had on the admission of qualified white applicants. The author of *Naked Racial Preference: The Case against Affirmative Action*, Cohen was hardly an unbiased observer, and he used the information he got through a freedom of information request to stir the objections of Republicans in the state legislature. Among these, State Representative Deborah Wyman contacted the Center for Individual Rights, which had already succeeded in challenging affirmative action policies at the University of Texas.[62] From a list of possible plaintiffs among rejected white applicants for undergraduate study, the CIR enlisted Jennifer Gratz, who applied in the fall of 1995 while Duderstadt was still president, and Patrick Hamacher, who applied two years later, when Lee Bollinger had become Michigan's new president.

The resulting case was known as *Gratz v. Bollinger*, but it was very much Duderstadt's policies that were being challenged. CIR brought a second case, *Grutter v. Bollinger*, against Michigan's law school. In 2003, the Supreme Court ruled 6–3 in favor of the plaintiffs in *Gratz*, on the basis that the university's use of a point system that benefited underrepresented ethnic groups was too mechanistic in its use of race as a factor in admissions. Michigan had already revised its system of undergraduate admissions away from weighting racial factors so heavily, so the decision was not earth-shattering, even though minority presence dropped in subsequent years. More significant was the 5–4 decision authored by Sandra Day O'Connor upholding the law school's goal to sustain a diverse student body. Although the decision referred specifically to the desirability of a color-blind society, the court majority contended that race-conscious policies, though they should be limited in time, were still necessary and might be so for another twenty-five years. By a narrow majority, the court was still not ready to discard Justice Blackmun's imperative that race would have to be taken into account in order to combat racism.[63]

Although the Michigan cases confirmed that affirmative action remained acceptable up to a point, Reynolds's declaration, issued in 1989, that "we have set the terms of the civil rights debate," proved largely true in the years after he left the Department of Justice.[64] Even though Congress had blocked his promotion to associate attorney general, Reynolds, when Attorney General Edwin Meese subsequently named him counsel to his office, assumed a central role in naming and recruiting candidates for nomination to the high court. His legacy materialized especially with the ascension of William Rehnquist as chief justice and the subsequent appointment of Antonin Scalia. Just as notable, although Justice Clarence Thomas was in the minority in *Grutter*, the court subsequently moved increasingly in his direction in opposition to color-conscious decisions.[65]

* * *

For those who had been active in civil rights efforts as undergraduates, it was possible to maintain some consistency, despite the shift in the national political climate over the course of their careers. As one of the first Yale undergraduates to volunteer for Aaron Henry's gubernatorial campaign in Mississippi, Jon Van Dyke maintained his commitment to equal justice, writing in favor of affirmative action and seeking out a more racially integrated atmosphere than he found in the East, first by moving to California, then to Hawaii. As a law professor at the University of Hawaii, he continued to support preferential programs for a number of minority groups, including indigenous peoples of Hawaii, whose rights he pursued for a number of years in print and in court.[66] Although Gary Saxonhouse bypassed the opportunity to join Freedom Summer in order to wed, he later remarked that his career as an economist at the University of Michigan specializing in Japan was very much informed by his earlier civil rights activities. "I do actually see a lot of what I'm doing today as combating racism," he reflected. "But a different kind of racism."[67] Joseph Rich argued policy with William Bradford Reynolds when the two men overlapped at the Department of Justice. Rich retained his position, however, until, finally in 2005, angered by what he considered the politicization of the Civil Rights Division under George W. Bush, he resigned.[68] He ended his career with the Lawyers' Committee for Civil Rights Under Law, the nonprofit organization formed in 1963 at President Kennedy's request to involve the private bar in providing legal services to address racial discrimination. Stephen Bingham never forfeited his right to practice law, and through supporters in California he joined a law firm in San Francisco after his acquittal. Private practice was never his love, however, and he subsequently returned to public interest law in the Bay Area. Discouraged by the direction of national politics, he concentrated on local efforts to secure rights he once had believed would be assured by federal legislation.[69]

Other members of this class could recount particular civil rights efforts over the years.[70] The real test for most of these men, however, lay in how they navigated race relations in their daily lives, and in this William Drennen made a special contribution. Born to a well-to-do family in Charleston, West

Virginia, Drennen spent a year in the city's newly integrated high school before prepping at Episcopal High School in Alexandria, Virginia. As a Yale student, he followed an established path, playing football as a freshman, joining the DKE fraternity, and generally having a good time. He was aware of civil rights efforts because students living next door ran a tutoring program intended to serve New Haven's black youngsters. He embraced the selection of his black football classmate, Stan Thomas, into DKE, even as the national chapter threatened penalties for doing so. When it came to becoming active in protests, however, he dismissed the prospect. "I was unaffected and generally uninterested in the movement," he confessed. "In truth I was much more interested in art and architecture and girls and football and drinking and partying than I was in politics. Politics was the pigeonhole into which I put the integration issues." Besides, he recounted, "Stan Thomas was not involved in the movement to integrate the Deep South; why should I be?"[71]

After a rough journey through the navy during the Vietnam War and a period of drug-induced stupor abroad on his release, Drennen returned to West Virginia, where he recovered sufficiently to enter business. His interest in American history gained his appointment, in 1995, as the state's commissioner of culture and history. It was in this connection, following a speaking appearance from Appalachian native and distinguished African American Harvard professor Henry Louis Gates Jr., that Drennen got the inspiration to team up with Kojo (William T.) Jones Jr., a black boyhood friend, to construct a dual biography. "How would I have felt about my college years if I had had a classmate or a professor like Henry Louis Gates?" Drennen asked. "He was after all, only four years behind me at Yale. . . . If I had been able to engage the issues of race and political power in 1964, might my life have been different?"[72]

Edited with an additional section devoted to analyzing verbal differences between the two men by linguist Dolores Johnson, *Red White Black and Blue* stands as a brave attempt to bridge a substantial racial gap. Despite their ability to speak to their common childhood in Charleston, including the single year they went to school together, it is clear through their individual accounts that the two men see the world in very different terms. While Drennen echoes Reynolds's desire for a color-blind society, Jones rejects the premise in a biting response, commenting,

"Let's be a color-blind society, the even-steven concept. Let's all put down our arms and start the fight here on a level playing field, as if integration and affirmative action have already accomplished their goals." This is an argument designed to appease whites. It employs the Abraham Lincoln philosophy on the slavery issue, . . . and I suspect even Bill Drennen subscribe[s] to this kind of even-steven concept.

This is the fallacious, illogical reasoning that is being used in most government circles as a way to keep the black minority from achieving economic parity. Sure. And then give us another two hundred fifty years to catch up.[73]

Most significantly, the autobiographical portion of the book ends with two very different sentiments. While Drennen states his regrets for the many obstacles that remain to achieving an integrated society, Jones instead stresses his disappointment that there has not been greater solidarity among African Americans as each generation has struggled to achieve its goals. As Dolores Johnson notes, the two men may use the same language, but their experiences have been so sharply differentiated that they "enter the irrational worlds of stereotype, rage, and withdrawal." While each man found the experience of critiquing each other's writing transformative, in the end, Johnson concludes, they failed to find common ground. They succeeded in accepting each other as individuals, without, however, understanding or accepting each other's ideology.[74]

Neither Jones nor Drennen can be faulted for not resolving the dilemma of how best to live in a world that is nominally integrated yet without the full realization of equal opportunities presumed in a color-blind society. The ideal was forged in the 1960s. The path to realization was clouded in years thereafter. That two such well-educated men of privilege as Stephen Bingham and William Bradford Reynolds, each idealistic and responsible in his own way, could end up at such far ends of the civil rights spectrum would have been surprising in 1960. Fifty years later, their differences make more sense. Observations and judgments made and reinforced through experience have created different lenses through which to see the civil rights challenge. That these two men and others in their generation continue to see things in such opposing terms confirms the continued dilemma of race in America. Even as we try to communicate, let alone act, we are challenged to breach a deep divide created from our own social constructions over time. Not even the common privileges of class have bridged that gap.

And it is to privilege that we return. In an authoritative essay on the state of racial inequality in America issued in 2005, three scholars at the University of Pennsylvania confirmed America's mixed record in combating discrimination since the 1960s. "By the end of the century, legal and formal barriers that had excluded blacks from most institutions and from the most favorable labor market positions had largely disappeared," they report. "Black poverty had plummeted, and black political and economic achievements were undeniable." Clearly there was reason for celebration. "Yet," they continued, "for many people—both white and black—the sense remained that racism still pervaded American society, operating in both old and new ways, removing some barriers but erecting others." After demonstrating a range of areas where African Americans still faced disadvantages in not arriving at the starting line at the same time—to use a metaphor Brad Reynolds was fond of employing—and not having the same resources with which to compete, the article concludes by urging that progress be measured not on the basis of assuring abstract individual rights, but through a lens that accounts for accumulated privilege.[75] "It was through . . . differentiation—the accumulation of many small and not-so-small distinctions—that black social structure came increasingly to resemble that found among whites and that black inequality endured despite individual and group mobility."

Such findings, these scholars assert, underscore the limits of individualist solutions to group problems, the approach that Reynolds championed and has since become Republican orthodoxy. "Solutions that promote individual social mobility without attending to the processes that reproduce inequality lead to differentiation—the mobility of a fortunate minority who pull away from the rest," they conclude.[76] "The belief, even the hope, that the nation would glide into color-blindness was foolish," another critical review of contemporary views of civil rights adds. "Indeed, there are good reasons to believe the current goal of a color-blind society is at least as naïve as the optimism of the 1960s and conveniently masks color-coded privileges."[77]

And was this not exactly what Justice Blackmun was arguing, in terms that had to resonate especially with those fortunate enough to have an Ivy League education? While historian and critic of affirmative action remedies Hugh Davis Graham argues persuasively that Blackmun regretted the need to embrace affirmative action at all and hoped such remedies would not continue to be necessary much longer, the justice nonetheless acknowledged the presence of privilege in admissions policies that had certainly been present in the formation of Yale's class of 1964. "It is somewhat ironic to have us so deeply disturbed over a program where race is an element of consciousness," he mused, "and yet to be aware of the fact, as we are, that institutions of higher learning, albeit more on the undergraduate than the graduate level, have given conceded preferences up to a point to those possessed of athletic skills, to the children of alumni, to the affluent who may bestow their largess on the institutions, and to those having connections with celebrities, the famous, and the powerful." That being so, he concluded, to put his widely quoted statement in context, "I suspect that it would be impossible to arrange an affirmative action program in a racially neutral way and have it successful. To ask that this be so is to demand the impossible. In order to get beyond racism, we must first take account of race. There is no other way. And in order to treat some persons equally, we must treat them differently. We cannot—we dare not—let the Equal Protection Clause perpetuate racial supremacy."[78]

That affirmation held sway for more than thirty years, surviving even its greatest challenge in 2013 when the Supreme Court, by a 7–1 margin, chose not to reject the consideration of race as one of a number of factors affecting admissions decisions at the University of Texas. The court nonetheless required the university to assure the lower court that it could not achieve a satisfactory level of diversity through a race-neutral process, thus suggesting that the ongoing debate over affirmative action was far from over.[79] Ominously, the Court, in *Schuette v. Coalition to Defend Affirmative Action*, in the following year upheld a 2006 voter referendum in Michigan banning race as a consideration in admission to public universities. A force in fighting such practice, Jennifer Gratz—the lead plaintiff against the University of Michigan in *Gratz v. Bollinger*, decided in 2003—was exuberant, telling a reporter for *Politico*, "There are always those who want to stand in the schoolhouse door, if you will," alluding to attempts to stop public school integration in the 1960s. "I think that this ruling took us one step closer to equality."[80]

Just as significantly, the Supreme Court, in a 5–4 decision, upended established civil rights law in 2013 by negating Section 4 of the Voting Rights Act, in effect terminating provisions that required a select number of states with a history of discrimination to pre-clear any changes in voting procedures with the Department of Justice. Not surprisingly, the decision provoked outrage from liberals, even as it garnered support from William Bradford Reynolds, who had sought just such an outcome when he headed the Civil Rights Division of the Justice Department and now could take pride in efforts he had taken over the years to forge a conservative majority on the court.[81]

No two people in the class of 1964 remained further apart than Bingham and Reynolds, not just in their positions on civil rights but in their entire worldviews. As much as they both believed in equal justice, they were not about to agree on how best to achieve the goal that loomed so large during their years in college. While they could count a number of classmates who took up the civil rights challenge in other, less polarizing ways, the American dilemma of racial injustice, as it had been prominently addressed since the 1950s, remained unresolved into the twenty-first century. As much as members of the class of 1964 had embraced the goal of achieving a color-blind society, agreeing on actions appropriate to that goal remained elusive, even fifty years after the first student sit-ins and the Freedom Rides that marked the onset of their college careers.

4

War and Peace

An acute observer of the effects of the Cold War and its aftermath, '64's Thomas Powers still remembers the night the accused spies Julius and Ethel Rosenberg were executed: June 19, 1953. As a twelve-year-old Boy Scout, he was attending a regular troop meeting in the gym of the Siwanoy School in Pelham, New York. "Sing Sing prison, where the Rosenbergs were scheduled to be executed at eight o'clock, was also in Westchester County," he recounted, "and the whole troop—twenty or thirty kids—believed that so much power would be drained by the electric chair that the lights in the gym would dim. The moment came and went, but the lights did not dim. For a few moments we believed they had been spared, but word soon circulated from a radio report that they died on schedule."[1]

Powers's memory, vivid and unique as it was, provides but one bit of affirmation of the pervasive presence of a Cold War message that suffused the lives of young people growing up in the 1950s. Not just hopelessly inadequate "duck and cover" exercises that sent students under desks intended to protect them from a nuclear blast, but films depicting the iron and bamboo curtains as literal walls between the free and communist worlds were powerful presences in school programs during those years. For students who had arrived at Yale in the early 1960s, if the Bay of Pigs fiasco and the Cuban missile crisis were not sufficiently immediate to convince them of the communist threat, then the Soviet Union's decision to arrest and charge visiting Yale political science professor Frederick Barghoorn with treason in November 1963 brought the message home. Only President Kennedy's personal intervention shortly before his death assured Barghoorn's release.[2]

A writer by profession, Powers became over time a respected critic of U.S. national security policy, what former-military-officer-turned-critic himself, Andrew Bacevich, calls "Washington Rules," based on the belief that international peace and order require the United States "to maintain a global military presence, to configure its forces for global power projection, and to counter existing or anticipated threats by relying on a policy of global interventionism."[3] Rooted in the Cold War tenets that coincided with Yale '64's period of socialization and given particular power in John F. Kennedy's call "to pay any price, bear any burden, meet any hardship, support any friend, oppose any foe, in order to assure the survival and the success of liberty," these "Washington Rules" demonstrated remarkable staying power. Even as Powers was joined by a number of classmates in questioning those tenets, they found themselves largely in conflict with those in power, not the least their classmates John Ashcroft and Joseph Lieberman. In the contest to redefine America's place in the world during and after the Cold War lay another source of the divide that extended from the 1960s into the twenty-first century.

* * *

No doubt Vietnam—what journalist Myra MacPherson has called "the San Andreas fault in the hearts and minds of Americans"[4]—fundamentally challenged presumptions that had informed the Cold War thinking that did so much to define American attitudes and experiences in the years after World War II. Naval veteran William Drennen confirmed as much for his college classmates, as he wrote at the time of his twenty-fifth Yale reunion in 1989, "For whom of us in the Class of '64 was Vietnam not a landmark—we, who would change the world to make it a peaceful, verdant paradise, found life head-on at war, [a] stark contrast to idealized visions of freedom and optimism of Yale's academic enclaves. For some of us the war was journalism, for some of us it was protest, for most of us it was avoidance. For none of us it was nothing. Our personalities are all marked with scars of our interaction with history in the Indochinese peninsula."[5]

Unlike college classes that followed in the mid-1960s, Yale '64 did not perceive Vietnam as an issue, let alone a divisive one, during its college years. There were a few hints of the war's relevance—a *Yale Daily News* story about a few Yale faculty, including law professor Thomas Emerson (referred to by friends as well as critics as "Tommy the Commie"), questioning the U.S. commitment to Vietnam, and a disturbing documentary shown to members of the Yale Socialist Union that evoked considerable hostility from the audience.[6] Quietly, a few classmates slipped away to enlist in the military before

It was a virtual straight line for '64's John Wilbur from captain of the Yale wrestling team to military service, a path he was familiar with from his father and his generation. The effect of his service remained elusive, however. Returning to Vietnam in 1999, he recalled the events that put him frequently in harm's way, but he struggled to draw greater meaning from the conflict. Courtesy of Beverly Wilbur.

graduating, eventually making their way into combat, but that happened only after graduation. Few paid any attention, so they remained largely ignorant of either the personal or political implications of American involvement.

Born to the generation that fought World War II, raised under the tenets of the Cold War, and charged to include military service as part of their leadership obligation, the members of the class of 1964 were well poised to extend their fathers' own wartime legacy. As John Wilbur recalled, "Even though my college years were 1960–64, we were dyed in the fabric of the Fifties generation with no premonition of the future as the Sixties turned out to be. The Cuban Missile Crisis and racial civil rights said it all for the major issues of our day. Entering the military to become an officer was as natural a post-graduate opportunity as graduate school is today."[7] Wilbur was a powerful swimmer and captain of the Yale wrestling team, and his decision to join the navy SEALs represented a clear extension of his own identity as he had fashioned it in college. Moreover, by following his father's path into military combat, he could be counted among those whom historian Robert Self observes did not doubt in the mid-1960s that "military service was a sure path to manhood and a claim on meaningful citizenship."[8]

Overall, 40 percent of this class served in the military, a good number of them in Vietnam. When called to serve, many did so enthusiastically, none more than Bruce Warner, who according to his childhood friend and college roommate, Tyler Smith, was eager to see combat if the opportunity arose. A talented athlete who lettered in baseball as well as hockey, a fixture on the premier social circuit, and a man with a rich legacy of Yale forebears, Warner represented everything that had been honored in Yale tradition for generations. Hoping to return to work at Hotchkiss following service in the Marine Corps, Warner married before shipping to Vietnam, where he was wounded in battle and died from his injuries back in the United States in March 1966. Twenty-three years later, his widow, Mimo Robinson, wrote movingly of "my childhood sweetheart, a blond, blue-eyed, broad shouldered young man with his high ideals and grand expectations of teaching and coaching in his old school once he had 'come to the aid of his country.'" Voicing her own disillusionment with a war "for which no one seemed remotely grateful," Mimo nonetheless could believe that even through "the heat, the filth, the deception, and disillusion of a year in South Vietnam," Bruce had maintained his fortitude. "I remember the letter that I got when he had only been there for two months telling me about the death of a good friend who had been at Quantico with us and I think of his pain. Fortunately though, while he was there, he felt pain, but amazingly, never seemed to question the cause."[9]

Others who survived their service in Vietnam would come to question the cause, but that came later. Like Warner, '64's Gill Cochran initially embraced the challenge. On entering Yale from Groton School, he joined army ROTC, believing that he was both expected and destined to follow his father and grandfather's steps by doing military service. He selected the infantry because it had the handsomest uniform, never imagining that eighteen months after graduation he would be in the rice paddies of Vietnam, where he soon replaced a platoon leader who had been killed. Cochran considered himself lucky. He had a superior officer who helped him make the transition, and though he led a number of what were routinely referred to as suicide patrols, he experienced only five firefights and lost only two men. Returning home to taunts that he was a baby killer, he retorted angrily with an essay in the *Yale Alumni Magazine*, "Dissenting from Dissenters." He even conveyed his message, in a speech at Groton, that American troops were at the right place at the right time.[10]

Quite another group of graduates elected military service simply to get their obligation out of the way. Among these was Daniel Kapica, one of a small group of white ethnic students actively recruited to Yale in the early 1960s. An active Catholic in Saint Thomas More House as an undergraduate, and pressed by his mother to enter the priesthood, he listed future theological study at Lumen Vitae in Brussels at the time of his graduation. Instead, after being advised by a possible employer in New York that there was a job waiting for him in advertising if he completed his military obligation first, he joined the army.

Hardly the enthusiast for his assignment that Bruce Warner had been, Kapica nonetheless accepted a number of further bits of advice that left him not in intelligence, as he had originally intended, but in the Eleventh Airborne infantry assault team that was preparing to make the army's first helicopter attacks in Vietnam. Assigned to An Khe in the Central Highlands with what was now known as the First Cavalry, Kapica was wounded in one of the first major battles of an escalated war, in October 1965.[11] As he recovered from his wounds, he was sufficiently bothered by reports of rising protests to the war at home to write an anguished letter, published in the *Yale Alumni Magazine* for December 1965. "Yale taught me to give of myself, of my talents and of my experiences," he wrote. "Will my generation continue to hoard the wisdom of education and to be afraid to give of themselves to God, to Country, and to Man? The pompous idealistic clans which shout anti-Vietnam slogans are making a debacle of these principles which I and Yale cherish. Not only are the G.I.'s in Vietnam without adequate books, fatigues, medical supplies and even cigarettes, but also they are without the unanimous support of their own generation. I am insulted and so are 165,000 others who, out of volition or conscription, are giving of themselves for you." Once recovered, Kapica returned to active service, earning accolades for heroism as he took command of his unit and guided it to safety while vastly outnumbered during a rescue mission near the Cambodian border.[12]

Both Kapica and Cochran viewed the war more critically in later years, joining the 70 percent of their classmates who, by 1989, believed the war had been a complete mistake. Cochran, when he returned home, struggled with alcoholism before he found a good psychiatrist, joined Alcoholics Anonymous, and entered a stable career in the law. Looking back in 2011 as he reflected about the connection between the wars in Afghanistan and Vietnam, he noted, "It took me 30 years to put it into perspective, to be finally able to say, we were in the wrong war." Kapica's experience was even more difficult. Marriage, a family, graduate school in business, and positions on Wall Street followed his return from service, but he could not hold his jobs, and his marriage was disintegrating. He too was falling victim to alcohol, a vice he had never indulged in at Yale. He tried unsuccessfully to get support from the Veterans Administration for what later was diagnosed as post-traumatic stress syndrome. Finally, during a marriage counseling session in 1987, he broke and simply walked away from his previous life. In place of the suburban home he had maintained outside of New York City, he lived on food stamps and welfare in a small apartment in a rough section of Elizabeth, New Jersey. It was only after an army friend sought him out and persuaded him to enter Alcoholics Anonymous that he began to reconstruct his life. It took some twenty years for him to forge his own guide to living—what he called "the Way of the Mangrove Seed," a mélange of New Age and Eastern philosophies—before he finally righted himself again. He came to see his embrace of the war and all that lay behind it as part of what he called the "unconscious Boy Scout bubble" he had embraced as he was growing up.[13]

In the immediate years after graduation, few who enlisted questioned the cause as it had been presented, of combating communist aggression and securing liberties abroad. William Drennen proved an exception. The son of a naval war hero and grand-nephew of a Congressional Medal of Honor recipient, Drennen attended Yale when Stanford failed to offer him a place in its navy ROTC program. A football player at Yale, very much caught up in the mystique of his own family's reputation for heroism, he extended his obligation in the service for a year so he could go to Vietnam. Assigned to river patrol, he chafed at the initial lack of enemy contact. Once that changed, he could not get enough of the action until the reality of casualties hit him. Stung by the loss of colleagues and what he perceived as the military's failure to counteract native insurgency effectively, he had become disgusted with the war by the time his tour of duty in Vietnam was over. Burdened by the knowledge that he was leaving behind a Vietnamese woman who was carrying his baby, he told himself he might someday return to take responsibility for the child. For the moment, however, he declared,

> I am just confused and unhappy and feeling guilty and I need to clear my mind. I need some space to think about things. I need to catch up with the world that's spinning round out there with Beatles and Stones. I need to go to rock concerts and anti-war rallies. I need to know where I fit. . . . When America is so screwed up that it would destroy a country in order to make it safe for democracy, I will not recognize laws or submit to being governed by such a social system. Let the LSD generation rule the world. I want to be free.

After leaving his lover with a diamond ring he bought at the PX for $110, he returned to the United States, where he took drugs and traveled widely in search of "a way of life that made sense," until, landing in a French prison, he sobered up, took time to read and reflect, and got his life started again.[14]

Such shifts in opinion as Cochran, Kapica, and even Drennen experienced were largely personal in nature and thus lacked political effect. From the mid-1960s on, however, in an environment of growing skepticism about the war, particularly on college campuses, the effects could be considerable and lasting, even for a military officer. Such was the case with '64's Robert Musil. Prepared for college at Garden City High School on Long Island, Musil entered Yale at the age of sixteen, encouraged in his decision by fellow Garden City graduate Inslee Clark, an admissions staff member who became director in 1965. Musil's father was a Swiss immigrant who worked his way up to a Wall Street position; his mother was a descendant of Thomas Hooker, a founding father of Connecticut. Attracted immediately to ROTC by a brochure he received even before entering Yale, Musil was impressed by the picture of a uniformed student standing before an ivied building, and he signed up in his early days on campus. The army's bureaucratic regimen gave Musil some pause about continuing in ROTC, but President Kennedy's appearance at the Berlin Wall convinced him he would ultimately face the draft, so he continued with officer training. He received his commission as a second lieutenant in July 1964, a week before Congress approved the Gulf of Tonkin Resolution authorizing the president to use military force in Vietnam without a congressional declaration of war.

Commissioned officers were allowed to put off active duty if they were enrolled in a graduate program, and Musil took advantage of this policy by entering a PhD program in English at Northwestern University. Assigned the position of freshman counselor, he grew increasingly uneasy with his responsibilities policing student social life, even as the war in Vietnam was escalating. Through the sister of a friend, he came into contact with Students for a Democratic Society. By his second year at Northwestern he was organizing against the war at the same time he was conveying his views through a course on war and literature. Still in graduate school in 1968, he threw himself into Eugene McCarthy's presidential campaign. He counseled draft resisters, even as he remained in military service.

By 1968, Musil was approaching the end of his graduate program, and the issue of active service became more pressing. He considered escaping to Canada, but his roots were too deep in the United States. Refusing orders was another option, though examples of punishment meted out to those who had done so were chilling. Teaching for the army was one possibility, but his application to West Point was denied. For the moment he avoided active military engagement by taking a position at Fort Benjamin Harrison in Indiana. There he used his experience writing for underground newspapers to help train twenty-six hundred military information officers. Even as he did that, he joined a concerned officers group that sued Secretary of Defense Melvin Laird for war crimes. He also continued his antiwar counseling through the Methodist Church. Somehow, his activities failed to incur reprimand, but that changed after he published an antiwar petition in the *Nation* in 1970.

Issued orders to report to Vietnam in December, Musil sought conscientious objector status. Given a few precedents, an excellent lawyer, and what he considered his class privilege, Musil applied for and ultimately received an honorable discharge from the army. Achieving his independence too late in the year to acquire an academic job, he took a position instead with the Central Committee for Conscientious Objectors. Thus he began a long association with peace organizations.[15]

Disillusionment with the war in particular and many of the assumptions behind it became common enough on university campuses in the mid-1960s. A number of Yale '64 members used their time in graduate school to protest the war, burning a draft card at Yale in one instance, joining the McCarthy or Robert Kennedy presidential campaigns in a number of other instances. At Harvard, '64's Jon Van Dyke went beyond protest to add to the formal, published critical assessment of the military measures that were widely expected to force the North Vietnamese to surrender. As a student in Henry Kissinger's seminar on national security in 1966 while at Harvard Law School, he was privileged to hear from top Washington-based experts on the war, including Secretary of Defense Robert McNamara, whose appearance on the Harvard campus Kissinger nervously monitored by phone as the surge of protesters built up outside the classroom building.[16] The previous year Van Dyke had defended the war on Harvard's side in a debate with Yale Law School. A summer of research on Vietnam as part of an internship at the law office of the State Department convinced him, however, that the war effort was misguided. His study of the intensive bombing campaign launched against North Vietnam in February 1965 started as a seminar paper for Kissinger, then appeared in book form in 1972, with a foreword from the distinguished Harvard Asian expert Edwin Reischauer. Despite "the most sophisticated and sustained bombing campaign history has yet known," Van Dyke reported, "the North Vietnamese had held fast, and all effort to use the campaign to force concessions or surrender at the bargaining table had failed." Looking back, he felt that Kissinger himself had understood the causes of U.S. failure in Vietnam, but once in a position of power he had embraced the same failed policy anyway.[17]

Such criticism did not emanate only from college campuses, but extended to those who found their way to Vietnam outside military ranks. In a book of reflections on Vietnam, John Wilbur described his frequent visits while in the military to a diplomatic compound in an upscale section of Saigon, where an assortment of journalists, young diplomats, and visiting businessmen—anyone with something interesting to say—would gather to argue the merits of the war.[18] He was drawn into the group through his college classmate Thomas McAdams "Mac" Deford, a Foreign Service officer, who by that time had drawn an assignment as an aide to Ambassador Ellsworth Bunker. Deford later recounted the speed with which he came to question the viability of the war effort. Arriving in Vietnam in June 1966, he was sent initially to work with a U.S. military unit training Vietnamese forces at the village and province level; his job was to coordinate USAID projects. Soon after settling in he attended the dedication of a school built before his arrival with AID assistance. As the province chief approached the ceremony by helicopter, the rotor wash blew the tin roof off the new facility. "We went ahead with the dedication ceremony anyway," Deford reports, "while I mentally wondered how most of the allocated funds had actually been divvied up." That was enough to convince him "that we weren't going to win. There were a bunch like me out in the provinces in the mid to late '60s—first assignment state department types, CIA officers, AID guys, navy SEALs, young captains and majors, some fluent in Vietnamese, many attracted to the country and its people, and we all knew it wasn't working."[19]

Another member of the Saigon circle of 1964 graduates was Robert Kaiser. The son of a prominent diplomat and labor official, Kaiser started a long and distinguished career with the *Washington Post* as an undergraduate intern. As soon as he received the physical exemption from the draft he had ardently sought, Kaiser began pestering his editors for assignment to the war, noting later, "It struck me then, as it strikes me now, that Vietnam would be the critical event for our generation. I wanted to see it, to know it." Early in 1969, he got his wish to join the paper's two-man bureau. Assigned with his wife to a grand apartment located over a car dealership, Kaiser found himself going to war by day, "flying by helicopter to the scene of battle," and returning in time for a martini and dinner. "We actually belonged to a country club in Saigon, the Cercle Sportif, that the French had left behind—a pool, tennis courts, nice spot for a quick, light lunch," he reported. "A South Vietnamese tank was stationed on the grounds, which abutted the presidential palace. 'Good Morning, Vietnam' gave you a strong whiff of all this. It was really crazy."[20]

Before he left for the war zone, Kaiser did all he could to prepare, including debriefing his colleague Ward Just, whose reporting, Kaiser believed, was the best coming out of Vietnam. Just's last column had described the war as unwinnable. Kaiser's last column from Vietnam built on that conclusion, but stressed that the war was unending—an irony for him, because when he had first come to Saigon, at the outset of the Paris peace talks, he was told by senior U.S. experts of his good luck that he would be able to see the end of the war before his eighteen-month assignment was up. "Alas," he wrote in the *Washington Post* in August 1970, "the war was not ending then, and it is not ending now. It may prove as difficult to end as it has been to win." In an unusually blunt essay, Kaiser pointed to a host of failures by Americans as well as their South Vietnamese allies. The war would drag on, he asserted, because the North Vietnamese were determined and the opposition had too much financial as well as military support to give in. "My feeling is that Americans who think they can fundamentally change (i.e. 'improve') a society like this one are just mad," he concluded. "The lesson of Vietnam should be that America can do no such thing. Our skills, our power and even our national character are not suited to the war in Vietnam, or to the war in Cambodia, or to any similar problem."[21] With the additional perspective of time, he added in a submission to his twenty-fifth reunion book, "My sense is that the war was critical partly because of the upheaval it caused, but more importantly because of the turning point it marked, particularly for our generation. Vietnam ended the American Century far ahead of schedule. The war taught us that happy-ever-after and boundless progress were American myths, not laws of nature."[22]

Thomas Powers could see some positive signs in the rising criticism of war policy, and he concluded in a 1973 assessment that public opposition had forced Lyndon Johnson to finally stop bombing North Vietnam. "The opposition often seemed pitifully weak compared to the power of the presidency," he admitted, "but in the end it prevailed."[23] Still, he could not overlook the way the president had ignored intelligence reports that questioned the effectiveness of the bombing. One report, according to Powers, went so far as to claim that "short of a major invasion or nuclear attack, there is probably no level of air or naval actions against North Vietnam which Hanoi has determined in advance would be so intolerable that the war had to be stopped." CIA director Richard Helms never pressed the point over objections from the White House, however. Moreover, when it came to another critical assessment of the enemy—the number of troops it had in Vietnam—Helms gave in entirely to military insistence that the official estimate remain below three hundred thousand, despite the objection of a young analyst, Sam Adams, who fervently insisted that the number should have been twice as high. Despite knowing that the figures had been reduced for political purposes, Helms ended up signing the estimate in November 1967, only months before the Tet offensive caught both the public and the military completely off guard.[24]

Powers's classmate George "Chip" Pickett was in a particularly good position to confirm Powers's assessment of an intelligence failure. The son of a military officer who spent thirty-six months in combat in World War II and rose to be a three-star general, Pickett was unusual among '64 graduates in expressing his pleasure being on the rifle range two weeks after graduation, compared to the college years behind him. After a year in Korea on the demilitarized zone and further time at Fort Bragg, he switched from infantry to intelligence, arriving in Vietnam in January 1968, shortly before the Tet offensive. His responsibility was to track enemy forces, a role he became particularly adept at after Tet, and one he continued on returning to Washington in 1969 after a year in country. As head of a small staff that tracked all enemy forces in Vietnam at the Pentagon's Defense Intelligence Agency, he witnessed the continued infighting between defense and intelligence agencies over how best to count enemy dead and thus to estimate the opposition's ability to continue fighting. Beset by numbers of war dead from other sources that he considered inflated, and prodded by a superior officer to make sure his own estimates agreed, he finally felt compelled to jump the chain of command to express his concerns to a to senior general. At his prompting, new steps were taken to ensure that the Joint Chiefs of Staff were not misled.[25] The issue ultimately receded in importance, but not without deepening public suspicions that the military was either incompetent or dishonest about reporting its war efforts.

* * *

America's withdrawal in 1973 and the subsequent conclusion of hostilities with Saigon's collapse two years later did not resolve either the debate over the war's justification or the proper course for defending American interests abroad as the Cold War continued unabated. With the American military record tarnished abroad and pressures to restore cuts in defense funding, however, the Reagan administration made it a priority to restore the "Washington Rules" that America remain a dominant military power throughout the world. Among the administration's most visible commitments was the Strategic Defense Initiative—popularly know as "Star Wars"—intended to provide an impenetrable shield against potential nuclear attack. The proposal sparked heated debate, prompting a number of members of the class of 1964 into unprecedented actions in response.

Not surprisingly, Robert Musil was among these, serving over a number of years as executive director of the Professionals' Coalition for Nuclear Arms Control, the SANE Education Fund, the Center for National Security Studies Military Affairs Project, and for fifteen years as executive director of Physicians for Social Responsibility—winner, with International Physicians for the Prevention of Nuclear War, of the 1985 Nobel Peace Prize.[26] His classmate Andrew Harris, in the aftermath of his difficult relationship with the military while serving an internship in Madison, Wisconsin, also joined Physicians for Social Responsibility, ascending over time to chair the Salem, Oregon, chapter for more than a decade. Subsequently elected national president, he worked closely with Musil during his time in office.[27]

Robert Lamson took yet another path in the effort to curb reliance on military action. Trained as an economist at the University of Washington in his hometown of Seattle after his graduation from Yale, Lamson joined the Institute for Defense Analyses upon completing his PhD. Formed in 1947 as a university consortium to assist military agencies in dealing with the nation's most pressing security issues, the institute became an object of antiwar protest in the 1960s on a number of the participating campuses, including Columbia. While he was at the institute, Lamson witnessed growing frustration and even opposition to the war among the military officers he worked with. Practically his whole economics section opposed the war and took to wearing black arm- bands to work to demonstrate their position. Returning to Seattle in the early 1970s to serve as budget officer for the University of Washington, he experi- enced another side of protest as student demonstrations hampered the work of the university. Frustrated by the disruption, he left to take a job heading the Boeing Corporation's computer division.[28]

During the 1970s, Lamson and his wife became involved with the Creative Initiative Foundation, which traced its roots back to the early twentieth century when the theologian and scientist Henry Burton Sharman of the University of Chicago began offering seminars seeking to unify science and religion, based on the belief that each searched for the same universal truths. In the late 1930s a Stanford law and business professor brought Sharman's six-week program for college students and professors to California, where it was offered under the name of the Sequoia Seminar Foundation on a property purchased in the Santa Cruz Mountains. Under the influence of the threat of nuclear war in the 1960s, the seminar turned directly to the consideration of the precariousness of life, offering programs extending beyond specific con- cerns with the Cold War to more personal topics, such as "The Quest for Meaning." In 1971 these activities were incorporated as the Creative Initiative Foundation.[29]

Creative Initiative combined religious dialogue with New Age techniques, including the study of Jungian psychology and encounter seminars. As important as the organization was in melding Lamson's personal with his professional life, he felt the organization was growing too inward in the early 1980s. Leaving that association behind him, he chose to run for Congress as a peace Democrat the year Ronald Reagan ran for reelection. He lost his race to an entrenched Republican but subsequently helped institutionalize what he had learned over several decades, as director of Business Executives for National Security. Formed in 1982, BENS embraced issues that had been close to Lamson's interests since college: U.S.-Soviet threat reduction initia- tives and widespread inefficiencies in support functions in the Department of Defense. Lamson's classmate Anthony Lee took a similarly distinctive turn in the 1980s.

After serving a relatively uneventful three years as a navy officer following graduation, Lee enrolled at Rutgers Business School in Newark, near his childhood home in Short Hills, New Jersey. Armed with an MBA and having just passed the CPA exams, he took a position with Arthur Andersen in San Francisco, where he had done an internship in the winter of 1969. Joined by his new wife, Margie, he settled down to a conventional lifestyle. The couple had relationship problems that were exacerbated by their inability to conceive. Feeling they needed help communicating with each other, they sought out, at the suggestion of friends and a coworker, the Creative Initiative Foundation in Palo Alto.

Lee described himself as a weak Episcopalian, but through Creative Initiative, which included weeklong seminars on the teachings of Jesus, he and Margie found both the basis of better communication and a greater spiritual purpose in life. They continued an association with the foundation in the late 1970s and were drawn in, especially in the early 1980s, through growing concerns about the heightening of Cold War tension. In those years, the foundation suspended its other programs to focus on educating the public about the threat of nuclear war. Particularly effective was the film *The Last Epidemic*, produced by Physicians for Social Responsibility to depict the effect of a one-megaton hydrogen bomb dropped on San Francisco. It was shown in hundreds of homes and community meetings, where its sponsors conveyed the message that nuclear weapons were only a symptom of the larger problem of an all-too-great willingness to resolve conflicts through war. After devoting three months to formulating a revised mission statement addressing the crisis, the newly named organization, the Beyond War Foundation, developed a three-part course to communicate the nature of both the crisis and its solution. As the movement expanded at the grass roots, it built an organization devoted to taking its message into homes across the country.

In 1982, Lee quit his job as the chief financial officer of a large construction company to volunteer full time for Beyond War. Supported only by modest family inheritances, the Lees set off to organize in Massachusetts. Sixteen other couples moved at the same time from the headquarters in Palo Alto to other states for the same purpose. Eventually there were thirty to forty teams and five hundred volunteers working in Massachusetts to overturn prevailing attitudes about the necessity of war. The position volunteers promoted was that war was obsolete and that people had to learn to resolve conflicts without violence. To make that truth operative, they had to change people's consciousness, one small meeting and one intense encounter at a time. The work was hard. Not everyone was receptive, and some were outright hostile. The effort continued for most of a decade, however, until the collapse of the Soviet Union, when the urgency of the nuclear arms race finally receded.[30]

* * *

Accompanying the Reagan administration's determination to restore military dominance was the advent of tough popular heroes as the pride of contemporary American culture. It was in this context that the appearance of an article calling for a new kind of American warrior—one that featured '64's Jack Cirie—had particular salience. One of a group of Connecticut "locals" who were actively recruited to join Yale's football program, Cirie was quickly recognized as a superior athlete. In addition to setting a school record of five interceptions his junior year when he was named the team's most valuable player, Cirie lettered twice in lacrosse and won two middleweight boxing titles. After deciding not to enter the Peace Corps and rejecting a possible path to business after a single interview, with Colgate-Palmolive, he signed up for marine officer's training. "I decided that what I wanted was a military experience, and for me that meant going to war," he later recalled. "I wanted to be in a position where everything was at risk, where you get a chance to see inside yourself."

Having early and often demonstrated his courage on the battlefield, Cirie became one of only several members of his class to sign up for a second tour of duty in Vietnam. Challenging the system was out of the question, but during his second assignment there, his assessment of the war grew increasingly critical. A poem, "Yellow on White and Black," which he composed in December 1970, shortly before his tour ended, read, in part,

> As if to say, we did our best,
> And who's to ask the how or why?
> Just, we were here, lived the fear,
> Yellow and white and black men die.[31]

Bound to a military career, he kept his reservations from public view, but on his retirement after twenty years of service in the mid-1980s, he determined to learn from his experience.

Still personally as well as professionally shaken from his combat experience, Cirie joined a growing movement out of the 1960s to understand and to act upon his inner beliefs. Telling a colleague he wanted "to find and express that part of himself that he'd never allowed to blossom—his creativity, his sensitivity, his aliveness, his spontaneity," he made his way to the Esalen Institute. For eight months he took a program in energy training under the direction of George Leonard. Jack told me, a colleague reported, "he'd found there a place to release the grief he carried around from seeing men die before his eyes in Vietnam, to let go of the rage he'd swallowed at the senselessness of the killing, to forgive himself for the men he'd killed. He told me, IPE [Interpersonal Training] was a place where he'd been able to let down some of

Seeking "a place to release the grief he carried around from seeing men die before his eyes in Vietnam," Jack Cirie undertook months of interpersonal training at the Esalen Institute before joining SportsMind in Seattle. His effort to help define the "moral equivalent of war" was cut short by his death in 1992. Reprinted from *Later Life*, the Yale 1964 twenty-fifth reunion class book.

the armor he'd put on to keep from feeling his pain—a place where he learned to feel again, to be vulnerable, to love and be loved."[32]

A veteran of both World War II and the Korean conflict, George Leonard helped bring "the Sixties" to national attention as the San Francisco editor of *Look* in the early part of the decade. In 1970, he left the publication to devote himself full time to the human potential movement, a name he helped coin before joining the educational staff at Esalen. Building on the insights drawn from his 1968 book, *Education and Ecstasy*, and his training in the martial art aikido, with roots going back to the medieval Japanese samurai, he developed a program fusing movement, meditation, and mind/body practices intended to guide an inner voyage to realize inborn genius.[33]

Leonard was impressed enough with Cirie to make him the centerpiece of an essay conceiving the future of American military power at a time of particular national angst in the aftermath of the fall of South Vietnam. "America has discovered a new hero, the latest in a lineage that goes back to Davy Crockett and Daniel Boone, to the Lone Ranger and the western marshal with the fast draw," Leonard asserted:

> He is an elite-forces man with the muscles of a Western body builder and the mind-set of an Eastern martial artist. He is Chuck Norris in "Missing in Action" and "The Delta Force," Arnold Schwarzenegger

in "Commando," and Fred Ward in "Remo Williams: The Adventure Begins." Above all, he is Sylvester Stallone in "Rambo: First Blood Part II." This is the new American warrior, a man who, lacking the gritty camaraderie of a John Wayne or the true urbane wit of a James Bond, slaughters commies and other enemies of the state by the score, cutting through bureaucratic inertia with a stream of machine gun bullets. This is the warrior as an American revenge fantasy, a vivid dream image of a single-minded, unrestrained action that would somehow erase the frustrations of Vietnam, Iran and Lebanon, and set things right in one miraculous catharsis of blood and gore.

Despite the popularity of the image, Leonard charged, "Rambo won't do. He's too sullen, self-centered, head-strong, delinquent and—face it—unreal. We need military men and women who are effective, who are professional, who live by a spoken or unspoken warrior's code, and who are dedicated to keeping the peace." Citing a 1910 passage from the philosopher William James, Leonard called for a "moral equivalent of peace," a way of living "to provide the challenges of combat without its horrors." "We need challenge and risk. We need to be pushed to our limits. And I believe this is what happens when we accept the warrior's code, when we try to live each moment as a warrior, whether in education, job, marriage, child-rearing or recreation."[34] For him, Jack Cirie exemplified that code.[35]

On completing his program with Leonard, Cirie joined a small training company called SportsMind in Seattle, which developed an experimental five-day program that included two days of outdoor high and low ropes course events, units on nutrition and exercise, and intensive review of attitudes, beliefs, and philosophy of life. To his close friend and former Yale football teammate, Patrick Caviness, he wrote, "I am designing, creating, and teaching the very things I want to learn the most: Integration of the body and mind, of the spirit and emotion; ways of positive transformation in the face of overwhelming odds (in our business, family, and personal lives); ways of accelerating learning—indeed learning to learn."[36]

Beyond his personal quest, Cirie anticipated helping the military achieve "a moral equivalent of peace" through the training of a new kind of warrior. He got his chance when the army hired him and fellow ex-marine Richard Strozzi-Heckler to provide several dozen Special Forces soldiers with training in aikido, biofeedback, and "mind-body psychology." His was one of a growing number of programs seeking the difficult balance of military action and peaceful intent.[37] What Cirie might have accomplished over time is simply conjuncture, as he died of an aneurysm on January 6, 1992. His own actions, however, represented a peculiar if not entirely unique synthesis of early New Frontier idealism and New Age mysticism, hardly a consensus approach to balancing international objectives between military and peaceful means. More frontally, the question arose as to how important the military buildup—most notably the Star Wars initiative—had been in precipitating the collapse of the Soviet Union.

George Pickett was in a good position to pronounce that effort a success. After he completed two years at Harvard Business School, the army permitted him to be assigned to Henry Kissinger's staff in the White House, where he worked under Andrew Marshall, widely regarded as one of the premier defense thinkers of the Cold War. Following Marshall to the Department of Defense, he spent several years focused largely on comparisons of U.S. and Soviet forces. Although he recognized that other factors mattered in the competition with the Soviets, including improved intelligence gathering through satellite surveillance and the recovery of U.S. conventional military strength after Vietnam, he believed that U.S. military investments, including what he called the much maligned Star Wars initiative, finally convinced the Soviets that they could no longer afford the costly arms race. Thomas Powers, in what must have been something of a surprise to the readers of his contributions to the *New York Review of Books*, agreed. Referring to the definitive Cold War policy of containing Soviet expansion, Powers noted, "Kennan often wrote in subsequent years that he did not intend an exclusively military form of containment, and that he certainly would never have proposed such a dangerous American reliance above all on nuclear arms. But time is what containment took and time is what the fear of nuclear war gave us. All other factors in the outcome of the Cold War fade beside that one. . . . The bomb won."[38] If there was some consensus on this particular point, however, it proved harder to forge agreement on defining the proper balance between military and diplomatic power in the post–Cold War era, a point brought home in the experience of '64's Chas Freeman, a career diplomat, who played a central role as the ambassador to Saudi Arabia during the Gulf War as the United States responded to Iraq's invasion of Kuwait.

* * *

Born Charles, but officially adopting "Chas," George W. Bush's favorite name for him, Freeman arrived as a freshman at Yale with many of the same social assets of his fellow prep school graduates, including his Milton classmates Stephen Bingham and Timothy Mellon, for many years his closest friend. Raised in the Bahamas and sent to Milton to be "re-Americanized," as his father put it, because he spoke with an English accent, Freeman sped through his undergraduate studies as a Spanish and Spanish literature major, graduating in three years to take a place at Harvard Law School. Unimpressed with what he was learning in Cambridge, Freeman took the first chance he got to enter the diplomatic corps, which he described as "a perfect escape from boredom and monotony." Using his facility with languages, he served, among other things, as translator for Henry Kissinger's landmark 1971 trip to China at President Nixon's request to open relations with mainland communists.

The Vietnam War posed a dilemma for Freeman as a junior Foreign Service officer in India. Asked to defend U.S. policy before a university audience in Madras, he toyed with the usual excuses of feeling ill or some other evasion. Realizing he was only putting off the inevitable demands to speak about the war publicly, he devised a rationale that America was in Vietnam to protect India from China. As shallow as the case for such an interpretation was, it sat well with Freeman's audience, turning it from an overtly hostile to an overwhelmingly supportive crowd. Such success prompted other invitations to speak on Vietnam, a topic he did not relish. As with others of his generation, the war's impact remained well after its termination.[39]

Freeman's appointment as ambassador to Saudi Arabia closely coincided with the end of the Cold War, marked by the tearing down of the Berlin Wall in 1989 and the collapse of the Soviet Union. While this triumph was received with great bravado in Western political circles, Freeman worried about the lessons policy makers were drawing from the war's conclusion. From what he called the neoconservative-influenced myth that the West's victory stemmed largely from military power, it followed, he believed, "for many that we should bear any burden and pay any price to sustain that superiority in every region of the world, no matter what people in these regions felt about this. . . . The answer was to make the preservation of global military hegemony our objective. With no real discussion and little fanfare, we did so."[40]

Saddam Hussein's invasion of Kuwait immediately put the United States and its allies to the test of this vision. Freeman fully supported the determination not to let Iraq inaugurate the new era by absorbing its neighbors with the intent of controlling a great portion of the world's oil supply, and he worked closely with the U.S. military and Saudi officials on logistics for launching an allied counterattack. Because Saudi Arabia's armed forces would have been no match for an Iraqi attack, King Fahd made short-term compromises to embrace Western military support in order to guarantee his country's survival. The military success that followed appeared to justify the alliance, but Freeman believed that the hard work necessary for securing the peace through diplomatic channels never happened, leading to what he considered an unsatisfactory resolution. "That war never really ended," he concluded, an argument that appeared to be confirmed in the aftermath of the September 11, 2001, attack on the United States.[41]

That attack, Freeman believed, only deepened the American reliance on military over all other forms of response. The extended conflict in Afghanistan and the botched follow-up to the invasion of Iraq that followed reflected the actions of policy makers who filtered the events of a new world order through a reconstructed view of the Cold War, which he felt mistakenly viewed military might as the primary weapon against terror. Pointing to the many errors of judgment that shaped the occupation of Iraq, he asserted in 2007, "The problems we confront in Iraq and on other less central fronts in our confrontation with anti-American terrorists are primarily political, not military. What we lack is not military might but political acumen. Our failings are not those of muscle but of the mind." For the *Washington Post*'s Robert Kaiser, the new war effort had the look of Vietnam all over again. Events in Iraq reminded him of Tet and the vanity of Richard Nixon and his principal aide, Henry Kissinger, who he believed had prevented an early end to the war because they insisted on a "decent interval" before acknowledging defeat. Reflecting his earlier reading of the Vietnam War, Kaiser concluded a 2004 assessment by writing, "Today we cannot know the consequences of any of the choices we may make in Iraq. We can only hope that the end won't be so long in coming this time."[42]

Joining this dialogue was Mac Deford. Retired to Maine after a stint with Merrill Lynch in New York City, he returned to his early Foreign Service interests by organizing a high-powered annual conference on world affairs and launching a weekly news column in the aftermath of the 9/11 attacks for the *Free Press*, based in Rockland, Maine. "There might not be much military similarity between Iraq and Vietnam but by God it's beginning to sound like Vietnam," he wrote in December 2003. Not unlike the earlier war, he noted, failed rationales and stalemate led to mounting domestic opposition. Challenging the Bush rationale that a democratic Iraq would lead to peace in the Middle East, Deford—a self-professed Arabist like Freeman from his Foreign Service experience—argued instead that the United States intervention had become widely perceived as an occupation. "Keep the focus on winning an unwinnable victory in Iraq to the detriment of real issues—and we're going to lose the Middle East," he warned.[43]

Deford's judgments coincided closely with those of Thomas Powers, who quickly came to consider the decision to enter Iraq a massive failure of intelligence. Writing in December 2003, he identified the invasion and conquest of Iraq as "probably the least ambiguous case of misreading of secret intelligence information in American history." Linking the rationale for intervention directly with the Tonkin Gulf resolution forty years earlier, he noted that "not a single one of the factual claims about Iraqi weapons and links to al-Qaeda has been robustly confirmed, and in most cases there has been no confirmation of any kind whatever." The situation looked no better in retrospect, as Powers added in 2010: "It is no longer a secret how the Bush White House pushed, cajoled, bullied, and deceived the United States into war with Iraq."[44]

Powers felt the war created a crisis for the Central Intelligence Agency that evoked Richard Nixon's abuse of power in the Watergate scandal. With so much pressure to bend to executive will, the CIA could no longer be trusted to "call them as they see them." Again using the 1960s as a reference, he compared the war over time with the bombing of North Vietnam, as another failure of nerve. Instead of providing the kind of critical assessment Jon Van Dyke had accumulated from public sources, the CIA, Powers charged, had failed to report in plain language whether the strategy in Iraq was working or not.[45] Powers argued that the CIA had connected many of the bits of information that an attack was coming in 2001, but "for reasons of his own President Bush did nothing." When I asked Powers in a 2010 interview what he thought Bush's reasons were, he suggested that the Bush administration was so committed to installing an antiballistic shield on a scale originally envisioned by Ronald Reagan, it did not want to acknowledge the danger of terrorism.[46] Regardless of whether Powers's position receives confirmation by future historians, the Bush administration's response to the 9/11 attacks, after early days of near universal acceptance, proved nearly as controversial at home as the Vietnam War had been in the 1960s.

* * *

To assure national security at home, President Bush called especially on his attorney general, '64's John Ashcroft. Never one to underplay the drama of his actions, Ashcroft recounted the message he believed Bush had directed at him the day after the 9/11 attacks:

> We were assessing damages, reviewing our situation and plans when President Bush abruptly stopped, turned, and looked toward me. "Don't ever let this happen again," the president said. Whether he intended the remark for anyone else in the room at the time, I don't know. But I took it personally. *Never again. Don't let this happen again.* Those words became my guidepost for the next four years. From that moment forward, I devoted myself to an intense, sometimes secret war with a mission many people thought was impossible: stopping terrorists from attacking again on American soil.[47]

1964's John Ashcroft brought a powerful sense of mission to his position fighting terrorism as George W. Bush's attorney general. Even as he defended his methods, they sparked enough controversy to deepen the nation's political divide. Illustration by David Levine. Copyright 2014 by Matthew and Eve Levine.

Ashcroft did not arrive without difficulty at a position of such consequence. After losing his Senate reelection campaign to Mel Carnahan, whose tragic death gave the deceased Democrat a last-minute boost and resulted in the seating of his wife, Jean, Ashcroft was tapped for attorney general, but only when several choices Bush had pursued proved untenable. Facing the stark partisan divide that had hardened in the 1980s and thereafter, Ashcroft underwent a difficult confirmation hearing not unlike the one that William Bradford Reynolds had faced in his nomination to be associate attorney general fifteen years earlier. Ashcroft's own description of the process captured well his antagonism toward those who faulted his suitability for the position. Newly installed chairman of the Judiciary Committee

Patrick Leahy "fired the initial shots in the conflagration." Senator Ted Kennedy "was particularly vehement in his inquisition. His face grew red and his voice increased in volume and pitch." As for the "liberal organizations given privilege by the media," he asserted, "it was their same old song, different day, different verse." Most offensive, he implied, was an effort to exploit his opposition while still Missouri governor to the appointment of African American Ronnie White to the Western District Court of Appeals. "This is race-baiting, pure and simple," Ashcroft suggested, in citing the Center for Individual Rights' Clint Bolick's defense of his position: "It is an effort on the part of the left wing and the Democratic party to inflame the base by injecting race." Despite the opposition, Ashcroft's nomination passed 58–42—not, however, with the support of his classmate Democrat Joseph Lieberman.[48]

Determined to make good his pledge never to let another attack take place on American soil during his tenure, Ashcroft zealously pursued the surveillance, detainment, and deportation of possible enemies to the state. As a chief vehicle for securing domestic security, he crafted the Patriot Act, which despite prompting criticism for its lack of respect for civil liberties, passed the Congress overwhelmingly and in record time. Using an approach he adopted from Robert Kennedy's aggressive war on organized crime in the 1960s, he determined to find any excuse he could—including the metaphorical equivalent of "spitting in the streets"—to arrest those who might pose a threat to the United States. Unapologetic for any of the actions that generated controversy during his time in office, Ashcroft asked rhetorically, "Why should we send our young people into danger around the world in our fight against terrorism if we are going to coddle and succor terrorists in our own country? It would be a travesty if because of our lack of moral resolve and the will to win we turn our country into a haven for terrorists that they no longer have in other lands."[49]

Ashcroft's primary targets were foreign aliens, almost all of whom were Muslim or Arab. The largest target of prosecution were immigrants who had violated their terms of entry, a great many in minor fashion. Hundreds were rounded up and held, most notably in notorious conditions in Brooklyn. The *Philadelphia Inquirer*'s Stephan Salisbury detailed in chilling detail the effects such actions had on Muslims in his community. In the two years after 9/11, some five thousand foreign nationals were detained, none of whom had been convicted of a terrorist offense five years later.[50] Still, for his part, Ashcroft could look back on his term with satisfaction. Accepting the complete militarization of the "war on terror," he acknowledged how difficult it was "knowing how or when to release detainees if there is no controlling, receiving authority to restrain these captured terrorists from restarting the battle."

Nevertheless, he concluded, "in answering the question of which party should bear the risks of indeterminate detention pending the definitive cessation of the war, the answer is clear. The attacked, innocent culture should not bear the risk of additional injury. The risk should be borne by the terrorist aggressor who assaulted the innocent."[51]

Such aggressive tactics inevitably attracted criticism, and a year after the terrorist attacks, Ashcroft found himself again before the Senate Judiciary Committee. Once again, Ashcroft's defense of his policies was unapologetic and his account of the process searing. Wondering whether the senators before him could possibly believe "the drivel spouted by the talking heads," he stated his determination not to let "the security of the American people to be sabotaged by political intimidation and senatorial histrionics." Charging civil liberties groups and their allies in Congress with fear mongering, he speculated that "the more liberal elements of Congress, no doubt, were disappointed that we were so successful in our attempts to secure our government's favor, that we could focus on fighting terrorism rather than feuding about emotional attempts to wedge one faction or group of Americans against one another."[52] Critics, in turn, found Ashcroft's assertion that challenges to his tactics "only aid terrorists" and "give ammunition to America's enemies" reminiscent of Richard Nixon's defense of his Vietnam War policies.[53]

As part of the national security team in the Bush administration, Ashcroft played a central role in gathering intelligence. One tool in the repertoire of federal weapons was the Foreign Intelligence Surveillance Act (FISA), which had been instituted in 1978, following extensive hearings under the chairmanship of Senator Frank Church, with the intention of protecting civilians from excess government intrusions in the form of wiretapping of the kind authorized by President Nixon at the height of opposition to the Vietnam War. According to the law, government requests to tap domestic civilian communications had to be approved by a special court established under the 1978 statute. The court was generally willing to extend permission for such requests, but the Bush administration, in widening the scope of the data it was collecting from U.S. citizens without warrant, found going through the court inconvenient and, in some instances, unacceptable.[54]

With authorization for Bush's Terrorist Surveillance Program set to expire in March 2004, the director of the Office of Legal Counsel in the Justice Department, Jack Goldsmith, after thoroughly reviewing the program, concluded that it was illegal and persuaded Ashcroft not to approve its extension. Vice President Cheney strenuously objected to what he considered an unwarranted restriction on the executive branch's ability to fight terrorism. Armed with a memo authorizing the extension, drafted by his chief legal adviser and a hard-liner on terrorism, David Addington, Cheney acted. At his request, two of the president's top aides, chief of staff Andrew Card and legal counsel Alberto Gonzales, were dispatched to get approval from Ashcroft, who had fallen ill with a near lethal case of pancreatitis. Worried for her husband's well-being, Ashcroft's wife, Janet, called Deputy Attorney General James Comey and pleaded with him to intervene. Already convinced that the authorization to extend the surveillance program drawn up by Goldsmith's predecessor John Yoo was sloppy and unacceptable, Comey reached Ashcroft in the intensive care unit of the hospital just before Bush's emissaries arrived.

In a scene that attracted considerable journalistic attention afterward, Gonzales asked how Ashcroft was doing. Ignoring the attorney general's response, "Not well," Gonzales pulled out the draft order and asked Ashcroft to sign it. According to Jane Mayer's authoritative account, "Ashcroft lifted his head off the pillows and delivered a strong denunciation of the TSP's legal framework. Then, spent, he sank back into the pillows, from which he wearily added that whatever he thought was irrelevant anyway, because, he said, turning to Comey, 'He's the Attorney General.'" The aftermath, according to Mayer, was that President Bush, in reviewing the program with FBI director Robert Mueller and Comey the next day, realized for the first time that the program was illegal.[55] Subsequent reviews of Dick Cheney's memoir contend that Bush took the unusual step of reversing a wartime directive when Mueller and Comey threatened to resign if he did not. The incident reportedly created a breach between Bush and his vice president that was never fully repaired for the remainder of his presidency.[56]

Another role the Department of Justice played in the months after the 9/11 attack was to provide guidance for treating prisoners captured on or off fields of battle. It was John Yoo, in the Office of Legal Counsel, who provided the rationales both for treating prisoners outside the Geneva Conventions, which America had embraced and respected since their inception after World War II, and for a range of interrogation techniques, including water-boarding, that many believed constituted torture. Although Ashcroft blocked Yoo's promotion to head the Office of Legal Counsel, he continued to defend administration interrogation policies, confirming in an interview with National Public Radio's Guy Raz on the tenth anniversary of 9/11 that he had signed off on the memos, even though he did not know their details until later. Claiming that such techniques had been essential to uncovering Bin Laden's location and bringing about his death, Ashcroft confided, "If you can learn things that will help you disrupt other terrorist attacks, I think it's very important to a free society in a wartime situation to be able to exploit that information—to develop it and exploit it."[57]

Try as they might, neither critics nor supporters of Ashcroft's aggressive tactics in the name of national security could escape the shadow of the Vietnam syndrome. Although much of the attention the press paid to Ashcroft's appearance before the 9/11 commission focused on his effort to blame commission member and former deputy attorney general in the Clinton administration Jamie Gorelick for enabling the attacks by making it virtually impossible for law enforcement agencies to share information with intelligence agencies,[58] the roots of such cautionary strictures went back to the Church Committee's recommendations in the mid-1970s. Responding critically to government spying on its own citizens, a practice Stephen Bingham cited in his own defense of fleeing the country in the aftermath of the 1971 tragedy at San Quentin prison, the Congress reacted by enacting a series of measures to curb executive power. It was those restrictions that Vice President Cheney and John Yoo, with Ashcroft's ardent support, sought to bypass in order to give the president a free hand to fight domestic terrorism.[59] At the same time, the breach of those restrictions stirred critical responses, including a detailed critique of interrogation practices circulated to members of the Yale class of 1964 by Gerald Shea, calling on his classmate Joseph Lieberman to vote against a measure exempting from prosecution government officials putting them into effect.[60]

* * *

Despite expectations to the contrary, the Obama administration did not mark a sharp turn in war policy from the Bush administration. Even as troop levels were drawn down in Iraq, they were built up in Afghanistan, which Obama had touted as "the right war." There Obama extended, to little effect, the philosophy of counterinsurgency trumpeted by Bush and John McCain, as the war dragged on and the ability of local forces to fend for themselves did not appear within reach anytime soon. Two years into the Obama effort, Mac Deford weighed in, questioning what he called "an updated boots-in-the hamlet version of the old Vietnam hearts-and-minds strategy." "And we all know how that ended. Or do we?" he asked. "Could it be that we have so little interest in history, with our minds focused on reality shows and Twittering, that Vietnam and its lessons are now of no more importance to us than the Spanish-American War?" Citing Andrew Bacevich's *Washington Rules*, Deford warned that America's inability to break out of the structural commitment to Cold War militarism was not only counterproductive, but pointed the way to "financial and moral bankruptcy."[61]

In another essay, assessing America's perceived decline—as reported in Thomas Friedman and Michael Mandelbaum's *That Used to Be Us*—Deford again disputed the idea that more might would right the American ship of state again:

> Looking back over the past decade at the wrecks of Iraq and Afghanistan and the sterility of the rest of our efforts in the Middle East, or some 30 years before that at the disaster we created for ourselves as well as for Vietnam and Cambodia, might give one a little doubt about America's role as pre-eminent world-shaper. Certainly, we've accomplished much at home in the last half century—the end of segregation, the empowerment of women, the removal of discrimination against gays—but maybe an America no longer convinced of its own exceptionalism and invincibility would not be a bad thing; maybe an America focused on solving the rest of our own problems, and not the world's, would be better for all. Not isolationism, just a healthy realization of the limits of military power.[62]

Closely associated with the lack of resolution of the wars in Iraq and Afghanistan was the continued failure to secure a lasting peace between Israel and its neighbors. With the neoconservative rationale for invading Iraq in order to ensure Israel's future security fully in tatters, President Obama seemed to be reversing course, as soon after his inauguration he addressed Arab satellite television and delivered an eloquent message in Cairo of conciliation to Muslims everywhere. He strongly affirmed the bedrock principle of years of negotiations to secure a two-state solution and put the respected negotiator George Mitchell to work making it happen. In retrospect, neither Chas Freeman nor Mac Deford was impressed. Summarizing the failures of the Obama team in September 2010, as peace talks were reportedly intensifying again, Freeman was especially critical, describing such gestures as obsessed with process and lacking in substance. Once again citing America's overreliance on military solutions, he told an audience gathered in Oslo, "We have become skilled at killing Arabs. We have forgotten how to listen to them or persuade them." Failing to take the Arab peace proposal of 2002 seriously, accepting Israeli policies, no matter how flawed, heavily subsidizing the country without gaining commitments in return, the United States, Freeman argued, had long ago given up any pretense of acting as an honest broker. He pleaded for a more balanced approach in the Middle East, one that could gain security and acceptance for a democratic state of Israel *and* eliminate "the gross injustices and daily humiliations that foster Arab terrorism against Israel and its foreign allies and supporters." America's future security, he argued, depended on such action.[63]

Mac Deford agreed. Despite hopes that the Obama administration would chart a different course as a truly honest broker for a two-state solution,[64] by

April 2010 he too had recognized the futility of the Mitchell trips to the Middle East. The longer peace was delayed, he warned, the more likely another war would break out, further endangering U.S. troops in the region and strengthening al-Qaeda. The U.S.'s inability to persuade Israel to contain the expansion of housing in occupied territory practically assured the failure of further negotiations. For their part, Palestinians, he felt, had virtually no other choice but to give up on the U.S. role as broker and seek recognition directly from the United Nations, forcing Obama into opposition that ultimately proved hugely unpopular in the rest of the world.[65] As Israel retaliated with a yet another settlement initiative in 2012, one that would effectively bisect the West Bank and sever Palestinian territories from Jerusalem, Deford concluded bleakly, "Well, that's it. That's the final blow . . . the two-state solution is dead. . . . For the foreseeable future, the US, driven by strong lobbying from AIPAC [the American Israel Public Affairs Committee] and other pro-Israel groups, will continue to vote with Israel, with the result, counter-productive for both countries, of an ever-harder-line Israel and the ever-diminishing influence of the US in the Middle East."[66]

The political calculation of not accepting the prevailing pro-Israel approach came home especially to Freeman as he was asked to become the chief of the National Intelligence Council shortly after Obama's election. Never enthusiastic about accepting the position, Freeman nonetheless indicated his willingness to be appointed. Before he could formally take up his duties, however, news of the appointment was leaked, provoking immediate opposition from the American Israel Public Affairs Committee, which he had criticized publicly some years earlier for imposing ironbound commitments to Israel that made it difficult for Foreign Service officers to be effective in other countries in the Middle East. The language had been harsh then, when Freeman charged AIPAC with achieving in Congress "an atmosphere of intimidation, worthy of the McCarthy era," in many respects imposed on "Arabists" like himself.

Not surprisingly, the prospect of Freeman's appointment evoked a forceful response. Steven Rosen, a former AIPAC staff member, immediately attacked Freeman on the website of the Middle East Forum, a neoconservative think tank, charging, "Freeman is a strident critic of Israel and a textbook case of the old-line Arabism that afflicted American diplomacy at the time the state of Israel was born." In the fight that followed, Freeman made clear his desire to see Israel survive and prosper, pointing to the current regime, however, as "doing itself in and taking us with it." Such positions failed to satisfy critics. After several months Freeman withdrew acceptance of the position, not without accusing AIPAC of "doing widening damage to the national security of the United States." For his final word, he declared, "I believe that the inability of the American public to discuss, or the government to consider any option for U.S. policies in the Middle East opposed by the ruling faction in Israeli politics has allowed that faction to adopt and sustain policies that ultimately threaten the existence of the state of Israel."[67]

Among Freeman's harshest critics in the nomination fight was his Yale classmate Joseph Lieberman. An observant Jew, whose religious belief became deeper over the years, Lieberman was both troubled by the Six Days War and profoundly grateful that Israel's victory was quick and complete. Ironically, he had no success in his first campaign for the U.S. Senate in obtaining support from pro-Israel political action groups, which were traditionally reluctant to support non-incumbents. Once in office, however, he became one of Israel's primary defenders, even on the ongoing controversy of building new homes on Arab land acquired in the 1967 conflict. Not incidentally, Lieberman, who had not been drafted for Vietnam thanks to a succession of deferrals, starting with his graduate education in law school followed by marriage and his first child, became increasingly hawkish. He appeared to join those in more conservative ranks who came to admire Israel's capacity to strike its enemies quickly and unapologetically.[68]

Lieberman's support of Israel played a major role in his defense of George W. Bush's policy in Iraq, so much so that he lost the Democratic primary in 2006 and won reelection only by running as an independent with Republican support. Subsequently, Lieberman remained aggressive in foreign policy, not the least working to blunt Obama's possible tilt toward an imposed peace settlement that he thought might penalize Israel. Stating on his Senate website his commitment to a two-state solution, he nonetheless asserted that "no peace is possible in the Middle East unless the Palestinians are absolutely willing to renounce terrorism, accept previous agreements with Israel, and recognize Israel's right to exist." In a position Israeli prime minister Netanyahu himself took in his charged August 2011 address to Congress, the site reported that Senator Lieberman "does not believe that Israeli settlements are the main obstacle to peace today, nor should we treat them as such. Rather, the central obstacle to peace in the region is the extremists, like Hamas and Hezbollah, and their state sponsor, Iran."[69]

Lieberman's close ties to AIPAC were well recognized and reported, and it was he who introduced Sarah Palin as John McCain's vice presidential candidate in 2008 to AIPAC's officers, who promptly proclaimed her a good friend of Israel.[70] Lieberman was not just true to his faith in challenging Freeman. Defending Israel could be considered good politics if he expected to run for reelection again in Connecticut. But it was in his ramped-up attack on Iran, considered a terrible threat to Israel once in possession of nuclear weapons, that Lieberman made his most distinctive efforts. None of his classmates writing on foreign policy—Powers, Deford, or Freeman—could agree with his aggressive stance, one that put military assertiveness well ahead of diplomacy.[71]

* * *

The world remained a dangerous place fifty years after the United States sent troops to Vietnam and attempted to overthrow Castro in Cuba, though neither of those countries appeared especially troubling in the post–Cold War era. Ironically, one member of the class of 1964 who was directly present at the 9/11 attacks in 2001, John Boardman, had served as a Foreign Service officer in both locations. As liaison to commandant of the Marine Corps General James Jones, he was in the Pentagon in 2001 when the plane hit the other side of the building. As smoke began to pervade the corridors, he followed orders to clear the structure and return home. Within weeks, however, he joined General Jones in Afghanistan to meet with American troops and senior leaders. Subsequently he traveled to Kuwait a week before troops moved into Iraq. A veteran of countless difficult international situations, including Pakistan, Korea, Nicaragua, and Sri Lanka, as well as Cuba, Boardman was not pleased by the way his country turned the attack on American soil into a war on terrorism. "It was a terrible attack, but it was basically a fluke that took place because of a whole series of intelligence failures and strange procedures on flight security," he claimed. "And we're making it like World War II and Pearl Harbor. Certainly fear of international terrorism should not be the organizing principle of U.S. foreign policy." No doubt his view was tempered not just by his experience as a diplomat, but also, as was the case for many in his generation, by Vietnam, albeit in an unusual way.

Assigned to intelligence following completion of officer training with the marines the summer after his junior year in college, Boardman, when he wasn't debriefing pilots returning from missions, spent much of his time in Vietnam on the beach drinking gin and tonics and watching movies on the outside screen at his base at Chu Lai, a marine tactical airstrip about fifty miles south of Da Nang. He did not see much of the country, aside from taking recreational time in Saigon and Da Nang. Assigned to foreign language school in California on his return, he fell in love with one of the teachers, Nguyen Ngoc Chat, the daughter of a Vietnamese nationalist leader and a doctor who had helped direct the refugee movement to the South after communists took control of the North in 1954. It was through Chat that Boardman came to appreciate the complexities of the country. While the couple were still dating, Chat's father became very ill, and she returned to Saigon to tend to him while the war was still raging. After his death, she sought to return to the

United States, but local officers prevented her from leaving without paying a bribe. Refusing the demand, she remained in Saigon, facing rising dangers in and around the city, while Boardman took a new assignment preparing to head an interrogation-translation team. His assignment was originally to go to Vietnam, but it was changed to Bangkok because of the need for a Thai speaker. Chat was finally able to join him there, and the two were able to marry. They returned to the United States in 1969, where John left the marines to join the State Department.

A number of Chat's family found refuge in the United States after the collapse of the South Vietnamese government in 1975. When they saw John after he returned home, they would accuse the United States of abandoning them, even as some of his American friends would claim that Ho Chi Minh was a wonderful leader and that the United States had been helping the wrong people. Caught in the middle, Boardman concluded that the U.S. effort was probably doomed from the start and that there were no clear winners in the war. However difficult it was to draw larger meanings from his service, by temperament as well as by training he had to keep balanced between competing interests as he worked his way professionally through the effects of Iran-Contra while in Nicaragua, Tamil rebels in Sri Lanka, and the Elián González controversy while he was stationed at the interest section in Havana between 1997 and 2000. As his final assignment—coming full circle from his early military service—he became deputy chief of mission in Vietnam in 2004, where he worked especially on issues of trade and public health.

John Wilbur too returned to Vietnam long after the war had ended. Using the psychic space that the interval of peace had provided to allow him to "think about going back without ever having to do again what I thought I had to do before," he set out in 1999 to revisit the places that had shaped his military service. The result was mixed. As vivid as his combat recollections remained—including a harrowing near-death experience during the Tet offensive—the geopolitical ramifications of his country's actions proved elusive. He liked the people he met as he traveled throughout the country and sympathized with their dreams for a better life. But larger meanings were hard to come by. He was not one to share his war experiences with friends, according to his wife, and his chance to make sense of them in print fell short of his and potential publishers' expectations.[72]

While John Wilbur found it difficult to put Vietnam into a larger framework, John Boardman drew on the broad range of his experience to adapt. A pragmatist in a world of competing ideologies, Boardman had witnessed the evolution from a period when the Soviet Union's dominance as the prime U.S. enemy suggested a clear grand strategy, to a much more complicated contemporary world beset by an ever-greater range of volatile issues.[73] As Mac Deford put it in a 2012 column,

The Cold War, with its bipolar rivalry of two nuclear-armed super-powers, is long gone, but arguably, as a result, the world has become a much more dangerous place. When it was divided between us and our allies and the Soviet Union and theirs, the superpowers had a remark-able degree of control, at least in terms of assuring things didn't get out of hand. Wars between Israel and Egypt, or between the two halves of Vietnam, or following the Soviet invasion of Afghanistan, could be contained. That may be much harder in today's multi-polar world at a time, unfortunately, when our leaders have ever less international expertise.[74]

Complicated as Boardman and his classmates found the twenty-first century, the war without end that John Ashcroft identified or that Joseph Lieberman sought to win continued to be treated a lot like the Cold War. It was hard in this light for critics of earlier engagements not to see some of the same pitfalls that burdened the country in the years during and immediately after their college years, even as defenders of American intervention clung to justifications rooted in the same period. Chas Freeman put his view suc-cinctly in a 2012 speech:

Since 9/11, Americans have chosen to stake our domestic tranquility on our ability—under our commander-in-chief—to rule the world by force of arms rather than to lead, as we had in the past, by the force of our example or our arguments. And we appear to have decided in the process that it is necessary to destroy our civil liberties in order to save them and that abandoning the checks and balances of our Consti-tution will make us more secure. Meanwhile, our military-industrial complex and its flourishing antiterrorist sidekick have been working hard to invent a credible existential challenge to match that of the Cold War. This has produced constantly escalating spending on mili-tary and antiterrorist projects, but it has not overcome the reality that Americans now face no threat from abroad comparable to Nazi Ger-many, Imperial Japan, or the USSR. The only real menace to our free-doms is our own willingness to supplant the rule of law with ever more elements of a garrison state.[75]

Revelations of the extent of domestic surveillance authorized by the Obama administration only furthered Freeman's concern. Citing as precedent Daniel

Ellsberg's unauthorized release of the top secret Pentagon Papers in 1971, Freeman in 2013 praised Edward Snowden's massive exposure of National Intelligence Agency practices. Snowden, he claimed, "has brought home to us that, while we Americans do not yet live in a police state or tyranny, we are well along in building the infrastructure on which either could be instantly erected if our leaders decided to do so. No longer protected by the law, our freedoms now depend on the self-restraint of men and women in authority, many of them in uniform. History protests that if one builds a turnkey totalitarian state, those who hold the keys will eventually turn them." Discounting the protection presumably offered by the FISA court, Freeman warned that "a massive, ongoing failure by our government to conduct its intelligence activities in a manner supportive of our liberties and our alliances with foreign nations" requires "urgent corrective surgery." "In the Cold War," he concluded,

> we Americans and our allies justly saw ourselves as threatened with nuclear annihilation or ideological subjugation. Someone in Moscow could turn a key and most of us would soon be dead. The threats before us are in no way comparable. Yet, in the face of a greatly lessened danger, our leaders have chosen—mostly in secret—to defend our freedoms and preserve our international standing in ways that diminish both. Our own government has become a vastly more potent threat to the traditions and civil liberties of our republic and to the rule of law than al-Qaeda could ever hope to be. . . . No one in Washington or anywhere else should be in a position to turn a key and deprive us or our posterity of the blessings of liberty. It is past time to rethink and radically downsize both the warfare state and the undisciplined surveillance apparatus it has given birth to.[76]

And so the debate continued: "So much talk—so much writing—such long labor before birth of the mouse!" Thomas Powers reflected in 2013. The arguments, over military intervention in the Middle East, over domestic surveillance, and over the nature of the threat to American security from abroad could have been crafted fifty years earlier.[77] The issues and their articulation remained eerily reminiscent of previous debates. Now it might be '64's grandchildren who would be fighting—or protesting—as the country remained divided, both in perception about how best to secure peace, and at what cost.

5

The Greening of '64

Appearing only months after the nation's first celebration of Earth Day in 1970, Charles Reich's *The Greening of America*, making the claim that a new and better consciousness was seizing America through America's youth movement, rocketed to the top of the *New York Times* best-seller list in December and remained there for most of a year. Not everyone shared an admiration for Reich's work, but one former Reich student cited the book favorably in the twenty-first century—the Yale class of 1964's most eminent environmentalist, Gus Speth. A founder of the Natural Resources Defense Council and the World Resources Institute, the chair under Jimmy Carter of the President's Council on Environmental Quality, and for ten years the dean of Yale's School of Forestry and Environmental Studies, Speth did not discount *Time* magazine's description of him as the ultimate environmental insider.[1] And yet, even as he sat as a Yale dean, he was both quoting Charlie Reich and sounding a good deal like him, blaming the failures to control climate change, among other environmental challenges, not on lack of information or insight, but on modern capitalism and an associated consumer ethos.[2]

Faulting Reich for being too enamored with the youth culture of the 1960s, Speth nonetheless asserted, "Reich was right that a new consciousness is both possible and necessary."[3] Citing, among other faults of capitalism, a commitment to economic growth at any cost, enormous investment in technologies designed with little regard for the environment, and government that is subservient to corporate interest and the growth imperative, Speth was taking a position that went well beyond the bromides acceptable to either national political party. In a series of books and major speeches issued between 2004 and 2014, he argued not just for the transformation of capitalism but a new politics to assure that capitalism's worst effects would be permanently curbed. "We can't recreate the 1960s and 1970s; we shouldn't even try," he declared. "But we can learn from that era and find again its rambunctious spirit and fearless advocacy, its fight for deep change, and its searching inquiry."[4]

The environmental movement that emerged in the late 1960s was not entirely new, following as it did landmark efforts to conserve natural resources dating back to the Progressive Era at the outset of the twentieth century. Yale's School of Forestry owed its origin in 1901 especially to Gifford Pinchot, Yale 1889 and subsequently the first chief of the U.S. Forest Service under President Theodore Roosevelt. Only one member of the class of 1964, Edward Arens, choose to enter the Forestry School, subsequently breaking new ground in environmental research built on his expertise in both engineering and architecture.[5] However, with the widespread impact of *Silent Spring*, Rachel Carson's searing 1962 critique of the ways carelessly applied science and technology were destroying nature and threatening life, it is not surprising that other classmates would have pursued careers in the field. As the grandson of the man who was credited with saving from logging the last major stand of redwoods outside San Francisco, Sherman "Toby" Kent picked up his ancestor's thread by serving for a number of years as an environmental educator and subsequently as director of the Connecticut Audubon Society.[6] G. Gordon Davis, looking for an alternative to practicing law in New York City, moved to upstate New York, where he served as general counsel to the Adirondack Park Agency and coauthored a book describing the importance of conserving that vast protected area.[7]

In the wake of Carson's striking revelations, environmental protection attracted a wide following. Although environmentalists generated some antagonism early on from the political Left for diverting attention from issues of racism at home and war abroad, establishing the means to curb corporate exploitation remained very much a part of both the environmental and New Left agendas. The first Earth Day in 1970, which was originally conceived as a university-based teach-in following the model of antiwar demonstrations, attracted not just twenty million participants but a diverse spectrum of speakers, reaching well across ideological and partisan lines. Congress suspended business for the day, and two-thirds of its members spoke at Earth Day events. In addition to Democrats Ted Kennedy, Walter Mondale, and Edmund Muskie, speakers across the country included Republican senators Charles Percy, John Chafee, Clifford Case, and Bob Packwood, as well as self-identified leftists Rennie Davis, I. F. Stone, and George Wiley of the

National Welfare League. According to Philip Shabecoff's authoritative account, Earth Day marked the advent of a mass environmental movement: "After Earth Day, nothing was the same."[8] Gus Speth's career trajectory in his early years after graduation built on established traditions of environmental regulation. But his efforts also represented something new that owed its power especially to the liberal spirit of the early 1960s.

* * *

Speth's own emergence as an environmental leader would have been surprising even to him while he was at Yale. A chemistry major into his junior year, he switched to political science when he learned how few electives he would be allowed were he to complete the requirements for a chemistry degree. By his final year, he was sufficiently credentialed to be allowed to put together his own program through individual tutorials. Working with the eminent southern historian C. Vann Woodward and political scientist Robert Dahl, both of whom had considerable effect in reshaping his personal as well as his political views, Speth finished his undergraduate career brilliantly by being one of two seniors named Rhodes Scholars. By the time he entered Yale Law School in 1966, his previous worldview, grounded in his upbringing in the white South, had collapsed, and he was primed to embrace change as it engulfed him.[9]

Speth's tenure at the law school marked a period of growing student ferment, directed largely at gaining a greater say over the curriculum and how it was delivered. True rebellion did not break out until the year he graduated.[10] Speth's own postgraduate path seemed initially conventional, a coveted clerkship with Supreme Court Justice Hugo Black. Before he took that position, however, he began to envision a new kind of environmental organization. The idea was to take advantage of growing support for public interest law to form a defense fund for the environment, a parallel effort to the way legal services were being made available to those who normally were not well represented.

Indeed, Speth's inspiration had come from two articles appearing in the *New York Times* the same day, one on the NAACP Legal Defense Fund, the other announcing plans for national legislation to protect the environment.[11] Here was a chance for lawyers to step in on behalf of threatened natural resources for which representation might mean the difference between survival and extinction. One of the first faculty members to support the idea, ultimately joining the new organization's board of directors, was Charles Reich. Speth had taken a graduate seminar with him in law school, subsequently serving as a teaching assistant in his enormously popular undergraduate course, "The Individual in America," through which Reich developed and refined his arguments for what became *The Greening of America*. Reich himself was a former clerk for Justice Black, and it was his letter of support, Speth believed, that made possible his own position with the Supreme Court justice.[12]

Officers at the Ford Foundation liked Speth's idea, but they wanted the young lawyers behind it to have a stable base, and thus they brokered a partnership with Stephen Duggan and Whitney North Seymour, Wall Street lawyers whose introduction to environmental litigation originated in fighting Consolidated Edison's plans for a power processing plant behind Storm King Mountain on the Hudson River. Seymour, however, accepted the position of U.S. attorney for New York before the new organization, the Natural Resources Defense Council, could be formed. In his place a "seasoned" thirty-four-year-old John Adams assumed the role of director, in March 1970. In his words, "We had succeeded in uniting two very different groups and styles—the aggressive initiative of the Yale group and the seasoned experience of 'establishment' lawyers and old-style conservationists. Together we would bring about change within the system. I thought of what we were doing as 'responsible militancy.' "[13]

Joining Speth in the initial Yale contingent were three other former law school classmates, John Bryson, Edward Strohbehn, and Richard Ayres. Forty years later they were honored with the law school's highest alumni award. Looking back, Ayres attributed his commitment directly to the upheaval of the 1960s, explaining "there was a whole series of issues which people my age saw as part of one seamless web of need for social change—ending the war, a better criminal justice system, dealing with poverty, and protecting the environment, which was a newly emerging or reemerging issue at the time." In their more critical view, conservatives saw the establishment of the Natural Resources Defense Council as part of an expansive Ford Foundation effort to give an establishment veneer to the burgeoning field of public interest law and Charles Reich as a pioneer among legal scholars politicizing the instruction of law at elite institutions like Yale. Where Adams emphasized the "responsible" element of the initiative, conservatives pounced on its "militancy."[14]

While there were important precedents in the 1960s,[15] Speth recalled the 1970s as a golden age for environmental legislation, citing the creation of the Environmental Protection Agency and the President's Council on Environmental Quality, the Clean Air Act of 1970, and the Federal Water Pollution Control Act of 1972, among other actions. Such progress was possible in part because President Richard Nixon anticipated a challenge for reelection from Edmund Muskie, who was effectively honing his own environmental record. Administration of the new legislation in the early days was uneven, however, and the Natural Resources Defense Council determined not just to advance legislation but also to monitor its implementation. Charging, for instance, in 1974 that the Environmental Protection Agency had missed fourteen deadlines required by the 1972 Water Pollution Control Act, Speth and Strohbehn challenged EPA's decision to further put off the regulation of secondary waste-emitting plants. When it appeared two years later that EPA intended to weaken rules governing penalties for spills of hazardous chemicals into waterways, Speth again raised objections. In dozens of lawsuits filed in the first part of the 1970s, NRDC attacked clear-cutting, strip-mining, and breeder reactors, in additional to pollution in all forms.[16]

Speth's prominence in the movement brought him to the attention of Jimmy Carter, whose presidential campaign he assisted in 1980. Shortly after his inauguration, Carter asked Speth to join the Council on Environmental Quality, making him chairman in 1979. Speth's appointment to the council drew immediate praise, as did Carter's pro-environment policy laid out early in his term. Arguing that "environmental protection is consistent with a sound economy," Carter claimed that new jobs in clean energy would more than make up for positions lost in polluting industries. In assuming this position, he adopted the argument for channeling activity into what Speth called "environmentally benign" areas, such as waste reduction technologies, the improvement of public transportation, and solar energy, and away from capital-intensive activities such as interstate highways, interceptor sewers, and massive water resources projects and fossil energy developments that caused stress to limited natural resources.[17] Now on the inside of government, Speth maintained a relentless pro-environmental position. When President Carter appeared to shift his emphasis from conservation to energy independence toward the end of his term in office, Speth held his ground in what a *New York Times* reporter perceived as a difference with the president. Speaking at a White House briefing, Speth asserted, "We must not lose sight of the fact that, despite other pressures, the American people still feel deeply about the quality of the environment."[18]

As Speth's efforts demonstrated so well, law proved a particularly powerful vehicle for addressing threats to the environment, and he was not alone among his classmates in taking advantage of the new opportunities that followed legal training. Named a Henry Fellow for a year of graduate work in Oxford, '64's Angus Macbeth entered Yale Law School with Speth in 1966. He too took Charles Reich's course, finding it a refreshing alternative to the more traditional offerings that dominated the curriculum. He joined the Natural Resources Defense Council after a year's clerkship with U.S. District Judge Harold Tyler, replacing one of NRDC's founders after he moved to California. Admitting that there was considerable tension between the senior partners at the organization and the Yale graduates, Macbeth nonetheless committed himself to extending the battle at Storm King to protect fish from the damage that could be expected from Consolidated Edison's construction of a power storage generator that would empty into the Hudson River. He represented fishermen in the region, who formed a precedent-setting association to protect their livelihoods through litigation. Macbeth found the work exciting because the field of environmental law was entirely new, and he was caught up in the early idealism of the movement. After an interim appointment to the U.S. attorney's office in New York in 1975, he joined the Carter administration as deputy assistant attorney general for the land and natural resources division. He subsequently served as chief of the pollution control section from 1977 to 1979.[19]

Also recruited to the Carter administration was '64's Peter Bradford, as a member of the Nuclear Regulatory Commission. Bradford completed a degree at Yale Law School in 1967, following an undergraduate career that focused on a history major and reporting for the *Yale Daily News*. Learning about a position working with the dynamic young Democratic governor of Maine, Kenneth Curtis, Bradford had decided after law school to pass up possible work with a private firm or a government agency in Washington. His experience as a summer intern with Ralph Nader investigating the Federal Trade Commission had honed his commitment to protecting consumer interests and helped him secure the job with Curtis. His initial interview with the governor had not even broached the environment, but by the time he took his position in the fall of 1968 a new possibility for the state had arisen, which soon captured much of his time: a proposal to take advantage of deep water off the coast to establish New England's first oil refinery. No student either of Charles Reich or the environment directly, Bradford was forced to learn on the job about the difficult tradeoffs anticipated between protecting a pristine coastline and providing economic relief to a region forced to accept higher prices as long as refining remained confined to other parts of the country. Bradford provided his own clear-eyed assessment of the complicated and messy pursuit of competing interests in a 1975 book on the battle that ensued.[20]

The refinery was never built, the result of opposition both from competing oil refining interests in the South and Southwest and from local environmentalists. Clearly sympathetic with the positive economic impact Governor Curtis claimed the refinery would have on the state and the region, Bradford nonetheless could appreciate the importance of securing environmental safeguards, a goal he continued to embrace after the governor appointed him to serve on the Maine Public Utilities Commission. Bradford's pragmatic approach to the environment recommended him to the newly elected President Carter as he sought to fill three vacant positions on the Nuclear Regulatory Commission. Bradford was appointed in 1977.[21]

With the initial success of efforts to put in place new regulations and to enforce them, the environmental movement widened to include protection not just of air and water but living creatures as well, and in this area Michael Sherwood joined his former classmates in breaking new ground. A graduate of Stanford Law School, where he did legal services work in East Palo Alto while still a student, he took a job with the Legal Aid Society of Hawaii on graduation. A subsequent position with the U.S. attorney's office for the District of Hawaii in Honolulu in 1969 led him into environmental work when he decided to prosecute trespassers in a wildlife refuge. The appointment of a new U.S. attorney prompted him to leave that office and to set up a public interest firm with a former public defender. Some of his work involved landmark environmental cases, but he found the burden of maintaining the business difficult. Thus when he was approached while at a conference in San Francisco by the Sierra Club Legal Defense Fund director James Moorman about joining his staff, he overcame his reluctance to leave Hawaii and moved to California.

It was in his new position that Sherwood had the chance to test the strength of the Endangered Species Act of 1973. While there had been a few precedents to the law, they lacked real teeth. Under the new legislation, however, new precedents could be set. Building on his earlier breakthroughs, Sherwood litigated about half his cases in Hawaii over the next ten years. The first, and most significant case, involved the palila, a finch-like bird whose habitat was confined to only one mountain area on the Big Island. With threats to the palila's habitat looming, Sherwood took the unprecedented action of naming the bird chief plaintiff and won a decision against Hawaii's Department of Land and Natural Resources in the Ninth Circuit Court of Appeals in 1978. Sherwood attracted his share of criticism for putting animals and plants ahead of development, but his commitment did not flag. In subsequent court actions, he managed to add 186 species to the protected list in Hawaii, 150 in California, and another 200 nationwide. His website introduction in 2011, at what is now known as Earthjustice, read, "You won't see diplomas hanging on the walls of my office, [but] pictures of the various critters I've represented, and, maybe, helped to save." A picture of a palila held pride of place.[22]

Such actions by the 1980s were generating increasing opposition. In the process, what had been largely a bipartisan effort in the 1970s dissipated, a turn of events brought home especially to '64's Bruce Driver. As a law student at the University of Michigan, Driver was drawn into the environmental movement, not through formal classes, but through participation in the first Earth Day in 1970. Returning on graduation to New York City, where he had grown up, he took a job with a large law firm, only to decide at the end of six weeks that such practice did not sit well with him. Hoping to play a part in the burgeoning effort to protect the environment, he took a job with the Conservation Foundation in Washington. Following another job with a new lobbying organization, the Environmental Policy Center, where he became knowledgeable about strip-mining, among other issues, he sought to enter the legislative process himself. His immediate plan was to approach the House Democratic chair of the environmental committee, Morris Udall. Udall did not have a job opening, but he suggested Driver use his recent law degree as a point of entry with the ranking minority member of the committee, Philip Ruppe, a moderate Republican from Michigan. Driver got the job and threw himself into the work, spending as much as sixty to seventy hours a week in the position.

Driver felt that he was accomplishing a good deal and getting the support he needed from Republican moderates on the committee, which included Alan Steelman from Texas and Oregon's John Dellenback. By the mid-1970s, however, consensus was breaking down. One Republican member of the committee Driver served, Sam Steiger of Arizona, was not friendly. At a key point during deliberations of a House Rules Committee, on whether to send a bill regulating strip-mining to the floor, Steiger, who was attempting to kill the effort, saw Driver conferring with Congressman Udall. In a pique of anger, he lifted Driver by the nape of his neck and told him forcefully, "We're going to stop this bill."[23]

Driver was confident enough in Congressman Ruppe's support not to give ground to Steiger, but Richard Nixon's deteriorating position in the Watergate scandal forced him to drop his support for the bill after Steiger and his allies threatened to abandon their opposition to impeachment. This left moderate Republicans in limbo, and as Steiger further pressed Republican opposition, their support for the legislation lagged. When the bill finally passed, President Gerald Ford pocket vetoed it. With a new congressional election, Steiger became the ranking minority member of the committee, and he wasted no time telling Driver he was fired. Driver found another position, at the Federal Energy Administration, the predecessor of the Department of Energy, where he continued after that department's formation in 1977. With Ronald Reagan's election, however, he was told his brand of environmentalism was not welcome in the new administration, so he decided to leave. As he reflected years later, "I was there for the end of bipartisan support for environmental regulation."[24]

Indeed, Reagan's election represented a sharp turn against regulations that conservatives argued were stifling economic growth. Among the priorities the new president favored was the expansion of nuclear energy, and once again the contest over priorities involved another member of Yale's class of 1964, Peter Bradford. Slowed in its development both by high costs and growing public skepticism about its compatibility with good environmental practice, the nuclear field hit a major obstacle early in Bradford's term on the Nuclear Regulatory Commission with the partial meltdown on March 28, 1979, of one of the two generating plants at Three Mile Island in central Pennsylvania. While the NRC could not confirm any death or injuries directly related to the accident, public reaction was overwhelmingly negative, and plans to license additional plants were put on hold. Reagan had made acceleration of nuclear production part of his campaign for energy independence, and it was not surprising that Bradford, as a Carter holdover, was not embraced by the new administration. He found Reagan's choice of chairman, Joseph Palladino, easy enough to work with, but it was without regret that he left his position a few months before his term was to expire to accept a position as Maine's public advocate, representing utility consumers before the commission he once served on. Subsequently named chair of that commission, Bradford was no longer reticent to criticize the NRC under Reagan for underestimating the costs of generating energy through nuclear plants. Although he continued to believe, despite Three Mile Island, that the NRC had worked effectively to assure public safely, he discounted wildly overoptimistic contentions from the industry, fully supported by Republicans, that nuclear production was the primary answer to the country's energy needs.[25]

* * *

Other environmental issues served increasingly to divide the two national political parties in the Reagan years, but the one lasting topic that especially heighted both the stakes and the intensity of the argument was global warming. The issue had come to Gus Speth's attention as a member of the Council on Environmental Quality when President Carter charged the CEQ and the Department of State with preparing a report on "probable changes in the world's population, natural resources, and environment through the end of the century." While that work was proceeding, Speth was approached by environmental scientist Gordon MacDonald and Rafe Pomerance, who was then president of the Friends of the Earth. Responding to their concerns about climate disruption, Speth promised to bring the matter to the president if they would prepare a credible memorandum on the subject.

Speth found the report he received in 1979 from MacDonald and three other scientists alarming, and its release in July made national news. Its message that the continued release of carbon dioxide into the atmosphere through the burning of fossil fuel would result in the warming of the earth's atmosphere, in what today is well recognized as a "greenhouse effect," was scarcely known at the time. And it appeared when the Department of Energy was reportedly promoting massive development of unconventional fossil fuel resources—"synthetic" oil made from coal tar sands, and oil shale—which environmentalists worried would release toxics into the air and water. Because the government did not treat carbon dioxide as a pollutant, it did not have any program to deal with it. Speaking as chair of the Council on Environmental Quality, Speth addressed the dilemma directly, thus affirming his opposition to the direction the Department of Energy was taking, as he charged, "The country needs to address the carbon dioxide issue squarely before going down the syn-fuels road."[26]

When the Department of Energy produced a counter-memorandum to MacDonald's claims, the administration asked the National Academy of Sciences to assess the scientific basis for concern about man-made climate change. Its report, issued in late 1979, fully confirmed MacDonald's assessment by warning of the dangers of waiting too long to see how trends developed. Boosted by that information, the CEQ's own report, issued in early 1980, extended the argument for what was intended to be a broad audience. In his foreword to the report, Speth described the carbon dioxide issue as presenting "the ultimate environmental dilemma" and warned against experimenting with great systems "in a way that imposes unknown and potentially large risks on future generations." Asserting "our duty to exercise a conserving and protecting restraint," Speth urged "every effort to ensure that nations are not compelled to choose between the risks of energy shortages and the risks of carbon dioxide."[27]

Speth further clarified his evaluation of the crisis, telling the Fifth National Conference of the Environmental Industry Council in February 1980, "The issues that persist today are not just questions of esthetics, or comfort, or an idealized notion of 'the good life'; they are clear threats to the health and welfare of the American people. They simply cannot be put aside until a time when it is more convenient to focus on them." Nearly twenty-five years later he could write, "Political leaders then and since have been on notice that there was a new environmental agenda—more global, more threatening, and more difficult than the predominantly domestic agenda that spurred the environmental awakening of the late 1960s and the first Earth Day in 1970."[28]

One of the contributors to *Global 2000*, a second well-known report from Speth's CEQ, issued in 1980, was Speth's Yale '64 classmate Thomas Lovejoy, a conservation biologist, who coined the term "biological diversity" the same year. A biology major as an undergraduate, Lovejoy continued graduate study at Yale under G. Evelyn Hutchinson (who is credited with founding the modern field of ecology), and his early fieldwork in Brazil led to a lifetime passion to protect endangered species. His dire prediction of the consequences of what he believed could be a two-degree rise in world temperature was controversial enough that the *Global 2000* study director required him to be the only contributor to sign his essay. Lovejoy's predictions of global extinction rates were widely circulated thereafter, even as they generated criticism from conservatives who faulted his documentation.[29]

Lovejoy's leadership and influence only grew in the 1980s and later years, as he assumed leadership positions at the National Wildlife Federation, the Smithsonian Institution (where he was twice a top candidate to be secretary), and the Heinz Center for Science in Washington, D.C. His commentary on global warming in a number of books and articles helped keep the scientific and moral arguments for dealing with climate change at the forefront of informed discourse. His view, stated most forcefully in 1992, was that "unless there is major change, the artificial heating of the planet is likely to generate a tsunami of extinctions equal to that currently playing itself out in the tropical forest regions of the world. And as biological diversity goes up in smoke with tropical deforestation, the CO_2 generated is augmenting climate change, which will cause a second major reduction in biological diversity."[30]

Despite the growing scientific evidence supporting the perils of climate change, the opposition to further environmental regulation intensified in the Reagan years, both inside and outside government. In 1982, William Tucker, an independent though libertarian-leaning journalist, issued a forceful response to environmental activism. Building on a critique he had published in *Harper's* of the opposition to Consolidated Edison's plans for a generating plant on the Hudson—the issue that had helped spur the formation of the Natural Resources Defense Council—Tucker, in *Progress and Privilege*, described environmentalism as "the ideas of aristocratic conservatism translated onto a popular scale." Environmentalism, he charged, had "entwined itself with the protection of privilege" to the point of blocking the progress that should inevitably follow from a free and innovative people. In describing the expansion of the upper middle class to the evolution of a "new 1970s-style liberal, making rhetorical gestures toward the poor, while wearing the vine leaves of environmentalism and consumerism," Tucker could well have been aiming at Yale '64's numerous environmental activists. To them, Tucker offered his declaration, "The problems of overcoming environmental difficulties are hard but not overwhelming. In fact, they will probably solve themselves."[31]

Such opposition, and the political environment that supported it, dampened but did not diminish Yale '64's efforts in the field. Bruce Driver helped challenge many Reagan initiatives to roll back environmental regulations while serving as counsel to the House Energy Conservation Subcommittee under the leadership of Richard Ottinger, Democrat of New York. When Ottinger retired in 1984, Driver moved to Colorado, where, with the support of Bruce Babbitt, then serving as chair of the Western Governors' Association, he took up the issue of water conservation, becoming in 1999 executive director of the Water Fund of the Rockies.[32]

In Hawaii, Driver's Yale classmate marine biologist John Culliney, after publishing a book in 1976 detailing the environmental threats to the continental shelf off the coast of New England, addressed even greater dangers. Despite perceiving a rich and complicated ecosystem in Hawaii that would have delighted Charles Darwin, Culliney feared threats to species of all sorts: "accelerating destructive development and outright environmental abuse . . . more shorelines under golf courses and more gated communities for the ultra wealthy; more ticky-tacky subdivisions, theme parks, malls, and other 'plastic satisfactions' spreading up over lands formerly zoned for agricultural uses." "Nearly everywhere in Hawai'i," he remarked coolly, "the dominant shade of green is the color of money, and environmental abuse in this mid-Pacific Eden continues apace." Hoping his darkly majestic book, *Islands in a Far Sea: The Fate of Nature in Hawai'i*, might reverse this perverse tide of development, he remarked, "I'm keeping hope alive, but it's harder and harder to do. Good people are trying to sustain the wonders of the biosphere, but we're still going downhill here and in the rest of the planet."[33]

Culliney's writing continued a tradition of environmental criticism in the spirit of Rachel Carson that included Thomas Lovejoy and also '64's John Stacks, a *Time* magazine writer and editor, whose 1972 critique of strip-mining, *Stripping*, helped spur the regulatory efforts that Bruce Driver worked to effect in the pre-Reagan years. In his biting commentary published shortly after he served briefly as a spokesman for George McGovern's 1972 presidential campaign, Stacks praised the environmental movement as "a thoroughgoing expression of what is doubtless a major quest of postindustrial society—the search for a new quality of life." Efforts to curb the devastating effects of strip-mining on both the natural environment and the communities nearby were going nowhere, however. "In case after case," he reported, "the strippers who rob the land also indirectly rob the people." Strip-mining, he charged, "has become an ugly and addictive habit of the American energy companies. . . . It yields enormous profits at enormous public costs. Like the rest of the energy market in this country, it has grown virtually without public regulation and certainly without national planning." A precious natural resource and source of tremendous national power, coal, he concluded, "has become a Robin Hood in reverse, robbing the poor to give to the rich. And the rest of the country has become an accessory to this larceny by permitting it to go on and grow without much restraint, and with pitifully little complaint."[34]

Daniel Berman added his own contribution to the environmental reform literature. Moving from his involvement in the civil rights movement while in college, Berman, while studying for a PhD in political science at Washington University in St. Louis, became actively engaged with union efforts to resolve occupational safety hazards. From 1972 to 1975 he headed up the Occupational Health Project of the Medical Committee for Human Rights, working out of Chicago and then San Francisco. The organizing strategy was to join local union leaders with medical and legal activists in regional grassroots organizations, a number of which still exist. With the support of the environmental critic Barry Commoner, among others, he published his research on work safety hazards, a stinging critique of failures to execute faithfully the Occupational Safety and Health Act of 1970. His 1978 book, *Death on the Job*, like Stacks's book, assumed that a roused public opinion would force government actions to rectify prevailing injustices.[35] With the advent of the Reagan era, however, Berman recognized that the gains of the 1970s were at risk. Moreover, he feared the dampening effect of the changed political climate in Washington was forcing a more conciliatory approach among environmentalists. He singled out the Natural Resources Defense Council as a case in point.

The issue in question involved Berman's home state of California, where NRDC's Los Angeles office brokered an arrangement using the concept of "Demand Energy Management" to provide incentives to the utility giant Pacific Gas & Electric to dampen consumption through the carrot of financial incentives from the state to invest in conservation. Such efforts were instituted with good effect in New York State through Peter Bradford's chairmanship of the state's utility commission under Governor Mario Cuomo in the late 1980s. In California, Berman argued, the arrangement proved problematic, as the company, after Republicans reworked the rules under which the arrangement originally operated, gutted any prospect of energy conservation. With government accepting the power of private utilities in particular to determine their own rates and sources of energy, issues of climate warming would never be adequately addressed, he charged. Historically, Berman contended, "the energy reform movement's biggest successes have come from public pressure against the utilities and other energy corporations, in order to limit their activities by statute and regulation."[36]

* * *

Gus Speth might well have pursued a more conciliatory approach domestically had he not concluded following his departure from government in 1981 that the crisis of global warming had to be addressed at an international level. As he described the situation some years later, "I remember thinking that we were building a fool's paradise here in America by concentrating on local environmental concerns while ignoring these global-scale ones."[37] With assurances—gained through a friendship born of his undergraduate days—that he was not a dangerous radical, Speth secured $15 million in funding from the John D. and Catherine T. MacArthur Foundation to form the World Resources Institute in 1982. Established as "a major center for policy research and analysis addressed to global resource and environmental issues," the institute adopted an ambitious research agenda that included evaluation of the devastating effects of deforestation, desertification, population growth, and world poverty, as well as climate change. It sought to produce studies, in its words, that would be "both scientifically sound and politically practical."[38]

A 1972 United Nations Conference in Stockholm laid the foundation for international cooperation by compiling a list of twenty-six principles detailing a new ethic intended to govern behavior toward the environment. An action plan followed, backed by the creation of the UN Environment Programme, located in Nairobi. Measurable results from such declarations proved difficult to achieve, however, and the conclusion at a 1985 conference in Villach, Austria, cosponsored by that UN program, warned that "as a result of the increasing concentrations of greenhouse gases, it is now believed that in the first half of the next century a rise of global mean temperature could occur which is greater than any in man's history." The World Resources Institute responded two years later by issuing an integrated simulation model that spelled out what differences coordinated actions might make. In his introduction to the report, Speth asserted that the risks of not acting were too great to be considered: "Given what is now known, major national and international initiatives—grounded in the best available science and policy analysis—should become a top priority of governments and citizens."[39]

Over the next several years, international agreements forged at the Vienna Convention for the Protection of the Ozone Layer in 1985 and the Montreal Protocol in 1987 succeeded in the virtual elimination in industrial countries of chlorofluorocarbons (CFCs), compounds used in aerosol propellants and refrigeration that damage the earth's stratospheric ozone shield as well as contribute to global warming. Taking heart from such efforts, Speth described a new environmental agenda for the planet, an agenda he believed should be pursed aggressively on an international basis, to increase sharply the efficiency with which fossil fuels are used; to introduce nonfossil energy technologies on a priority basis; to phase out CFCs completely in the United States; to promote a large-scale international effort to halt deforestation in the tropics and move to net forest growth globally; and to stabilize world population, before it doubles again, at as close to eight billion people as possible. Drawing on CBS broadcast anchor Walter Cronkite's early 1970s television series on the environment, "Can the World Be Saved?," for his own assessment, Speth choose to be positive. "One reason for optimism," he asserted, "is that science and technology are presenting us with answers. We are in the midst of a revolution in earth science and a revolution in industrial and agricultural technology, both with huge potentials in the areas we have been reviewing. . . . People everywhere are offended by pollution. They sense intuitively that we have pressed beyond limits we should not have exceeded. They want to clean up the world, make it a better place, be good trustees of the Earth for future generations."[40]

Speth's prominence warranted his appointment in 1992 as senior adviser to President-elect Bill Clinton's transition team, heading the advisory group on natural resources, agriculture, energy, and the environment. Clinton's support, as a candidate, for an energy policy that "lets Americans control America's energy future" rather than "coddling special interests whose fortunes depend on America's addiction to foreign oil" provided the basis for optimism that Clinton would reverse the Reagan administration's hostility to environmental regulation.[41] Rather than return to the federal government, however, Speth extended his international commitments by accepting appointment as administrator of the United Nations Development Programme, a position he held for six years and at that time the second-highest position in the United Nations. In 1999 he left the UN to become dean of Yale's School of Forestry and Environmental Studies.

Despite his role in working to forge international agreements that would be binding on other countries, an approach Republicans steadfastly opposed while George W. Bush was president, Speth nonetheless joined the growing consensus on policy at home, that incentives rather than regulations represented the best route to energy conservation. His answer to the question raised in his 1989 article, "Can the Earth Be Saved?" was to harness market mechanisms without government micromanagement as the best way of resolving the problem of reconciling growth with conservation. Such an approach seemed warranted by tax policies introduced in the 1970s providing a strong disincentive to using leaded gasoline, which virtually eliminated the use of highly toxic lead in gasoline. Thomas Lovejoy's proposal for relieving debt obligations for countries that adopt significant conservation measures, popularly referred to as debt-for-nature swaps, extended the concept internationally.[42] So too when the Obama administration took office with promises to invest in renewable energy resources, it placed its biggest bet for conservation on a Republican-initiated idea to use market forces to curb energy use.

In 2003 Senators Joseph Lieberman and John McCain introduced the first "cap-and-trade" legislation proposal to curb global warming. Speth embraced the approach in his 2004 book, *Red Sky at Morning*.[43] Following the model of the successful acid rain trading program of the 1990 Clean Air Act, Lieberman's bill would have required a reduction in carbon dioxide emissions to the 2000 level by 2010 and a reduction to 1990 levels by the year 2016. The bill generated support not just from environmentalists, but from industry working in cooperation with environmental organizations, most notably the U.S. Climate Partnership. Formed in January 2007, with support from the Pew Center on Global Climate Change, this coalition strongly supported cap-and-trade legislation, which had remained mired in Congress through the last years of the Bush administration.

Obama's election gave new life to the bill, yet with a vote approaching in the summer of 2010, Lieberman had lost not just McCain's support and that of the bill's other Republican backer, South Carolina senator Lindsey Graham, but many of the bill's potential protections to the environment had been bar-gained away to satisfy different energy interests.[44] The exchange between two columnists for the *New York Times* as a vote approached was revealing. A plea from Thomas Friedman for Republicans to come forward in the name of national security as well as environmental reform evoked only an indifferent response from Ross Douthat, who retorted, "It's possible that the best thing to do about a warming earth—for now, at least—is relatively little." According to the experts he chose to cite, a warmer world will also be a richer world, and "economic development is likely to do more for the wretched of the earth than a growth-slowing regulatory regime." Not every danger has a regulatory solution, he concluded, "and sometimes it makes sense to wait, get richer, and then try to muddle through." No Senate Republican supported the bill, which Democrats finally removed from consideration.[45]

The effort to take the fight against global warming to a national and inter-national level necessarily complicated prospects for broad agreement, and at least one Yale '64 graduate, policy scientist Ronald Brunner, argued for a more decentralized and incremental approach. He supported a national carbon tax in a 2010 book with Amanda Lynch, but fearing continued stalemate and a lack of political will in the United States and internationally, they argued for "adaptive governance," an approach based on factoring the global prob-lem into thousands of local problems, each more tractable scientifically and politically than the global one. Describing "climate engineering" as part of the increasingly obsolete tradition of scientific management, they pointed to better results from locally generated initiatives, the kind Bruce Driver had become a part of in Colorado and Brunner had written about in his previ-ous work. "In short, the emerging pattern of governance is marked by more decentralized decision making," Brunner and Lynch asserted, and "by wider participation in policies more procedurally rational than technically ratio-nal, and by applications of local knowledge sometimes supplemented but not replaced by scientific inquiry."[46] While this approach did not win supporters at all levels, it was embraced in a number of areas before and especially after failures in the United States to ratify the Kyoto Protocol—an international effort to reduce greenhouse gas emissions—and to enact national cap-and-trade legislation.[47]

Among those also acting locally with global goals in mind was '64's William Duesing. His embrace of an environmental ethos while managing an organic farm outside New Haven in the 1960s had been fully imbued with every embodiment of the counterculture. By the early 1970s, however, the Pulsa commune Duesing had been so much a part of had dispersed, requiring new means both for sustaining a living and keeping 1960s ideas and ideals alive. Duesing never accumulated much in the way of material goods—air conditioning, a fancy car, or electronic equipment—but he did organize, locally and regionally, becoming active in the Connecticut chapter of the Northeast Organic Farming Association. Ultimately he became executive director of the eight-hundred-member organization. During the late 1980s he cofounded and chaired the New Haven Ecology Project, which culminated in the formation of a successful charter school for the environment, Common Ground High School at New Haven's West Rock.

While Duesing still referred in the twenty-first century to how LSD trips in the 1960s had opened his eyes to the power and beauty of nature, he could be very practical in the lessons learned about the environment. From 1990 to 2000 he served as creator and coproducer of a weekly program for WSHU Public Radio in Fairfield, Connecticut. Mixing practical advice for gardening throughout the seasons with critical assessments of commercial agriculture and its products, he maintained a sharp and discerning critique of the costs of modern capitalism. His programs, which garnered him a paltry $25 each for days of preparation, made their way into a book, *Living on the Earth*, produced by an enthusiastic listener. The message, contained succinctly in the conclusion to one chapter, was, "Let's 'Just say no' to more oil and nuclear energy, and use conservation, solar energy and intelligent life-style changes to improve our environment and the quality of our lives." Through lectures, training programs, and networking, Duesing continues to advance a strong conservation ethic, as well as promoting the increasingly popular notion of buying produce close to home. "So much time spent close to and tending the earth," he reports, "has informed my thinking and brought great happiness."[48]

John Jeavons took his work in farming a step further to reach an international audience. A westerner by birth and a graduate of Camelback High School in Phoenix, Jeavons took a position with USAID on his graduation from Yale. Finding his effectiveness limited, however, he left after nine months to take a job with Kaiser Aerospace and Electronics in 1966. Three years later he became chief of business services at Stanford University. Soon anxious to find a more creative job, Jeavons, like Duesing, determined to try his hand at farming. While working at Stanford, he performed his own research on small-scale farming and related subjects. This led him to take a three-part seminar in the biodynamic / French intensive method of farming promoted by Alan Chadwick, the English master gardener and student of the Austrian philosopher Rudolf Steiner. From that moment, he reported, I "read everything about intensive gardening techniques that I could get my hands on (and) began practicing in a backyard garden of my own." Intent on expanding his effort, he sought the support of a local organization, Ecology Action, which his wife, Betsy, had worked with to create a recycling program in 1971.

Charged with finding the space to develop a community garden, he managed in 1972 to locate land at Stanford's industrial park. As modest as his financial aims were at the time—he and his wife had set a goal of living on only $6,000 a year—the costs of sustaining this experiment to vastly improve the yield on an unpromising piece of land piled up. Only when a psychic who had read about the project and thought it was in financial trouble appeared without warning in 1973 with a $1,100 donation was the undertaking saved. Jeavons's publications subsequently sustained the project and gave it international prominence.[49]

Jeavons's goal after becoming director and president of Ecology Action was to increase crop yields by as much as 400 percent with biologically intensive practices. Driven by concerns that the spreading depletion of farmable soil along with desertification would soon compromise the world's food supply, Jeavons made it his mission to simplify Chadwick's approach as easily adaptable methods for individuals to sustain themselves on greatly reduced plots of land. As author, teacher, and a frequent speaker at international conferences, Jeavons advanced his own sustainable agricultural method known as Grow Biointensive sustainable mini-farming. Jeavons's website in 2012 declared that GB—when practiced correctly—nurtures healthy soil fertility, produces high yields, conserves resources, and can be used successfully by almost everyone. Most important, he reports, in a world of increasing water scarcity and desertification, his method has the capacity to use as little as 33 percent of the water customarily used per pound of food produced. "Our goal," he declared, "is to help this system be known and used locally . . . on a worldwide basis."[50]

Jeavons's work represented well the power of local actions to induce larger consequences, illustrating a prime argument of E. F. Schumacher's popular 1973 publication, *Small Is Beautiful*. Such efforts needed a sustained ethos, however, and even as political actions were fracturing nationally, '64's Strachan Donnelley determined to revitalize one philosophical position that predated the divisions rooted especially in the 1980s. The son of a highly successful philanthropist and businessman, whose wealth derived from his position as chairman and president of R. R. Donnelley & Sons, a publishing house established in 1864, Donnelley might well have returned to Chicago to enter the family business, as his father urged him to do. Instead, he opted for the study of philosophy, first at University College, Oxford, then at the New School in New York, where he received his PhD in 1976.[51]

Like his friend Gus Speth, Donnelley was an admirer of Aldo Leopold's classic 1949 volume on environmental ethics, *A Sand County Almanac*.[52] As president in the 1990s of the Hastings Center, a bioethics and policy organization formed in 1969, Donnelley launched a new Humans and Nature program. Impressed by the blow that evolutionary biology had dealt to any conception of a universe directed by God, Donnelley nonetheless saw a path for mankind to assume its own moral responsibility for the world's stewardship. Following Leopold, such a path, he asserted, would have to be not of man over nature but man with nature. "We can no longer be exclusively or centrally concerned with our human selves, communities, and their well-being or happiness," he wrote. "We may remain only co-creators, along with nature, of the earth's and our future."[53]

Donnelley revealed the basis of his own understanding of moral responsibility by telling the story of his indoctrination into hunting. As a child, his father took him frequently to Hennepin, Illinois, where he owned a farm with two small lakes. There, in the early morning, the child of only ten or twelve years shouldered his gun and brought home his prey, finding in the experience a power that thrilled him beyond his understanding. As an adult looking back on that time, Donnelley described his feelings as pre-Darwinian and pre-Leopoldian. "Now I can hazard a guess at what was happening to me. I was experiencing deep, well-honed predator instincts, interests, and satisfactions. I was implicated in predatory relations that psychologically and behaviorally bound me to natural landscapes, to evolutionary and ecological time and space. Never again could I deny an aboriginal membership in historically deep biotic communities." Once a recognized member of a biotic community, Donnelley contended, we cannot let ourselves off the moral hook. We must address the injustice done to the earth and become its stewards: "We need to grow up, culturally and morally."[54]

Any such effort was inherently political, if not in a narrowly partisan sense. Hence Donnelley's first effort to promote his thinking was to create a demonstration project close to the area where he grew up in Illinois. The Hastings Center devoted a special supplement to its regular publication in 1998 to lay out the elements of this program, to which Donnelley gave the name Nature, Polis, Ethics. Inspired by William Cronin's analysis, through an ecological lens, of Chicago's early development in his landmark history, *Nature's Metropolis*, Donnelley projected a new definition of civic responsibility for the Chicago region, informed by what he called "a new art of moral ecology, that

is, the concurrent consideration and mutual coordination of long-term obligations to humans and nature." With the support of the Gaylord and Dorothy
Donnelley Foundation, as well as the Chicago-based John D. and Catherine T.
MacArthur Foundation, the program projected by planners, preservationists,
and environmentalists conceived the convergence of elements of the "smart
growth" movement with a "substantive ethical vision and conception of
the human and natural good."[55] Donnelley died of stomach cancer in 2008,
but his work continued through a foundation, the Center for Humans and
Nature, that he himself helped fund.

* * *

As powerful as the environmental movement had appeared in its early years, it
appeared to flag in the new century, prompting calls for renewed action to meet
what was increasingly described as a growing crisis. Among the leading voices
sounding an alarm was '64's Robert Musil, whose approach to environmental conservation and global warming built from public health concerns that
naturally followed from years of antinuclear activism. As executive director of
Physicians for Social Responsibility, he joined a coalition of national environmental organizations in Washington determined to revitalize the environmental movement at the grassroots level following setbacks in the Reagan years
and in the period of Republican control of Congress in the 1990s. Building
on his religious convictions and the inspiration of the civil rights movement,
he took a decidedly optimistic view that the combination of altered personal
behavior and collective pressure on political bodies, at home and abroad,
could reverse a dire situation. "You and I are going to have to become far more
energy efficient in our own lives and demand the same of industries and public policy," he wrote in summarizing his work as an activist and professor at
American University in Washington. "We can attack the demand side of our
huge appetite for power and electricity. Then we must move rapidly to renewable fuels—wind, solar, biomass and biofuels, even tidal power—that generate
the energy we need without adverse health effects, pollution, security risks,
and mountains of waste left for future generations."[56]

Following his departure from Yale in 2008, Gus Speth joined the faculty of
the University of Vermont Law School, a pioneer in developing environmental legal education. Given the impasse in Washington, his contributions to
the ongoing debate became increasingly critical. Contending that the United
States had reached a point of "uneconomic growth" that "hollows out communities" and "rests on a manufactured consumerism," he declared that
"Americans need to reinvent our economy, not merely restore it. We will have
to shift to a new economy, a sustaining economy based on new economic

Gus Speth, being arrested at a Keystone XL pipeline protest at the White House, August 2011, part of his ongoing effort to bring the intensity of 1960s protest to the compelling issue of global warming. Courtesy of Shadia Fayne Wood.

thinking and driven forward by a new politics. Sustaining people, communities and nature must henceforth be seen as the core goals of economic activity, not hoped for by-products of market success, growth for its own sake, and modest regulation."[57] Once again he was evoking his earlier ode to activism, to "find again its rambunctious spirit and fearless advocacy, its fight for deep change, and its searching inquiry."

In August 2011, Speth acted on his belief when he was arrested and jailed along with environmental activist Bill McKibben as they protested the $7 billion Keystone XL oil pipeline, proposed to run from Alberta, Canada, to the Gulf Coast. Speth's classmate Wallace Winter was among the more than twelve hundred people arrested in the following days.[58] Conservatives pounced on the controversy, not just to support their claim that environmentalists were blocking new jobs and a path to energy independence, but to demonize opposition to the project. Echoing William Tucker a quarter century earlier, the *New York Times*'s Ross Douthat referred to the opposition as "the decadent left, which fights for narrow interest groups rather than for the public as a whole . . . for a small group of activists and donors, keeping the pipeline out of their national backyard is all that counts, even if American workers pay the price." That message was subsequently picked up and circulated widely in a video titled *If I Wanted America to Fail*, produced by Free Market America, an advocacy organization formed in 2011 to roll back environmental regulations.[59]

By way of contrast, the *Huffington Post*'s John Fullerton pointed out that the protest coincided with the anniversary of Martin Luther King Jr.'s "I Have a Dream" speech at the March on Washington in 1963. "The peaceful protesters, led by Bill McKibben, Gus Speth, and others," he declared, "are shining a light on the consequences of continued investment in and expansion of tar sands oil production—what climate scientists say would make catastrophic climate change inevitable." Noting how individual freedoms to consume coalesce into injustice for all, Fullerton revealed his own dream for a time "when many more of us are moved to confront that cold and careless injustice with the kind of determination and courage that our friends protesting and being arrested at the White House are demonstrating today." [60]

Speth provided his own prescription for a new era the following year. Like his earlier publications in the new century, *America the Possible: Manifesto for a New Economy* put the environment, most especially the crisis represented by global warming, at the heart of his argument. But the scope of the volume was wider, as he described his agenda as "system change, not climate change." As he had in his earlier work, he called for the forging of a new consciousness, only instead of invoking Charles Reich he cited Bill Clinton's former secretary of labor, Robert Reich, among other progressive critics of late capitalism's damaging effects. This was not a soft, cultural analysis, but one incorporating ideas from some of the most perceptive economic and social critics of the twenty-first century. "The only future they find truly attractive," he proclaimed, "is a Great Transition involving deep, systemic change—'a values-led shift in which citizens of the world drive fundamental change towards a just, sustainable, and livable future.'" Implementing a broad agenda of initiatives to mobilize progressive organizations in working to achieve greater equality in the cause of economic sustainability as well as social justice, he argued, would require a "rebirth of marches, protests, demonstrations, direct action, and nonviolent civil disobedience" reminiscent of 1960s activism.[61]

Speth's passionate arguments coincided with heightened activism on the left—most notably the Occupy movement—and an outpouring of media attention to growing economic disparities in America, a theme he addressed in his book, declaring that current conditions could well threaten the American dream as it had come to be associated with the promise of upward mobility for those who worked hard to achieve security for themselves and their families.[62] Among his allies might well have been David Schoenbrod, for a while his college classmate before Schoenbrod graduated a year early to take a Marshall scholarship to study economics at Oxford. An active Democrat in his youth, who worked for Hubert Humphrey through his college years, Schoenbrod was invited before he graduated from Yale Law School in 1968 to join the Humphrey for President national campaign staff. He rejected the offer because of Humphrey's support for the Vietnam War. Instead, he took a clerkship with Spottswood Robinson III, lawyer for one of the chief plaintiffs in *Brown v. Board of Education* and the first African American appointed to the powerful U.S. Court of Appeals for the District of Columbia.[63]

Schoenbrod's first job, before joining Speth at the Natural Resources Defense Council, was at the Bedford-Stuyvesant Restoration Corporation, where his work in community organizing involved him in early efforts to stop the horrible effects of lead paint on children. Married to Rhonda Copelon, who was two years behind him at Yale Law School and subsequently a pioneer human rights lawyer working out of the Center for Constitutional Rights,[64] he joined through her the company of young radicals caught up with Marxist doctrine and communal living. After that marriage ended in the mid-1970s, he formed a lasting union with a man, describing the relationship not as the product of a previously suppressed sexual preference so much as a good match that could only be conceivable in the aftermath of the sexual revolution.[65]

Frustrated at the inability of community development corporations to secure justice for their clients in court, Schoenbrod joined NRDC shortly after it formed. Over seven intense years he won several victories in court that forced the EPA to use its authority under the Clean Air Act to protect public health from lead and in particular to get oil companies to reduce lead in gasoline. As codirector with Ross Sandler of the council's Project on Urban Transportation, he achieved the unlikely victory of setting in motion legal directives resulting in upgrading the antiquated subway system in New York City in order to make mass transit more competitive with the automobile.[66]

By all counts, Schoenbrod should have been pleased with his victories as an environmental litigator, but his experience opened his eyes to faults in the system. He was upset that the Clean Air Act protected children from lead in gasoline far more slowly than its sponsors promised. The upshot of the delay, he calculated, was that fifty thousand people died from lead in gasoline, about the number of American deaths in the Vietnam War. To gain under-standing of the problem of translating congressional promises into effective results, he left NRDC to be a professor at New York Law School. There, as he stepped back from the activism that had captivated him throughout the long 1960s, he came to challenge core beliefs behind the early environmental movement, that environmental protections were best secured through central government agencies, most notably the Environmental Protection Agency, and backed by court actions of the kind he had instigated for years.

In a series of articles and in four books published by Yale University Press, he argued that environmental goals widely shared in the 1970s were not being met, not because of any inherent ideological differences, but because members of Congress had fallen into the habit of establishing environmental rights without incurring responsibilities for securing them. By giving the Environmental Protection Agency powers to implement its goals, Congress could bask in righteousness for promising clean air, for instance, even as achieving targeted levels for reducing pollution remained entirely beyond anyone's control. Courts, he contended, only made the problem worse. "States and cities," he asserted, "cannot be run effectively through court decrees that are as thick as phone books. When judges impose such decrees, it is the voters who lose. They lose the ability to hold elected officials accountable for the performance of governmental institutions."[67] Schoenbrod capped his argument in *Saving Our Environment from Washington: How Congress Grabs Power, Shirks Responsibility, and Shortchanges the People* (2005) by citing Speth's favorite environmental philosopher, Aldo Leopold, in his belief that conservation best grows from the bottom up, rather than the top down. Further challenging prevailing attitudes, he asserted, "There is also no shame in caring about the economic losses caused by high-modernist environmental protection . . . there are savings in eliminating our unnecessarily undemocratic, centralized, inflexible, unjust, and joy-killing way of protecting the environment."[68]

In the process of his writing and teaching, Schoenbrod formed associations with groups on the right, as a fellow at the American Enterprise Institute, a collaborator with the Cato Institute, and a contributor to the editorial pages of the *Wall Street Journal* and the *City Journal*, a publication of the Manhattan Institute, famous for helping inform the policy initiatives that made Rudy Giuliani a Republican star. Not a Republican, or even a conservative by his own definition, Schoenbrod nonetheless had moved away from his ideological roots in the 1960s to a pragmatist position that set him far apart from the grand aspirations spelled out by his former classmate and colleague Gus Speth. Far from denying the existence of environmental problems, he nonetheless argued that actions should be coupled with realistic assessments of their costs and measured approaches to identifying the entities best suited to secure results. Citing the 2009 House bill aimed at curbing carbon emissions (known as Waxman-Markey) as a prime example of an ineffective top-down program masquerading as a cap-and-trade approach, he cited the effort dealing with acid rain a decade earlier as a more effective approach to providing individual incentives for conservation. Elsewhere, he linked ongoing reliance on federal environmental action to the mistrust built up over the years around civil rights policy, arguing that in this instance the states were capable of acting responsibly on their own.[69]

Starting at opposite ends of the political spectrum as college students, David Schoenbrod and Gus Speth converged in the 1960s and early 1970s around common liberal commitments to saving the environment through active government intervention and stewardship. In later years, their approaches to environmental action diverged. While Schoenbrod sought to make the existing system work more effectively, Speth pressed for a much more radical alteration, of politics and belief, as much as specific policy actions. As much common support as there was among members of this class for environmental reforms,[70] the differences between Speth and many of his classmates remained significant. For even as he joined others who continued to seek justice for the land and its creatures, Speth insisted on acting upon the even higher stakes of addressing the fate of the earth itself.[71] And this was a step not all his classmates were ready to contemplate, let alone take.

6

God and Man

Douglas Grandgeorge, a top student at the tiny Somonauk,
Illinois, high school sixty miles west of Chicago, read William F. Buckley
Jr.'s *God and Man at Yale* the summer of 1960, as part of his preparation for
study at Yale. In retrospect, he could not have found Buckley's lament that
religion was dead at Yale any more inaccurate. "Religion," he recalled about
his time as a member of the class of 1964, "was everywhere. We talked about it
in science classes. The problem of God was the first thing we dealt with in philosophy. The great lecture of the week was in the chapel. Religion permeated
everything." Ordained a Presbyterian minister in the 1980s, he became pastor
of New York City's Central Presbyterian Church, originally funded with the
considerable assistance of John D. Rockefeller and made famous in the 1920s
by Harry Emerson Fosdick's daring theological interpretations. Grandgeorge
felt a thrill of recognition in Fosdick's spirit every time he mounted the pulpit.[1]

Having organized a statewide conference on human rights while he was
still in high school, Grandgeorge was immediately pulled into the civil rights
cause at Yale. His mother had been an active supporter of civil rights as chair
of the Illinois Women's Fellowship of the Congregational Church, and he had
been personally shocked when an aunt he was visiting in Florida reprimanded
him for using the bathroom especially set aside for her black maid. Bill Coffin
became an early and lasting influence on him, and he might well have joined
Coffin as a Freedom Rider had his family not insisted that he not miss two
weeks of school in order to participate. Sustained by his social as well as his
religious convictions, Grandgeorge continued to gravitate to Sunday chapel.
In the process, he grew especially close to three fellow midwestern classmates,

all of whom planned to pursue their religious interests after college. Elon
Peterson wanted to become a Lutheran minister even before he arrived at Yale
from Hopkins, Minnesota. Vincent Taus made his way to Yale from Salem,
Ohio, intending to become a Congregational minister. Gary Martin, a brilliant New Trier (Illinois) High School graduate and anthropology major,
experienced a religious conversion on Easter Sunday his junior year and
shifted his studies in order to enter the Episcopalian ministry. Grandgeorge
thought he would pursue an academic career as a theologian.

The deaths of Peterson, Taus, and Martin in an automobile accident on
their way back to the Yale campus from Peterson's twenty-first birthday party
in New York City on December 7, 1963, devastated Grandgeorge. Walking
outside downtown New Haven about a week after his friends' deaths, he
recalled his tears mixing with the rain pouring around him and thinking,
"I can't get through this if God is not going to make this right." Clearly the
philosophical God he had come to know as a student was no longer adequate.
Before he could even consider entering the ministry, then, he devoted his life
to service, working in New York first with the elderly, later with AIDS victims,
and eventually with the homeless as director of the city's largest shelter. It
was several decades before the call to the ministry finally came and he was
"ordained almost against my will." Still suffering the loss of his Yale friends,
he reported, "I found myself propelled into the Everlasting Arms as a necessary alternative to despair."[2]

Grandgeorge's life course appeared to owe very little to the 1960s for the
shape of its trajectory. To his own later embarrassment, he gave up a possible
student deferment at Harvard to enlist for military service that clearly would
have taken him to Vietnam, were it not for a history of migraine headaches
that exempted him. He grew up trusting the government and believed that
if the president and Congress were behind the war, it had to be necessary—a
matter of faith he retained until it was shattered by America's invasion of Iraq
in 2003. He was shocked at the social changes that took place in Yale College
in the immediate years after his graduation. Still, the circuitous path he took
to the ministry and the liberal interpretation of his mission, whatever form
it took, reveal an affinity with the set of changes that marked shifts in belief
and religious practice in the wake of the 1960s upheaval. Like so many other
aspects of American life as it was previously known, religious belief diversified and fragmented in the latter part of the 1960s. In matters of faith, nothing
remained certain or predictable.

Bill Buckley sought to persuade Yale to declare "active Christianity the
first basis of enlightened thought and action" as a basis not just for educating its charges but preparing them for national leadership.[3] Asked to hold
the line against experimentation, Yale 1964's graduates nonetheless proved

susceptible to alterations of even the most intimate matters of belief. While some managed to maintain continuity with the religion of their childhood, and others made defending traditional beliefs a lifelong cause, for many others religion became something entirely new in the wake of modern cultural change. As personal as these matters might have been, they nonetheless had lasting public consequences.

* * *

Statistically, this class seemed to remain within the mainstream over time. Despite the effects of a sustained revolt against authority, church and synagogue included, these men reported a decade after graduating from Yale that by a 4–1 margin they believed in God. Only twenty-seven respondents to a class poll said they were less religious than they had been in college, while thirty-seven described themselves as more religious. In line with prevailing tendencies that had witnessed a drop in weekly attendance at religious services from a high of 49 percent in 1955 and 1958, only 8 percent reported such devotion in 1974, while 45 percent reported not attending services at all. Fifteen years later the number attending weekly services was up to 17 percent, and the proportion of those not attending had dropped to 30 percent. Seventy-four respondents reported being more religious, while another forty-one reported being less religious.[4]

Fifty years out of Yale, James Turchik, a Roman Catholic, let his classmates know how important his faith had been to him over time. "By reading and studying the Scriptures, I have learned priorities in my life which remain: God, family, and my vocation," he wrote. "These priorities are enhanced by the grace given through the gifts of the Holy Spirit including wisdom, knowledge, faith, healing, prophecy, miraculous powers, and the other discernments given to some but not all in the Church." Turchik's classmate Roger Thompson, recalling his ordination at age twelve as a deacon in the Mormon Church, reported, "Over my lifetime, I have come to believe that all things point to a personal God who knows and cares about us. . . . I try to nourish and cultivate my faith regularly, much as I did as a Yale undergraduate. I strive to be honest and honorable in my business dealings and be open to the promptings of the Holy Spirit. The precious fruits of my faith and spiritual journey have given me hope for eternal life with my eternal companion, satisfying answers to the purpose of our existence, opportunities for service, and invaluable support during trying times."[5]

Such testimonials would have gone unnoted in another time, were it not for associated declarations of an entirely different kind. On the one hand, there was Nate Jessup praising the tenets of Scientology as a guide for a spiritual journey "in the direction of ever more self-determinism and ability to help others." Then there was Frank Hotchkiss, confessing that religion never had had any interest for him until he discovered Buddhism. "This is not some New Age-y creation," he wrote on the Yale '64 website. "It's based on great insights from the distant past as to how to create value in your life. And those insights are compelling. . . . So that's why I became a Buddhist 40 years ago."[6]

Even more telling was Van Lanckton's account of his conversion to Judaism. He grew up in a very religious family—his father was a Congregationalist, his mother a pious Presbyterian—in Darien, Connecticut, where Jews were excluded by gentleman's agreement. In attending Mount Hermon Academy, he was not aware of Jewish students, if there were any. His exposure to other beliefs as a freshman at Yale through an interfaith discussion group organized by Bill Coffin may have had some long-term effect on him, but more significant, he thought, was getting to know Joe Lieberman. He was impressed that Lieberman was always sure to have change in his pocket because if a homeless person asked for help, he was obliged to respond. It was that concept of *tzedakah*, of justice, or more broadly an obligation to improve the world, that Lanckton found compelling later on. The prospect of marrying a Jew as he neared completion of Harvard Law School in 1967 prompted him to investigate Judaism further. And it was in that exploration, at a time when issues of social justice were so prominently discussed, that he discovered a faith that met his needs. Here, he believed, was a faith that appealed both to his conscience and his intellect. As he later reflected, "Unlike the Christianity I had known, I found that Judaism valued questions. I learned that we could challenge God. Abraham argued with God to prevent destruction of Sodom and Gomorrah. Moses argued with God to spare the Israelites after the Golden Calf. I decided that my place in life was as a Jew, not a Christian."

As the ultimate extension of his conversion, thirty-five years later Lanckton retired from the practice of law and in 2003, at age sixty, entered the newly formed Rabbinical School of Hebrew College in Newton, Massachusetts. There he studied full time for the next six years in order to be ordained as a rabbi. Those studies further sharpened his evolving belief. "I no longer think of God as having supernatural power to alter events through external, conscious intervention," he reported. "I believe that we can never know God fully; God would not be God if humans could do that. I hold instead, informed by Rabbi Harold Kushner and Rabbi Art Green and Rabbi Neal Gillman, among others, that God operates as a force to reduce chaos, just as imagined in the opening verses of Genesis. Humanity acts as God's partner in that sadly incomplete work. The disorder that remains is the cause of suffering, random consequences for which I don't blame God."[7]

Lanckton's altered belief system was especially striking but hardly unique among his classmates. Peaslee DuMont too grew up in a distinctly religious household, raised in his mother's Catholic faith, even though his father was a Unitarian Universalist. He became highly energized at Yale his sophomore year through a student group that gathered once weekly to discuss in depth the experiences of early Christians. "Here we were, pre-Vatican II, having an experience that would really cut away the legalism and say this is not what it's all about," he recalled. "This was about a spirit that was alive. This was about eternal life being present here and now." Determined to take a year off before attending medical school, he spent a year in India on a Fulbright Scholarship teaching English and using his free time to investigate Eastern religious traditions. His decision to visit India was inspired by a lecture he had heard at Yale by Bede Griffiths, an English-born Indian Benedictine monk, who was visiting the United States.[8] DuMont's experience abroad set him on a course, deepened by his subsequent exposure to maverick theologian Matthew Fox, to describe his own faith as "a radically open Catholicism."[9] Increasingly put off by the Catholic hierarchy, he came to the point of saying that he was becoming "more catholic and less Roman." To affirm the melding of his traditional faith with Eastern influences, he opened his daily meditation with the sign of the cross before entering a round of tai ji.[10]

If openness and fluidity were possible among Roman Catholics, that was even more true among Protestants, if Jon McBride's experience was any indication of new currents affecting belief. Looking for a church in which to bring up his first child, McBride found himself attending St. Columba's Episcopal Church in Washington, D.C. Listening to a sermon from his Yale classmate, Stephan Klingelhofer, then serving as a seminarian in residence while studying at Virginia Theological Seminary, McBride was suddenly overwhelmed by tears, even as he felt a sense of peace washing over him. It had been a period of stress; a business venture had come unraveled just as the McBrides learned that a second child was on the way. What mattered most, however, was that this experience reversed a dogged sense, reaching back to McBride's childhood and deepened by a profound sense of loss with John Kennedy's assassination, of being urgently alone in the world. As the tears flowed, McBride recalled, "I experienced myself connected to all that is, a part of the 'wholeness' of life. Nothing was lost. I could still acknowledge, even celebrate my own uniqueness, and yours, as separate and distinct facets. Of the same stone. A new all-inclusive perspective was gained. Alone and connected. A loop had closed. A magnificent paradox. I was waking up from a 37-year nap. And it was okay."[11]

McBride described his revelation not as becoming "born again" so much as becoming at peace with the church and the guidance it could provide.

He subsequently pursued a series of "personal growth" seminars. Then, by chance, he encountered a woman at a Yale alumni event who had recently founded the Washington Center for Attitudinal Healing. Through her he learned about *A Course in Miracles,* a collection of lessons, one for each day of the year, that cut through conventional doctrine to provide a more contemporary, if somewhat controversial, interpretation of Christ's teaching.[12] Other reading in the New Age domain followed, including Eckhart Tolle's *The Power of Now.* McBride insisted that he had not embraced New Age beliefs as such, yet his actions as well as his language continued to reflect the personal transformation that started at St. Columba's.

Experiencing a new sense of self-awareness and connectedness drew McBride into new paths in both his public and private life. At home, he reported, "what resulted was a new openness and willingness/ability to communicate with parents and sister. And a keen awareness of how tough it is to stay 'conscious' with spouse and two kids. . . . It's hardest for me to stay awake, to really 'be there' at home where I live every day." In his chosen profession, executive search consulting, McBride perceived himself as a "hearthunter" rather than a "headhunter," noting that he was more interested in who the candidate is than in what he or she has done: "I looked for individuals for whom doing what my client needed done was a natural expression of who they 'are' as opposed to something they knew how to 'do' well and, if you paid them enough, they'd do it for you." Influenced by a presentation, "Beyond War—a New Way of Thinking," by his classmate Anthony Lee at a Yale reunion, McBride reported becoming active in the Beyond War effort. By embracing a new way of thinking, he suggested, human beings could experience a new way of being, "connected" around a determination to survive. "Out of Tony's presentation I experienced a synthesis of my military experience in the Vietnam era and my subsequent journeys into separateness and joining," he recalled. "It's become quite clear to me that nuclear weapons both pose a dangerous threat and offer an extraordinary gift. They let me see in the physical world what has been a spiritual truth since time began—we do unto ourselves as we do unto others. You can't 'nuke' somebody else without 'nuking' yourself."[13]

If Catholics and Jews had increasingly made their way into the accepted lexicon of established faiths in America alongside Protestants, the 1960s added much else that was different. In this, '64's Christopher Schaefer's life course was telling. Born in Bad Nauheim, Germany, in 1942, the son of a scientist who conducted research on carbon dioxide on a German submarine during World War II, Schaefer immigrated with his family to the United States in 1950 to join his father in Groton, Connecticut, where the senior Schaefer worked at the submarine base. He maintained a German connection when he attended a Waldorf school, an institution inspired by the insights into the development of children and of human consciousness by the Austrian philosopher and scientist Rudolf Steiner. At Yale Schaefer shifted his study from science to the humanities and would have continued in philosophy in graduate school had he not been discouraged by the difficulty of securing a teaching post in the field. Instead, he entered Tufts University's Fletcher School of Law and Diplomacy, where, in the spirit of the times, he focused on issues of war and peace. After a fellowship at the Brookings Institution in Washington, D.C., he joined MIT's Department of Political Science.

Schaefer loved teaching, and he loved the students he encountered. Over time, however, he became increasingly uncomfortable not just with the Vietnam War and its justifications, but also with MIT's support of it through the strategic hamlet program and other contracts with the Department of Defense. He also realized that as a young academic of twenty-eight, he had limited life experience and was primarily teaching the ideas of others. Given his antiwar position and his interest in neo-Marxism, it was not surprising that after he resigned his position at MIT, he wrote in his tenth reunion report in 1974, "I have gradually come to the conviction that there is a fundamental crisis in American society which cannot be remedied by social tinkering or political reform. I am presently in Europe trying to figure out how I can usefully act on this feeling when I return to the United States."[14]

What Schaefer did not report was that his commitment to social causes had led him to becoming spiritually active and engaged. Even while at Brookings he was reading widely in Buddhism and other spiritual philosophies and religions, interests that were deepened as he and his wife hosted in their home visiting speakers about Waldorf education and the spiritual teachings of Rudolf Steiner. Those interests coalesced particularly in anthroposophy, the study of human relations with the spiritual world through the schooling of one's inner life. That practice built on Steiner's contention that every human being (*anthropos*) has the inherent wisdom (*sophia*) to solve the riddle of existence and to transform both self and society. Translated to the Waldorf school experience, this meant taking a spiritual view of education as the means of gradually unfolding a child's capacity. Behind that notion is the critical assumption that children are not just helpless little beings, but they are full of wisdom and insight, and teachers have a responsibility to allow them to become who they are meant to be because they have been on earth before. Steiner's philosophy, in essence, according to Schaefer, is that human beings have the potential for developing spiritual cognition and spiritual insight through a process of self-development.

Over time, Schaefer and his wife, Signe, poured their energies into the Waldorf experience, starting a Waldorf school in Lexington, Massachusetts,

studying anthroposophy abroad, then returning to direct and teach in a
Waldorf administration program at Sunbridge College in New York State.
Looking back on their lives' work, both Chris and Signe, whose two children
went all the way through Waldorf schools, reflected on what their experiences
would have been like had they followed more conventional careers as some of
their friends had. For his part, Chris had no regrets, despite the prestige and
attention that would have come to him if he had continued as a member of
MIT's faculty. "I certainly have been able to do the work I believed in, working on questions of human relations and community development in diverse
settings as well as helping the Waldorf school movement both nationally and
internationally," he recounted. Explaining his role in the Occupy movement
near his home in Western Massachussetts, he further reflected,

> On a much smaller scale, we've been able to live our beliefs and pur-
> sue our spiritual interests. We didn't have to compromise what we
> regarded as essential. We both feel good about these choices. I actually
> find myself now in a mental and psychological state that is very similar
> to what I felt in the Vietnam years, while I was teaching at MIT, as the
> wars in Afghanistan and Iraq, or the U.S. Empire Project as I see it,
> when coupled with the financial crisis of 2008 make me again question
> our political and economic elites. We live in an oligopoly of wealth in
> which ordinary working Americans and minorities are getting a bad
> deal. Real wages have not increased significantly for most Americans
> since the mid-eighties.

Last but not least among the reasons he listed for his involvement was the
statement that "by practicing non-violence, we give voice to a moral and spiritual dimension to social change, and to the effort of building a society which
honors the physical, social, and spiritual nature of the human being."[15]

Clearly, both the social concerns of the early 1960s and the turn inward
of the later years of the decade and into the 1970s had considerable effect
on belief. Inevitably, the break between reason and belief would widen in a
form of spirituality that was entirely new, as it did for '64's Alexander "Sandy"
McKleroy. Raised an Episcopalian and prepped at the Episcopal church school
St. George's in Rhode Island, McKleroy experienced a crisis of faith at Yale of
the kind most feared by Bill Buckley. Seeking to bolster his beliefs through a
course on religion and philosophy offered by Professor John Smith, McKleroy
instead lost his faith. Exposed to Freud and Nietzsche, among others, he
entered a period of atheism. "For me, it was extinction, there was just the
black," he recounted. When called to Communion, he found he was unable to
participate. Although he started law school in San Francisco in 1964, he did

not take to his studies. Relieved on physical grounds from possible military service, he set off for Europe to see the world. Back in San Francisco in 1967, he threw himself into the life of the counterculture, surviving financially on modest fees from the music he provided for some of the street theater that was making headlines at the time.

McKleroy might have appeared to have been drifting, but an experience that year changed his life, setting him on a spiritual quest that never ended. One afternoon, after a period of fasting and proper rest, he turned on some *Victory at Sea* music and launched what he called a guided marijuana trip. "I actually went through a death thing," he explained. "I thought, 'My heart's beating. I think I'm dying,' but part of me said, 'Let's see what is going on.' And I had this amazing epiphany. . . . I had this feeling of the absolute goodness of the universe, an experience of light that completely turned me around. I was on the spiritual path from that point." From that "zeitgeist of Haight-Ashbury," he recalled, "the universe reblazed in glory through the catalysts of the psychedelics and psycho-spiritual literature." And from this "ineffable ecstasy of divine unity" his "passing and necessary atheism" was extinguished forever. A full immersion in self-discovery followed, through the study of Eastern religion, yoga with Swami Satchidananda, a full course in est, and time in a Tibetan ashram in Scotland before returning to the United States, where he did some teaching and found his life partner, whom he married in 1974 after living together with her for three years in Haight-Ashbury.[16]

Even as McKleroy taught Spanish, first in a private school in Oakland, then in several public schools in the Bay Area, he continued his spiritual journey. "It was very exciting to be in on the beginning of the whole New Age business," he recalled. He continued practicing yoga through the Baptiste Institute in San Francisco and earned a certificate in holistic health from the now defunct Holistic Life University, also in San Francisco, taking a special interest in herbology. His early spiritual beliefs were nourished through participation in Landmark Seminars, a series of encounter experiences passed on from Werner Erhard based on est principles, but with less of a confrontational structure. Aimed at improving personal growth through improved communication and self-evaluation, Landmark drew McKleroy and his wife to it frequently, prompting them to renew their commitment to each other as recently as a May 2012 session. McKleroy also embraced Life Expos, annual gatherings of spiritual seekers to conventions of provocative and uplifting speakers.[17] It was the Bruno Groening Circle of Friends, however, that capped McKleroy's journey as he entered his sixties.

Groening was, in McKleroy's estimation, a natural saint whose ability to convey spiritual energy to others, even after his death, had the power of healing that went beyond any medical explanation. Groening's prophecy, according to the Circle of Friends, stated, "Everyone has to die, so do I, but I will not be dead. And when someone calls me, I will come and continue to help, if it is God's will." McKleroy joined the organization in 2006, becoming a community leader both in San Francisco and in the Berkeley-Oakland area where he was living. The effort proved too demanding for him, and he scaled back to work only in his own community, but with great success, from the number of healings he witnessed and heard about. The process involved "absorbing the Heilstrom." The Circle of Friends instructed practitioners like McKleroy to sit on a chair in a quiet room, both feet on the floor, and "open hands palms up on your thighs. Open your heart and mind and ask for energy to come. Think of something pleasant and positive. . . . Disengage all negative thoughts—of illness and worries. The Heilstrom moves into the body via our antennas—our hands, feet and head, and can completely fill it with new energy. Sit and absorb the energy daily, even if for just 15 minutes, for health maintenance and longer for healing."[18]

McKleroy found the experience fully energizing and fulfilling. He could see a relationship to other movements to address social ills, which he was very much aware of and concerned about. Describing himself as mostly on the political left and a participant in the Occupy movement, he nonetheless felt the Circle of Friends approach was a better means of solving problems. He realized that his approach would take a long time to achieve social transformation, but he believed it more promising than the left's continual harping about problems. Never at ease with the artifice he witnessed as a relative outsider from the West when he attended St. George's and Yale, he embraced principles advanced in the Landmark seminars and practiced in his own life, to go beyond looking good—a condition he applied to the Yale of his undergraduate years—to seek personal transformation by declaring a new way of being instead of trying to change in comparison with the past. In his later life, McKleroy contends, he aims to continue to get bigger and bigger as a human being, finally overcoming obstacles that held him back in previous years. It is a process aided by the continued ritual of smoking marijuana, which, he asserts, has great medicinal effect as well as offering a positive boost in creativity.[19]

* * *

If the struggle to reconcile established beliefs with new elements of spirituality and practice proved difficult for laymen, it was even harder for clergy. None would dare predict today the career paths of the three midwestern Yale men who died in 1963, had they lived to enter the ministry. But for three of their classmates who were able to pursue the ministry, the course was anything but straightforward.

Born and raised in Kalamazoo, Michigan, Thomas "Tim" Bachmeyer had never heard of prep schools nor met a preppie, he said, until he met William Bradford Reynolds in his freshman German and English classes. Once he overcame his culture shock at Yale, he threw himself into religious activities, most notably the Wesley Foundation, the New England Methodist Student Movement, and Yale's Board of Deacons. Together with John Ashcroft, his roommate of four years, Bachmeyer limited his social life largely to Yale football games and the master's beer parties in his Branford residential college, where the two teetotalers would strum guitars and sing silly songs. Despite his relative cultural isolation, Bachmeyer found career inspiration in Yale's Methodist campus minister, Arthur Brandenburg, and found his church youth work, along with his association as a deacon with Bill Coffin, liberating. Although he did not sign up to go to Mississippi, he solicited funds for SNCC his sophomore year, and he followed the civil rights struggles around the country his last years in college. With the inspiration of Bill Coffin and periodic sermons in Battell Chapel from Martin Luther King and other national civil rights leaders, he found his social conscience and sense of social justice deepened.

On graduation, Bachmeyer attended the University of Chicago Divinity School, where he was caught up in the era's ferment. Immediately at hand on Chicago's South Side was the community organizing work of the Reverend King and Ralph Abernathy, not to mention student occupation of the university's central administrative building. Issues of social justice infused his life, and he decided that writing rather than personal activism would best build on his interests in religion and philosophy. That determination materialized in his 1968 master of divinity thesis, in which he applied sociologist Erik Erikson's theory of the eight stages of development to the life course of Martin Luther King. Deeply shocked by King's assassination, which he learned about as he was driving back from his own parish assignment on the South Side in 1968, Bachmeyer came to believe that he was in the midst of an important historical transformation and that spirituality was central to the struggle for social change.

Even as he was completing his doctoral degree, Bachmeyer's own quest for spiritual truth was evolving. His final ordination board required candidates to sign the same twenty-two-point statement passed down from John Wesley in 1722, committing to a life free of drinking, smoking, and premarital sex. Bachmeyer had lived up to that pledge himself, but he felt its demands were out of touch with the times and too focused on personal morality in an era of the struggle for social justice. His own search for spiritual integrity was confounded when one of his ministerial examiners suggested he sign the pledge with the understanding that he would not necessarily abide by it. Although he was initially assigned to the teaching ministry, his own vision of his calling finally shattered when, returning to Michigan, where ministers were expected to stay close to home, he found that typical assignments were in small towns he had never heard of—an ironic reversal of his first experience of Yale. He found himself too independent to live the commitment to a parish church, and so he finally abandoned any prospect of offering pastoral care. Instead, Bachmeyer took a position teaching at the Catholic St. Francis School of Pastoral Ministry in Milwaukee.

By the time he arrived in 1970, Roman Catholic seminary education was undergoing upheaval. Hired to help create a new degree curriculum in line with contemporary behavioral science, he viewed with alarm the growing influence of humanistic psychologists Abraham Maslow and Carl Rogers. Coincidentally, the number of students prepared for the priesthood dropped as growing numbers of graduates sought secular callings. Seeking to establish a better balance between science and faith—what Bachmeyer described as "reconciling faith with psychological and sociological facts on the ground"— he collaborated with his fellow Protestant colleague William Johnson Everett, a 1965 graduate of Yale's divinity school, to write their own interdisciplinary text. Its goal was to demonstrate how theology, psychology, and sociology had certain affinities among their respective schools.[20] That joint effort represented Bachmeyer's personal integration of formal intellectual interests and religious belief, as a commitment to the social component of religious faith and a practical search for an authentic spirituality. At this point in life, as he continued to pursue the personal independence that characterized his professional career, he and his wife separated.

After his marriage ended and while in psychotherapeutic training, Bachmeyer met and married his second wife, who was preparing to be a social worker and shared his interests in personal and spiritual authenticity and social change. When they married they shed their respective Methodist and Roman Catholic traditions and joined an Episcopal Church, where their children were baptized. Together they continued their spiritual quests, eventually exploring Hinduism and Buddhism. As the appeal of teaching diminished, Bachmeyer left St. Francis to start up his own counseling practice, where, as he said, he helped clients "deal with their emerging personal energies underlying the social roles they had achieved." Central to his own new role was six years of clinical training in transactional analysis, an approach to psychotherapy stressing personal growth launched in the 1950s by psychoanalyst Eric Berne and popularized especially in the experimental 1970s through Dorothy Jongeward's book *Born to Win*.[21]

After a dozen years in counseling Bachmeyer shifted careers again, this time as a professional fund-raiser specializing in planned giving. He considered his work another way of counseling people how to act on what they valued most in life by leaving a lasting charitable legacy. As he shifted jobs over time, his wife, Ellen, took on a number of therapeutic roles, including that of an equine massage therapist, for horses and their riders. It was through expanding this energy work that she met Marti Spiegelman in northern California, an experienced teacher and practitioner of several ancient indigenous healing traditions conveyed through nature and the energy of the earth. Ellen Bachmeyer traveled with Spiegelman to Machu Picchu and Siberia to study ancient healing traditions, while Tim incorporated her teachings in promoting the healing of body and soul, even as he relied himself on that wisdom as he recovered from two life-threatening illnesses. In 2011 he launched a mentoring practice called Personalized Leadership Training, intended to boost individuals' innate leadership capacities by integrating their own inner resources, sense of social responsibility, and personal sense of the transcendent. Coincidentally, his thirst for social responsibility, so inspired by the 1960s, turned to the protection of the natural environment and wildlife, as a board member of the Florida Wildlife Federation and as president of a small international charity supporting indigenous traditions and economic justice in a small community in Peru.[22]

As one of the few other Yale '64 graduates who studied for the ministry, Frank Basler pursued an equally eclectic career. In seventh grade, he declared himself an atheist in reaction to an unsatisfactory explanation from the local Roman Catholic bishop that the deaths of a number of children in a parochial school fire was the will of God. He maintained his skepticism in his first years at Yale, but he found himself drawn into Bill Coffin's sphere at Battell Chapel, where he became a deacon his senior year. Introduced in high school to the power of religious experience to fill an empty interior world through William James's *Variety of Religious Experiences*, he turned to religion and philosophy to help ease bouts of depression. Uncertain about his career direction, he applied to the liberal Union Theological Seminary in New York, assisted with a Rockefeller Brothers scholarship. Basler loved the educational experience there, despite his inability still to call himself a believer. While in New York, he reconnected with Bill Coffin, who was then pastor of Riverside Church, adjacent to the seminary and the flagship of liberal Protestantism. He also began Jungian analysis, building on an interest in Carl Jung he had developed at Yale.

Struggling with his faith, and especially the notion of Jesus as divine, Basler made only a halfhearted search for a church ministry. In the summer before he graduated, he found an internship in a "shopping center ministry" at the Oakbrook Shopping Center outside Chicago. There he learned about a network of ministers formed to address the world of work, not as it had been traditionally organized but in a less autocratic and more people-centered basis. The effort was very much a part of the times. With degree in hand, Basler took a position directing the Rochester, New York, Downtown Ecumenical Ministry, an effort by five downtown churches to build relationships with the surrounding business community. Here, he thought, was a way of overturning the past through a coordinated faith-based transformation of the way work was organized. Already a veteran of the 1963 civil rights effort in Mississippi, he became active in peace efforts and demonstrated at the Democratic National Convention in Chicago in 1968. One of his Union professor's arguments, that God is found in "doing politics," was among his greatest intellectual influences.

Basler stayed in his position with the downtown churches for four years and put the ministry on solid footing as a management training organization with business, church, and community organizations as clients. But he found the effect of his efforts limited, and he decided he needed graduate training in organizational behavior to be more effective. Studying at MIT's Sloan School of Management, he came under the influence of Chris Argyris, recently arrived at Harvard from Yale and a pioneer in the field of organization development, which used behavioral science insights to plan approaches to change. The solution Basler took away was to move from hierarchy to teamwork, stressing free choice, transparency, and internal commitment. Choosing to see the breakdown of authority in positive terms at the time of his tenth reunion at Yale, Basler wrote hopefully about the emergence of new forms of shared power: "The liberation movements of the past ten years are part of what I see as a very long-term trend of power redistribution. Authority based on position, role, or wealth is gradually being supplanted by authority based on competence to accomplish mutually chosen goals. In organizations, control through boss-subordinate relationships will be replaced by networks of self-regulating teams, eliminating hierarchy as we know it. Intra-personally the authority of the rational ego is being supplanted by that of less restrictive modes of consciousness."[23] The values behind the theory were compatible with his earlier thoughts about the ministry, but they had gained secular form, and his career subsequently reflected that shift.

Basler's first job out of MIT was back in the Chicago area with the G. D. Searle pharmaceutical company. In 1977, two years after he arrived, Donald Rumsfeld became company president, and one of his first acts was a dramatic downsizing that cut the number of headquarters employees by more than half. The management development department was decimated, and Basler left for another job. Positions in two other companies followed, but neither fulfilled his hopes, leading him to the conclusion that corporate life was not for him. Instead, boosted by his wife's employment as a director of a group home for adolescent girls, he ventured to form his own consulting practice, where he was better able to combine his early social and religious ideals with his MIT management training.

The practice grew, and as it did, Basler decided to enter therapy at the Westchester Institute for Training in Psychoanalysis and Psychotherapy. He wanted to address his continued periodic depressions and his tendency to overreact to authority figures. After years of analysis and study, he was certified as a psychoanalyst, but he did not practice, since psychoanalysis was still not eligible for insurance reimbursement in Connecticut, where he lived. Significantly, although he had remained unchurched during this period, as he approached the end of his training he started to attend the Benedictine Grange, where he was again exposed to mysticism and began meditating. His life was changing again. Then, it took a dramatic turn.

When Bill Coffin died in 2006, one of the eulogists at his funeral asked, "Who was this man?" He answered, "A pianist. An agent of the CIA." And, finally, "Bill was a follower of Jesus!" Basler, for whom Coffin had been an important spiritual guide, was in attendance and found the experience profound. "I could see Christ in Coffin's life," Basler recalled. "He loved Jesus. I loved Bill, so, OK, I must love Jesus, too." With his faith given new immediacy, Basler took up practices that could only have happened in the aftermath of the 1960s, Buddhist meditation and new ministry training leading to his being authorized in 2011 by the United Church of Christ to look for church employment. Echoing Gus Speth's call for a new consciousness to counter prevailing aspects of materialism, he spoke of challenging the prevailing culture of individualism, which he believed threatens the planet.[24]

Surveying this range of belief, Bill Buckley would have been hard-pressed to identify trends to assure him that Yale was doing its job in conveying sufficiently established religious traditions as well as beliefs. Even those who might have come closest to his model seemed destined by the age to take a turn outside of tradition. That was true of James Miner's experience in the ministry. Even though his career as an Episcopal minister approached a Buckley ideal, it could not avoid the drama of the social changes emerging in the 1960s. The son and brother of Yale men, Miner never seriously considered attending any other college. Although he elected a religious studies major, his coursework emphasized a broad liberal arts education rather than specific religious training. Service as a deacon his senior year brought him into close contact, through weekly reading groups, with Bill Coffin. Deacons also regularly interacted with the outstanding religious minds of the era through the guest sermons in Battell Chapel. Those experiences notwithstanding, Miner did not elect to enter seminary until well into his senior year. When he did make that decision, he shunned the advice of family and friends to take more time to gain additional experience and to consider further options. Instead, he followed the lead of a Yale divinity student he met through his work as a deacon, who recommended that he attend the Episcopal Theological Seminary of the Southwest in Austin, Texas. Gaining the permission of his bishop in Ohio—only because, Miner later thought, he did not take his commitment entirely seriously—he took up his religious training in the fall of 1964.

Miner's new school, one of only two Episcopal seminaries west of the Mississippi, was founded in 1951 by John E. Hines, an activist priest and later bishop of Texas. Unlike traditional schools of its kind, Southwest began with immersion in social sciences and literary criticism, only then following with the standard courses in theology. With its high ratio of faculty to students, this small school offered a collaborative approach to education that Miner found fresh and inspiring. Despite the sudden departure of a significant number of faculty in the months before he arrived—the product of ideological conflict within the church that resulted in hard times for the seminary financially—the activist mission embraced by its founders remained. Building on the revelations of what poverty and injustice might mean, through his experience as a college volunteer in the hardscrabble Farnham Court housing project in New Haven, Miner embraced the prevailing spirit of reform by engaging in antipoverty causes while at Southwest. Armed with his degree, Miner accepted his first assignment, to a parish in Sandusky, Ohio, which allowed him to extend his interests and concerns in a community undergoing the disinvestment that accompanied deindustrialization. His next assignment, to Youngstown, coincided with the closure of the research and development division of Youngstown Sheet and Tube, a venerable steel company and a pillar in the community.[25] As many as two hundred PhDs and their support staffs were suddenly out of work, with predictable results of personal hardship, depression, and even suicide.

Miner's subsequent career included ministries in Medina and Columbus, Ohio, as well as six years as administrative assistant to the bishop of Ohio, John Harris Burt, a social activist, who fought, unsuccessfully as it turned out, to enable workers to buy the mills where they worked, in the midst of the collapse of the steel industry. Miner described Burt's passion and commitment in terms evocative of Bill Coffin. "He was the kind of guy who gave local clergy courage," Miner recalled. "His commitment energized me." With cutbacks in federal antipoverty programs, Burt, with Miner's active support, introduced community development efforts that vested considerable power and responsibility in local communities to determine their own priorities and to execute them with grants from the church. Burt thus created a privatized version of the War on Poverty's concept of "maximum feasible participation."[26] As the rector of Trinity Church in Columbus following Burt's retirement as bishop of Ohio, Miner continued his social engagement, offering the church as sanctuary for social justice efforts as well sustaining an active antipoverty ministry. Providing the last beds for the homeless on any evening, Trinity initially offered space in its own sanctuary and subsequently initiated a voucher program with area hotels and motels so beneficiaries could have private bathroom facilities. Even after his retirement, Miner remained active in antipoverty work, serving for six years as president of the Hunger Network in Ohio.

Miner's activism placed him within a liberal theological tradition very much associated with the 1960s, and as such he might well have been looked at askance by Bill Buckley. Looking back on those years, however, Miner shared some of Buckley's concerns even as he reflected the temperament of a number of his Yale classmates. Continuing to serve on a number of other antipoverty committees, Miner still could see some value in the conservative pushback to church activism. He disagreed with many of the church's reactions to policy dilemmas, describing them as "knee-jerk liberal," doing the right thing in the short term, perhaps, but falling short of addressing larger structural issues. In making these judgments, Miner was not far removed from social scientists who felt that more than charity was needed to curb systemic poverty. Unlike these academics, however, Miner blamed the failure of activism on its growing distance from considered spiritual beliefs. "The evangelicals got it right in one sense," he reflected. The work of a minister "is the conversion of souls. When people get converted they begin to behave differently and maybe the world would change a bit when that happens." That being said, Miner reacted pointedly to a 2012 column by the conservative Catholic Ross Douthat that criticized the Episcopal Church for its liberalism. In the column, Douthat stated that the church was "flexible to the point of indifference on dogma, friendly to sexual liberation in almost every form, willing to blend Christianity with other faiths, and eager to downplay theology entirely in favor of secular political causes."[27]

Not so, Miner retorted:

> What is missing from this view, in my estimation, is that it does not recognize that we live in a postmodern world. Like it or not, we live in a pluralistic world. Christians no longer enjoy the privileges and cultural hegemony of Christendom. Gay people are gay, poor people are poor, people of color are people of color, and many of the injustices of the world persist because there are strong cultural, social, and economic arrangements designed precisely to keep things that way. Critical thought has recognized that and "named the demons."

Reflecting the argument the religious historian Robert Ellwood has advanced that the 1960s forced the end to any sustainable metanarratives in favor of a greater pluralism of belief, Miner asserted, "Once Pandora's box has been opened, the demons cannot be stuffed in again. Simply to turn a blind eye to all of this would lead to the greatest sort of irrelevance, it seems to me. One cannot go back to a pre-critical naïveté or innocence." Rather, it was the church's obligation in a postmodern era to document and understand both past and current traditions and then test them in a process of either affirming or discarding them.[28]

* * *

With so much change and adaptation at hand, the continuity in belief of Yale '64's two politicians, Joe Lieberman and John Ashcroft, is striking. Yet in their shared orthodoxy exist differences that help reveal how what otherwise might be considered a shattering of belief over fifty years nonetheless adds up to a religious divide.

In college Joseph Lieberman's observant Judaism stood out. More than one classmate recalled years later the special kosher meals Lieberman picked up in the college dining halls. In a 2011 event in New Jersey promoting his book about cherishing the Sabbath, Lieberman confessed that it was not until the death of his beloved grandmother, while he was studying at Yale Law School in 1967, that he became committed to worshipping regularly at a synagogue. That did not mean he had not been previously devout. While in college, he made a point of setting aside time for prayer, and over time he became ever more devoted to maintaining the Sabbath, despite pressures to engage in weekend events. When he and his first wife divorced, Lieberman cited as a primary cause religious differences in the degree of commitment to orthodoxy. In his second wife, Hadassah, he found a high level of religious compatibility. "Belief in God and observances of religion have enabled me to order my life and bring purpose and pleasure to my day," he wrote in his twenty-fifth reunion class book.[29] Lieberman's role both in seeking public constraints on lewd language and images in popular culture and his early condemnation of Bill Clinton's sexual activity with Monica Lewinsky were widely credited with influencing his selection as Al Gore's running mate in 2000.[30]

If anything, John Ashcroft remained even more consistent in retaining his beliefs—evangelical principles he had grown up with as a devout member of the Assemblies of God church. His paternal grandfather set the family tradition by becoming an evangelical preacher following his recovery from a near-fatal gasoline explosion. His father, J. Robert Ashcroft, extended the faith by becoming an evangelical while still in his teens and entering the ministry in 1932. Following a pastorship in West Hartford, Connecticut, after World War II, J. Robert moved his family to Springfield, Missouri, where he joined the staff of the Assembly of God's Central Bible Institute. In a long career that combined education with writing, J. Robert rose to prominence in his church, with considerable impact on his son John. "Hearing him pray was a magisterial wake-up call," Ashcroft recalled. "While many kids wake up to the smell of coffee brewing or the sound of a rooster crowing, I have cherished memories of entering the day as this man's outspoken prayers filtered throughout the house."[31]

As an adult, Ashcroft routinely started his day, inside and outside government, with a prayer and proved a leading organizer of prayer groups within the U.S. Senate after his election in 1994. When he launched an exploratory committee to run for president in 1998, he made his religious beliefs, including opposition to abortion under any circumstances, the centerpiece of his campaign. If elected, he promised, he would kneel and pray for divine guidance before taking office. Every time his course faltered, he considered the setback a chance for redemption. "My theory about elections," he wrote, "is mirrored in what I believe about all of life: for every crucifixion, a resurrection is waiting to follow—perhaps not immediately, but the possibility is there." As the legal reporter Jeffrey Rosen commented in an *Atlantic* profile at the height of the controversy surrounding adoption of the Patriot Act, Ashcroft drew from his father the view of himself as an instrument of some higher power.[32] Following his government service as attorney general, he was appointed a distinguished professor of law and government at Regent University, the interdenominational Christian school founded in 1978 by televangelist Pat Robertson as Christian Broadcasting Network University.[33] Even as he followed the well-beaten path out of government service into the lucrative position of a lobbyist, Ashcroft fashioned a self-image of rectitude intended to contrast with the sleazy activities that most famously landed Jack Abramoff in jail.[34] Just as importantly, he threw himself back into the activities of the growing Assemblies of God church, seeking in the process to restore prevailing liturgy to purer biblical form. Contending that the church had become too modern, he agreed to participate in individual services only if he was given charge of the liturgy.[35]

These two men's party affiliations quite obviously set them apart, a product in part of their contrasting social, geographic, and ethnic roots. Party difference was most manifest when Lieberman voted against Ashcroft's confirmation as attorney general. But beyond the label of party, there were significant differences, most notably Lieberman's tolerance of a pluralist view of belief that Ashcroft did not and could not share. In college and afterward, Lieberman retained a passion for civil rights, a product of his own minority status as well as his exposure to civil rights through Bill Coffin. He later credited his college exposure to social injustices for his support for ending discrimination against gays in the military.[36] Ashcroft, on the other hand, retained the individualist perspective that William Bradford Reynolds applied to civil rights policy and considered issues of sexuality within the rigid moral code of the traditionalist. His was not the religion of Lieberman or Lanckton, to ask questions, but a set of beliefs intended to bring moral certainty to life in its public as well as its private dimensions. That split, even among what are generally considered compatible orthodox beliefs, said a great deal about the abiding differences not just in this college class but in the country.

In the ongoing debate over religious values the last word goes to James Miner. Reflecting the confidence in critical inquiry that was so central to his Yale experience, Miner described the ideal person of faith as a thinker, professor, and confessor. "A thinker," he explained,

> is someone who gathers the data and ruminates upon it, and the data is from the world and from the tradition. That's what you would call critical theology. Then you might become a professor. You say, OK, I've drawn some conclusions, I'd like to profess what I believe to be the case and tell the truth as I see it about what I've seen here. The third step, and this is what pastors pray and hope for, is that congregants will become confessors. I stake my life on this, to the point where I'm willing to risk doing something, and what is guiding me is this thinking and this professing, this acknowledgment of what I believe to be true, which is pushing me into action and commitment.

Despite his reservations about contemporary trends in liberal theology, Miner remained optimistic that serious reevaluation of how social action emerges properly out of spiritual investigation was already well under way.[37]

In his faith, as in that of so many others, what Miner described as a postmodern era was a more open, more flexible attachment to religious doctrine, one that was nonetheless infused with a commitment to achieving greater social justice. Such beliefs existed before the 1960s, but in that era they assumed new and more diverse forms, some more formal than others. To a striking degree, members of the Yale class of 1964, while not characterized as a whole as driven by the social issues that emerged in the 1960s, nonetheless made those issues a significant part of their private, devotional life as much as they might have acted on them more publicly in their professions. When such adaptations took them in the direction Bill Coffin had laid out while they were undergraduates—toward a liberal embrace of social justice—their actions and beliefs did not go uncontested. As anachronistic as some of William Buckley's views about the importance of received wisdom may have seemed to some in later years, his position retained considerable power on the Christian right. After the 1960s, America may have been one nation under God in theory, but in practice God's presence was interpreted in such distinct and often opposing ways as to further deepen the national cultural divide.

7

Sex and Marriage

Few aspects of the 1960s became more contested over time than the changing mores associated with sex, the family, and marriage. While "sex, drugs, and rock 'n' roll" may have served as the rallying cry for those determined to put the 1950s firmly behind them, during subsequent years considerable monetary and institutional power aligned to restore honor and respect to the idealized, post–World War II nuclear family. Nevertheless, even as traditionalists bemoaned the acceptance of premarital sex, rising levels of divorce, and birth outside wedlock, to say nothing of the legalization of abortion and the institutionalization of rights for women and gays, national attitudes towards sex changed fundamentally.

One had only to consider the public reaction to the scandal that engulfed the Clinton presidency. While it was obvious that Bill Clinton had taken sexual license in the Oval Office, the public did not seem to care. He not only survived the effort to impeach him, but a number of his programs were enacted into law, and he maintained high public ratings. As humanities scholar Mark Lilla pointed out, as successful as the Reagan counterrevolution had been in setting the national policy agenda that forced Clinton to adopt conservative welfare and fiscal policies, the sexual revolution was here to stay. So successful have been both these revolutions, Lilla argued, that Americans "see no contradiction in holding down day jobs in the unfettered global marketplace—the Reaganite dream, the left nightmare—and spending weekends immersed in a moral and cultural universe shaped by the sixties."[1] The indifference to subsequent revelations of extramarital affairs conducted by Newt Gingrich and Robert Livingston (who was expected to succeed Gingrich as Speaker of the

House), even as they pressed for Clinton's impeachment for the same impropriety, confirmed as much.[2] However, on the broader plane of establishing equal rights for women, the issue that emerged so forcefully at the end of the 1960s, much remained to be decided. Instead of consensus, Americans in the twenty-first century remained divided both about the proper role of law in assuring women's liberties and about the cultural norms defining the roles both of men and women in the home and in the family.[3]

The class of 1964 arrived at Yale too early to fully encounter the sexual revolution while still in college. Not that sex didn't happen. It did, but in a much more clandestine and forbidden atmosphere. Public discussion focused largely on enforcement of the strict parietal rules governing the mixing of the sexes in student rooms. When Father John McLaughlin chose in the spring of 1964 to lecture undergraduates on the importance of confining sexual intercourse to married couples, he evoked a scathing column in the *Yale Daily News*, but not without attracting his own defenders, including a moderately

"This time when the swinging sixties come around, I'm not going to miss them."

Some members of the Yale class of 1964 were caught up in the sixties sexual revolution, others not. They all faced changing rules for sex and marriage, testing privileges traditionally associated with men as primary breadwinners and heads of household. *New Yorker*, October 24, 2011, cartoon by Jack Ziegler. *New Yorker* Collection/www. cartoonbank.com.

sympathetic editorial.[4] While the introduction of the birth control pill, with its revolutionary implications for separating sex from procreation, coincided with their college admission,[5] prescriptions for this form of contraception were initially confined to married couples. In Connecticut, the pill was not even legally available until the Supreme Court lifted the state's prohibition on birth control in *Griswold v. Connecticut* in 1965.[6] For those active in college, then, sex remained something of a covert activity, which sometimes ended in unwanted or at least unexpected pregnancies. For the former, there were at least some illegal abortions;[7] for the latter, there was the alternative of early marriage. For the great majority of these men, both expectations and practices remained largely what they had been for at least a generation. As with the Vietnam War, the biggest social changes that would ultimately affect these men's lives came after their collective college experience.

These men were largely socialized in traditional homes, typical of the immediate postwar era.[8] There were exceptions, but for the most part the work their mothers did took place in the home. When their names appeared in the newspaper, most often it was in the society pages. An exception was Frederick Buell's mother, Marjorie Henderson Buell, the acclaimed creator of the *Little Lulu* comic strip character. Yet she published under the pen name Marge and chose to live a very private life with her husband and two children in Malvern, Pennsylvania, doing virtually no entertaining and making no connection to her public identity. Successful as she was professionally, she did nothing to upend her traditional role in the nuclear family. Women expressed their hopes for their children, as Sydney Lea's mother did, by pushing them to achieve academic excellence. In Elizabeth Jane Lea's case, however, her hopes for her son stemmed largely, he thought, from her own educational disappointment. Lacking the means to pay for Radcliffe College, she had looked to a wealthy uncle for help. But, like many traditionalists, he declined. Women, he believed, should not attend college. Consequently, while she was active in her community philanthropically, Mrs. Lea never took up a career.[9] David Plimpton's mother, Ruth Talbot Plimpton, proved herself an unusually forceful presence, talking her way into Radcliffe and out of a number of serious jams while serving abroad with her physician husband (and later Amherst College president), Calvin Plimpton. The author of several books, including one on Crossroads Africa, which drew her son into contact with the organization in his teens, she nonetheless served, as many wives did, as a particularly effective complement to her husband, even as she bore prime responsibility for raising five children.[10]

Following a trend building over a half century in what historian Margaret Marsh calls "masculine domesticity," the fathers of Yale 1964 were very much present in the home, as companionate husbands, attentive parents, and contributors to household activities.[11] During the 1950s, advice givers began to promote equality among married couples, with men assuming more parental responsibilities and making sure that sex was "mutually satisfying." The husband's primary role, however, remained that of a stable provider. "The bride who wants to do her full job will plan from the start to create the kind of home her husband wants, and to do it with no more assistance from him than he willingly offers," psychologist Clifford Adams wrote in his Making Marriage Work column for the *Ladies Home Journal* in 1950. If a husband "offers to dry the dishes, thank him for the favor," he suggested, "rather than regard it as your right."[12] Writing in 1974, historian Peter Filene reported, "Men and women may have been feeling and behaving as equals in bed, but in the kitchen and living room they remained markedly unequal." The twentieth-century family had evolved from a patriarchy to a democratic team, but the average nonemployed wife still performed between fifty and fifty-six hours of family work per week, in contrast to her husband's seven to thirteen.[13]

A 1962 survey of students at Yale, Cornell, and Mount Holyoke on gender relations suggested that Yale men might be open to alternative models for marriage, as 61 percent responded positively to the statement that "a woman's place is in the home is totally outmoded." An even greater number—65 percent—agreed that the chief breadwinner should be "head of the household."[14] In this, respondents sounded very much like the Ivy League student who told sociologist David Riesman a few years earlier, "I want someone who would stay home and take care of the children. But on the other hand I want someone who can stimulate me intellectually, and I don't know if those things are compatible. If a woman goes to Radcliffe and takes up economics, she isn't learning how to bring up children."[15]

As the members of the class of 1964 began to enter marriage, they selected partners overwhelmingly from among college women, a good number of whom had their own professional as well as personal ambitions. *The Feminine Mystique*, Betty Friedan's influential 1963 manifesto urging women to seek greater measures of fulfillment outside the home, was still fresh enough not to have changed entirely women's expectations. But it was clear by the mid-1960s, when these men began marrying, that rules governing sex and marriage were changing. Elements of civil rights egalitarianism and concepts of self-actualization combined to help fuel early feminist sentiment.[16] As Stephanie Coontz reports, in the two decades following the mid-1960s, "marriage lost its role as the 'master event' that governed young people's sexual lives, their assumption of adult roles, their job choices, and their transition into parenthood. People began marrying later. Divorce rates soared. Premarital sex became the norm. And the division of labor between husband as breadwinner and wife as homemaker, which sociologists in the 1950s had believed was vital for industrial society, fell."[17] Between professed ideals of equality between partners and adherence to prevailing views of the chief breadwinner's dominance in every household, something had to give.

* * *

For men of the old school, marriage and a degree from a prestigious university represented a form of social capital, preferably confirmed by a wedding announcement with a "suitable partner" in the *New York Times*.[18] John Armor was among those in the class of 1964 who came from a privileged background. His grandfather, George Maxwell Armor, was past chairman of McCormick & Co. in Baltimore, and his mother, Annie Linn Henley, was a direct descendant of Charles Linn, one of the founders of Birmingham, Alabama. Undoubtedly the family envisioned John marrying one of the Baltimore-area debutantes who had been groomed to marry men like him. Shortly after graduation, however, he hastily married a local New Haven nursing student, hardly the union his family had hoped for or expected. When that marriage failed, Armor again married, this time another medical professional and Playboy Club worker whom he met in a gasoline line during the energy crisis of 1973.[19] Strachan Donnelley married Vivian Hilst, a student he met while teaching at Valparaiso University in Indiana. The marriage was a strong and lasting one, but at the time of their union in 1968 members of the prominent Chicago-based Donnelley family expressed misgivings because the bride came from uncharted social territory in Kansas. More striking were the marriages to white women of two of '64's African Americans, Stanley Thomas and Arthur Reagin. While both marriages ended in divorce, they lasted long enough to bring forth biracial children at a time when such family formations were rare and, in some parts of the United States, still prohibited by law.[20]

Clearly some members of Yale '64 were breaking old taboos, often with considerable penalties. When Henry Putzel proposed to Anne Bolton Smith, for instance, her family refused to approve the union because he was Jewish. With the exception of Anne's sister, the Bolton Smiths did not attend the wedding. Jim Rogers also entered into a "mixed" marriage, only this time the family objected because he was not Jewish. Rogers had met his wife while traveling through Europe. When they announced their engagement, her mother traveled all the way to Oxford to confront Rogers and try to undo it. As Rogers recalled, her family "were just mortified that she was so involved with this 'goy,' just could not bear it, even when we got married. We did, but they were right." The marriage lasted only three years.[21]

As Tyler Smith and Stephen Bingham discovered, a turn to 1960s activism could take its toll on a new marriage. In other, unexpected ways, changing mores caught up with some members of the class of '64. Gordon Davis, for instance, after only a short marriage, discovered that his wife had "lit out for Haight-Ashbury with an impecunious boyfriend she'd known for two weeks, leaving behind everything she couldn't stuff into a backpack and the boot of her Porsche."[22] Michael Arons thought he represented a solid alternative as a family man for the woman he married, an educational administrator, while completing his residency in psychiatry at Harvard. Before completing her undergraduate degree at Berkeley in 1966, his wife had lived with what Arons described as "a long-haired, dope-smoking philosophy graduate student." Married after a short courtship in 1970, the couple had two children and settled down in Reston, Virginia, to the great satisfaction of her parents, whose other daughter's marriage, to the fellow medical resident who had introduced Arons to his wife, had ended. With the death of Arons's mother-in-law, however, any reservations his restive wife had about divorce dissipated. She left the marriage, very much to his disappointment. He described the experience as "especially ironic and sad since having a wonderful family life was my highest priority."[23]

In line with national trends, divorce was no stranger to this class. As David Steigerwald puts it, "The old song that unhappy couples should stick it out 'because of the kids' hardly played in the age of liberation."[24] By the time of '64's tenth reunion, 6 percent of those reporting had already ended a marriage. Fifteen years later, another survey reported that the overwhelming number, 345 of 400 reporting, were married.[25] Of these, however, eighty-seven were in second marriages, and another eight were in their third. Fifty-three were not married, with this group including at least some of the fourteen self-identified homosexuals and possibly the three who identified as bisexual. Another fifteen admitted to be contemplating divorce. About a quarter surveyed, 121, admitted to having had extramarital affairs; 214 said they had not. Significantly, wives who responded to the survey, while recording a similar rate of divorce to the men (41 of 192), reported a lower level of infidelity (28 of 193). Not only that, women tended to trust their husbands more than they should have. Although the number of men and women surveyed pretty much matched each other in the number of spouses who suspected infidelity (31 men, 28 women), a much larger number of men, 121, admitted infidelity than women, 23.[26]

This last statistic suggested that while marriage bonds were loosening generally, men retained more control over their partnerships than women, a reasonable conclusion when women were still largely expected to follow the lead of their husband's professional life.[27] That being said, the advent of the

women's movement did not leave them untouched. Reflecting the restructur-
ing of the household economy that marked the period since their graduation,
the same 1989 poll reported that women, by a 2–1 margin, worked.[28] A comparable number, 60.4 percent, confirmed that feminism and "liberation" had
affected their marriages. Nearly 59 percent of the men answered the same
question affirmatively. As '64's Donald Edwards recollects, the most pervasive topic of conversation among his classmates returning to New Haven for
their tenth reunion was the change in rules between the sexes. As he put it,
describing the relationship with his wife, a 1963 Wellesley graduate whom he
met as a blind date to his senior year prom, "As each of us has changed, our
relationship has changed, and the changes have not been easy." Edwards's wife
found a job where she used the master of arts in teaching degree she earned
at Yale, but when children arrived, she left her full-time position, providing
dance instruction on a part-time basis as the children grew up, and returning
to full-time work as a lay minister only after they had left the home.[29] Her
story of adaptation to the husband's role no doubt was repeated by many of
the 67 percent of women who worked while in a Yale '64 marriage. In this
light, the experience of Lucy Moore is instructive.

* * *

Two days after her marriage to '64's Robert Hilgendorf in June 1968, Moore
and her husband jumped into a brand-new blue-and-white Ford Bronco and
headed west, from Cambridge to Chinle, Arizona, the heart of Navajo country. Hilgendorf was one of twenty-four lawyers selected for a new government
program designed to provide legal representation to American Indians. The
newlyweds shared both a sense of adventure and a desire to do good. Still
reeling from the assassinations of Martin Luther King and Bobby Kennedy,
they were acutely conscious of the challenges ahead, for themselves and for the
nation. "The country seemed doomed to self-destruction at home and abroad,"
Moore wrote in introducing a memoir of their days on the reservation. "John
F. Kennedy, assassinated just five years earlier, was still an inspiration to many
of us, and we wanted to live up to his expectations, to do something for our
country. We were determined to use our valuable education, our fortunate
background, our youth and energy to improve the lives of others."[30]

Hilgendorf was part of a significant cohort of Yale '64 graduates who chose
the newly formed field of public interest law over private practice. Like others
who arrived at what constituted a foreign country—whether it was a Peace
Corps posting abroad or a domestic inner city or reservation mission—he had
adjustments to make. On his first day at work, he discovered that his effort
to dress respectfully in a coat, white shirt, and tie reminded his first client of

Finding their own "new frontier" in Chinle, Arizona, the Hilgendorfs spent eight intensive years working with Navajos, an experience that grew from their common commitment to service and social justice grounded in the 1960s. Courtesy of Lucy Moore.

Mormon missionaries, who were not especially welcome on the reservation. The alternative of wearing jeans, he was told, would make him look like a cowboy, which, while no closer to the truth, was preferable. Adjustments were made easily enough, and Hilgendorf had little trouble establishing himself in his new community. As Lucy noted, "He had a role that was very clear, at least to himself. He was the first lawyer ever to practice in Chinle. . . . A lawyer didn't wonder where the path was. He just stepped onto it and proceeded." Bob's life of doing good, she reflected, "was easier than mine."[31]

Moore's concern about her own role was typical among her peers. As part of a minority of the 1966 Radcliffe graduates who chose not to continue in graduate school, Moore first took a job working with Robert Coles, the Harvard child psychiatrist, professor, and author who had been actively involved in Freedom Summer in 1964. As she dated Bob Hilgendorf, she moved on to a position at the Boston Welfare Department, giving away, as she put it, as much money as she could to needy clients in Roxbury and Dorchester. Her work represented a logical extension of her upbringing by socially progressive parents in Seattle and her commitments as an undergraduate to civil rights and antiwar activism. But, she recalled, "I was not passionate about anything related to a career. I assumed I would find interesting things to do with my life and wasn't worried about what those things might be. When Bob and I got married I thought, 'Ah-ha! This is what I am supposed to do next.'" Like so many women before her, it seemed natural to go along with her husband's choices, which fortunately in this case she supported wholeheartedly.

But now, thrown into an entirely different world from the one she had become accustomed to as a young adult, she was faced with the challenge of establishing her own identity.[32]

Moore did indeed find interesting things to do in Chinle that were satisfying both to her and Bob. As their presence in Navajo country extended well beyond their original two-year commitment, she found work, attended to traditional domestic chores, and bore two children. In a variety of ways, too, she became a force in the community. She worked as a Head Start teacher, sold car insurance, helped start a day care center, and served two terms as justice of the peace. She found the decision to leave after eight years wrenching, but she justified the move to New Mexico, where Bob joined the staff of the state attorney general for a few years before entering private practice, as a chance to recalibrate her frenetic life, a decision reenforced by a life-threatening illness to the younger of the couple's two sons.

As part of the adjustment, Lucy took up woodworking. Although the toys she made found customers, the work never paid enough to cover the cost of the wood, let alone sustain a business. Bob encouraged Lucy to find a more professional career, both for her sake and the sake of the family. He suggested she go to law school, but she declined. The thought of more school and of joining a mainstream profession did not appeal to her. When Bob persisted with the idea of law school, she compromised and worked as a paralegal for several years. That adjustment made, the marriage still did not last. With the children older, Lucy charted her own way by helping found an environmental mediation firm. She speculates that being single may have contributed to her taking more seriously the idea of a career. Over the next two decades she built her mediation practice and has become one of the leading mediators of complex multiparty conflicts in the country.[33]

Moore's challenge to go beyond an establishment career, even as she assumed the traditional roles of wife and mother, was central to the changes affecting women in the 1960s and thereafter. Miriam Horn puts it well in her account of Hillary Clinton's 1969 class at Wellesley. The question for this generation of women, Horn notes, was how to reconcile "their youthful aversion to the establishment and what Hillary called in her commencement speech 'our prevailing acquisitive, competitive corporate life' with their determination to claim power for women, break into male professions, support themselves, provide well for their children, change the world. . . . The women of '69 recognize themselves as characters in the present drama over the meaning of gender, over family structure and the rearing of children, over the relationship between the self and society, between the private and public realms."[34] Yale men who married or entered long-term partnerships faced the same set of questions, though from an entirely different position. Their role as full-time

workers was assumed and virtually assured, they thought, with the right education and connections. As the sexual revolution advanced and deepened out
of the 1960s, however, the standards by which their parents had lived and they
had come of age absorbing were sharply challenged.

As part of the effort to work through issues of marriage and the family,
Moore helped form a women's group while in Chinle, but it did not prove
central to her life. In the end, she recalled, "I found I had little sympathy
for the women's movement, which seemed something of a luxury belonging
to another world where day-to-day survival was not the norm, as it was in
Chinle. I had some pride in believing that if you want to have an impact and get
something done, you can figure out how to do it, even if you are sitting in the
middle of Navajo Country with no particular degree in anything. I thought
I had a more realistic, let's-get-things done, down-to-earth attitude, and the
women's movement sounded academic and whiney to me at the time."[35]

Owen O'Donnell's wife, Kristina, also joined a women's group in the
1960s. When she graduated from Stanford, one of a small group of women
undergraduates there in the mid-1960s, she was told she could be a nurse or
a teacher. In assuming the latter role, she started teaching social studies at
Novato High School in Marin County, outside San Francisco. Responding to
the dramatic social changes taking place in that city, where Owen was starting
his career as a lawyer after graduating from Stanford Law School, she invited
a gay speaker to the school. When the school blocked her effort, she filed suit
through the American Civil Liberties Union. When that effort failed for reasons that had little to do with the content of the case, she began to consider
other careers. Her change in status coincided with the emergence of feminism
and her decision to join a women's consciousness-raising group. Her husband
recalled being comfortable enough with his wife's embrace of feminism, realizing that raising children was a two-person job. But he felt excluded from
his wife's activities with the other women when she refused to discuss them,
describing her attitude in retrospect as militant. Not to be deterred, he contacted the husband of one of the other women in the group to suggest forming
a group of their own.[36]

Kristina O'Donnell's women's meetings lasted only six months. In line
with earlier patterns of women's work, at least initially, she shifted her career,
to accommodate the domestic demands of her marriage. After her first
child was born, he cried endlessly when she left the house for her teaching
job. Determined not to let that happen again with the second child, she quit
teaching and opened a poster gallery with her sister in San Francisco, where
she could watch her child during business hours. For his first year and a half,
he napped during the day in the gallery's kitchen. When that business failed
to prosper, Kristina went to work for a nonprofit organization that placed

volunteers in public schools. Drawn into fund-raising, she found that she was good at it. She concluded that if she had to work so hard to raise money for someone else, she ought to try making some money herself. Once relieved of the burdens of early child rearing, she did just that, becoming a highly successful retail broker and a pioneer among women employees at Merrill Lynch's San Francisco office.

Owen O'Donnell, in the meantime, stayed with his men's group, meeting every Tuesday night for a dozen years. Consisting of fewer than a dozen men—all heterosexual—the group considered a range of issues, including careers, but the focus was primarily marriage and sex. Nothing was held back—whether it was issues with a spouse or girlfriend, or an extramarital affair. O'Donnell found the experience helped him release some of the tensions within his marriage by providing an outlet outside it, concluding that the effort strengthened his commitment over time. Having been part of a senior society at Yale helped make him comfortable in such discussions, he recalled, but he was further assisted by an outside participant clearly not a part of the undergraduate experience: a family therapist. For six years, this therapist joined the group, leaving periodically when the men felt she had met their needs, only to be asked to return again. According to O'Donnell, she brought a feminist point of view to discussions and "pushed us to think about our relationship with women and how we dealt with them."[37] His marriage not only survived over time; it thrived. Whether it was the existence of peer groups outside the marriage that boosted the O'Donnell marriage, clearly the couple was not alone in experiencing the vicissitudes of changing relations between the sexes, a point brought home especially in the life of Nicholas Danforth.

* * *

Writing under the heading "Daddy, where were you during the war of the sexes? Or, how I infiltrated the women's movement—and lived to tell about it," Nicholas Danforth, in his contribution to the Yale twenty-fifth reunion book, detailed his encounters with feminism, fatherhood, and family, in his personal as well as his professional life. "Remember the so-called women's movement?" he asked. "Turns out it was a movement for men, too, which makes it twice as important, twice as complicated. It was a movement which I think affected me more than most classmates, because I actually focused my work on problems related to the sexes." Recounting a two-year stay, immediately following graduate work at Columbia, in Lesotho, where women bore the double burden of working eighty-hour weeks for "slave wages" while still managing family duties, Danforth detailed how he came to apply this dramatic lesson of unfairness to a variety of circumstances, from supporting the fight to make abortion legal to efforts to promote sexual abstinence among African men. Reflecting the feminist mantra "the personal is the political," he sought to apply in his own family the values he promoted publicly. Proud of his role as a committed parent, he nonetheless alluded to a dark side in concluding his class reunion book submission:

> The noisy street battle of the sexes of the '60s and '70s, like the Vietnam war, continues to be fought, but now without fireworks, inside the home. The misunderstanding and backlash resulting from the idea of breaking out of traditional sex roles may be subdued, but it is persistent. For me this issue is close to home—as well as to my work. My wife and I, as liberated from traditional roles as any couple I know, do not find it easy to fulfill each other's images of spouse. Once attracted to her self-reliance and commitment to work, I find her as George Gilder warned I would, too immersed in work, important though it is, and spending too little time with family. She appreciates the role I play as primary parent, and I appreciate that she earns twice as much as me, but we both wonder sometimes that maybe the conservatives were right, that maybe our role reversal has gone too far.[38]

The personal dilemma conveyed at the heart of Danforth's reunion statement had its roots in a complex and conflicted sexual history, which in different ways reflects the transitional period of the early 1960s. Raised in an old family farmhouse built in stages beginning in 1760, he shared a single bathroom in the intense, often intimate presence of three sisters. Consequently Danforth discovered secrets girls rarely shared with male counterparts and became aware, from an early age, of the social and psychological as well as physical makeup of the "opposite" sex. What could have been a sexual awakening was tempered by his socialization according to well-established New England norms of propriety. Lest he forget, when his summer experience with Crossroads Africa at age eighteen resulted in close friendships with two African American women, his father, fearing either relationship would end in pregnancy, sent him a telegram reminding him of his youth and his Yankee roots. The relationships remained platonic, but through them the connections between gender, sexuality, and race began to coalesce in Danforth's mind.

At Yale in the early 1960s, Danforth felt liberated, identifying with the newly independent nations he had visited, but at the same time his proper Bostonian upbringing, emphasizing delayed gratification, continued to affect his sexual growth. If he finally broke his resolve to remain a virgin (ironically, with the persuasive daughter of a psychiatrist, on her father's office couch, while her father was out of town), he maintained his reserve into his early years out of college. While attending graduate school in New York, he fell in love with a lifelong friend, but he refused to go beyond petting. Instead, he put the object of his affection high on a spiritual pedestal. Disappointed in what she apparently saw as his indecision and insecurity, she broke off the relationship to marry an old boyfriend, subsequently bearing him two children.

Danforth's initial experience in Africa prompted his decision to take up the new area of black studies within Yale's American Studies program, and at graduation he pursued a master's degree in international relations and African Studies at Columbia. His first intense love affair behind him, he rejected job offers from the Foreign Service and the CIA because of his objections to the Vietnam War. Instead, he accepted a Ford Foundation grant to work in the government of the newly independent nation of Lesotho, inside South Africa, where another personal relationship deepened his interest in international development, particularly women's rights, as well as sexual and reproductive health.

Danforth worked with several of the new Lesotho government ministries to promote community development, small industries, diamond mining, and adult education. Through his work, he gained a good deal of expertise that would serve to advance his career over time as a writer and consultant. It was the contact, which grew sexually intimate over time, with a local woman working with him in the government, however, that had the most significant impact on his avocation. One of the first Zulu women to graduate from the local university, she opened his eyes to African women's lives, including their roles, usually as single mothers and heads of household, and their relationships with men, most of whom worked outside Lesotho in South African mines and factories. She explained many of the economic, political, emotional, and sexual problems faced by girls and women, especially the countless poor, rural, and divorced women throughout Africa whose husbands had abandoned them, beaten them, neglected them for other wives, or were simply unable to earn enough to support them or their children.[39]

Returning to the United States in 1969, too old to be drafted, Danforth found a temporary position with New York Mayor John Lindsay's Office of Environmental Affairs, where he set up an internship program in advance of the first Earth Day being planned for 1970. His real interest, however, was in the new field of "women and development," especially as it related to couples' reproductive and sexual health, including family planning. Naturally drawn to the emerging feminist movement, he joined the New York chapter of the National Organization for Women, not, however, without upsetting some female members who at first did not welcome his presence at their meetings.

Finding the opportunity at the Century Foundation to study women in the U.S. labor force, he seemed to be settling into a recognizable career path. That changed through his association with Roy Lucas, a recent graduate of New York Law School, who shared Danforth's office and his interest in women's reproductive rights.

As a law student, Lucas had developed a legal theory that the implied right to privacy established in the 1965 *Griswold* case overturning Connecticut's ban on the use of contraceptives should also apply to the right of a woman, and her doctor, to terminate a pregnancy. Through many conversations over lunch the two men formed a plan. Promising to do the legal research and writing if Danforth would raise funds and manage staffing and budgets, Lucas persuaded him to join in establishing the James Madison Constitutional Law Institute, a nonprofit law foundation. The institute's primary purpose was to advance a state abortion ruling to consideration before the U.S. Supreme Court.

The Madison Institute set up its office in a small town house at 4 Patchin Place in the West Village, the home of poet e.e. cummings from 1924 until his death in 1962. It was as cramped as the funds they raised for the cause. The staff initially consisted of Lucas as president, Danforth as vice president, and two part-time clerks. They were joined in 1971 by three barely paid summer interns, including a male friend of Danforth's from Yale Law School. Danforth remembers wondering constantly where money to sustain the work of the institute would come from. Although the board of directors included a few impressive names, including the noted New Deal lawyer Thomas "Tommy the Cork" Corcoran, very few foundations or individual donors were confident enough in the organization and its approach to make donations. Most feminist groups were also skeptical. Danforth met Betty Friedan at a mutual friend's party in Greenwich Village, but instead of gaining her support, he was regaled by Friedan's displeasure that the Madison Institute was staffed largely by men.

The Supreme Court announced in 1970 that it would review two "class action" cases representing pregnant women whose rights had been restricted: *Doe v. Bolton* from Georgia, whose more liberal law allowed some abortions, and *Roe v. Wade* from Texas, whose strict law prohibited all abortions except to save the life of the mother. Lucas had other legal obligations, and as the court date approached in the summer of 1971 and work on the *Roe* brief languished, he appealed to Sarah Weddington, a twenty-six-year-old lawyer who had argued the original Texas case, for help. At the insistence of other supporters of the effort, she was designated as the sole attorney to argue the case, much to Lucas's displeasure. Danforth, however, recognized the appropriateness of the shift, siding with Weddington while encouraging Lucas to cooperate with her. In her book about those years, Weddington described Danforth as "the glue that held the institute together" during the difficult days leading up to the argument before the court.[40]

For his part, Danforth struggled to complete the nonlegal social science research for the appendix that accompanied the *Roe* brief, an unusual and somewhat controversial effort to provide the justices background data showing that existing state abortion restrictions discriminated against poor, rural, and younger women and made abortion unsafe and costly without preventing most illegal abortions from happening. When the *Roe* brief and appendix, along with the *Doe* brief from the attorneys in Georgia, were finally completed just in time, the institute could not afford to pay the printers the overtime they required. At the last minute Danforth was able to secure a $15,000 donation from a respected Boston philanthropist, Thomas Cabot, who later told an audience at MIT that it was one of the smallest but most important donations he ever made. The brief arrived just in time.

Weddington argued *Roe* effectively in 1971 but before only seven justices; so, after President Nixon appointed Justices Rehnquist and Powell, she had to argue the case a second time in October 1972 in front of the full bench. By then the institute, after being renamed the Population Law Center, with Danforth as the executive director, had run out of funds and was about to close. Pessimistic about *Roe*'s prospects, Danforth reacted with tears of joy when he walked out of his apartment on the morning of January 22, 1973, and saw the banner headline that *Roe* had carried by a 7–2 margin. Years later, when Danforth again met Betty Friedan, she congratulated him for his role in *Roe* and apologized for her earlier criticism.

Danforth's nascent feminism, as it advanced from his African experience and materialized in the *Roe* case, gained personal strength through the developing relationship with his future wife, Turid Sato, a fellow graduate of Columbia's international affairs program. The two had met at an alumni party shortly after Danforth's return from Lesotho. A native of Norway, a graduate of Sarah Lawrence, and one of the first women admitted to the Young Professional Program at the World Bank, she impressed Danforth immediately. At a second encounter in November 1969, the two joined the massive "new mobilization" protest in Washington against the war in Vietnam. Danforth remembers thinking that if so many international development professionals in Washington were women like her—antiwar, pro-choice, politically savvy environmental activists—he had found his professional niche. The relationship culminated sexually for the first time three years later when Turid joined Nick for Christmas while visiting him in Boston, where he was studying for a second master's degree at the Harvard School of Graduate Education.

Nick Danforth, with Betty Friedan, at the UN Conference on Women, Beijing, 1995. Once cool to his work at the Madison Institute on behalf of the winning side in *Roe v. Wade*, Friedan ultimately made peace with Danforth and his efforts on behalf of women's equity. Courtesy of Nicholas Danforth.

The following year Danforth worked in the Middle East and Asia for the UN Population Fund on a global program to encourage male involvement in family planning and mother-child health. Sato traveled for the World Bank, mostly to Africa. They had romantic meetings in Switzerland, France, Thailand, and Norway, and decided during a particularly happy week together near St. Tropez in 1974 that they would get married at his family's farm outside Boston the following year. At a traditional Norwegian-style wedding ceremony in the garden, they ended their three-day celebration galloping off into the sunset in traditional Norwegian regalia on one black and one white horse. Like so many of their peers, they placed notice of their marriage in the *New York Times*.[41]

The honeymoon seemed to continue for years. Nick's international consulting for the UN, Planned Parenthood, and USAID, combined with Turid's increasing World Bank responsibilities in Africa, Asia, and Latin America took them to many exotic spots, and the World Bank paid for first-class travel for both of them to Norway for "home leave." In 1980, through his continued friendship with Sarah Weddington, who was then advising President Jimmy Carter on women's issues, Danforth was selected by the Carter administration as the sole nongovernmental male delegate representing the United States at a UN Conference on Women, held in Copenhagen. Ironically, although Nick planned to stay in his hotel with Turid, a World Bank delegate, she was barred by security from joining him because she had not taken his name.

The couple remained sexually happy and faithful in those years, with the exception of some minor dalliances both enjoyed, without jealousy, during their many years of separate travels. Recalling the spirit of the advancing sexual revolution, Danforth remembers one late summer afternoon in the mid to late 1970s, when two other couples joined him and Sato on the family farm for the usual skinny-dip in true Nordic style. Afterward the couples shared showers together, then sat naked in front of a warm fire. Someone passed around a marijuana joint, which they all shared with plenty of laughter. Most of the six took turns giving each other gentle massages, including some casual sexual touching. Afterward, when they had dressed and the marijuana had worn off, they sat down together for supper and talked about what had happened. All agreed that they were surprised to find they were not shocked or jealous at the pleasant, mildly erotic intimacies all but one of them had shared. From that point on, both Nick and Turid hardly ever worried about brief sexual intimacy with others, particularly when one or the other was "on the road," as long as pregnancy and infection were avoided.

This openness continued for years. After buying a town house on Embassy Row in the Kalorama section of Washington, Nick and Turid carried on their Scandinavian traditions by installing a four-person sauna on their top floor and a redwood hot tub for six on their roof deck. They often joined their many guests, women and men, naked in their tub after a sauna, under the moon and stars, looking out over the rooftops toward the Capitol, the Washington Monument, the Potomac River, and Virginia beyond. Turid was particularly popular with her foreign male World Bank colleagues, and she regularly invited, on separate occasions, two different members of the House of Representatives (both, fortunately, liberal Republicans) for a jog and dinner followed by a sauna and a soak. Nick always approved, proud that Turid attracted such interesting guests, and often joined them. He remembers, in addition to the two congressmen, various ambassadors and diplomats, several top Washington lawyers, a few African government ministers, a spouse of a current prime minister, a future prime minister, and a future male U.S. senator who was invited by a neighbor. All seemed to enjoy their rather famous hot tub, though not simultaneously, during those festive and sometimes patriotic occasions, such as the Fourth of July.

During the 1970s, Nick and Turid both felt their lives were too complicated to contemplate having a child, but as she approached forty, Turid starting talking about her desire to be a mother, at one point threatening to leave Nick if he resisted. So in 1980 she took a sabbatical from the World Bank, moved to the Boston farm with Nick, and studied international energy issues at MIT. With careful, couple-focused family planning she became pregnant, extending her leave another six months to facilitate the transition. Their child, Thomas, was born two months early, weighing only three pounds, in September 1982.

Turid was unconscious during the emergency delivery, but Nick rushed to the delivery room in time to see his son born. "I was pouring tears," he recalled. "I was so into that tiny but beautiful boy, bright pink, screaming for life, but I was so scared he might not survive. I'd seen several babies born in African hospitals, and I'd heard how men could be converted to loving, life-long fatherhood in the delivery room, but still, this experience with my own son was amazing." Turid, on the other hand, "was out cold. As I'd quickly attached to Tom, she emerged from anesthesia sort of out of it and terribly weepy. I had only once seen this tough, strong, Viking woman so sad, when she wept at the grave of her father in Norway where he died in the war."[42]

Thomas proved a dynamic addition to the family, drawing Nick's ever greater affection. In a 2011 interview with me, Nick admitted that he could not be described fully as the primary parent (as he had claimed in his twenty-fifth reunion book), but he did affirm that he often played with Tom in ways that left Turid on the sidelines. Nick took major responsibility for tracking Thomas's progress in school, gymnastics, karate, and music lessons. As a couple, both parents relied on a nanny, often Norwegian, to be with Tom when schedules required it. They staggered international trips, however, so that one parent would always be home, and several times they took him along. Tom had been around the world twice by the time he was five and went to visit his family in Norway every year, either in summer or at Christmas.

During this period, Turid began spending more and more time with one of her World Bank colleagues, both while they were in Washington and often during travel abroad. Nick had been the colleague's friend too, and they sometimes all worked together on international development. One night after the three dined out together, Turid confessed that she had been secretly holding hands with her colleague. She told Nick she was in love and wanted a divorce. Nick resisted for weeks, arguing that they had much to build on as a family. She insisted on separating, however, saying she wanted to be with her colleague and admitting he had secretly been her lover for years, sleeping together on World Bank missions and even at the family home while Nick and Tom were asleep nearby. In 1990 they each hired respected lawyers who skillfully fanned the flames associated with their separation. Their divorce was nasty, costly, and very complicated.

Despite Nick's efforts to share custody of Tom, after the divorce he was only allowed to see his son every other weekend. For seven years Nick and Turid's relationship remained strained. Turid left the World Bank to start a consulting business with her partner. Nick moved to New York for two years, where he became the first full-time USAID consultant focusing on engaging men in sexual and reproductive health. He then moved back to the fifteen-acre family farm near Boston, which had now become his own. He continued to see Tom on most weekends and vacations, but Tom went to Washington schools and lived primarily with Turid and her partner in the Washington home.

In 1997 disaster struck. A former employee of Turid's, who for many years had also been a close family friend, had become deeply depressed. He had a falling out with both Turid and her partner over money and other personal squabbles. One afternoon in October, the employee entered the home office he had once shared with Turid and her partner, brandished a pistol he had easily bought in Virginia, and—in front of two witnesses—shot Turid dead before killing himself. Thomas, age fourteen, returned from school to a home surrounded with the police cars. Without telling him what had happened, officers took him to a police station for questioning. After four traumatic hours of confused questions, he was finally told that his mother and her killer, his friend from childhood, were both dead.[43]

Nick brought Tom to live with him in the family home in Massachusetts, where they shared many happy times. But Tom refused all therapy for what was clearly post-traumatic stress following his mother's murder. He failed to graduate from high school or attend college. After smoking marijuana, Tom became addicted to heroin for over two years and died of an overdose in 2008.

For over two decades Nick Danforth has lived with his partner, Robin Jones, a highly respected doctor at Massachusetts General Hospital in Boston who has been repeatedly selected as one of Boston's top child neurologists. Young patients and parents visit her from many states and countries. For a while in her forties she had wanted a child; Nick preferred otherwise. Now they are both content to be child-free. She is glad to see children as patients all day instead of being a full-time parent

Danforth continues to work on sexual and reproductive behavior change as a consultant and researcher, does occasional consulting overseas, and is in his second decade as a resident scholar in the Woman's Studies Research Center at Brandeis University. He continues to see himself as a feminist, favoring major changes in gender roles and relationships. He deplores the widespread tendency to rush into romanticized, sexualized marriages, and he does not object to the many young people who postpone marriage and parenting or choose to help prevent climate change by remaining child-free. He particularly criticizes youth who have been socialized to think they must be married and have children to be happy and what he considers society's overemphasis on having many children. He laments statistics indicating that despite all the forms of birth control now widely available to prevent or terminate pregnancy (and likely to become more available under the Affordable Care Act), the United States continues to have far higher rates of unintended and teenage pregnancies than other industrialized countries. Still very close to his three sisters, who live near him, he continues to use the old family bathroom, noting "It's got newer fixtures, but only one female in it now."[44]

* * *

Nick Danforth's adaptation to new sexual mores in his personal as well as his professional life was complicated and sometimes painful, but it was no more complex than the challenge gays from traditional backgrounds had adjusting to a universe the 1960s had upended. By any external measure, '64's Robert Ball's marriage to Julia Wilson and the birth of a daughter in 1970 followed a normal trajectory. With most of the work for a PhD in Spanish and comparative literature behind him, Ball began teaching at Stanford, where he published a number of scholarly articles and settled into what appeared to be the good California life. Not long into his marriage, though, he met another man in group therapy, who like him was married with a child. Before long they were lovers, hiding their relationship from their spouses for nearly a year before they each sought a divorce in order to be with one another. As Ball put it, "My wife was not amused." Once liberated, the two men threw themselves into the San Francisco gay scene, including the city's notorious bathhouse culture. There they embraced recreational sex until the AIDS epidemic cast a pall over them and their gay comrades. Thankful to have survived the epidemic and eager to start life anew with children they had adopted, Ball and his partner moved from the Bay Area to a 535-acre ranch in Bozeman, Montana. As he wrote in his submission to his twenty-fifth reunion book, "If anyone had told this devoutly Catholic bookworm in 1964 that I would end up as a sheep rancher in Montana, in a longer-term quasi-marital relationship with another man, with four adopted disabled boys that I share with him, I would have laughed myself sick!"[45]

Ball's breakout from closeted homosexuality to liberation was facilitated by the shift in mores after his graduation. At Yale, he did everything he could to repress his feelings, including a spiritual quest that led him from the rigid Southern Baptist tradition he had grown up with into the Catholic Church, where he thought he would find support, at least for his intellectual interests in philosophy and religion. He made the commitment formally his senior year after spending the previous year in Zurich learning Greek, specifically to advance his reading of the Bible, and German to read philosophy and religion. He learned soon enough that the Catholic Church was not congenial and concluded that his decision had been motivated in large part by an effort to deal with his own sexuality. On discovering their son's orientation by reading a letter sent to him by a classmate he had had a clandestine encounter with between his junior and senior years, Ball's parents acted forcefully by sending him to a psychotherapist for treatment. Ball acquiesced sufficiently to take a teaching job out of college for two years at Governor Dummer Academy (now the Governor's Academy) so he could continue to see his therapist in nearby Newton, Massachusetts. When the therapist declared him "cured," Ball proceeded to marry in 1967.[46]

Ball came from an extended family, which included Ralph Ball, his father's gay younger brother. Though never disinherited, Ralph was clearly marginalized in the family. He moved to New York, where he lived a flamboyant life and acted, as Robert Ball put it, something like a sissy. Ball knew he did not want to be like his Uncle Ralph, but there were few alternative models for his generation. After he left his marriage and committed to his partner, the two of them decided to form a family for others who had been rejected. They did so working through Aid to Adoption for Special Kids, a favorite charity of Henry Winkler (Fonz of *Happy Days*). In 1984 they got their first referral after several rejections. Their son was not violent, but he was difficult, and he was about to be ejected from a group home. Ball and his partner felt that the Bay Area was not an ideal place to bring up children with difficult life histories, so they decided to move to Montana. Ultimately, they adopted five children, ranging in age from eight to fourteen.

Once he divorced, Ball realized he could not afford to support his former wife and child on a university salary, so he became a stockbroker, doing well enough to sustain his new life before and after moving to Bozeman. But the pressures of his new family were tremendous, and they took their toll. After most of two decades together, Ball and his partner, both feeling burned out, separated. Ball subsequently moved to Minneapolis, where, through his former partner, he met Mark Schuler, a neuropsychologist. The new relationship solidified, and on August 24, 2013, three months after Minnesota approved gay marriage, the two men married. "We wanted to project our belief that we were 'married' in reality many years ago and society is just now catching up to it," Ball reflected. One of his five adopted children is gay. He remains close to his daughter by marriage, although she has complained that her needs were pushed aside all too often by the many demands of Ball's adopted children. Although more a sympathizer than an activist for gay rights, Ball marched together with his ex-wife and his eight-year-old daughter in 1978 to protest

Proposition 6, which would have banned gays and lesbians, and possibly any-one who supported gay rights, from working in California's public schools.[47]

Unlike Ball, Colston Young never married, touting his situation as the best of all worlds in an extended submission to his tenth reunion book. A stellar athlete at the Lawrenceville School in New Jersey and at Yale, where he let-tered in lacrosse and mingled jauntily with fellow athletes in Delta Kappa Epsilon, Young returned to Lawrenceville as a member of the development office and history faculty before leaving to take a law degree at the University of Virginia. After two years in a San Francisco law firm, he joined the Public Defender's Office in Alameda County. Well aware of the paths his classmates were taking, he reported in 1974 that he remained unmarried, "though cer-tainly not without attachments of varying duration. Gone are expectations of fatherhood, aspirations of substantial wealth, and the felt need to do many things expected by 'others.'" To make his point especially clear, he addressed his classmates by congratulating

> those of you who are finding fulfillment in wife and children, and I congratulate myself for the self-knowledge that I prefer the ridicu-lously high degree of personal freedom I now enjoy to the restraints and routine of raising a family and especially for having learned that truth without dragging any other humans in on an unsuccessful attempt to live out that scenario. If the price of such freedom were loneliness, then the alternative would be more tempting. . . . There is such a joy in creating new relationships that grow into intimacy and in living through the natural duration of passion and excitement and caring, however brief or extended, that the term "married bliss" strikes me as a contradiction.

No one who knew Young in college would have questioned his sexuality as anything but hetero, and yet news of his death in 1992, conveyed by his older sister, presented quite a different picture. "As an openly gay man since the 1970s, he must have known the sting of discrimination but he never lost his sense of pride," she reported. "He had a marvelous style and he exuded confidence. . . . The year he died, one of the millions of victims of the AIDS plague, he was named California Defender of the Year by the California Public Defenders Association."[48]

* * *

One of the lasting consequences of the sexual revolution was the way fluid relationships between the sexes could lead to reinvention. Michael Price, for instance, reported in 1998 not just the graduation of his two children from college the same day, but the arrival of a newborn, now twenty months, her mother "a Peruvian woman now living in Boston who I have been see-ing for several years—since soon after my separation from my now ex-wife." Confessing that he considered divorce "one of the few changes recently which I do not look upon as positive," he noted finally a surprise when "three years ago I learned I had a 31-year-old Ethiopian daughter from my time there in the Peace Corps." Now located in Ontario, Price's daughter had visited him in Boston, and he subsequently visited her and his granddaughter in Canada. "After the initial shock, it has made my life richer," he concluded.[49]

Jim Rogers did not report to his classmates his second marriage, in 1977, a partnership he entered into ninety days after the two met. The marriage lasted only three years. Rogers made the most of his bachelorhood in subse-quent years, however, detailing in a best-selling book his adventures traveling around the world on a motorcycle with a woman he said he loved and who was a good deal younger than he was. That romance ended, and he did not marry again until 2000, this time to another younger woman. For the new millennium, he became the father of two children, who he determined ought to be trained from infancy in Mandarin. To assure the best results, the family moved from New York City to Singapore.[50] Even more striking was Brooks Carder's acquiescence in a directive to find a new wife, issued by Synanon director Charles Dederich, who insisted on a change in marital partners for all members of the commune. Carder was willing to make the change, even though it took a few tries living with other women before he finally settled down into a lasting second marriage. "It was a great opportunity for me," he recalled. "My first wife was a good person and quite intelligent and produc-tive. I was never really fond of her. I just didn't like to talk to her. Through that process I ended up with my present wife, not immediately but eventually, and I have been happily married for thirty years."[51]

With the model of a professional mother before him, a gynecologist who taught a pioneer course on marriage and the family at Ohio State University, Peter Harding was very much committed to establishing an equal relationship with his wife, Peggy, whom he married in 1971, noting in his tenth reunion book, "The women's movement affects my life by helping to redefine men and women, giving me as a man more freedom to enjoy my full self." On the way to that union, however, Harding reported experimenting with sex with men as a means, he said, of getting to know his own feminine and more intuitive side. That process continued, he reported, as his wife taught him Gestalt ther-apy. Determined to break the rules that defined his early years, he still consid-ers himself "try-sexual," declaring, "I will try anything."[52]

Even a self-professed conservative could reinvent himself through relationships, and this was especially true of John Armor, whose marital history
was anything but normal, despite the distinction of being the only member
of the class of 1964 to be featured in the *New York Times*'s Wedding of the
Week. In his fourth marriage, and hers, lay a tale of what conservative critics of the sexual revolution were up against. In the months before he died
in 2010, Armor appeared before a number of Tea Party gatherings, dressed
as Ben Franklin, touting an originalist view of the Constitution and urging
his audience to be vigilant in defense of American liberties from the threat
of government coercion. An active blogger and contributor to legal opin-
ions for the American Civil Rights Union, formed in 1998 to counter liberal
civil rights and civil liberties efforts (and whose board of directors included
William Bradford Reynolds), Armor was ideologically pure, driven, and conservative. Marriage was another question. Conservative as he was, Armor was
no Rick Santorum railing against sexual permissiveness rooted in the 1960s.[53]
Rather, he fit the profile of a great number of Americans, who might well be
conservative on a whole range of social and political issues, but whose own
sexual histories could not have been considered mainstream before the sexual
revolution. Hardly a serial womanizer, he was nonetheless a serial husband,
one who despite his keen attention to the details of constitutional law was less
than stellar in making legal arrangements adequate to assuring the well-being
of his wife upon his death.

The reason for the *Times* feature was not the frequency of the marriages
of the two but the circumstances of their first meeting thirty-six years earlier. John was a newly minted lawyer, trying to survive in a newly formed
private practice. Michelle Mead was a twenty-one-year-old student at
Goucher College. They were brought together in court, where Armor was
defending Michelle's estranged husband from charges of assault and battery.
As John sheepishly confessed, "In those days, I would have defended anyone if the check didn't bounce." Despite the adversarial situation, Michelle
was smitten by John, who she thought in those days looked remarkably like
Robert Redford. Armor won the case, but when his client left the country
shortly afterward, he had to contact Michelle regarding the disposition of
personal property left behind in the marital home. Michelle, who had neither a driver's license nor a vehicle, insisted that John help her move her
things from the marital house to her college dorm room. "You got the bas-
tard off," she said flatly. "You owe me one!" To the surprise of both, John
showed up at the Mary Fisher dorm as demanded, in what Michelle later
described as "his hideous lemon yellow station wagon." What should have
been an awkward situation led instead to an almost immediate physical

attraction. As Michelle laughingly recalls about that evening, "He was one happy camper."[54]

At the time John already had three children from his first marriage. Balancing time with them and his burgeoning law practice, as well as dealing with constant interference from his mother, proved a tremendous strain on the relationship. What the *Times* failed to mention was that John met his second wife while engaged to Michelle. The gasoline line flirtation had lasted all night, and although John came home at 5 a.m. the next day repentant and apologetic, Michelle terminated the engagement. John married the buxom former Playboy bunny three months later. Unable to face the prospect of living in the same city as John and his new wife, Michelle left the country for nineteen years, marrying twice before ultimately returning to the United States.

Newly divorced and looking to make a fresh start, Michelle was inspired by Susan Shapiro's *Five Men Who Broke My Heart* to review the men who had once been important to her life. In recalling her own loves lost, she found that John Armor rose to the top of the list. Discovering through an Internet site that he was mounting a challenge to Charles Taylor of North Carolina's Eleventh Congressional District, Michelle contacted John again, quipping "I always knew you'd wind up dead, in jail, or running for Congress." As they exchanged news of themselves, John assured her that he was happily married to his third wife, whom he had met on the Internet when she had written to compliment him on his online essays on conservative politics and the Constitution.

All assurances to the contrary, John's marriage ended swiftly when his third wife decided to move to American Samoa without him. Shortly after her departure, John was flying to Manhattan, where he and Michelle arranged to meet again at her neighborhood Irish pub. Despite the initial shock of how much time had changed them physically, they had a wonderful evening together. John immediately wanted to resume where they had left off, but Michelle was understandably cautious. She had a secure job in New York and was reluctant to make the difficult transition to rural North Carolina, where John was living on the family's country property in Highlands. She did so, however, assuming some of the challenges involved in helping John move his starry but impractical idealism into more practical directions to make himself a credible political candidate. When an Episcopal minister refused to marry the couple because John had not yet been divorced for a year, John suggested marriage at the local county courthouse. Michelle refused, stating "I won't get married in a place where you can get a dog license." She insisted on waiting the full year, which resulted in the church wedding of her dreams and full *New York Times* treatment.

Michelle was no longer the self-described "long-haired hippie chick" John had first met when she was in college, and their seven-year age difference meant they clearly fell on opposite sides of the divide that marked the sexual revolution. John revealed that his primary source of knowledge in sexual matters came from his study of the 1972 illustrated manual *The Joy of Sex*, as well as the "how to" Playboy Advisor.[55] Spontaneity was not his strength, according to Michelle, who said she sometimes had to go to extremes—once dancing in the doorway clad in only a bowler hat—to lure him away from his devotion to Fox News. As drawn to him as she was, Michelle felt that John was not at ease with his own sexuality, a trait he shared with a number of men of his generation with no female siblings, and who compounded the problem by attending all-male prep schools.[56]

John Armor died in August 2010 of complications from colon cancer surgery. As the treatment leading up to the surgery was neither particularly painful nor debilitating, his death came as a shock. Although John had written a hopeful posting about his recovery shortly before he died, he took a sudden, and tragic, turn for the worse. Michelle, who had fought the cancer every step of the way with him, arrived at the hospital five minutes after his death. John was a lawyer who took up all manner of causes throughout his life. By insisting on making his own will, however, he left an impossible situation for his widow. While the original text of the will leaving the majority of his estate to his wife was found on his computer, the executed will, which Michelle had previously seen, was never found. As a result, the house and property in Highlands were sold at auction, as were John's personal effects. Left with only what the state of North Carolina required for a surviving spouse, Michelle was relegated to buying back at auction items to remember John by—his cane, his poker chips, and books that had been personally inscribed to him. Having twice followed John's lead in life, Michelle was now left alone to cope under the most difficult of circumstances.[57]

* * *

Michelle Armor's ability to adapt allowed her to realize personal happiness over the years, but often at the cost of financial security, a situation heightened at the time of John Armor's death. Her disadvantaged position highlights what sociologists have called a patriarchal dividend, an inherent advantage to men not just in monetary terms, but in maintaining authority, respect, and access to institutional power and control over one's life.[58] Despite his own uneven work history, John Armor had both the monetary and social capital to do what he wanted in life, including the pursuit of a number of political interests that offered only limited financial return. His position was strong enough that he appears not to have looked to marriage as social capital at all. That does not mean that he did not care about family. A novel he published in 1988 appeared to project his own desire to broadcast his political voice in a new media age. But behind the story of a blustery broadcaster there lurked the stain of regret, most notably of children distanced from a parent through divorce, a theme that appeared in more than one of his classmates' midlife reunion submissions.[59] Even marital autonomy had its costs, but the advantage still lay with men, as even the most balanced marriages most often involved some significant sacrifice on the woman's part.

Thomas Roderick's union with Maxine Phillips in 1981, for instance, represented a close match in beliefs and interests out of years of activism dating back to the 1960s. A 1967 graduate of Juniata College in Pennsylvania, Phillips secured a graduate degree in mental health journalism from Syracuse University. She met Roderick in 1977 through Judson Memorial Church in Greenwich Village, when he succeeded her as chair of the social concerns committee. Together they became involved in left-wing politics, Phillips with the Democratic Socialist Organizing Committee (DSOC) and Roderick with the New Action Party for Peace, Justice, and Joy, started by his East Harlem Block School colleague Dorothy Stoneman. Both organizations worked to rebuild a progressive agenda in the aftermath of attacks on 1960s idealism during the Nixon years. Through a life-planning course at the church, Phillips decided to leave her position as director of conferences and communications for the Child Welfare League of America and become managing editor of *Democratic Left*, the publication of the DSOC, where she worked closely with its dynamic leader, Michael Harrington.[60] Phillips rose to become DSOC's executive director, then faced a dilemma as the birth of her first child approached in 1985. The couple shared household responsibilities, but Roderick had recently taken up the challenge of building a new organization to teach peacemaking skills to children and teachers in the New York City public schools. So Phillips cut back her professional commitments and became managing editor of *Dissent*, the independent socialist quarterly founded by Irving Howe and Lew Coser in 1953. Never the part-time position it was supposed to be, the *Dissent* job nonetheless offered flexible hours that enabled her to pursue a career, even as she bore the primary burden of domestic duties.[61]

No doubt a number of men moved closer over the years than their fathers ever had to sharing domestic responsibilities. Many saw marriage as a possible crucible for egalitarian ideals, to use historian Jessica Weiss's term, in line with the social changes of their early years out of college. John Hanold suggested as much when he wrote in his tenth reunion book that the women's movement had affected him profoundly. The son of a college-educated woman who gave up her job as a medical researcher to bring up eight children and to support her husband's career rise to the presidency of the Pillsbury Company in Minneapolis, Hanold was determined, as was his wife, Pamela, a Smith graduate, not to repeat the mistakes his parents had made. They consciously shared their financial resources and household responsibilities. When his wife chose to shift careers by pursuing graduate study, John supported the decision over objections from his strong-willed mother, who thought Pam ought to be staying at home with the couple's young children. When John lost his job at Honeywell, just as Pam was accepted into law school, he insisted his wife act on her plans, ultimately making his way through the financial strain when he found another job at Honeywell at lower pay. When illness prevented Pam from taking a full-time job after passing the Minnesota bar, the couple stayed the course together, continuing to act on principles of shared responsibility as well as affection for each other.[62] The Hanolds' life decisions were the product of negotiations within the family. Their marriage continued through difficult times, the product, John asserts, of purposeful decisions on both their parts. Other classmates, demonstrating Weiss's point that modern marriage itself is negotiable, divorced, the great majority of them marrying once again. Even as relationships shifted, however, these men demonstrated Weiss's contention that "male prerogatives of leisure, authority and sex diminished; they by no means disappeared."[63]

* * *

In the drive toward greater gender equity ignited in the 1960s and building strength in the 1970s as these men married and formed families, couples faced the daunting challenge of working through issues of parenting and employment largely on their own. Despite the institution of what William Chafe calls "negative rights" for women as well as African Americans, through the removal of impediments to freedom and equal access to opportunity, more "positive rights," in government, labor, and education, were needed to assure that the opportunities opened through those rights were actually realized. "Thus freedom to attend a law school meant little if the best law firms refused to hire women and blacks, or if promotions were partially determined by business lunches at private clubs," Chafe notes. Ideally, changes toward greater equality within households would be supported externally, but that proved not to be the case. Most businesses resisted the institutionalization of flexible hours, and government was slow to press affirmative action for women in particular, let alone fund day care that would have freed both spouses to pursue full-time employment while they had young children at home. Left largely on their own, couples had to navigate the difficult balance of maximizing income

while also accommodating household duties and the aspirations of both partners. Attempting to overcome the basic incompatibility of the achievement
ethic with the goal of gender equality, husbands, Chafe points out, needed not
only to cooperate in their wives' aspirations, but also accept the loss of an older
pattern of complete service to the male career.[64]

Chafe reports that the issue of gender equity was "particularly relevant to
the young, affluent college graduates who on public opinion polls appeared as
converts to the norm of egalitarian relationships, and who were in a situation
more conducive than most to the development of new modes of male-female
interaction." Certainly his observation applies to Yale '64, though as we have
seen, these men acted unevenly in addressing changing gender roles, a product of their own uneasy position on the emerging cultural divide. In this they
were not alone. Writing on the occasion of the fiftieth anniversary of the publication of *The Feminine Mystique*, Stephanie Coontz reported that progress
toward gender equality and its embrace by the American public stalled in
the 1990s. What resulted, she recounts, were compromises among couples
caught up, as she puts it, "between the hard place of bad working conditions
and the rock wall of politicians' resistance to family-friendly reforms."[65] Most
of the men surveyed in one report she cites, when they realized they could
not achieve an egalitarian ideal, expected their partner to assume primary
responsibility for parenting so they could focus on their work. The members
of Yale '64 would have recognized that situation. If they gained from their
wives' employment and the promise of more satisfying relationships with
their immediate family members, it could also be said of this generation that
the promise of equality between partners was less a reality than a prospect
that it could be different for future generations.

8

Culture Wars and the University

Universities played a critical role in the expansion of the American economy in the years following World War II, advancing knowledge that boosted discoveries of huge importance at home at the same time they contributed to the military research and development called for in the execution of the Cold War abroad. As they became sites of contest during the student rebellion of the 1960s, more than parietal rules and controversial war contracts came under fire. Social controls over students loosened, reflecting changes in prevailing social mores. Curriculums shifted toward greater inclusivity, taking into account the dramatic rights revolutions taking place in the United States and around the world at the time. Some of the most honored campus traditions withered as universities became even more involved in the world outside their once cloistered campuses. Inevitably, such changes, however much they might be accepted within the academy, would be challenged, from alumni, social critics, and legislators. As with so many of the controversial issues stemming from the 1960s, Yale '64 members found themselves centrally involved in the currents of academic change and the subsequent fallout in American culture.

Yale was not immune from change, and one member of the class of 1964 who thought the university had gone too far in bending to the demands of critics was Pierre Canu, an active member of the Yale Political Union's Party of the Right as an undergraduate, who became actively involved in the Goldwater campaign as an aide to the Republican National Committee immediately after graduation. Ten years out of college, he blasted the Yale faculty and administration as

a closed minded little clique of knee jerk radicals and social revolutionaries . . . they have so structured the admissions policies, courses
and degree programs as to foster their particular social, economic,
and political point of view which is totally repugnant to me and, fortunately, is completely rejected by the great majority of our fellow
Americans. . . . Yale is no longer turning out a solid proportion of
well-balanced men (and women) but is instead rapidly becoming the
Mecca of the alienated, the dropouts, the drug culture, the revolutionaries, etc.[1]

As harsh as it was, Canu's critique was not an isolated point of view. As
changes to university policies across the country—many of them in response
to student pressures—advanced out of the 1960s, politicians including most
notably Ronald Reagan and Spiro Agnew made "liberalizing education" the
object of public debate. If both campus protests and external criticism waned
in the 1980s, the criticism of university practice revived in the 1990s as part
of what came to be labeled "culture wars," a phenomenon that extended to
equally liberalizing practices in museums and the arts.[2] At the head of a virtual industry of critics, located largely on the right, were two former *Ramparts*
editors, David Horowitz and Peter Collier, as well as Allan Bloom, Dinesh
D'Souza, and Roger Kimball. In *Tenured Radicals* and an accompanying volume, Kimball deepened the argument circulating in conservative circles that
a generational turn, by undercutting the foundations of liberal learning and
civic affairs, had weakened if not corrupted modern American life. The leading culprits were leftist intellectuals, many of them tenured in the aftermath
of the 1960s upheaval.[3] As literary theorist Brook Thomas describes the conservative backlash, "Just as the Cold War worked to preserve democracy by
containing communism and the War on Drugs hopes to shut off the import
of drugs across the border, so the cultural wars will be won and the American
mind reopened by closing off the subversive influence of disgruntled academics who threaten the purity of the body of great works representing our
cultural heritage."[4]

That position gained support in a 1990 book by former Yale English professor Alvin Kernan, decrying changes in the treatment of American literature. He bemoaned not just contemporary modes of academic discourse
but a much larger shift that extended well beyond universities deep into cultural practice. "Not only our traditional institutions, the family and the law,
religion and the state, have in recent years been coming apart in startling
ways," he asserted. "The death throes of the nuclear family, along with the
changes in other major social institutions, make the death of romantic literature seem but a trifle here."[5] Elsewhere Kernan used similar language to that

used by demographer Daniel Yankelovich to describe changes in intellectual life in the 1960s, shifts of huge tectonic plates—demographic, cultural, and technological—capped by revolutionary challenges to established authority and "'empowering' a much wider intellectual competence." Science, he claimed, set the stage with relatively theory, but postmodern literature "took uncertainty to its nihilistic extremes in the humanities and social science, 'demystifying' traditional knowledge, replacing positivism with relativism, substituting interpretation for facts, and discrediting objectivity in the name of subjectivity."[6] Kernan, and some of the critics he joined, may well have been thinking of his former student, Yale '64's Stephen Greenblatt.

A three-year graduate of Yale College, Greenblatt returned to Yale Graduate School in 1966 after two years of study at Cambridge University, to take up work for his PhD. There he worked under Kernan's advisement, completing his degree in only three years. At a time when Yale's English Department could place its advanced degree candidates virtually any place they wanted, Greenblatt sought a position at Berkeley. He had visited San Francisco the summer before he started his PhD program at Yale and was, in his words, "blown away" by the emerging countercultural scene he witnessed, including concerts by Janis Joplin and Jimi Hendrix. As he looked to his future, he felt drawn by what he described as a "classic California experience of not feeling the need to conform to an entrenched authority structure."[7] He had every right to expect an interview and an offer to follow at the annual Modern Language Association meeting, where job searches officially began. Disappointed that the interview did not materialize, Greenblatt asked Yale's director of graduate placement, Marie Boroff, what had happened. He was startled to hear that the Yale English faculty, anticipating that they were going to make him an offer themselves, had not authorized her to arrange for a Berkeley interview. Flattered as he was by the prospect of remaining with the leading English department in the country, Greenblatt persisted in pursuing a position at Berkeley. In the fall of 1969, he joined the faculty there. The promising son of Yale had rejected the father.[8]

Berkeley in 1969 was volatile, to say the least, a place one literary critic has described as a time capsule that preserved a simulated appearance of the 1960s.[9] For Greenblatt, the place was charged with "a sense of excitement, of disorder, of the dream of reconstituting the world, of the sense that hierarchies were breaking down." He found this mix both maddening and exhilarating. In his second semester, student strikes that turned violent shut down classes on campus, forcing Greenblatt to hold seminars at his home, a political act in itself, as he put it, "one at odds with both the left, which was demanding that classes cease until the university and society were reconstituted, and with the right, which was demanding that order be restored before the university could reopen for business." He did find the opportunity to collaborate with faculty in other departments exciting, however, and the core of his colleagues became close enough that his wife liked to refer to it as his "cell." Reflecting his new associations and the texts they were reading, Greenblatt's teaching diversified to include a course titled "Marxist Aesthetics."[10]

The turn away from Yale and to the left was not entirely surprising. While in England, Greenblatt had studied with the radical historian Raymond Williams, whose commentary on the literary consequences of the class struggles of the seventeenth century Greenblatt found "complicated, subtle, and compelling." At Yale Graduate School, he had bridled under directives to analyze literature for its intrinsic aesthetic qualities following the prevailing mode of New Criticism still dominant at the university. His dissertation, on Sir Walter Raleigh's poetry, though winning the department's highest prize, nonetheless incorporated enough history to suggest that he would not long be representative of the preferred Yale mode of study. In the mid-1970s he met the French critic Michel Foucault, just arrived for his first visit to Berkeley and a special object of Kernan's contempt for treating literature "as a capitalist institution and a disguised instrument to hegemony, to be exposed as mere establishment propaganda."[11] For his part, Greenblatt recounted, "I couldn't believe it! Each sentence was more magical and beautiful than the last. I kept rushing out and saying to friends, 'This guy's amazing!' And they'd ask, 'What's he saying?' And I'd try to explain, but it would sound like I was completely out of my mind." Most striking, Greenblatt reflected later, was "the revelation that even something that seems timeless and universal has a history. Even our most basic and deeply held feelings—toward sex, identity, masculinity, femininity and love, for instance—can be traced to certain historical events and occurrences."[12]

No doubt there were signs of Foucault in Greenblatt's breakthrough book, *Renaissance Self-Fashioning*, which appeared in 1980. A study of the emerging nature of identity in the early modern period, *Self-Fashioning* extended beyond any one theoretical influence, however, to incorporate insights from anthropology and other social sciences. In examining the emerging power of the self in the sixteenth century to determine its own representation, Greenblatt advanced a view of literature suggesting it was socially constructed. Drawing directly from anthropologist Clifford Geertz's assertion that "there is no such thing as a human nature independent of culture," Greenblatt sought to redefine the role of the literary critic. To capture the full value of a text, scholars could no longer examine it in isolation from the world that produced it, as the New Critics had done. Rather, it had to be seen as part of a larger system of public signification. "Language, like other sign systems," he wrote, "is a collective construction; our interpretive task must be to grasp more sensitively the consequences of this fact by investigating both the social presence to the world of the literary text and the social presence of the world in the literary text."[13] Here, his debt to Foucault became clear in the realization "that things that just seem given are not given, that they're made up." In the literary traces of actions as well as words, Greenblatt sought to identify the formation of attitudes—toward love, toward colonialism, toward women—as they have been "made up." Then, reflecting the voice of his own revolutionary times, he reflected, "If they're made up that means they can be changed."[14]

Shortly after *Self-Fashioning* appeared, Greenblatt gave his approach a name: new historicism, which he described as less a doctrine than a practice, asserting that "historicist critics have on the whole have been unwilling to enroll themselves in one or the other of the dominant theoretical camps." In a manner that has proved central to his writing, Greenblatt told a personal story to establish the distinct trajectory of his commitment to this mode of inquiry. Referring to the course he once taught on Marxist aesthetics, he admitted the influences on him of those he described as "troubled in relation to Marx," including the highly influential Walter Benjamin. "I remember someone finally got up and screamed out in class, 'You're either a Bolshevik or a Menshevik—make up your fucking mind,' and then slammed the door. It was a little unsettling, but I thought about it afterwards and realized that I wasn't sure whether I was a Menshevik, but I certainly wasn't a Bolshevik. After that I started to teach courses with names like 'Cultural Poetics.'"[15] Just as his classmate Stephen Bingham found the old Marxist ideology limiting, Greenblatt too turned to an alternative approach for the evaluation of literature, one that would allow critics to "hold on to our aesthetic pleasures" while at the same time advancing "our desire for critical innovation; our interest in contingency, spontaneity, (and) improvisation."[16]

Greenblatt's approach to literature became institutionalized with the founding, in 1983, of the new academic journal *Representations*. Leaving no doubt who was behind the new enterprise, Greenblatt was listed as cochair of the editorial board and was author of the first essay. The journal quickly attracted the scholarship of leading figures in the humanities and established new historicism as a leading approach to literary theory. Not surprisingly, Kernan found fault with the approach, noting that while "my own formalist view was that the primary meaning of any literary work was best found by going right down the middle of a text," new historicists "assume that all writers are politically subversive."[17]

The timing of the new publication was significant. The turbulence of the 1960s may have receded, but the Reagan counterrevolution was very much in effect. Greenblatt was no protester, on the picket lines or in the ghetto, noting in a 2009 interview that he had no illusions that any act of academic discourse could have had the power to force Lyndon Johnson to end the war in Vietnam. Still, there was an edge in his writing that signified a challenge to literary if not political authority. Much more important than addressing contemporary politics, in Greenblatt's mind, was "a necessary change in the discourse of the profession." "It seemed politically important," he recounted,

> that the human imagination was not the possession of a tiny num-
> ber of well-tenured academics and a tiny number of artists, but that
> the whole reason literature existed was because the imagination was
> democratically distributed across large populations in different places,
> including women, as well as men, and gays and Jews and blacks . . .
> the central issue was to understand that the boundaries in which we
> had been trained to study the human imagination were too narrowly
> drawn. We had to grasp that imaginative creation was going on in lots
> of other places and could be detected for good and ill in phantasmatic
> commitments other than the tiny number of books we had identified
> as the canon.[18]

In this belief, he drew the opposition of yet another of his former teachers, Harold Bloom.

Born in 1930 and the recipient of a PhD at Yale in 1955, Bloom was well advanced in a career at Yale that would span more than fifty years, making him, along with Greenblatt—since 2000 university professor of humanities at Harvard University—one of the most visible figures in the profession. As their writing focused on similar topics, the two men necessarily jostled for position within their highly competitive field of inquiry. When he was in New York in 2011 to receive the National Book Award for his immensely successful book, *The Swerve*, Greenblatt told several classmates a striking story about himself. Perhaps it was Greenblatt's absence of credit to Bloom, who originally conceived the idea of identifying the changing path of literary history as a "swerve,"[19] that prompted the story, although it could just have been Greenblatt's own inclination to connect the drama of his own life with that of his writing. Whatever the origin, the scene in question was Princeton University several years earlier. Greenblatt and Bloom were to be featured in a named speaker series. Some days in advance, Greenblatt received from Bloom a copy of his prepared remarks. They were scathing, though not entirely out of character with exchanges the two men had had professionally over the years. Greenblatt prepared a reply in kind. Once given the podium at Princeton, however, Bloom switched his text, saying only nice things about his younger rival and receiving the audience's sympathy when Greenblatt was not deft enough to alter his own witty but wicked response. "I had to admit some

Some critics accused Shakespearean scholar Stephen Greenblatt of helping spark a generational turn that both diminished humanities scholarship and contributed to cultural decline. His acclaimed scholarship, and the way he dealt with issues fundamental to his life, offered its own defense. Illustration by David Levine. Copyright 2014 by Matthew and Eve Levine.

admiration as witness to my own beheading," Greenblatt could reflect, even as Bloom delivered his blow.[20]

The public exchange between these two scholars represented more than academic performance. Although it has been pointed out that both men consciously moved away from the New Criticism training they received at Yale,[21] they did so in strikingly different fashion. The cause lay less in their contrasting personalities and intellectual interests than in the shifting cultural ground on which each man stood as he came to professional prominence. It was not that Bloom was not interested in the historical grounding of literature. His own critical approach emphasized the influence of one writer on another, a necessarily historical process. At the same time, as one critic noted, "what he desires most is not to engage history but to make his own history in the face of the giants of English poetry."[22] Bloom's 1973 book, *The Anxiety of Interest*, established that approach in decidedly Freudian terms, as the oedipal process of one poet overthrowing the dominance of his progenitor. For Bloom, however, the idea of democratizing literature in line with changes emanating in the 1960s, as Greenblatt described his own goal, was perverse. Indeed, Bloom characterized *The Anxiety of Interest* as taking a stand against the "great awakening of the late sixties and early seventies. . . . I did not consciously realize this then, but my meditation upon poetic influence now seems to me also an attempt to forge a weapon against the gathering storm of ideology that soon would sweep away many of my students."[23]

As befit a man of words, Bloom defended the canon stridently, labeling the rising generation of critics, including the new historicists, a "School of Resentment" willing to sacrifice literary merit in order to score political points. "The flight from or repression of the aesthetic is endemic in our institutions of what still purport to be higher education," Bloom declared in a typical salvo. "Shakespeare, whose aesthetic supremacy has been confirmed by the universal judgment of four centuries, is now 'historicized' into pragmatic diminishment, precisely because his uncanny aesthetic power is a scandal to any ideologue. The cardinal principle of the current School of Resentment can be stated with singular bluntness: what is called aesthetic value emanates from class struggle." One breaks into the cannon, he argued, "only by aesthetic strength, which is constituted primarily of an amalgam: mastery of figurative language, originality, cognitive power, knowledge, exuberance of diction. The final injustice of historical injustice is that it does not necessarily endow its victims with anything except a sense of their victimization. Whatever the Western Canon is, it is not a program for social salvation."[24]

Alvin Kernan used his own term to characterize Greenblatt and his associates as "professors of disenchantment," a label conservatives were quick to seize upon. Among those weighing in was the journalist George Will, who used a *Newsweek* column to contend that Greenblatt had outrageously suggested that Shakespeare's *Tempest* reflected "the imperialist rape of the third world." Greenblatt shot back, "It's very difficult to argue that *The Tempest* is not about imperialism," noting, however, that it was about many other things as well. "It is . . . all but impossible to understand these plays without grappling with the dark energies upon which Shakespeare's art so powerfully draws," he retorted. "Like most teachers, I am deeply committed to passing on the precious heritage of our language, and I take seriously the risk of collective amnesia. Yet there seems to me a far greater risk if professors of literature, frightened by intemperate attacks upon them in the press, refuse to ask the most difficult questions about the past—the risk that we might turn our artistic inheritance into a simple, soporific lie."[25]

Greenblatt's defense stirred only further criticism from conservatives. Contemporary literary critics, Roger Kimball asserted, are "not opening up literature but subverting it." For his part, Kernan tore into Marxism, new historicism, and feminism for totally discounting

> the moral integrity and the truthfulness of the literary text. These modes of literary interpretation have discounted literature by accusing it of ignorance at best, bad faith at worst, of playing a purposeful and cunning part in the imperialistic and financial power games of Western society, imposing and strengthening the hegemony of one class, or sex, or ideology, or race over others. In these views, literature, not long ago considered to be the most authentic language of humanity, expressing its highest abilities and aspirations, diminishes to propaganda, its structure or form to the rhetoric of persuasion, and its values to ideology.[26]

Greenblatt has never been one to deny the personal investment of the author in his subject. Describing the practice of "cultural poetics" at the outset of *Renaissance Self-Fashioning*, he acknowledged "the impossibility of fully reconstructing and reentering the culture of the sixteenth century, of leaving behind one's own situation; it is everywhere evident in this book that the questions that I ask of my material and indeed the very nature of this material are shaped by the questions I ask of myself." Rather than shrinking "from these impurities," however, Greenblatt accepted them as "the price and perhaps among the virtues of this approach." In an epilogue to the book, he elevated his feeling for literature to the level of existentialism.

In a flight home to Boston one day, Greenblatt's seatmate asked him a favor. Apparently preparing to visit his mute and gravely ill son in the hospital, this stranger requested that Greenblatt soundlessly mouth the words he expected his son to convey when he reached his bedside: "I want to die." Try as he might, Greenblatt could not manage to do it. Distressed at his inability to meet the stranger's request, Greenblatt recounted his realization "in a manner more forceful than anything my academic research had brought home to me, of the extent to which my identity and the words I utter coincide, the extent to which I want to form my own sentences or to choose for myself those moments in which I recite someone else's. To be asked, even by an isolated, needy individual to perform lines that were not my own, that violated my sense of my own desires, was intolerable."

That was the dilemma the critics of the new historicism missed by reducing Greenblatt's insight to a particular ideology. The deeper he got into his research, Greenblatt reported, and the more he realized how much middle-class Renaissance males had gained a sense of their own agency, the more he saw how they were at the same time fashioned by cultural institutions: family, religion, and the state. Indeed, he found, "the human subject itself began to seem remarkably unfree, the ideological product of the relations of power in a particular society. . . . If there remained traces of free choice, the choice was among possibilities whose range was strictly delineated by the social and ideological system in force." As author and critic, Greenblatt could well have considered his discovery merely academic, but his final words in the book belie that conclusion. Noting the impossibility of abandoning self-fashioning, which itself would be the equivalent of abandoning the craving for freedom and accepting death itself, he concludes, "As for myself, I have related this brief story of my encounter with the distraught father on the plane because I want to bear witness at the close to my overwhelming need to sustain the illusion that I am the principal maker of my own identity."[27]

The critique of new historicism, when it has come from those associated with Yale, not just from Kernan and Bloom but also from Robert Bork, tells more about the passing of a generation than the faults of scholars who emerged in the 1960s. Born to the "Greatest Generation" and a veteran of World War II, Kernan arrived at Yale following his graduation from Williams College as a PhD candidate prepared to study with the greatest of the New Critics. Unlike Greenblatt, he stayed on to teach after receiving his degree, entering the administrative ranks as associate provost with the ascension of Kingman Brewster to the university presidency in 1963. In that position, Kernan was increasingly put off by rising student militancy and the willingness, he thought, of faculty as well as students to excuse a brutal murder as a number of Black Panthers accused of killing a fellow Panther suspected of being an informer came to trial in New Haven in 1970.[28] "Many Americans viewing the marches and the costumes on the nightly news found it all titillating," he wrote of that academic year when he stepped in to serve as provost, "but it was a direct challenge to the rational principles on which Western society was built, and university administrators like myself suddenly found ourselves in the front of a great culture war, defending against assaults of the irrational." Three years later, he left to become dean of the graduate school at Princeton, where again his anger continued to mount with what he perceived was a turn away from scholarship to politics.[29]

Robert Bork was somewhat younger than Kernan, born in 1927, but he was every bit as bitter. From the perspective of the 1990s, Yale Law School seemed a wonderfully civil and intellectually exiting place to teach until the arrival of the class entering in 1967. "Unlike the traditional liberal students of the second- and third-year classes whom they frightened as much as they dismayed the faculty, these students were angry, intolerant, highly vocal and case-hardened against logical argument," Bork recalled. As part of a generation of what he calls barbarians who never grew up, this new group followed on the heels of Yale '64's first law graduates who finished that year, including Joseph Lieberman, and joined those who had delayed their admission, including '64's Gus Speth and Angus Macbeth. As one of only two registered Republicans on the Yale Law Faculty, Bork was bound to set himself apart from his colleagues in some fashion, but the depth of venom he directs at other professors is striking. Moreover, he draws from his personal experience the judgment that the "sixties" lay at the root of a radical decline in American culture.

Complaining in his 1996 diatribe, *Slouching towards Gomorrah*, of "philosophies claiming that words can carry no definite meaning or that there is no reality other than one that is 'socially constructed,'" Bork puts himself directly in opposition to Greenblatt and his colleagues: "A reality so constructed, it is thought, can be decisively altered by social or cultural edict," the result being "a prescription for coercion." Had such attitudes dissipated over time, the problem would have been minor. Instead, Bork insists, "As the rioting and riotousness died down in the early 1970s and seemingly disappeared altogether in the last half of that decade and in the 1980s, it seemed, at last, that the Sixties were over. They were not. It was a malignant decade that, after a fifteen-year remission, returned in the 1980s to metastasize more devastatingly throughout our culture than it had in the Sixties, not with tumult but quietly, in the moral and political assumptions of those who now control and guide our major institutions." American culture, he declared, "is complex and resilient. But it is also not to be denied that there are aspects of almost every branch of our culture that are worse than ever before and that the rot is spreading."[30]

* * *

For Bork, the problem was not simply that of a lost "son of Yale," but a radical turn left throughout higher education. If he looked beyond Greenblatt to other '64 scholars, he might have included William Roth among those who brought their activism into the classroom. After writing about disabilities and participating in the movement to assure accessibility to public places, Roth joined the faculty at the University of Albany, where, in 1984, he founded the pioneer Center for Computing and Disability. His 1992 book, *Personal Computers for People with Disabilities*, provided a state-of-the art guide in line with his longtime interest in the cause. The nature of his writing shifted in the new century, however, as he challenged the effort to weaken America's network of social welfare policies. Introducing his 2001 book, *The Assault on Social Policy*, as neither bipartisan nor impartial, he underscored his conviction "that current social policy is inadequate, undemocratic, even disgraceful." In several contributions to his subsequent coedited book on globalism, Roth asserts that experience has taught that government "is not perfect and cannot be relied upon for cherished values like social justice." Instead, he calls on grassroots activists to assure a future marked by "human decency and freedom, social justice, sustainable growth, and democracy" by changing the current system of industrial capitalism.[31] No doubt, Roth was revisiting issues that had first animated his social activism in Berkeley in the years immediately after his graduation from Yale. As he did so, he joined Greenblatt in paying attention to the way language represents power, in an essay, "The Social Construction of Disability," that combined his critical abilities with political advocacy.[32]

Another member of this class whose scholarship owed much to the 1960s was Frederick Buell. A wrestler in college, Buell gave up the sport midway through his undergraduate years to take up rugby instead. He was so taken with his English major, however, that he found himself bringing books of poetry to his matches and continuing to read until it was time for the action to begin. Among the prime influences on him in the major was Alvin Kernan, whom he described as a great teacher. Also influential, however, was Charles Reich—then a fellow in Pierson College—who befriended Buell his senior year. It was through Reich, Buell reported, that he gained his first interest in contemporary politics, especially the Vietnam War.[33] Following matriculation at Yale Law School in the fall of 1964, Buell organized the first faculty forum on the war before a large audience. Although he loved the legal method and became increasingly active in antiwar activities in New Haven, Buell found that he deeply missed literature. In 1965 he left law school to enter the PhD program in literature at Cornell. "I went back into total concentration on aesthetics for a while," he recalled. In 1969 Buell was in Germany finishing up his dissertation on the poet W. H. Auden when demonstrators virtually shut down Cornell—a favorite target, along with the Black Panther trial in New Haven, of critics who lambasted academic leadership for pandering to radical demands.[34] Ironically, Buell rediscovered his own political voice while abroad, where he joined some American expatriates in organizing against the Vietnam War. On his return to the United States, he took a job teaching at Queens College in New York.

Buell found Queens College an exciting place to teach in the 1970s. There he created courses on politics and literature, drawing on his study of Auden, among other writers. He also taught creative writing, reflecting his own production as a published poet. As the borough of Queens diversified in the later 1970s and 1980s, so did the student body. With the help of outside funding, Buell initiated a course in multiculturalism of the kind that has since drawn the ire of traditionalists in the field, including Alvin Kernan. For his part, Buell considered as an asset the perspective his racially and

ethnically diverse students brought to literary texts. Although their reading of a passage might differ from the dominant critical consensus, their
alternative views proved worth exploring. "Staying with the old traditions,"
Buell explained, "means that the traditions themselves tend to die. By entering a multi-cultural discourse, those traditions can be renewed through new
interpretations over succeeding generations." Then, as diversity at Queens
seemed more and more part of an international phenomenon, Buell developed courses on globalization and culture and led the initiative to create a
world studies program.

Buell's productivity gained him tenure and a stint as department chairman, but the free spirit unleashed in the 1960s pointed him away from
administration. With the experience of the Beat writers of the 1950s in mind,
he spent a number of summers traveling without a set agenda, to South Asia,
to North Africa, and to Latin America. He described these trips as motivated
partly by cultural curiosity, partly by the desire to trek in mountain, desert, and rain forest ecologies, and partly a spiritual journey allowing him to
pursue an interest in comparative religion. Such trips not only helped inter-
nationalize his view of literary culture, but also encouraged him to adapt
some of the practices he encountered to his own teaching. In the 1990s, he
introduced courses combining contemplative practice, creative writing, and
environmental literature, even as he continued a serious study of aikido. Such
practice, he believed, built on American as much as Eastern traditions, given
the importance of Eastern philosophy and religion to American environmental writers, from Emerson, Thoreau, and Whitman to the present. In the late
1990s, that work encouraged him to participate in creating an environmental
studies program at Queens.[35]

From the advent of his career, Buell infused his writing with a political
sensibility. His study of Auden—well known as a leftist who flirted with
Marxism—nonetheless was no more reductionist than Greenblatt's writing
was. As Buell asserts in the introduction to the book he adapted from his dissertation, "Clearly, one cannot rest content with determining what poems 'say'
about politics and then take that as an indication of what the poet 'believes' at
any point in time; to do so is to have a reductive understanding of the nature
of both poetry and belief. Instead, one must pose a variety of complicated
and indirect questions about the poem, the poet, and the political situation,
questions that lead, by different ways, to a fuller understanding of how they
are interrelated."[36] Seeing Auden as both responsive to the spirit of difficult
times and determined to fashion his position as a "modern" poet, Buell inter-
rogated Auden's politics without suggesting that they alone determined his
cultural production. No less than Greenblatt, Buell explored issues central
to his own life. His 1994 book, *National Culture and the New Global System*,

encompassed issues derived both from his travels abroad and his teaching literature through a multicultural lens. The book focused on how globalization was transforming cultural and social experience worldwide, and how it was beginning to supplant national perspectives in politics, sociology, economics, and, above all, cultural theory and production.

By his own admission, Buell's subsequent book was unabashedly political. A study of how environmental crisis as a political, scientific, social, and cultural issue changed and developed since the time of Rachel Carson, *From Apocalypse to Way of Life* (2003) began by detailing the efforts of anti-environmentalists, from the Reagan years to the beginning of the Bush era, to hijack the rhetoric of reform for their own purposes. Identifying this counteroffensive with a larger pattern of culture wars, he credited conservatives with having successfully countered environmental rhetoric and slowed reform. "The strategy of going with the left-liberal flow, and then turning it against itself," he asserted, "proved an extremely potent form of political aikido." Buell then showed nonetheless how the environmental movement had in fact steadily expanded, not shrunk, since Carson, in scientific analyses, in sociological thought, and in a growing body of environmental-cultural theory, literature, and film. By 2012, as environmental politics again changed, and the rhetoric and analysis of environmental crisis again appeared as a mainstream concern, he was well into a related book on fossil fuels and culture. This was a topic he considered particularly important for readers in a post–Hurricane Sandy era, when CO_2 in the atmosphere had already passed well beyond the safety zone of 350 parts per million.[37]

The writing of Buell's classmate T. H. Breen was less overt in addressing contemporary social problems, but in many ways it was equally critical. A history honors major in college, Breen remained at Yale to work with one of the country's leading colonialists, Edmund Morgan, publishing his dissertation, a study of early Puritan political ideas, in 1970. His early career seemed quite in line with contemporary scholarship, but Breen admitted his own personal transformation while at Yale. Deeply touched by Martin Luther King's challenge at the 1964 graduation ceremony to work for justice and equality, he came, like King, to condemn the war in Vietnam, going so far as to consider refusing induction, had not a wife and the birth of a daughter exempted him from service. "I not only condemned our imperial adventure in Asia, but also defined my interpretation of the American past around questions of popular resistance to irresponsible rule," he recalled.[38]

After teaching at Yale for four years and joining the faculty at Northwestern University, he shifted his scholarly emphasis to more directly investigate issues of contemporary concern. Acutely aware of the shift in the historiography of slavery as the civil rights revolution advanced, he challenged a prevailing belief that skin color had always determined status in America. His study with Stephen Innes of seventeenth-century race relations on Virginia's Eastern Shore concluded that before the 1660s talented free blacks managed to succeed quite well in a racially mixed society, so long as they maintained access to the primary source of wealth, which was property. In the years before people of color where confined to slavery, it was property that guaranteed freedom. It was the aggregate effect of large plantations putting small proprietors at risk that compromised the prospects of free blacks in the early colonial era.[39] Breen did not hammer the point home, but the implication of his study, published the year Ronald Reagan was elected president, was that class matters and that material deprivation as much as color consciousness has been critical in limiting the collective well-being of African Americans.

In subsequent work, Breen took up more fully the question of popular rule. His 2004 book, *Marketplace of Revolution*, described in highly contemporary terms the actions of ordinary Americans who were drawn together through a burgeoning consumer culture to the point of inventing an action appropriate to their shared material condition—the boycott. While in his own lifetime it had become fashionable to condemn consumer culture, he concludes that that perspective "underestimates the capacity of men and women to comprehend their own political situation. It is true that goods can corrupt. But in certain circumstances they can be made to speak to power. The choice is ours to make."[40] He extended his effort to locate the sources of liberty in the acts of common people in his 2011 volume, *American Insurgents, American Patriots: The Revolution of the People*. Focusing her book review on Breen's emphasis on the raw anger of a people who "surged forward in the name of rights and liberty," historian Jan Ellen Lewis could not help but be reminded of contemporary Tea Party activists. Such was hardly Breen's intention. While Tea Party sympathizers may have disagreed, Breen argued that the intent of early insurgents had been more unifying than divisive and intended to advance the principle of equality as well as protect existing material rights.[41]

To construct this broadened vision of American life, Breen, like Greenblatt, recognizes the limits to his own efforts to reconstruct the past. "Facts," he states, "most often melt under close scrutiny." Authoritative political and legal documents that survive "turn out to have been the voice of special pleading, the testimony of partisans in which winners always speak louder than losers." Recognizing there are "no 'truths' . . . out there waiting to be discovered," Breen abandons any illusion of positivist certainty in favor of the fundamental historian's craft as "an interpretive exercise, a sorting out of conflicting perceptions and an appreciation of the narratives that humans have always invented to make sense out of their lives."[42]

As much as Breen's work was rooted in the nation's origins, his writing ultimately spoke to contemporary concerns, as did the best work in the humanities, even that about dead white men, which returns us once again to the contribution of Stephen Greenblatt. Despite the effort of some critics to place him into a convenient academic niche, Greenblatt has managed to transcend each of those binding characterizations to self-fashion a view of human experience that is both sound academically and a powerful reflection of who he is. Nothing better exemplifies his approach than his 2004 volume, *Will in the World*.

* * *

The mystery of who Shakespeare was has for generations confounded scholars, who for lack of documentary evidence have had to guess at even the rudiments of his life. We know he had a strong educational foundation, without, however, the benefit of a college degree that so many of his peers revered. We know he married, though little remains to suggest why he spent so little time with his wife and family. We know too that he eschewed strong religious sentiment, though it would have been hard for him to avoid being troubled by the upheavals that shook every level of living as England shifted radically between irreconcilable Protestant and Roman Catholic domination. Greenblatt's solution to these mysteries is simple, but in scholarly terms, problematic: look to the plays. No less than his classmate Frederick Buell, Greenblatt would not attempt to draw a one-to-one relationship between elements of Shakespeare's poetry and his life. But patterns—of theme, of language, of allusion—point to elements of what could have been Shakespeare's life. Moreover, these elements gain clarity and power through their connection to the times. Eloquently crafted for an educated general audience, *Will in the World* serves effectively as a demonstration of the new historicism.

As one traces Greenblatt's arguments, it is impossible to miss the nearly unrelenting speculative nature of his suppositions. And yet the argument proves both seductive and compelling. Consider first the role of religion in Shakespeare's life. Through the evidence of a will naming a beneficiary that well could have been our William Shakespeare, Greenblatt places him shortly after completion of his high school education in Lancashire in the north of England, where the religion of his ancestors, Catholicism, managed to survive despite its suppression throughout Elizabethan England. It is there that the sixteen-year-old Shakespeare, while employed as a teacher, could well have come into contact with the pious Edmund Campion, who had returned to England after becoming a Jesuit priest with a secret mission of conversion. "Whether he actually met Campion in person or only heard about him from the flood of rumors circulating all through 1580 and 1581," Greenblatt speculates, "Will may have registered a powerful inner resistance as well as admiration."

Shakespeare's admiration could have stemmed from the priest's determination to sustain his Catholic heritage, in marked contrast to Shakespeare's father's suppression of his views in order to sustain a position as an alderman dependent on Protestant favor, to say nothing of protecting his own life. Indeed, Greenblatt reports, Campion was prosecuted, tortured, and ultimately hanged, and from that lesson Will learned to mask his own religious sensibilities. While his early history plays were safely set in the fifteenth century, they were populated with restive people taking extreme risks in playing dangerous games of power. His image of these people could well have been taken from the families he would have closely observed during his sojourn in the north. At the same time, with the example of Campion before him, Will was not going to sacrifice his own prospects to become a successful actor in what Greenblatt describes as a glorious, but treasonous, suicidal crusade: "If his father was both Catholic and Protestant, William Shakespeare was on his way to being neither."[43]

Greenblatt does not leave the subject there, but rather heightens the importance of this early suppression on Shakespeare's part to further infer from one of his greatest plays, *Hamlet*, the ways in which even the denial of ritual could reveal the man. Central to this interpretation is the death of Shakespeare's young son Hamnet (a name Greenblatt points out was virtually interchangeable with Hamlet) shortly before he wrote the play. The death that Hamlet is called on to avenge is that of his father, so could there be a connection? Greenblatt thinks so, once again referring to Shakespeare's father's anguished effort to reconcile his outer life with his inner beliefs. This time the specific issue was purgatory. Under Protestant rule, Greenblatt reports, all forms of praying for the dead were outlawed, a particularly devastating blow to Catholics who believed the trials they were likely to face in purgatory could only be alleviated by the prayers of the living. Greenblatt has only the slightest evidence for his supposition, except for its suitability, given the constraints on John Shakespeare's life, to the presumption that Will's father could well have taken out a kind of insurance policy for his own salvation, called a "spiritual testament." Fearing the possibility of death without the Catholic last rites of confession, anointment, and Communion, he could have declared his penance in advance, adding a request believed crucial to his fate, that those who loved him do what the state had declared illegal: pray for him upon his death.[44]

Once again, Greenblatt uses his own imaginative power to envision a scene in 1596, as Shakespeare's son is laid to rest. Hamnet has been brought up largely by his grandparents. Could John Shakespeare have prevailed upon his now successful son to pay for Masses for the dead child, even as he would have wanted Masses said for his own soul? Greenblatt cannot answer his own speculation, yet he proceeds to suggest that "Shakespeare must have still been brooding over it in late 1600 and early 1601, when he sat down to write a tragedy whose doomed hero bore the name of his dead son." And how would the play bring us back to this supposition about Shakespeare's own life? There is little doubt that despite the Protestant denial that purgatory even existed, that the ghost demanding that Hamlet avenge the murder of his father appears from just that place. Hamlet's indecision to act appears to acknowledge the impossibility of committing a crime in the name of someone, Catholic tradition declared, who was seeking to purge his sins in order to ascend to heaven.

The irresolvable religious question behind the action of the play allows Shakespeare, and his audience, an outlet not otherwise available to them. If Shakespeare attended church, as it appears he did, neither doctrine nor ritual gave him solace at such difficult times as those when he stood over the grave of a young son. So what resources did he have? "Shakespeare appreciated how crucial death rituals in his culture had been gutted," Greenblatt argues. "He may have felt this with enormous pain at his son's graveside. But he also believed that the theater—and his theatrical art in particular—could tap into the great reservoir of passionate feelings that, for him and for thousands of his contemporaries, no longer had a satisfactory outlet. . . . He responded not with prayers but with the deepest expression of his being: *Hamlet*." In short, the death of his son and the impending death of his father constituted "a psychic disturbance that may help to explain the explosive power and inwardness of *Hamlet*."[45]

As often happens in his work, Greenblatt's disquisition on purgatory turns out to have a personal connection, revealed at the outset of an earlier book that informed this particular discussion in *Will in the World*. His father, Greenblatt reveals, was obsessed with death throughout his life, the product, Greenblatt believes, of a traumatic childhood experience when the teacher of his father's Hebrew school class insisted that his pupils visit the home of a railway worker who had been struck and killed by a train. There they were instructed "to stand around the mangled corpse—which was placed on great cakes of ice, since it was the summer in Boston and very hot—and to recite the psalms, while the man's wife wailed inconsolably in a corner." The story immediately resonated when Greenblatt discovered at his father's own death that, without notice and without involving his own family, he had left a behest to an organization to say kaddish, the Aramaic prayer for the dead, for him. The revelation that even such practice existed, let alone that his father would bypass his own family to have it executed, was one of those startling revelations that demanded inquiry. And so it was that Greenblatt set off to examine an equally suppressed tradition, compelled by commingled motives to exercise his trade—"the historical and contextual work that literary critics do"—while also seeking "its own compelling imaginative interest" as a result of a personal discovery.[46]

Greenblatt's argument, moving back and forth, from the plays to their creator, and always acutely aware of the world out of which these master-pieces emerged, gains its own power from the representation of dynamic contradictions at the heart of Shakespeare's world. In another book, he claims that while Shakespeare remains "the embodiment of human free-dom," he acquires that status only out of an understanding of the con-straints on that freedom. Far from accepting Bloom's contention that the plays owed nothing to the society out of which they emerged, Greenblatt ticks off the constraints Shakespeare had to contend with. Living in a world of absolutist claims of an all-powerful God and what Greenblatt identi-fies as "an entwined set of linked absolutes: love, faith, grace, damnation, redemption," Shakespeare "directed his formidable intelligence to absolutes of any kind. These limits served as the enabling condition of his particular freedom."[47]

We can see that dynamic at work in *Will in the World* as illustration of what Greenblatt elsewhere calls "the circulation of social energy." Reiterating his oft-repeated view, "there is no escape from contingency," Greenblatt chal-lenges especially the position embraced so dearly by Bloom that it is the text in and of itself where meaning resides. "Indeed in the case of Shakespeare (and of the drama more generally), there has probably never been a time since the early eighteenth century when there was less confidence in the 'text,'" he asserts. "There are textual traces—a bewildering mass of them—but it is impossible to take the 'text itself' as the perfect, unsubstitutable, freestanding container of all its meanings." The Elizabethan theater, he suggests, should be looked at as it existed, as a social as well as a cultural phenomenon. The crit-ic's role, then, is to ask "how collective beliefs and experiences were shaped, moved from one medium to another, concentrated in manageable aesthetic form, offered for consumption."[48]

Placing Will in the world, rather than treating his genius as static and largely inaccessible to anyone but experts, Greenblatt succeeds in ground-ing his subject in everyday life. Although only the last chapter of *Will in the World* makes that approach overt, as Greenblatt teases out what the last years of Shakespeare's life must have been like when he returned to Avon, the tech-nique permeates the whole volume. As the *New Yorker*'s Adam Gopnik puts it, Greenblatt's achievement is to unveil a perspective "rooted not in moral principle, much less a religious dogma, but in the observer's eye for how many daily things . . . escape a single rule. . . . The double life that Montaigne writes about, and which he experienced high up in his tower, Shakespeare experienced in rented rooms and summer visits. As readers and writers, we remain blessed that the reigning poet of the language is so vocationally, so happily, the ordinary poet of our company."[49]

Making Shakespeare "the ordinary poet of our company" fits well with the best academic work emerging in the post-1960 era. More specifically, it reflects a world that was itself sharply divided, with even such fundamental concepts as liberty and justice contested in ways virtually without precedent in the previous generation. If Shakespeare achieved a kind of double consciousness in determining not to be Catholic or Protestant but to grapple with the effect of the hold of religion over human lives, Greenblatt can himself be credited with a kind of double consciousness, one that is suggested initially in his treatment of Jews in *The Merchant of Venice*. Although virtually invisible in Elizabethan England following their expulsion in 1290, Jews remained the object of merriment at their expense, a feature of contemporary life Shakespeare was not beyond exploiting in his plays. Such might be expected of his treatment of Shylock, not the least his forced conversion to Christianity, the object of presumed merriment in the play. Yet something more profound is happening, Greenblatt contends. Drawing a parallel with a real-life execution, of Roderigo Lopez, a Jewish attendant to Queen Elizabeth, whose profession that he loved the queen as much as he loved Jesus Christ failed to absolve him from charges of treason and prompted the derisive laughter of witnesses to his death, Greenblatt suggests that Shakespeare, who must have been aware of the circumstances of Lopez's execution, has revealed too much of Shylock's humanity to allow his audience a similar pleasure with his own forced conversion to Christianity. "The play has given us too much insight into his inner life, too much of a stake in his identity and his fate, to enable us to laugh freely and without pain." Unlike Marlowe's *The Jew Of Malta*, to which *The Merchant of Venice* is often compared, Shakespeare's play forces its audience to see beyond farce to the tragedy of an action that, for Shylock, could be considered the equivalent of death.[50]

In another essay on *Merchant* prepared for the *New York Review of Books* in 2010, Greenblatt allows a contemporary reference to creep in when he says of Shylock, in deciding not to carry his hatred of Christians to its ultimate end, that he "refuses to be a suicide bomber." Appearing in a journal of contemporary opinion, the allusion seems more inadvertent than it actually is. In fact, Greenblatt insists, in line with his argument that Shakespeare has given Shylock his humanity, that his renunciation of his Jewishness is the equivalent of suicide, for with it, he becomes invisible, without identity, and thus without meaning.[51] Greenblatt is not speaking directly of himself when he makes this observation. Still one cannot help but recall his comment in *Self-Fashioning*, describing his refusal to accommodate the request of a father for his dying

son: "I want to bear witness . . . to my overwhelming need to sustain the illusion that I am the principal maker of my own identity."

Even as he has fashioned a picture of Will in the world, Greenblatt has
left traces of his own life in a contentious and riven nation. The son of pious
Jews, Greenblatt reveals that his family's synagogue and the family itself left
Roxbury at an early stage in his life for suburban Newton, where upward
mobility was the norm for the grandchildren of immigrants like himself.
Returning many years later to his first home, the measure of change is starkly
written in the abandoned house of worship he previously attended and the
shuttered apartment house he once lived in. The final words of his account
leave no question about the failed promise of his college years, that African
Americans and Jews would ascend the ladder of success together. As he is
standing outside his former home, a concerned resident calls him over, speaking, Greenblatt reports, "in the tone of quiet urgency with which my mother
used to enjoin me not to go to the zoo, not to wander off from the haven
of the apartment: " 'Then get out quickly,' she added. 'It's not safe for you
to be here.' "[52] Even if the circumstances were different at Yale, when he was
told that as a Jew he was preying on university resources, a similar sense of
displacement still had to be there. Yale ultimately proved a fine academic
training ground for Greenblatt, but what a liberation first Cambridge and
then Berkeley had to be. If by then, all the verities he had grown up with
seemed steeped in contradiction, why was criticism not a way of examining
and evaluating the deepest meanings of the human condition? Where better
to examine issues of power, authority, love, and betrayal than in the work of
Shakespeare and his contemporaries?

* * *

On the surface, Sydney Lea's lifework appeared to take a very different course.
Trained in Yale's PhD program in comparative literature, immersed in the protest atmosphere that pervaded the campus to the point of relinquishing his
draft card to William Sloane Coffin at a protest meeting in 1968, and hired
at Dartmouth in the early 1970s, he appeared well on his way to becoming
yet another tenured radical. The label did not stick. Rather than conform to
the established path to academic success through scholarly publication, Lea
took up writing poetry. Denied tenure at Dartmouth, he held a succession of
positions over the years, remaining tied to academic life but not entirely of it.
Occasionally, issues rooted in the 1960s appeared in his poetry, as he alluded to
his brother's protest against segregation and his own sense of unease taking in
a Cannonball Adderley performance in North Philadelphia, near where he had
tutored black children the year before, even as he noted that "Dr. King and his

followers were being brutalized in Selma, Alabama."[53] In one poem—"Fourth of July"—he comes close to being political by conjoining the memory of being mugged with the idealism of his youth:

> The Kennedy era, this was, when things kept getting better,
> so we imagined. And so I kept wanting to get a say, too—something
> about a new day dawning, maybe, or I hoped so, really[54]

But such lines proved the exception. Poetry should have ideas, Lea supposed, but to be overtly political only diminishes its power. "At its heart," he believed, "his or her poetry is different from theory, and different from opinion of any kind."[55]

Turning away from the charged issues that dominated his years at Yale, Lea took up instead the depiction of everyday life where he lived, in rural New Hampshire and Vermont. As he explained in his twenty-fifth reunion class book in 1989,

> I'm the first to admit that, compared for instance to saving the ozone layer, to achieving international racial justice, to providing adequate shelter for all the skinny people in our fat nation, my own passionate concerns are literally pastoral. Yet through them—through my friendships with clerk and yeoman alike, through my fascination with the behavior of wildlife, through the hours of time (including tedious time) with my children, through my tiny efforts to assist those who need assistance hereabouts—I fancy that I participate at least feebly in that grand mission that Wallace Stevens proposed for poetry: "to help people live their lives." I don't mean that my writing in and of itself will do any good for the guy living in that bombed-out trailer up in Orfordville, but that the desire to imagine his condition is a prod to political and personal action on my part. And such action in turn is a prod to the poem. That guy has to fit somewhere. As Eliot said, the task after all of a poet—and I'm wishing it on everyone, obviously—is to "imagine new wholes."[56]

Emphasizing his turn from the dominant mode of academic discourse, Lea allied himself with Flannery O'Connor's description of herself as "an author congenitally innocent of theory, but with certain preoccupations." If he had successes—and he certainly did, with an enviable publishing record and appointment, in 2011, as Vermont's poet laureate—he chose to describe them in modest terms, as "little Himalayas," climbed hill by hill over some sixty years. "I conquer my small Everests one by one," he wrote.[57]

Lea encountered the people who drew him initially to his mission through a family summer campsite in a remote corner of Maine. There he became intrigued with a last generation of Americans virtually untouched by modern conveniences, from power tools to writing itself. Hearing them perform at Saturday night socials, Lea discovered they were marvelous raconteurs. "Some of them were poets, even if they could not read or write, they'd make the stuff up in their heads," he recalled. "When I came to Dartmouth I sought out their equivalents in New Hampshire and Vermont. I was fascinated by their lore and their storytelling skills. That probably has as much to do with my desire to be a creative writer as anything I ever did in school. I was trying to get some of that storytelling magic onto the page to the extent that my abilities permitted." Realizing he could never authentically convey a dialect without sounding condescending, Lea turned to poetry in an effort "to capture some of the rhythms or cadences of that language without having to imitate it."[58]

Very much a formalist, Lea nonetheless altered form to fit the topic, so that very few poems looked, let alone sounded, alike. Throughout, however, he remained preoccupied with the power of places and the people who animated them. His subject was not the modern, conflicted cities that captured headlines, but communities close to nature, tied to its rhythms, and caught up in the inexorable tides of life and death. Inevitably, critics compared his work to that of Robert Frost,[59] Vermont's first poet laureate. "My effort," he recounted, "to capture actual conversations going on within the confines of form is not as rigorous as his. That form is often self-invented or even ideally unobvious, but it is for whatever reason a factor in what I try to do."[60]

Indeed, Lea's own assessment of Frost could well be applied to himself. Frost's poetry works so well, Lea argues, because it is accessible, but also because its ultimate meaning remains ambiguous, resting always on a higher plane than the concrete "facts" that fill the foreground. "He is a Casbah of a poet, this fellow, and no matter the issue or instance, we can never absolutely learn our way around," Lea suggests. Citing Frost's well-known poem "The Road Not Taken," Lea chides those who would embrace it as "a cliché of undaunted self-actualization . . . the working motto of the New Age bliss patrollers." Like his other work, seen in full, this poem "vexes," to the point of forcing consideration and reconsideration, not simply of the implied message, but the range of the reverberations that follow from the poem itself.[61]

Lea is no imitator of Frost, yet from the same familiar territory arise similar truths. Without taking on Everest-like challenges, as he says, Lea has found a certain elevation. It is hard to image him confronting the chairman of the National Endowment for the Humanities, as Greenblatt had done, as part of the ongoing cultural wars engulfing so many of his colleagues.[62] Rather, Lea could conclude, "I am interested, as I've been since I first read Wordsworth's

Lyrical Ballads at age fifteen, in how a sensibility, in my own case a poet's, may find sustenance and even song—in quotidian life among quotidian personalities, my own included. I have, for better or worse, imagined that my extended residence in postage-stamp-sized towns, where I know just about everybody, allows me to read the great issues of the world—life, death, love, hatred, character, ecology in all its meanings—in small script."[63] In that goal, he could stand with the leading humanists of his generation. The methods might have changed over the course of his professional career, as they were bound to, but the questions addressed remained those central to the course of human history.

Reviewing the work of humanities scholars over the past half century, it is hard to imagine why anyone outside of academic life would feel threatened by the course of research and teaching these scholars might pursue. Historian Robert Self reminds us, however, that behind the declarations that social and sexual relations could be remade because they had been constructed by society (as Greenblatt and Buell both claimed) lay a direct challenge to the body politic as it had existed before the 1960s. As activists refashioned the social contract to broaden women's citizenship, protect racial and sexual difference, and permit greater freedom in private lives, they helped shift the locus of both power and privilege. For those most directly threatened by a change in the status quo, such changes as they were analyzed and celebrated on university campuses and related cultural institutions could not be considered merely academic.[64]

Conclusion

After a Long Journey, a Lasting Divide

The members of this class are divided against themselves, and one is struck by how much of their time is spent earnestly wrestling with the conflict between their reality and their ideals. They grapple with the trade-offs between equality and privilege . . . between convenience and social responsibility . . . between rebellion and convention.

David Brooks, *Bobos in Paradise: The New Upper Class and How They Got There* (2000)

Writing in a decidedly more optimistic period at the turn of the new century, syndicated columnist David Brooks thought he detected a new ruling consensus in America. The "new upper class" synthesized the key former antagonists of the 1960s: bourgeois capitalists and countercultural bohemians. Presided over by a new leadership elite of bourgeois bohemians—or "bobos"—this meritocracy, as he identified it, had created a new set of social codes providing coherent structure to national life and imposing social discipline on the rest of society. Brooks grouped George W. Bush and Al Gore as well as Maureen Dowd and John McCain in this portrait as he took the ultimate leap of faith by declaring that "the culture war has ended, at least within the educated class."[1] It seems his optimism was premature.

In fact if this new upper class existed, its cohesion was ephemeral. In the new century, its members had dissolved into vehement opposition to each other. Moreover, their disparate elements attracted criticism from across the political spectrum. From the right, libertarian political scientist Charles Murray decried the meritocracy's physical as well as social isolation from the rest of society, especially from the white working class. On the left, MSNBC's Christopher Hayes similarly blamed it for making a priority of its own perpetuation. "The meritocracy offered liberation from the unjust hierarchies of race, gender, and sexual orientation," Hayes declared, "but swapped in their place a new hierarchy based on the notion that people are deeply unequal in ability and drive. . . . At its most extreme, this ethos celebrates an 'aristocracy of talent,' a vision of who should rule that is in deep tension with our democratic commitments."[2]

If Brooks misread the internal consistencies of this new elite, it was nonetheless hard to challenge his contention that it drew its lifeblood from America's top educational institutions, not the least the Ivy League universities. In this, little had changed since the day in May 1960 when admissions letters found their way into the homes of the first undergraduate classes to matriculate in the 1960s. It was not just that two 1960s Yale graduates, George W. Bush and John Kerry, squared off for the presidency in 2004.[3] Just as visible in the 2012 campaign were the Harvard credentials of Barack Obama and Mitt Romney. It did not go without comment either that every member of the current U.S. Supreme Court had at least one Ivy League degree, four of them more than one. So, too, the press duly noted that when President Obama made a point of simultaneously nominating three candidates for the Court of Appeals for the District of Columbia Circuit in June 2013, every one of them had a Harvard law degree.[4] That two of these candidates were women and the other African American only served to reinforce Joseph Soares's argument that when the nation's top universities opened their doors to clientele that looked different from the white male Anglo-Saxon elite that preceded them, the outsiders became insiders and tapped into familiar positions of social privilege in order to build their successes.[5] As Brooks put it himself, in describing how a new meritocracy had replaced the ruling elite still in place into the mid-1960s, university admissions officers were responsible. "The proportion of Ivy League graduates in *Who's Who* has remained virtually constant throughout the past 40 years," he reported. "But the schools maintained their dominance by throwing over the mediocrities from the old WASP families and bringing in less well connected meritocrats."[6]

Brooks painted his social observations with a broad brush at best, and consequently his judgments do not begin to capture the complexity of the lives of the men described in this book. It is nonetheless impossible to deny that the members of the class of 1964 are part of a ruling elite, albeit one that has experienced tensions between equality and privilege, convenience and social responsibility, rebellion and convention. Those tensions surfaced in debates about civil and women's rights, as well as more private matters of marriage and spiritual belief. Angus Macbeth provided a particularly telling example of how privilege could combine with rebellion in recounting his experience at the 1967 Pentagon antiwar protest. Having made his way to the front lines of the march, only to be turned back by national guardsmen armed with bayonets, he subsequently ended his day at a cocktail party at the home of Secretary of Defense Robert McNamara, thanks to an invitation from McNamara's son-in-law, a Yale Law School classmate.[7] "High principled, privileged, well-educated, too," Tyler Smith reflected about his college peers. "Groomed for leadership, but so much victims of our own civilized greed. I want to clean up the environment, but I buy disposable diapers and carry my health food home in plastic bags."[8] As ironic as these examples are, they are proof that even as their privileged position within the establishment was frontally tested over time, these men remained ideally positioned to guide the transition from the old set of rules to the new.

We see that commitment in David Schoenbrod and Angus Macbeth's pragmatic effort to find a working congressional majority to support "nonpartisan proposals for smarter, more flexible regulatory programs to protect the environment, encourage green technology, and stimulate the economy. to craft practical environmental regulations."[9] Similarly, Stephen Greenblatt located himself in the middle ground when he described his own scholarly contribution: "I would say that . . . finding a way to move on from the positions that energized me in the late '60s . . . I wanted to hold onto the spirit of the generational insurgency in which many of us participated and at the same time to honor the tradition and the achievements of preceding generations."[10] So, too, the effort to mediate could be found in Nicholas Danforth's determination to reconcile his personal and professional commitments to women's equity, in Tim Bachmeyer's desire to connect his faith to "facts on the ground," and in Jack Cirie's intent to pursue "the moral equivalent of peace" as a representative of a new mode of military thinking. Such reconciliation remained difficult, however, for at the heart of the upheaval of the 1960s was a set of difficult contradictions.

For these men, the most obvious contradiction was illuminated through the civil rights movement, where they discovered that the rights of citizenship, largely taken for granted by those most privileged, were anything but equal in application. The early battle for justice under the law during the class's undergraduate years proved compelling, especially with the visible example of William Sloane Coffin. Not every student actively joined in, but Yale '64 was well represented at every juncture: Bob Kaiser, Joe Lieberman, and Brad Reynolds's presence at the 1963 March on Washington for Jobs and Freedom; Steve Bingham, Tom Powers, and Joe Lieberman participating in the mock election in Mississippi. The civil rights laws enacted in the mid-1960s appeared to resolve the untenable contradictions in democratic practice, in ways that Joseph Rich, among others who helped enforce the laws, found personally and professionally gratifying. Civil disorder and black militancy complicated the picture, however. So did the debates about how best to satisfy the ultimate goal of a color-blind society, including conflict over affirmative action in university admissions.

Racial injustice was not the only contradiction that demanded attention in the later 1960s, of course. Once the veil had been lifted to reveal the extent of unequal treatment under the law, further core assumptions naturally came under scrutiny, not the least of which was confidence in America's unerring righteousness in defending freedom around the world. If American Cold War militarism had once been defined, as historian Robert Self puts it, as an international instrument of liberty,[11] Vietnam tested that vision, as did so much that followed in the name of national defense. Unlike subsequent classes, those who graduated in 1964 still found military enlistment an acceptable postgraduate choice. As execution of the war soured, however, and its conduct became increasingly contested at home, many who served joined those who did not in challenging familiar Cold War presumptions. In the years after Vietnam, a workable alternative approach to world affairs, like fully achieving a fair and just society, proved difficult to define, let alone to put into practice.

If environmental justice appeared to be a unifying concept at the outset of the 1960s-inspired movement, its utility was short-lived. The "responsible militancy" of the Natural Resources Defense Council and related activism captured well the melding of rebellion and convention at the heart of the early environmental movement but ultimately generated its own counterrevolutionaries. And while Gus Speth's leadership in the field generated considerable support from his classmates, not everyone was willing to follow him to the point of rejecting the prevailing consumer ethos that David Brooks located at the heart of the bourgeois-bohemian synthesis.

Clearly these men, educated not just in an all-male environment, but one that elevated manliness to a high plane, found the adjustment to a movement for women's equality difficult. Whatever privileges they held by matter of race or status were further enhanced by their gender, especially as the primary agents of authority, as well as income, in the families they formed. No matter how conscientious and self-aware the relationships might have been, old habits, as well as practical considerations of assuring both a good family income and care for children, made equity within marriage difficult.

No member of the class of 1964 better exemplified membership in the modern meritocracy or the determination to reconcile the clashing perspectives that emerged from the 1960s than Joe Lieberman. If he had arrived in 1960 as an outsider to Yale and the establishment, he quickly took on the cloak of the new upper class, which served him well as a campus leader in college and law school, as a practicing attorney in New Haven, as a state senator, and as U.S. senator for twenty-four years. His effort to position himself in the political center through repeated calls for bipartisanship were legion. Yet well before he retired from the Senate in 2013, whatever centrist position he might have held was lonely indeed. The *New York Times* columnist Gail Collins was not being entirely facetious when she described Lieberman in an August 2012 column as "practically the only person in America who claims to have no idea who he's going to vote for."[12] Clearly the center had not held. What lessons, then, could be drawn from a review of Lieberman's career?

When I arrived for my interview with Lieberman in May 2012 in the city he grew up in—Stamford, Connecticut—he was wrapping up a meeting with a group of constituents in his cousin's law office. "I'm a great list maker," he assured his visitors as they prepared to depart, "and your cause is high on my list to address before I retire at the end of the year." As the assembled posed for a group picture, Lieberman was the same thoughtful, gracious presence that had carried him to so many successes fifty years earlier some thirty miles up the road in New Haven. This was the perfect setting to hear Lieberman's reflections on his life. Directly across the street had been the Jewish Community Center where his parents—both children of immigrants—had met at a community dance. Stamford High School was nearby, as was the condominium he and his wife, Hadassah, had moved to from New Haven after his divisive yet successful Senate reelection campaign in 2006. His roots were here, and looking back Lieberman could still marvel at how far life's path had taken him. Yale's role in that journey, he stressed, was transformative.

The convergence of Yale's educational opportunities with the Kennedy presidency and the civil rights movement formed the heart of that experience. The personal and the political came together for him in the concept of the American dream: that anyone who worked hard in America should be able to reap its considerable benefits. That concept formed the heart of Lieberman's first editorial as chairman of the *Yale Daily News* and recurred in his moving eulogy for the fallen President Kennedy. He spoke eloquently to its hold on him and America at his thirtieth Yale reunion, shortly after emerging as one of the most visible Democratic survivors in the tide that swept Republicans into control of Congress in 1994. He returned to the concept when he announced his candidacy for president in 2003.[13] Remembering how patriotic his grandmother had been, Lieberman recalled how, even in the largely Protestant neighborhood where he grew up, neighbors would stop to wish her a good Sabbath as she made her way to synagogue. "So I had this feeling that America was the land of opportunity," he recounted. "I mean I inhaled the American ethic, and I was living it. I was driven by the combination of the optimism that comes from a religious upbringing I had and the sense of gratitude that here I was in a country that allowed you to do that. And Yale was an important part of this. . . . It gave me a sense of what was possible. . . . That's probably part of why I'm so involved in so many forms of civil rights. That's why I'm so grateful that Coffin challenged me at that moment to go to Mississippi, because part of my vision of America is that the founders established these extraordinary founding goals—inadequately realized—and our lives have been the history of a journey to extend the basic promises to reality."[14]

Coffin, Lieberman admitted, could be tough on him, as he was in 1965, when Coffin criticized him for supporting the Vietnam War at the first open forum on the subject at Yale. Lieberman could not help smiling as he recounted his last exchange with Coffin only months before he died in 2006. Knowing Coffin was ill, Lieberman wanted to pay tribute to the man who had had such an impact on him. Having reached the ailing minister by phone and conveyed his gratitude, Lieberman was caught off guard as Coffin responded in his typically brusque manner. "Thanks," Coffin said. "And incidentally I can't believe some of the positions you are taking." "Even as I told him how much he meant to me," Lieberman recalled, "I also gave him the opportunity one more time to chastise and challenge me."

Lieberman considered the foreign policy positions he had taken over the years the logical extension of values he had embraced in the Kennedy years, not the least Kennedy's charge in his 1962 State of the Union Address "to seize the burden and the glory of freedom."[15] Citing an essay he had published in the *Washington Post* the day before our interview urging greater support for Syrian dissidents, he asserted, "If you like freedom, you follow it wherever it goes."[16] Lieberman admitted that he had been hurt by the stinging criticism that met his support of the Iraq War. Nonetheless, he believed that he had been vindicated to some degree by his reelection to the Senate as an independent in 2006. Still, he found it troubling to end his political career outside the party of John Kennedy. For years he had been buoyed by the company of others he considered centrists like himself. He relished the opportunity to team up with Bill Clinton in the politically moderate Democratic Leadership Council years after Clinton, as a Yale law student, had assisted Lieberman's first successful campaign, for state senator. Two years after Democrats had rebuked him on the war, Lieberman gravitated to his friend and sometime centrist, John McCain. Like Ronald Reagan before him, Lieberman felt at the end of his career that he had not left the Democratic Party so much as it had left him.

Clearly not everyone agreed with Lieberman's assessment of the Democratic Party, but his political path and the way he chose to describe it remain instructive. The message of the early 1960s—the good 1960s, as some have chosen to call it—was, as Lieberman described it in 2012, a message of freedom, to be realized at home and extended abroad. Women's and gay rights naturally followed from the civil rights campaign as matters of justice as well as inclusion. Vietnam, as much as the Peace Corps, was cast as an effort to bolster greater self-sufficiency and self-determination internationally. As those claims, and the rationale behind them, collapsed under scrutiny, and as laws guaranteeing freedoms at home proved unequal to aspirations for greater equality, the liberal tradition that could embrace an integrated, if simplified, view of human liberties at home and abroad shattered.

When Lieberman traveled to Mississippi in the fall of 1963, he was unsettled by his exposure to unvarnished racism, but not to the point of adopting a new, more radical perspective. Rather, he affirmed a sentiment, already central to his own worldview, that the opportunities uniquely pro-vided by the American way of life should be equally available to all. Merit, not social or economic circumstances, should determine success, a dictum that was nicely summarized in Martin Luther King's formulation that his fellow citizens be judged by the quality of their character, not the color of their skin. In later life Lieberman could no more adjust his vision of domes-tic policy to promote affirmative action—a clear affront to the bootstrap myth behind the American dream—than he could abandon his confidence, honed by Kennedy's New Frontier ambitions, in the power of military might to advance democratic institutions abroad.[17] Holding fast to both precepts of liberty as he understood them in the Kennedy era, Lieberman later found himself uneasily straddling the liberal divide that embraced activist rights policies at home while seeking alternatives to such activism as it relied solely on military power abroad. If he remained liberal on civil rights, he continued to adhere to a hard-line foreign policy, as affirmed when, upon retirement from the Senate, he accepted a position cochairing the conservative American Enterprise Institute's American Internationalism project. Described as an effort to build bipartisan consensus for "American diplomatic, economic, and military leadership in the world," the project was quickly identified with the same neoconservative personnel who had engineered America's decision to invade Iraq.[18]

The futility of Lieberman's position at the political center in 2012 reflected the stalemate in Washington and the breakdown of traditional political prac-tices, but it also revealed something more fundamental: that politics not only serves to reflect social and cultural differences but helps aggregate them by limiting policy choices. The excitement that permeated college campuses in the early 1960s touched young people of all persuasions. As disparate as the life histories of those involved in Students for a Democratic Society and Young Americans for Freedom became over time, they shared much in the early 1960s as part of grassroots youth movements that combined ideology and activism with hostility to ruling elites.[19] Both organizations sought to topple the prevailing liberal consensus, and to a considerable degree that happened, as the two parties realigned around the issues that most animated the long 1960s.

No doubt contested views of racial equality had a good deal to do with that realignment and the political polarization that followed. Pivotal was the Nixon administration's calculated effort to attract the support of white voters whose anxiety about the progress of civil rights had loosened their allegiance to the Democratic Party enough to vote for Alabama governor George Wallace in 1968, a "southern strategy" laid out in detail by Kevin Phillips in his 1969 book, *The New Republican Majority*.[20] When women pressed their own cause for equal rights, Republicans reacted strategically again, by appealing to defenders of the traditional male breadwinner's dominance, a concerted effort detailed by GOP feminist Tanya Melich and credited by historian Robert Self with deepening the emerging cultural divide rooted in the 1960s. As Self puts it, "Between the 1960s and the 2000s, Americans went to war with one another. . . . By the dawn of the twenty-first century, the contest over civic conceptions of gender roles and sexuality had become deeply etched in competing narratives of national identity. How one understood feminism, abortion, gay rights, welfare, and 'family values' signaled one's political allegiances."[21]

The "moderate" Republican Ripon Society, which I headed in the early 1970s, itself fell victim to the era's polarizing politics. Inaugurated at a gathering at the Harvard Faculty Club in December 1962, Ripon attracted a group of largely Ivy League men to the proposition that young Republicans could match the verve and imagination of the landmark Kennedy administration.[22] The society went on to advocate a number of programs embraced by President Nixon, including revenue sharing and support for black enterprise, as well as family assistance to simplify as well as rationalize federal support for people of limited means. It also contested the southern strategy, most famously generating damning assessments of Nixon's choices for Supreme Court vacancies, G. Harrold Carswell and Clement Haynsworth. Generally pro-choice and antiwar, the Ripon Society nonetheless split over Nixon's execution of the Vietnam War and federal provision of universal child care, a position that *Ripon Forum* editor George Gilder savaged in anticipation of his own forthcoming antifeminist treatise, *Sexual Suicide*, and Nixon's veto of child-care legislation that was still being sought fifty years later.[23]

Marking Ripon's half-century anniversary in 2012 as one of the few Ripon founders who remained a Republican, Gilder joined an e-mail exchange to insist that "moderation will prevail." Others, including Tanya Melich, looked back angrily at what their party had become. "Those Republican leaders, who knew better but were willing to join forces with those who wished to stop women from gaining full opportunity, are as much to blame for the present state of the Republican Party as those who played the backlash strategy for crass, short-term gain and have been running today's national party. Hopefully, their power is now diminished," she asserted in reference to Barack Obama's reelection. "I have trouble processing any regrets about Ripon's demise after the great win this November. I'm happy that women, who were ignored so long by so many Republican and Democratic strategists, finally proved that they could determine who would be President, who would win the Senate."[24] Not entirely dead in 2012, Ripon had for the previous twenty years utilized its nonprofit arm as a cover for bringing together Republican politicians and lobbyists under the guise of educational travel abroad.

As controversial as the 1960s themselves proved to be, and as closely associated as they were in the public mind with the actions and whims of the political Left, the impact of the political Right must also be acknowledged. That the political Right responded with conscious efforts to turn the most divisive elements of the period to political advantage is one of the period's lasting legacies. Parties had always sought to exploit their opponents' vulnerabilities, but starting in the late 1960s the Nixon administration reached new extremes when Vice President Spiro Agnew led a particularly divisive charge against Democrats, and even against Republicans such as New York senator Charles Goodell, who challenged administration policies, most notably in Vietnam. Reviving a tactic of tainting its critics through guilt by association, established most notoriously in Joseph McCarthy's anticommunist crusade during in the 1950s, Agnew denounced not just antiwar organizers as "an effete corps of impudent snobs who characterize themselves as liberal intellectuals" but turned to calling any number of critics "Radical-libs."[25] Nixon's reelection team extended the formula with a vengeance to George McGovern as they successfully made him the symbol, in the words of one historian, "of spinelessness, countercultural excesses" and the representative of the radical takeover of his own party.[26]

The 1972 Watergate break-in that led to Nixon's resignation was another effort to undercut opposition by all means possible. One of its chief perpetrators, G. Gordon Liddy, said as much when he proclaimed, "The experience of the past ten years left no doubt in my mind that the United States was at war internally as well as externally."[27] FBI authorization of spying on college campuses as well as among civil rights activists represented an extension of the same "politics as war" mentality. After subsiding for a few years, this strategy of "positive polarization," as the Ripon Society called it derisively, gained new life when conservative presidential candidate Patrick Buchanan revived what he declared was a "culture war" at the 1992 Republican National Convention, accelerated into the Clinton presidency, when President and Mrs. Clinton were made out to be emblems of the "bad 1960s," and continued famously when Newt Gingrich kept the war on the 1960s alive as part of the "Contract with America" that helped sweep Republicans into control of Congress in 1994.[28] One can only credit Brooks with especially wishful thinking that the culture war ended with the termination of the Clinton presidency.

That culture war, James Davison Hunter suggests, while rooted in personal disagreements like those among the members of Yale '64, nonetheless intensified through public debate. Over time, these disagreements have become so rooted in different ways, in Hunter's words, "of apprehending reality, of ordering experience, [and] of making moral judgments," that they have contributed both to the institutionalization and the politicization of two fundamentally different cultural systems.[29] The account of Yale '64 does not provide a perfect picture of that clash of worldviews, orthodox versus progressive, but it does demonstrate the many ways in which a more fluid and contingent set of expectations and beliefs crystallizing in the 1960s challenged and undercut prevailing and generations-old standards of conduct and modes of thought.

In the end, Yale '64 remained part of the nation's preeminent establishment, but without the kind of authority that flows from a unified outlook of the kind Brooks anticipated. Having complicated the triumphal sense of accomplishment that flowed from parents shaped by the tribulations of the Great Depression and World War II, these men found that a new, alternative consensus to the one that shattered in the 1960s proved elusive. Largely satisfied with their own lives and the boost Yale provided them, they nonetheless had yet to witness a new synthesis capable of reconciling the structural elements that enabled their own success with the demands for equal opportunities raised at so many levels in the 1960s.[30]

Robert Kaiser captured his classmates' dilemma well. Writing from the perspective of having observed fifty years of history-in-the-making from his perch at the *Washington Post*, he praised the era's three liberations—of African Americans, of women, and of gays. Indeed, he marveled at the marriage of his gay brother to a longtime companion in 2013 and the election of a black president in 2008. Such triumphs, however, did not soften his conclusion:

> Our country is in an awful mess, and our generation helped put it there. . . . When we left New Haven half a century ago, America was entering a time of great excitement, triumphs and disasters. I was full

of optimism, and although the '60s and '70s were the very definition of a mixed bag, my optimism survived them both. But the tumult of those decades sowed the seeds of what would follow. Our failure in Vietnam, then the debilitating impact of Watergate, then (from about 1973 onward) the end of broadly shared and ever-increasing prosperity, all discredited government, bred cynicism, eventually enshrined greed—and undid my optimism.[31]

Kaiser's dark view about the fate of the nation was not universally shared, but it was reflected in a number of other comments anticipating this class's fiftieth reunion. "Today we seem to have become a society where greed is the motivator," asserted Jack Huggins, whose career arced from a first job with the Dow Chemical Corporation to the position of director of the Nature Conservancy's watershed program. "We preach the 'need to be competitive,' but I am not sure what we are competing for. Certainly we are not competing for the dignity of the individual or the preservation of the environment. Our class has helped lead these changes to society and I am doubtful that this is a great legacy."

Former U.S. senators Joseph Lieberman and John Ashcroft prepare to address their 1964 classmates at their fiftieth Yale reunion, May 30, 2014. Asked to speak to the topic "Did We Blow Our Chance?" Ashcroft in particular evoked strong responses from the capacity audience, finally giving conservatives something to cheer after sitting on their hands during earlier discussion of social issues emanating from the 1960s. Despite the widespread opposition to Lieberman's support of the war in Iraq, he was received warmly, drawing from his natural charm and status as a Yale insider to overcome any possible hostility that might have been directed his way. Photo by the author.

Deploring the lack of leadership, nationally and internationally, to deal effectively with climate change in particular, Gordon Davis railed, "To such posterity as may survive, we acknowledge our embarrassment and offer our regrets.
It's true that some of us saw it coming as clearly as Canute predicted the rising
tide. But like Canute, we were helpless to prevent it. At least that's our pathetic
excuse." Added Richard Howe, "Today our country is characterized by divisive
hyperpartisanship that has weakened our economy and diminished our standing in the world and stands in sharp contrast to the Yale I attended 50 years
ago, where people were still divided but showed respect for each other and
used their intelligence to resolve conflicts."[32]

Like everything else, such views remained contested fifty years out of college. Yet Richard Berk's comment from his tenth reunion book—"from liberalism to radicalism to cynicism (but still trying)," with the emphasis on
"still trying"—appeared to hold with a great number of these men. For each
class member who had turned away from public life, there were counterparts
determined to maintain the causes of earlier years. Reflecting on a career
building affordable housing, Joseph Wishcamper reported, "I still want to be
and do the most I can. As much as ever, my goals are about making things
I can influence better, especially in my work, community and myself. I get
up early and go full tilt every day." Looking to the next five years, Wallace
Winter declared, "I have chosen to be an activist for a sustainable planet.
What does that mean? In my case, it means trying to be a vegetarian, taking
Quaker spirituality and simplicity seriously . . . supporting our local community supported garden." Continuing his work in sustainable agriculture,
John Jeavons cited individual points of inspiration: Kenyan gardens thriving
in a six-year drought, inner-city children growing vegetables at school, the
Mexican government adopting biointensive rural training programs. "They
give me hope that we can still grow a better future. We just have to dig in and
get our hands dirty. Together." Robert Musil, regretting that "our young and
idealistic hopes of the 1960s have yet to be realized," took the ultimate step of
challenging his classmates—"1,000 prominent, well-established and talented
Americans"—to form a Yale '64 action network. Such a force, he imagined,
might appear together "at the White House and Congress, on campuses, at
churches, in shareholder meetings, to demand an end to fossil fuels, ram-
paging gun violence, economic insecurity, a world at war. Imagine when our
grandchildren speak of legacies, when they whisper in awe the name of Yale
'64, the class that started the tradition of alumni social action. That would be
a legacy."[33]

What Doug McAdam said of those who volunteered for Freedom Summer
in 1964 could be said of these men: that they were fortified by class privilege, manifest in "the sense of personal efficacy or felt mastery over one's

environment that often characterizes those who are economically well off."[34] That did not mean, however, that they, or peer graduates from other elite institutions in the mid-1960s, managed to achieve the lofty goals that were set for their generation as they came of age. They were diverse enough from the outset not to have arrived at the same conclusions as to how best to apply the lessons of service and applied intelligence so central to their Yale education. That was to be expected. But what they did not anticipate was how deeply contrasting experiences and changes in outlook over the course of the long 1960s would widen differences between them to the point of becoming part of a solidifying national cultural divide. If they were not caught up themselves in the war to define American culture—and to see one side or the other of it manifest in public as well as in private affairs—their lives were nonetheless constrained by its effects. What best can be said of these men is that they did not remain on the sidelines. In their own explorations of, and adaptations to, a world largely redefined in their own lifetimes, they left a valuable legacy: the commitment to work through persistent contradictions in American life and to leave a record of their own actions and perceptions for future generations to build upon.

Notes

Introduction

1. Owen Johnson, *Stover at Yale* (New Haven, CT: Yale Bookstore, 1997), 385–86, special edition reprinted for the inauguration of the Yale Bookstore, November 21, 1997.

2. Leno quoted in Warren Goldstein, "For Country: The (Second) Great All-Blue Presidential Race," *Yale Alumni Magazine*, May/June 2004. Whether the physician Dean qualified as rich did not matter. Apparently his Yale credentials were enough to convince Leno that he was. By the time Leno spoke, Joe Lieberman had dropped out of the race, depriving Leno of yet one more Yale target for his humor.

3. Nicholas D. Kristof, "George W. Bush's Journey: Ally of an Older Generation amid the Tumult of the 60s," *New York Times*, June 19, 2000.

4. Edward P. Morgan, *What Really Happened to the 1960s: How Mass Media Culture Failed American Democracy* (Lawrence: University Press of Kansas, 2010), ix–x.

5. Bernard von Bothmer, *Framing the Sixties: The Use and Abuse of a Decade from Ronald Reagan to George W. Bush* (Amherst: University of Massachusetts Press, 2010), 2.

6. Robert G. Kaiser and Jethro K. Lieberman, eds., *Later Life: The 25th Reunion Classbook; The Class of 1964* (New Haven, CT: Yale University, 1989), 181. William Strauss and Neil Howe place the birth year of most of these men, 1942, in the silent generation, which they identify as "adaptive." They locate the outset of the baby boom generation in 1943, providing a rationale for choosing a year somewhat earlier than is generally agreed upon, and give it the label "idealist." They list as sample members for each period respectively Barbra Streisand (b. 1942) and Janis Joplin (b. 1943). Reflective of the transitional nature of this cohort, Yale '64 could well be described as both idealist and adaptive, though a case could be made that Bob Dylan (b. 1941) more closely reflects this group's sensibilities. William Strauss and Neil Howe, *Generations: The History of America's Future, 1584 to 2069* (New York: William Morrow, 1991), 279–80, 299–300.

7. Karl Mannheim, *Essays on the Sociology of Knowledge*, ed. Paul Kecskemeti (London: Routledge & Kegan Paul, 1952), 29, cited by Rebecca E. Klatch, *A Generation Divided: The New Left, the New Right, and the 1960s* (Berkeley: University of California Press, 1999), 3.

8. Wade Clark Roof, *A Generation of Seekers: The Spiritual Journeys of the Baby Boom Generation* (San Francisco: HarperSanFrancisco, 1993), 3.

9. Leonard Steinhorn, *The Greater Generation: In Defense of the Baby Boom Legacy* (New York: St. Martin's Press, 2006), 14.

10. A. Whitney Griswold, "A Proposal for Strengthening the Residential College System in Yale University," 1958, A. Whitney Griswold Papers, box 212, folder 1958, Yale University Archives. I am

grateful to my Rutgers colleague Carla Yanni for sharing this document with me. *Yale Daily News*, October 3, 1963.

11. For an account of this change in the direction of Yale College admissions and its effect see Joseph A. Soares, *The Power of Privilege: Yale and America's Elite Colleges* (Stanford, CA: Stanford University Press, 2007).

12. Jon Margolis, *The Last Innocent Year: America in 1964—the Beginning of the "Sixties"* (New York: William Morrow, 1999); James T. Patterson, *The Eve of Destruction: How 1965 Transformed America* (New York: Basic Books, 2012), xiii.

13. Miriam Horn, *Rebels in White Gloves: Coming of Age with Hillary's Class—Wellesley '69* (New York: Times Books, 1999).

14. Katharine T. Kinkead, "The Brightest Ever," *New Yorker*, September 3, 1960.

1. Bright College Years, 1960–1964

1. Michael Rossman, *The Wedding within the War* (Garden City, NY: Doubleday, 1971).

2. Daniel Yankelovich, *New Rules: Searching for Self-Fulfillment in a World Turned Upside Down* (New York: Random House, 1981), 175.

3. So confident was Yale into the late 1950s of its own undergraduates' future, the college did not support an office devoted to career counseling or job placement. "It was assumed that every Yale man had a job waiting upon graduation," Nicholas Lemann reports in *The Big Test: The Secret History of the American Meritocracy* (New York: Farrar, Straus and Giroux, 1999), 142.

4. Yale Office of Institutional Research, *Yale Book of Numbers: Historical Statistics of the College and University, 1701–1976*, compiled by George W. Pierson, online. According to the same source, private school students constituted 64 percent of the class as late as 1950. The regional breakdown of the class of 1964 included 39 students from New Haven, 186 students from other parts of New England, 179 from New York State, and an additional 413 students listed from other areas identified as east of the Mississippi River.

5. According to Jerome Karabel, *The Chosen: The Hidden History of Admission and Exclusion at Harvard, Yale, and Princeton* (Boston: Houghton Mifflin, 2005), 332, in 1959 69 percent of applicants from Andover were admitted, at a time when under a third of all applicants were accepted. Of Andover students in the bottom half of the class, Yale accepted fourteen, compared to Princeton, five, and Harvard, four.

6. The son of Andrew Mellon, Franklin Roosevelt's influential secretary of the treasury, Paul Mellon was generous to Yale; his gifts included financing of the Yale Center for British Art and two new residential colleges completed in 1962, Ezra Stiles and Morse. Both Peter Woodward and Peter Wallace died early in life, Wallace from a hiking accident following his sophomore year. According to Mike Wallace's obituary in the *New York Times*, April 9, 2012, it was his son's death that inspired the senior Wallace to become a serious journalist after a period when he had bounced between doing entertainment and quiz shows and the occasional cigarette commercial. Maynard Mack followed his father's path as a professor of English, spending the bulk of his career at the University of Maryland. Joe DiMaggio, despite the fame associated with his name, maintained a very distant relationship with his father. He died only months after his father, following a period of extended drug and alcohol abuse. See *Yale 1964: The Class at 50* (Hagerstown, MD: Reunion Press, 2014), 770. DiMaggio's time at Yale briefly overlapped with another troubled child of stardom, '64's Michael Ross Walker, the son of actor Robert Walker and Phyllis Lee Islay, whose stage name was Jennifer Jones. After a nasty divorce with Walker when Michael was still an infant, Jones married David Selznick in 1949 and, after his death in 1971, art collector Norton Simon. The younger Walker had a brief career acting without completing college. He died in 2007 of cardiac arrest, following administration of propofol, the same drug that killed Michael Jackson two years later. Ibid., 847.

7. Katharine T. Kinkead, "The Brightest Ever," *New Yorker*, September 3, 1960.

8. Thomas Barton, letter to the editor, *Yale Alumni Magazine*, September/October 2004.

9. Ron Rosenbaum, "The Great Ivy League Nude Posture Photo Scandal," *New York Times Magazine*, July 15, 1995.

10. Karabel, *Chosen*, 327. Among the physical elements alumni were asked to attribute to applicants were: attractive, awkward, effeminate, flabby-soft, forceful, good looking, neat–well groomed, and sloppy-untidy. Joseph A. Soares, *The Power of Privilege: Yale and America's Elite Colleges* (Stanford, CA: Stanford University Press, 2007), 48.

11. Griswold's personal concern for the morals of undergraduates and information from the university handbook are recounted in Gaddis Smith, "An Inside View of Yale, 1948–2002," in *Time and Change: Yale 1962 40 Years Later* (Hagerstown, MD: Reunion Press, 2003), 12–13.

12. *Yale Daily News*, September 10, 1960; William Roth, *Movement: A Memoir of Disability, Cancer, and the Holocaust* (Jefferson, NC: McFarland & Co., 2008), 63. Yale was hardly alone in its restrictions. As *New York Times* education editor Fred Hechinger and Grace Hechinger wrote in 1963, college rules governing the sexes were becoming increasingly contested—not without sympathy among college students for keeping them in place, however, in stark contrast to campus attitudes only a few years later. "College Morals Mirror Our Society," *New York Times Magazine*, April 14, 1963. At Barnard in 1964, one student recalled, "Men could visit you in your room, but three of your four feet had to be on the floor." Cited in Annie Gottlieb, *Do You Believe in Magic? The Second Coming of the Sixties Generation* (New York: Times Books, 1987), 239. Harvard was no less restrictive in enforcing a dress code, according to Roger Rosenblatt: "As late as 1969, students in the Houses were still required to wear ties and jackets in the dining halls at lunch and dinner—the so-called coat-and-tie rule. . . . Many of them complied with the rule. Others who did not were spoken to." *Coming Apart: A Memoir of the Harvard Wars of 1969* (Boston: Little Brown, 1997), 88–89.

13. *Yale Daily News*, September 14, 1961.

14. David Allyn, *Make Love Not War: The Sexual Revolution; An Unfettered History* (Boston: Little, Brown, 2000), 94–95.

15. Telephone interview and e-mail from Thomas Trowbridge, November 30, 2011. A May 14, 1964, *Yale Daily News* editorial, "An Archaic Rule," slammed the university's parietal rule, charging, "it can do little or nothing to stamp out the 'vices' it condemns," adding, "the student who wants it can get it." By way of contrast, the prospect of extending visiting hours for women in Harvard dorms prompted the editors of the *New England Journal of Medicine* to claim that such permissiveness would have the effect of condoning "informal concubinage under the college roofs with the approval of college authorities." Carolyn Herbst Lewis, *Prescription for Heterosexuality: Sexual Citizenship in the Cold War Era* (Chapel Hill: University of North Carolina Press, 2010), 26. Before he died in December 2011, Evans, one of two members of the prominent Mellon banking family in the class of 1964, left $50 million to Yale to construct and name the new home of the University's School of Management and Business.

16. *Yale Daily News*, September 15, 21, 1960.

17. Lawrence S. Pratt and Kenneth deF. Solstad, "Freshmen History," *Yale Classbook 1964* (New Haven, CT: Yale Banner Publications, 1964), 267.

18. Karabel, *Chosen*, 334–35; Lemann, *Big Test*, 145–46; Brooks Kelley, *Yale: A History* (New Haven, CT: Yale University Press, 1974), 450–53. Kelley reports (p. 431) that as late as the 1950s, as many as 55 percent of the university's faculty were Yale graduates.

19. Karabel, *Chosen*, 321.

20. Robert A. Caro, *The Power Broker: Robert Moses and the Fall of New York* (New York: Alfred A. Knopf, 1974), chap. 2.

21. Calvin Trillin, *Remembering Denny* (New York: Farrar, Straus and Giroux, 1993), 35–36, 92.

22. Ibid., 41. Sixty-one percent of Trillin's classmates were private school graduates.

23. Confined to a single paragraph in the 1964 yearbook entry on clubs, Haunt was described, accurately enough, as an organization "which provides a little bit of heaven in the form of a beer keg in the Pierson [College] courtyard before football games."

24. For an explanation of the term "shoe" see Dan A. Oren, *Joining the Club: A History of Jews and Yale*, 2nd ed. (New Haven, CT: Yale University Press, 2000), 178–79.

25. Telephone interview with Robert Lamson, May 21, 2012. Former assistant dean of students Henry Chauncey, Yale 1957, remembers that George W. Bush had a similar reaction to the way his classmates ribbed him after the day he arrived on campus in 1964 wearing a cowboy hat and boots. Interview with Henry Chauncey, Woodstock, VT, July 27, 2011.

26. Telephone interview with George Sheckleton, November 2, 2012.

27. Telephone interview with Frank Franklin, September 30, 2011.

28. Gary Saxonhouse interview with Jodi Lynne Wilgoren, February 23, 1992, Wilgoren Collection, Yale University Archives. Karabel, *Chosen*, 331, quotes Yale admissions officer Inslee Clark before he was named director as saying his office did not want to recruit at such schools where Jews predominated when they would have to turn down the majority of applicants despite their high grades and college board scores.

29. Telephone interview with Wayne Minami, October 28, 2011.

30. Interview with Richard Berk, Philadelphia, May 4, 2011.

31. Benjamin Fine, "Militia Sent to Little Rock; School Integration Put Off," *New York Times*, September 3, 1957. Skype interview with Patrick Caviness, April 20, 2011.

32. Jim Rogers, *Investment Biker: Around the World with Jim Rogers* (New York: Random House, 2004), 3–5.

33. Telephone interview with Joseph Wishcamper, June 4, 2011.

34. Joseph I. Lieberman, with Michael D'Orso, *In Praise of Public Life* (New York: Simon & Schuster, 2000), 32.

35. Although Ashcroft did not pursue football as a varsity sport after his freshman year, according to a November 25, 1963, report in the *Yale Daily News* it was his role as quarterback of Yale's Branford College team that led to victory over Harvard's Elliott House in the intramural championship game played the afternoon President Kennedy was shot and killed.

36. Interview with Gus Speth, South Royalton, VT, July 20, 2010.

37. Skype interview with James Rogers, December 21, 2011.

38. Geoffrey Kabaservice, "The Birth of a New Institution: How Two Yale Presidents and Their Admissions Directors Tore Up the 'Old Blueprint' to Create a Modern Yale," *Yale Alumni Magazine*, December 1999. According to a November 23, 1963, article in the *Yale Daily News*, while the percent of privately educated students matriculating at Yale had dropped from 80 percent to just over 50 percent between 1938 and 1960, Yale still led all colleges in the number of its undergraduates whose families were listed in the social register. Together Harvard, Yale, and Princeton accounted for 45 percent of such listings, with Yale garnering the largest share at 21 percent.

39. Lemann, *Big Test*, 145; interview with Henry Chauncey Jr., July 27, 2011; Oren, *Joining the Club*, 198.

40. The number of African Americans in each class rose significantly after Howe left his position as dean of admissions, to approximately ninety in each class in the years between 1975 and 1997, or 7 percent. Soares, *Power of Privilege*, 113.

41. Interview with Arthur Reagin, Laurel, MD, June 26, 2012. For a visual record of the hostile reaction of whites to school integration in Washington see Fredrick M. Miller and Howard Gillette Jr., *Washington Seen: A Photographic History, 1875–1965* (Baltimore: Johns Hopkins University Press, 1995), 214–15. Both George Bundy Smith and Inez Smith Reid were ultimately appointed federal judges, Smith to the New York Court of Appeals, Reed to the District of Columbia Court of Appeals.

42. Reagin interview, June 26, 2012; Robert G. Kaiser and Jethro K. Lieberman, eds., *Later Life: The 25th Reunion Classbook; The Class of 1964* (New Haven, CT: Yale University, 1989), 351–53. A record-breaking sprinter at Yale, Mottley subsequently won a silver and a bronze medal at the 1964 Olympic Games in Tokyo, the first ever garnered by a representative of Trinidad and Tobago. Profiles from the Ivy League's Black History, at http://ivy50.com/blackhistory/story.aspx?sid=5/11/2007.

43. Telephone interview with Stanley Thomas III, December 8, 2011; e-mail from Patrick Caviness, January 12, 2012. Brooks Kelley, *Yale: A History*, 452, reports that until 1962, when the *Report of the President's Committee on the Freshman Year* (the Doob report) recommended that the practice be ended, bursary work was required from any student receiving scholarship aid. Thereafter, such work was available on a voluntary basis and not a condition of grants or scholarships. An executive for Time Warner for a number of years, Stanley Thomas died in 1995. Caviness's close association with Thomas, deepened by their role as teammates, nonetheless stood in contrast to the circumstances of his own early education. As Lani Guinier reports, the all-white high school Caviness transferred to in 1957 was built to accommodate whites from Little Rock's more affluent neighborhoods, who left Central the same year it admitted its first black students. "From Racial Liberalism to Racial Literacy: *Brown v. Board of Education* and the Interest-Divergence Dilemma," *Journal of American History* 96 (June 2004): 104.

44. Erich Segal, *The Class* (New York: Bantam Books, 1985), 16.

45. Stephen Greenblatt, "China: Visiting Rites (II)," *Raritan* 4 (Spring 1985), reprinted in *The Greenblatt Reader*, ed. Michael Payne (Malden, MA: Blackwell, 2005), 283–84; Karabel, *Chosen*, 211, 358.

46. J. Chuck Mokriski, "More House: The Early 1960s," at http://www.stm.yale.edu/TheEarly1960s. php.

47. David Finkle, "Shame: Stepping Away from All the Wrong Places," in *Time and Change: Yale 1962*, 124–25.

48. Telephone interview with Robert Ball, October 20, 2010.

49. Paul Monette, *Becoming a Man: Half a Life Story* (San Francisco: HarperSanFrancisco, 1993), 106.

50. *Yale 1964 at 50*, 255–56.

51. Roth, *Movement*, 59, 61.

52. Warren Goldstein, *William Sloane Coffin: A Holy Impatience* (New Haven, CT: Yale University Press, 2004), 106; Karabel, *Chosen*, 330–31; Oren, *Joining the Club*, 205–11. The percentage of Jews at Harvard and Cornell had reached nearly 25 percent by 1952, Oren reports, but Yale's proportion of Jews remained almost precisely at 10 percent throughout the decade.

53. Oren, *Joining the Club*, 202. The report's recommendation to include women as "a substantial portion of each class" garnered the support of the *Yale Daily News* editorial page for April 18, 1962, which noted sadly that "the realization of this delightful prospect appears to be at least several undergraduate generations ahead."

54. *Yale Daily News*, October 8, 9, 1963.

55. *Yale Daily News*, October 24, 25, 26, 1963. There is some evidence that the recommendation to admit women was intended only as a diversion to counter opposition to refashioning the place of freshmen in the college. See Oren, *Joining the Club*, 219. The *Yale Daily News* contingent recognized a false lead when they saw it, and the effort to rouse the admissions office to action was undertaken in good fun, so much so that one of the instigators of the effort, '64's Mac Deford, was amused years later when he was approached by a researcher seeking to pin down his historic role in bringing women to Yale. Telephone interview with Mac Deford, June 4, 2011.

56. For a full account of the contested debate over coeducation see Karabel, *Chosen*, 410–27.

57. Telephone interview with Daniel Berman, August 24, 2010; *Yale Daily News*, March 15, 1961.

58. *Yale Daily News*, September 27, 1960. The paper subsequently endorsed Nixon in its October 24 edition and made fun of Galbraith following an October 26 appearance on campus that drew two hundred people. A faculty poll, reported October 30, recorded a 5–1 margin for Kennedy.

59. Cited in David Farber, *The Rise and Fall of Modern Conservatism: A Short History* (Princeton, NJ: Princeton University Press, 2010), 75.

60. *Yale Daily News*, September 28, 1960; John A. Andrew III, *The Other Side of the Sixties: Young Americans for Freedom and the Rise of Conservative Politics* (New Brunswick, NJ: Rutgers University Press, 1997), 17, 59.

61. *Yale Daily News*, October 7, 1960, February 17, March 2, February 20, 1961. Friedberg's letter in the *News* calling for support in opposing a committee "which threatens freedom of thought, speech, and action" appeared March 9, 1961. The editorial was written by the new chairman, Lance Liebman, who was elected that spring over the staunchly conservative Michael Uhlmann.

62. Telephone interview with Wallace Winter, September 28, 2011.

63. *Yale Daily News*, December 1, 11, 1961.

64. *Yale Daily News*, April 19, 1962.

65. *Yale Daily News*, April 18, September 17, 1962; interview with Stephan Klingelhofer, Washington, DC, December 14, 2010.

66. E-mail communication with Keith Huffman, January 8, 2011.

67. *Yale Daily News*, October 24, December 6, 1962; telephone interview with Wallace Winter, September 28, 2011.

68. *Yale Daily News*, October 18, 1960; Manning Marable, *Malcolm X: A Life of Reinvention* (New York: Viking, 2011), 171. Lehrman's reaction is my own memory. After a stint in his family business, he became prominent among conservative Republicans, running unsuccessfully for governor of New York before returning to his love of history, supporting a variety of programs and activities through the Gilder-Lehrman Institute. Serving on a one-year Carnegie Teaching fellowship in 1960, Lehrman was influential in my own decision to accept a similar appointment at the time of my graduation four years later.

69. *Yale Daily News*, January 12, February 8, 1961.

70. *Yale Daily News*, February 10, 16, 21, April 7, 1961. E-mail from Frederick Truslow, 1961, September 17, 2010; discussions with A. Tappan Wilder, Yale 1962, Washington, DC, December 14, 2010, March 29, 2011. Like Yale's established senior societies, Saint Anthony Hall issued a limited number of invitations to join an organization whose activities were strictly confined to its own members. The difference, however, lay in the organization's commitment to selecting members in their sophomore year, making the organization larger and more diverse than the more secret of the secret societies, whose membership was confined to fifteen seniors each year.

71. *Yale Daily News*, February 22, 23, 1961; Andrew, *Other Side of the Sixties*, 191.

72. Goldstein, *William Sloane Coffin*, 111.

73. Ibid., 113–15; William Sloane Coffin, *Once to Every Man: A Memoir* (New York: Atheneum, 1977), 149–62; *New York Times*, May 25, 29, 1961.

74. Coffin, *Once to Every Man*, 153.

75. Raymond Arsenault, *Freedom Riders: 1961 and the Struggle for Racial Justice* (New York: Oxford University Press, 2006), 272, 275, 279–80; Goldstein, *William Sloane Coffin*, 116–19; Taylor Branch, *Parting the Waters: America in the King Years, 1954–63* (New York: Simon & Schuster, 1988), 475–76; *New York Times*, May 24, 1961; *Yale Daily News*, September 20, 1961.

76. Richard H. Parke, "Chaplain at Yale Tells of U.S. Plea," *New York Times*, May 29, 1961.

77. *Yale Daily News*, October 30, November 13, 17, 1961. As governor of Oklahoma from 1975 to 1979 and United States senator from 1979 to 1994, Boren, a Democrat, maintained conservative positions consistent with those he held as an undergraduate.

78. Coffin, *Once to Every Man*, 163, 165–67.

79. *Yale Daily News*, October 4, 16, 1961.

80. *Yale Daily News*, October 9, 16, 1961.

81. *Yale Daily News*, September 30, 1960, October 27, 30, 1961. David Scharff, Yale 1962 and a member of Saint Anthony Hall, told me in a conversation in Washington on December 14, 2010, that the Yale administration made it clear to the organization that it would not tolerate a reversal of the offer, a position that the membership fully supported on its own. Fellow Saint Anthony Hall member Gordon Davis, 1964, though from Richmond and a detractor of Coffin for "tarring all southerners with the same brush," confirmed his complete support for Mottley's election along with his fellow inductees in a January 20, 2012, telephone interview.

82. *Yale Daily News*, November 2, 7, 9, 30, December 4, 1961, February 5, 1962; *Time*, May 17, 1963.

83. *Yale Daily News*, October 5, 1962.

84. William Sloane Coffin Papers, Yale University Archives, Series 1, box 4, letters.

85. *Yale Daily News*, April 25, 29, 1963.

86. Char Miller, *Fathers and Sons: The Bingham Family and American Mission* (Philadelphia: Temple University Press, 1982), 218. Bingham adapted this language directly from Peter Countryman. See Bingham's coverage of the Northern Student Movement, *Yale Daily News*, November 9, 1962.

87. John Dittmer, *Local People: The Struggle for Civil Rights in Mississippi* (Urbana: University of Illinois Press, 1994), 200–201. A report of Lowenstein's talk appeared in the *Yale Daily News*, May 10, 1963. Lowenstein's biographer, William Chafe, reports that he originated the idea of a mock election following the analogy rooted in South Africa, a day of mourning that Lowenstein felt could be turned into a day of voting. SNCC leaders disputed that account, believing that the idea emerged from a collective process and other, less visible campaigns they had organized for congressional seats. William Chafe, *Never Stop Running: Allard Lowenstein and the Struggle to Save American Liberalism* (New York: Basic Books, 1993), 181–82.

88. Lowenstein's speech appears not to have been covered by the *News*. This quote is from Jodi Lynne Wilgoren, "Black and Blue: Yale Volunteers in the Mississippi Civil Rights Movement, 1963–1965," Senior Essay, Yale University, 1992, 14, copy in the Yale University Archives. Wilgoren draws this quote from Lowenstein's papers at the University of North Carolina, Chapel Hill. In a May 1, 2012, e-mail to me, Bingham reiterated the importance of that moment in Coffin's home, writing that "decades later I addressed the Berzelius [senior society] delegation about my adventures and recall that what I felt the most important lesson I wanted to convey was that at some point(s) potentially life-transforming opportunities will present themselves and it's important to be willing to take the risk to respond. It's clear that if I hadn't raised my hand in Coffin's living room, my entire life would have been completely different. It was the 'fork in the road.'"

89. *Yale Daily News*, October 17, 1963, October 22, 1963.

90. *Yale Daily News*, October 22, 29, 30, November 5, 1963. In his interview with me in South Royalton, VT, July 20, 2010, Speth explained that at the time he felt compelled to come to the defense of his native South, a position he would not have taken only a few years later.

91. Lieberman, *In Praise of Public Life*, 34.

92. *Yale Daily News*, October 3, 28, 1963.

93. Kevin Sack, "Trip South in '63 Gave Lieberman a Footnote, and Hold, in History," *New York Times*, September 26, 2000; Lieberman quoted in Wilgoren, "Black and Blue," 23. Lieberman supports the latter emphasis in his 2000 book, *In Praise of Public Life*, 35, when he admitted feeling "a definite sense of danger during the entire time I was there, the same danger that would result the following summer in the murders of James Chaney, Mickey Schwerner and Andy Goodman—three young men about the same age as I."

94. Telephone interview with Jonathan Greene, August 24, 2010.

95. Interview with Thomas Powers, South Royalton, VT, July 20, 2010. Further details of the Yale student presence in Mississippi can be found in Taylor Branch, *Pillar of Fire: America in the King Years, 1963–65* (New York: Simon & Schuster, 1998), 156–59.

96. Telephone interview with Chip Nielsen, January 25, 2011. In a news account in his local paper, Nielsen, despite a moderate tone and acknowledgment that local whites had invited him to go duck hunting, adamantly stated that most people would be shocked to learn of the conditions he discovered while in Mississippi. "All of us returned with a tremendous feeling towards SNCC," he reported, "and all of us will return, and all of us will work in some way or another for them and for civil rights in all its phases." Clipping from the Rolling Hills, CA, paper, November 28, 1963, supplied by Chip Nielsen.

97. Interview with Frank Basler, Bridgeport, CT, February 4, 2011. The *Yale Daily News* reported the arrests of Basler and Nielsen's companions October 23, 1963. Former Mississippi governor Haley Barbour generated considerable controversy when he described in 2010 the citizens councils of his youth as nonviolent, but his assessment is generally confirmed by Arsenault, *Freedom Riders*, 278, who describes Mississippi officials, most of whom were citizen council members, going about business "with cool efficiency."

98. *Yale Daily News*, October 22, 1963.

99. Miller, *Fathers and Sons*, 222.

100. *Yale Daily News*, October 24, 1963; Chafe, *Never Stop Running*, 184–85. Bingham confirmed this account in a telephone interview January 22, 2011, though he subsequently questioned the term "model." According to a May 1, 2012, e-mail, he recalled that Aaron Henry provided the bail money for their release.

101. *Washington Post*, November 16, 1963.

102. *Yale Daily News*, October 30, November 1, 1963.

103. Martin A. Padley, "Senior History," *Yale Classbook*, 1964, 289.

104. *Yale Daily News*, November 27, December 6, 9, 1963.

105. *Yale Daily News*, December 9, 11, 1963.

106. *Yale Daily News*, March 11, 12, May 1, 1964; Bingham interview with Jodi Lynne Wilgoren, Yale University Archives; Wilgoren, "Black and Blue," 28.

107. Telephone interview with Stephen Bingham, January 22, 2011; "Closed Society," *Washington Post*, November 16, 1963. Progressive by the standard of Mississippi whites, Silver nonetheless expressed his apprehension about the prospect of white students joining the organizing movement during Freedom Summer. Predicting violence in the months ahead, he worried "there will be people who make mistakes" by staying in black households or joining blacks for meals. "It's silly to come down here just to be arrested. Many students seem to feel that if they don't get into a little trouble the mission hasn't been successful," the *Yale Daily News* reported him as saying, April 24, 1964.

108. *Yale Daily News*, June 15, 1964.

109. Reagin interview, June 26, 2012.

2. Into the "Long Sixties," 1964–1974

1. Telephone interview with Peter Harding, March 21, 2011.

2. *Ten Years Out: The Tenth Reunion Classbook, Yale 1964* (June 1974), 60.

3. Ibid., 2, 44, 61.

4. Telephone interview with Guild Copeland, June 4, 2010.

5. Started in 1961 by Joseph Blatchford, who was appointed director of the Peace Corps in 1969 by President Nixon, ACCION relied on the raising of private donations, a difficult task that Holcombe pursued for a number of years. He subsequently used those talents to serve as a financial development officer at Yale and Columbia. As a sign of how personally connected this class was with the Peace Corps as undergraduates, Peter Von Mertens reported that he met Peace Corps director Sargent Shriver when he was a nonresident fellow in Yale's Pierson College. After joining Shriver for a beer following a lecture he offered senior year, Von Mertens reported, "That night I made up my mind to join the Peace Corps." Following a two-year assignment to Nepal, Von Mertens returned to that country dozens of times over the years, working as a trekking guide, helping establish a literacy program, and assisting a small hospital in Eastern Nepal. *Yale 1964 at 50* (Hagerstown, MD: Reunion Press, 2014), 680.

6. Dartmouth and Princeton started similar programs the same year. William G. Bowen and Derek Bok, *The Shape of the River: Long-Term Consequences of Considering Race in College and University Admissions* (Princeton, NJ: Princeton University Press, 1998), 5.

7. Quoted in Paul Liberatore, *The Road to Hell: The True Story of George Jackson, Stephen Bingham, and the San Quentin Massacre* (New York: Atlantic Monthly Press, 1996), 23.

8. Telephone interviews with Thomas Rowe, September 28, 2010; Nicholas Allis, January 21, 2011; and Daniel Berman, August 24, 2010.

9. John Dittmer, *Local People: the Struggle for Civil Rights in Mississippi* (Urbana: University of Illinois Press, 1994), 253; Char Miller, *Fathers and Sons: The Bingham Family and the American Mission* (Philadelphia: Temple University Press, 1982), 224–25. The subject of the student movement in Mississippi is further detailed by James Marshall, originally a member of the Yale class of 1965, whose commitment to the cause cost him a year before he graduated. James P. Marshall, *Student Activism and Civil Rights in Mississippi: Protest Politics and the Struggle for Racial Justice, 1960–1965* (Baton Rouge: LSU Press, 2013).

10. Telephone interview with Stephen Bingham, January 22, 2011.

11. Miller, *Fathers and Sons*, 229–33; C. Payne Lucas and Kevin Lowther, *Keeping Kennedy's Promise; The Peace Corps: Unmet Hope of the New Frontier* (Boulder, CO: Westview Press, 1978), chap. 4. Bingham also expressed concerns that the Peace Corps was vulnerable to efforts to politicize its actions, a real fear in light of efforts on the right, especially among leaders in Young Americans for Freedom, who urged the agency to advance an anticommunist message. E-mail from Stephen Bingham, May 1, 2012; John Andrew, *The Other Side of the Sixties: Young Americans for Freedom and the Rise of Conservative Politics* (New Brunswick, NJ: Rutgers University Press, 1997), 84.

12. Bingham interview, January 22, 2011; Liberatore, *Road to Hell*, 33–34; Miller, *Fathers and Sons*, 235–36. In his May 2012 e-mail to me, Bingham amplified his Marxist views by noting that he found many allies—in thinking and action—within the National Lawyers Guild, whose founding slogan in 1937 was "Human rights are more important than property rights." Some of its founding members were also members of the Communist Party.

13. Liberatore, *Road to Hell*, 33–41. Bingham interview, January 29, 2011. For a thorough examination of the upheaval on the Berkeley campus, including the violence that engulfed the effort to establish a People's Park and the FBI's complicity in fomenting that turmoil, see Seth Rosenfeld, *Subversives: The FBI's War on Student Radicals, and Reagan's Rise to Power* (New York: Farrar, Straus and Giroux, 2012).

14. Howard Zinn, *SNCC: The New Abolitionists*, 2nd ed. (Boston: Beacon Press, 1965), 272–73; Frank R. Parker, *Black Votes Count: Political Empowerment in Mississippi after 1965* (Chapel Hill: University of North Carolina Press, 1990), 219, n2; Bingham interview, January 22, 2011. Eric Bruner suggests in *And Gently He Shall Lead Them: Robert Parris Moses and Civil Rights in Mississippi* (New York: NYU Press, 1994), 211, that Allard Lowenstein's decision to distance himself from Freedom Summer was the result of his opposition to the National Lawyers Guild's involvement in the project.

15. The upheaval at San Francisco State is recounted as part of the larger rebellion on college campuses in the late 1960s by Howard Brick, *Age of Contradiction: American Thought and Culture in the 1960s* (New York: Thwayne, 1998), 170.

16. Bingham interview, January 22, 2011. As much as has been written critically about the Panthers, the most recent scholarly assessment places them within a continuum of black self-help organizations in the Bay Area. See Donna Jean Murch, *Living for the City: Migration, Education, and the Rise of the Black Panther Party in Oakland, California* (Chapel Hill: University of North Carolina Press, 2010), and Robert Self, *American Babylon: Race and the Struggle for Postwar Oakland* (Princeton, NJ: Princeton University Press, 2003). For an account of the ways the Panthers were unfairly demonized in the news media see Edward P. Morgan, *What Really Happened in the 1960s? How Mass Media Culture Failed American Democracy* (Lawrence: University Press of Kansas, 2010), 203–13.

17. Interview with Michael Price, Allston, MA, December 6, 2011. Hardly a complete account of the strike, Roger Rosenblatt's *Coming Apart: A Memoir of the Harvard Wars of 1969* (Boston: Little Brown, 1997), provides some sense of the turmoil at the university in the late 1960s.

18. The Boston highway controversy is highlighted in the film *Divided Highways*, produced for public broadcast by Lawrence R. Hott and Tom Lewis in cooperation with WETA-TV in Washington, DC.

19. Todd Gitlin, *The Sixties: Years of Hope, Days of Rage*, rev. ed. (New York: Bantam, 1993), 392.

20. Thomas Powers, *Diana: The Making of a Terrorist* (Boston: Houghton Mifflin, 1971).

21. Telephone interview with Tyler Smith, February 11, 2011; Richard Rosenkranz, *Across the Barricades* (Philadelphia: J. B. Lippincott Co., 1971), Log, 40–41. For details on the Columbia strike and what provoked it see James Kilpatrick Davis, *Assault on the Left: The FBI and the Sixties Antiwar Movement* (Westport, CT: Praeger, 1997), chap. 3. Davis reports that it was the student protests at Columbia

that prompted FBI director Hoover to initiate a counterintelligence program within the service on the model originally established not just to identify but to disrupt and disperse members of the Communist Party within the United States.

22. Rosenkranz, *Across the Barricades*, Postlog, 41–42.

23. Tyler Smith interview, February 11, 2011. Smith continues to practice architecture in Hartford today.

24. *Yale Daily News*, October 7, 1963.

25. Rosenkranz, *Across the Barricades*, Prolog, 1–3.

26. Ibid., Epilog, 4.

27. Robert G. Kaiser and Jethro K. Lieberman, eds., *Later Life: The 25th Reunion Classbook; The Class of 1964* (New Haven, CT: Yale University, 1989), 371. Joining Roth in Berkeley and in the Free Speech Movement was his friend and classmate Shannon Ferguson. Having left Yale his senior year short of the credits he needed to graduate, Ferguson ultimately received his BA from Berkeley, but not before being arrested in Sproul Hall and sentenced to community service. Following completion of his degree, he went to work for the Child Development Group of Mississippi, the nonprofit equivalent of Head Start formed when the state refused to support the federal program. He was drawn to the position from an interest in the civil rights effort in the state that took him for a time to Tougaloo College and his association with Marian Wright, one of CDGM's founders whom he knew when she was at the Yale Law School. Interview with Shannon Ferguson, Washington, DC, December 13, 2010; "Profiles: A Sense of Urgency," *New Yorker*, March 27, 1989.

28. Interview with Richard Berk, Philadelphia, May 4, 2011.

29. Telephone interview with Ward Cates, December 6, 2010; Ward Cates, "Yale, Public Health and Me: A Personal Odyssey," talk at the Yale School of Public Health, November 8, 2004, copy supplied by Ward Cates.

30. Telephone interview with Andrew Harris, February 17, 2011.

31. Jonathan Greene, for instance, reported in an August 24, 2010, interview that he secured exemption on the basis that his wife could not be expected to fulfill the janitorial duties the couple had incurred jointly as part of their rental agreement in New York City. Typically, those who did not have student or family exemptions reported the intervention of their employers or the perception that they were passed over when an excess of eligible (usually not college-educated) men were available to fill quotas in the metropolitan areas they lived in.

32. Telephone interview with Robert Hilgendorf, February 18, 2011.

33. *Ten Years Out*, 72.

34. Telephone interview with David Plimpton, January 17, 2012. The descendant on his grandmother's side of Massachusetts Bay colonial settler Thomas Hastings and the son of Calvin Hastings Plimpton, who served as president of Amherst College while his son attended Yale, Plimpton reported the unlikely assignment of carrying a personal message of goodwill from African National Congress president Albert John Lutuli (whom Plimpton had met in South Africa in the summer of 1963) directly to Martin Luther King Jr. in Atlanta. Like a number of his classmates, Plimpton was active in the Northern Student Movement, joining Peter Countryman in staging protests on Maryland's Eastern Shore in 1962.

35. Telephone interviews with John Clark O'Brien, September 13, 2012, and Wallace Winter, September 28, 2011.

36. Interview with Angus Gillespie, New Brunswick, NJ, March 31, 2010; Jonathan Rodnick submission, *Yale 1964 Class Directory: 40th Reunion* (2004), 180; obituary, *San Francisco Chronicle*, February 18, 2008, posted on the Yale 1964 class website at http://www.yale64.org/remembrances/rodnick.htm.

37. Telephone interview with Angus Macdonald, August 25, 2010; Angus Macdonald biographical statement e-mail communication, December 21, 2010. A statement posted on the am-cor website describes the company as a model green industry: "The am-cor panel production factory incorporates solar power generation to operate panel production machinery and air-conditioning. The am-cor System uses 70% less steel and cement to create ultra-strong building shells. Am-cor homes can incorporate SHA (solar home systems) and can be easily insulated since wall and roof structures are hollow. Both manufacture and product have very low carbon footprints." Two of Macdonald's model solar homes were featured in *Mother Earth* in 1984. Following the devastating earthquake in Haiti in 2010, Macdonald sought to establish a ferro-cement panel factory as part of a larger environmental community.

38. Telephone interview with Edward Ranney, October 31, 2011.

39. Philip S. Deloria, "The Era of Indian Self-Determination: An Overview," in *Indian Self-Rule: First-Hand Accounts of Indian-White Relations from Roosevelt to Reagan*, ed. Kenneth R. Philp (Salt Lake City: Howe Bros., 1986), 191–207.

40. Telephone interview with Philip Deloria, January 6, 2011; Philip S. Deloria, "The American Indian Law Center: An Informal History," *New Mexico Law Review* 24 (Spring 1994): 285–307.

41. Telephone interview with George Sheckleton, November 2, 2012.

42. David L. Shirey, "Pulsa: Sound and Light and 7 Young Artists," *New York Times*, December 24, 1970; Pulsa, "The City as an Artwork," in *Arts of the Environment*, ed. Gyorgy Kepes (New York: George Braziller, 1970), 217.

43. Leary's role at Harvard during the 1960s is recounted in Don Lattin, *The Harvard Psychedelic Club* (New York: HarperCollins, 2010). The *Yale Daily News* for November 30, 1961, carried an unsigned article on the front page on reports of hallucinatory drugs at Harvard. The Yale director of university health responded by claiming that drugs were not a problem on his campus, but they should be considered dangerous.

44. Pulsa, "City as an Artwork," 213. Pulsa's view of the ways artists could unlock the meaning of urban form finds additional resonance in Gyorgy Kepes's essay "Art and Ecological Consciousness," a contribution to the Universitas Project, a two-day symposium at the Museum of Modern Art: *The Universitas Project: Solutions for a Post-Technological Society* (New York: Museum of Modern Art, 1972), 150–59. For a more academic, postmodern reading of the Pulsa experience see Yates McKee, "The Public Sensoriums of Pulsa: Cybernetic Abstraction and the Biopolitics of Urban Survival," *Art Journal* 67 (Fall 2008): 47–67. Pulsa represented only a part of the upheaval at Yale's School of Art and Architecture, where planning students challenged the premises behind urban renewal in New Haven and attempted to act unilaterally to open admission to the school to minorities, challenging academic authority sufficiently to prompt the university to terminate the graduate program in city planning entirely. See Brian Goldstein, "Planning's End? Urban Renewal in New Haven, the Yale School of Art and Architecture, and the Fall of the New Deal Spatial Order," *Journal of Urban History* 37 (May 2011): 400–422.

45. *Ten Years Out*, 28.

46. Michael Wines, "Dissecting Romney's Vietnam Stance at Stanford," *New York Times*, September 12, 2012.

47. Telephone interview with Peaslee DuMont, August 24, 2012; website for Revision Health, the holistic medical practice DuMont opened in 2011, at http://revisionhealth.com/.

48. Edward Shorter, *A History of Psychiatry: From the Era of the Asylum to the Age of Prozac* (New York: Wiley, 1997), 274; Szasz obituary, *New York Times*, September 12, 2012.

49. *Ten Years Out*, 37.

50. Linda Sargent Wood, *A More Perfect Union: Holistic Worldviews and the Transformation of American Culture after World War II* (New York: Oxford University Press, 2010), 174–76; Donald Stone, "The Human Potential Movement," *The New Religious Consciousness*, ed. Charles Y. Glock and Robert N. Bellah (Berkeley: University of California Press, 1976), 103–6; telephone interviews with Peter Harding, March 21, 2011, November 15, 2012.

51. Bruce L. Maliver, *The Encounter Game* (New York: Stein and Day, 1973), 206; telephone interview with Brooks Carder, June 19, 2012.

52. Carder interview, June 19, 2012. For a detailed account of what it was like for a "square" to become a part of the Synanon game see William F. Olin, *Escape from Utopia: My Ten Years in Synanon* (Santa Cruz, CA: Unity Press, 1980), chap. 3.

53. Brooks Carder, "The Transition from School to Work in Synanon," in *Easing the Transition from Schooling to Work*, ed. Harry F. Silberman and Mark B. Ginsburg (San Francisco: Jossey-Bass, 1976), 79–84. In some ways, the attitude at Synanon about children conformed with that of other communes (which numbered as many as four thousand by 1970), that women would be freed from the exclusive burden of care, while children would gain the advantage of having additional role models in their lives. David Steigerwald, *The Sixties and the End of Modern America* (New York: St. Martin's Press, 1995), 254.

54. Interview with Brooks Carder, February 16, 2012. For a full account of the Synanon story see Rod Janzen, *Synanon: The Rise and Fall of a California Utopia* (Baltimore: Johns Hopkins University Press, 2001). The organization traced its origins to a decision Charles Dederich made in 1958 to pull a group of drug addicts out of a chapter of Alcoholics Anonymous in Santa Monica, California, and form

a new organization for their care. For a summary of Dederich's controversial life see his obituary in the *New York Times*, March 4, 1997.

55.   Paul Heelas, *The New Age Movement: The Celebration of the Self and the Sacralization of Modernity* (Oxford: Blackwell, 1996), 2.

56.   Abraham Maslow, "Synanon and Eupsychia," *Journal of Humanistic Psychology* 7 (1967): 28–35. See the profile of Maslow in Wood, *More Perfect Union*, chap. 5, 139–67. According to Wood (139), Maslow envisioned advancing a utopia—his "eupsychia"—as a democratic, just, and peaceful society. Although Carder rejected humanistic psychology himself, his decision to move to Synanon was solidified in reaction to the death of his UCLA colleague Ken Dallet, an early adherent to the humanist wing of the profession, who was believed to have committed suicide after being passed over for tenure by those hostile to his "soft" approach to the field. For a full review of this approach see Jessica Grogan, *Encountering America: Humanistic Psychology, Sixties Culture, and the Shaping of the Modern Self* (New York: Harper Perennial, 2013).

57.   Carder interview, February 16, 2012. Carder's ability to pursue mainstream business interests while still maintaining the Synanon lifestyle fits well with what Paul Heelas calls the "harmonal" aspect of the New Age, an ability to combine spiritual and personal goals with mainstream society: "One can liberate oneself from the baneful effects of modernity whilst living in terms of much of what the good life—as conventionally understood—has to offer." Heelas, *New Age Movement*, 31.

58.   Kaiser and Lieberman, *Later Life*, 75. In a pair of e-mails December 5, 2012, Carder explained, "We chose not to fight the revocation. What we fought was the size of the tax bill. What they did was to take the entire gross margin of our business over several years and allow no expenses against it because we didn't pay salaries most of the time. Our position was that we provided the living expenses for these employees and that that should be deducted from the gross margin to come to some reasonable profit figure. Certainly the organization as a whole was not making a profit at all." In defense of the organization, he noted that "about 20,000 addicts passed through Synanon in its history with no cost to government other than the tax exemption. And there are hundreds of drug treatment programs today modeled after Synanon, the first therapeutic community for drug addiction."

59.   Tom Wolfe, "The Me Decade and the Third Great Awakening," *New West*, August 30, 1976, 27–48.

60.   *Ten Years Out*, 70, 19, 7; Kaiser and Lieberman, *Later Life*, 19, 13.

61.   Tributes to Bill Stage, from William Drennen and Karen Bahnson, memorial page, Yale 1964 website; *Ten Years Out*, 81. A smoker of Camels and herb, according to Drennen, Stage died of lung cancer in October 1991.

62.   *Ten Years Out*, 109, 30, 12, 26, 69.

63.   Ibid., 136. Liberatore, *Road to Hell*, 41, reports the photographs of the scruffy-looking Bingham were those taken by the Berkeley Police Department after Bingham's arrest in the University of California–Berkeley president's office.

3. Civil Rights

1.   Interview with Arthur Reagin, Laurel, MD, June 26, 2012.

2.   Paul Lyons, *The People of This Generation: The Rise and Fall of the New Left in Philadelphia* (Philadelphia: University of Pennsylvania Press, 2003), 16, 44.

3.   Interview with Thomas Roderick, New York City, November 10, 2010; Nat Hentoff, *Our Children Are Dying* (New York: Viking, 1966).

4.   For Looper's obituary see the *San Francisco Chronicle*, September 24, 2011. Together with Stoneman, Looper formed, in 1990, YouthBuild USA, with the goal of helping underprivileged youth build affordable housing, learn job skills, and acquire the tools to rebuild poor neighborhoods.

5.   Roderick interview, November 10, 2010; *Ten Years Out: The Tenth Reunion Classbook, Yale 1964* (June 1974), 73. Roderick provides a full account of his experience at the school in his book *A School of Our Own: Parents, Power, and Community at the East Harlem Block Schools* (New York: Teachers College Press, 2001). William Ayers, the educational theorist, who is well known for his role as a cofounder of the Weather Underground, provided a foreword to the book.

6.   Moved by a growing antinuclear movement and aided by Bill Coffin, who initially provided space at Riverside Church adjacent to Columbia University, where he was pastor, Roderick formed the New York chapter of Educators for Social Responsibility. Its goal was to mobilize educators to end the arms race and to educate a new generation of youth in peaceful ways of dealing with conflict. Subsequently renamed the

Morningside Center for Teaching Social Responsibility, the organization worked with hundreds of New York City public schools to help teachers and young people develop their peacemaking skills.

7. Interview with Joseph Rich, Washington, DC, December 13, 2010; Robert G. Kaiser and Jethro K. Lieberman, eds., *Later Life: The 25th Reunion Classbook; The Class of 1964* (New Haven, CT: Yale University, 1989), 362.

8. "Bingham Nephew Sought as a Visitor of Jackson," *New York Times*, August 23, 1971; Wallace Turner, "Bingham Charged in Prison Deaths," *New York Times*, September 1, 1971.

9. Fay Stender, introduction to *Maximum Security: Letters from California's Prisons*, ed. Eve Pell (New York: E. P. Dutton & Co., 1972), 9. Stender further revealed her disillusionment, writing on page 12, "Working in the prison has deepened my cynicism about liberalism. I am convinced that the prison is a totally lawless agency. Prison administrations attempt to conceal this. . . . Since I have begun to identify with the prisoners, it has changed my life. That is the real secret of why all these people write to me. They know that I really identify with them."

10. *Soledad Brother: The Prison Letters of George Jackson* (New York: Coward-McCann, 1970). For further corroboration of Jackson's claims see Min S. Yee, *The Melancholy History of Soledad Prison* (New York: Harpers Magazine Press, 1973). Telephone interview with Stephen Bingham, January 29, 2011.

11. Paul Liberatore, *The Road to Hell: The True Story of George Jackson, Stephen Bingham, and the San Quentin Massacre* (New York: Atlantic Monthly Press, 1996), 162, 175. Bingham interview, January 29, 2011.

12. Liberatore, *Road to Hell*, 164–68.

13. "Bingham Believed in Canada or Cuba," *Washington Post*, September 2, 1971; "Murder Suspect Leaves No Trace," *New York Times*, January 6, 1972. The view that radicals were largely the offspring of well-to-do and politically active parents who maintained permissive homes was widely shared at the time, as noted by Char Miller, *Fathers and Sons: The Bingham Family and the American Mission* (Philadelphia: Temple University Press, 1982), 238. That belief achieved particular traction in the arrest and trial of Patty Hearst, whom William Graebner describes as a primary symbol of the "out-of-control, self-indulgent, permissive sixties." William Graebner, *Patty's Got a Gun: Patricia Hearst in 1970s America* (Chicago: University of Chicago Press, 2008), 179.

14. One of the clearest signs of Jackson's intentions appeared in an interview published only weeks before his death, when he responded to a question about his hopes for parole by saying, "The whole truth is that I would hope to escape." Tad Szulc, "George Jackson Radicalizes the Brothers in Soledad and San Quentin," *New York Times Magazine*, August 1, 1971.

15. Liberatore, *Road to Hell*, 173. For Williams's role in the murder of Alex Rackley, suspected by Black Panthers of being an FBI informant, see Paul Bass and Douglas W. Rae, *Murder in the Model City: The Black Panthers, Yale, and the Redemption of a Killer* (New York: Basic Books, 2006).

16. Liberatore, *Road to Hell*, 243–48; Yee, *Melancholy History of Soledad Prison*, 240–42.

17. Liberatore, *Road to Hell*, 113–14; Bingham interview, January 29, 2011.

18. "Lawyer and Political Activist Stephen Bingham on the Assassination of George Jackson," *SocialistWorker.org*, March 3, 2006.

19. Yee, *Melancholy History of Soledad Prison*, 253.

20. Henry Weinstein, "A Lawyer Hunted in Prison Killings Is Active in Hiding," *New York Times*, September 22, 1974.

21. Cynthia Gorney, "Fugitive Lawyer Surrenders," *Washington Post*, July 10, 1984. Years later, Bingham's charges received particular support for his own experiences at Berkeley, in evidence of FBI abuse of power directed not just at students but faculty, including controversial chancellor Clark Kerr. Seth Rosenfeld, *Subversives: The FBI's War on Student Radicals, and Reagan's Rise to Power* (New York: Farrar, Straus and Giroux, 2012). Betty Medsger, *The Burglary: The Discovery of J. Edgar Hoover's Secret FBI* (New York: Alfred A. Knopf, 2014), tells the story of how the 1971 break-in at the Media, Pennsylvania, office of the FBI first exposed the secret spy program on college campuses.

22. Cynthia Gorney, "The Return of the Fugitive," *Washington Post*, January 6, 1986.

23. "Justice: After 15 Years, Not Guilty," *Time*, July 7, 1986. A particular irony of Bingham's good news was that the cover story for this issue featured Ronald Reagan under the headline, "Why Is This Man So Popular?"

24. Liberatore, *Road to Hell*, 214.

25. Kaiser and Lieberman, *Later Life*, 44.

26. Katherine MacDonald, "Bingham Acquitted of Role in Prison Massacre," *Washington Post*, June 28, 1986. For a report of Lowenstein's assessment at Yale of apartheid in South Africa see the *Yale Daily News*, May 5, 1963.

27. In an essay that first appeared in *Playboy* for January 1989, Peter Collier and David Horowitz decry criticism directed at the police in the 1960s, citing not just "a numbing barrage against what was derided as 'law and order,'" but also naming George Jackson specifically as the object of misguided efforts to proclaim him a political prisoner. They saw him as a murderer "who deserved to be locked deeper in the prison system rather than becoming [an] international [symbol] for American injustice." *Deconstructing the Left: From Vietnam to the Persian Gulf* (Lanham, MD: Second Thoughts Books, 1991), 22. See also Peter Collier and David Horowitz's essay "Requiem for a Radical," the highly personalized attack on Fay Stender, following her murder by a man who believed she had betrayed Jackson and caused his death, in *Destructive Generation: Second Thoughts about the Sixties* (New York: Summit Books, 1989), 21–66. Former editors at *Ramparts* who were very much a part of Berkeley's radical scene in the 1960s, Collier and Horowitz have resurrected their careers as conservatives who have repudiated their past.

28. Raymond Wolters, *Right Turn: William Bradford Reynolds, the Reagan Administration, and Black Civil Rights* (New Brunswick, NJ: Transaction Publishers, 1996), 309.

29. Ibid., 45; Frank R. Parker, *Black Votes Count: Political Empowerment in Mississippi after 1965* (Chapel Hill: University of North Carolina Press, 1980), 93–101.

30. John David Skrentny, *The Ironies of Affirmative Action: Politics, Culture, and Justice in America* (Chicago: University of Chicago Press, 1996), 166–71.

31. Hugh Davis Graham, *The Civil Rights Era: Origins and Development of National Policy, 1960–1972* (New York: Oxford University Press, 1990), 461–62; Hugh Davis Graham, *Collision Course: The Strange Convergence of Affirmative Action and Immigration Policy in America* (New York: Oxford University Press, 2002), 67–74. Thomas Sugrue reports that the Philadelphia Plan was instituted in part in response to real grievances among African Americans who were virtually closed out of premier positions in the building trades through entrenched patterns favoring family and friends of those already holding union jobs. Recognizing the importance of employment opportunities offering decent wages, civil rights organizations in Philadelphia and elsewhere organized campaigns to open such positions to blacks as early as 1963 and continued their efforts into the late 1960s, when their cause was embraced by Secretary Shultz and Assistant Labor Secretary Arthur Fletcher, perhaps the administration's most prominent African American. Thomas J. Sugrue, "Affirmative Action from Below: Civil Rights, the Building Trades, and the Politics of Racial Equality in the Urban North," *Journal of American History* 91 (June 2004): 145–73.

32. Skrentny, *Ironies of Affirmative Action*, 111–44, 67–110; *Regents of the University of California v. Bakke* (No. 7811) 18 Cal.3d 34, 553 P.2d 1152, online at Cornell University Legal Information Institute at http://www.law.cornell.edu/supct/html/historics/USSC_CR_0438_0265_ZX3.html.

33. Graham, *Collision Course*, 74–76; Skrentny, *Ironies of Affirmative Action*, 140–41. Skrentny juxtaposes this race-conscious approach with the classical liberal approach based "on the utopian American colonial belief in 'natural society' that prevailed in the early republic, that a fair and equal society will naturally occur when people are free" (15). This view, which he equates with the laissez-faire approach to public policy, naturally appealed to conservatives hostile to government intervention in social relations.

34. Drew S. Days III, "The Courts' Response to the Reagan Civil Rights Agenda," *Vanderbilt Law Review* 42 (1989): 1007–8.

35. There is some reason to believe that Al Gore, in introducing Lieberman as his running mate in 2000, made a point of Lieberman's civil rights commitments while an undergraduate precisely because Lieberman had expressed concerns about affirmative action in the mid-1990s. Saying he did not see how he could oppose a Republican-generated ballot initiative in California slated for 1996, Lieberman reportedly claimed that support for one race or gender over another was contributing to "breaking ties in civil society," making white males feel disaffected. John F. Harris and Dan Balz, "Affirmative Action Divides Democrats," *Washington Post*, March 10, 1995; "Washington Report," *National Minority Politics* 7 (April 1995): 30. As a candidate for vice president, Lieberman assured fellow Democrats that he supported affirmative action.

36. Dennis Deslippe, *Protesting Affirmative Action: The Struggle over Equality after the Civil Rights Revolution* (Baltimore: Johns Hopkins University Press, 2012), 52, 206. Deslippe reports that President Ford remained deliberately vague when pressed to reverse affirmative action policy and did not do so while in office (198–200). Ford's true sentiments may well have been revealed some years later when he signed an amicus brief in support of race-conscious admissions programs at the University of Michigan described later in this chapter. *Bakke* proved critical in sustaining the inclusion of black students in select colleges and universities, as the percentage of African Americans ages twenty-five to

twenty-nine who graduated from college rose from 5.4 percent to 15.4 percent between 1960 and 1995. Enrollment in law schools rose from 1 percent to 7.5 percent during the same period, while enrollment of African Americans in medical school rose from 2.2 percent in 1964 to 8.1 percent in 1995. See William G. Bowen and Derek Bok, *The Shape of the River: Long-Term Consequences of Considering Race in College and University Admissions* (Princeton, NJ: Princeton University Press, 1998), 9–10. In making their case for diversity among students in higher education, Bowen and Bok recount the negative effects on minority enrollment when admissions decisions are made on a strictly "race-neutral" basis.

37. Wolters, *Right Turn*, 5; Desmond S. King and Rogers M. Smith, *Still a House Divided: Race and Politics in Obama's America* (Princeton, NJ: Princeton University Press, 2011), 114–15, 123; Charles L. Heatherly, ed., *Mandate for Leadership: Policy Management in a Conservative Administration* (Washington, DC: Heritage Foundation, 1980), cited in Robert R. Detlefsen, *Civil Rights under Reagan* (San Francisco: Institute for Contemporary Studies, 1991), 60; Daniel T. Rodgers, *Age of Fracture* (Cambridge, MA: Belknap Press of Harvard University Press, 2011), 127–30.

38. Telephone interview with William Bradford Reynolds, February 16, 2012; *Clay v. United States*, 403 *U.S. 698* (1971). According to Bob Woodward and Scott Armstrong, Harlan shifted his vote after reading background material on black Muslims provided by one of his law clerks and becoming convinced of Ali's sincerity as a conscientious objector. His vote left the eight participating justices deadlocked until Justice Potter Stewart proposed an alternative reason for reversing the earlier conviction by citing a technical error by the Justice Department. That led to a unanimous 8–0 decision. See Woodward and Armstrong, *The Brethren* (New York: Simon & Schuster, 2005), 136–39.

39. Wolters, *Right Turn*, 6–7.

40. Reynolds interview, February 16, 2012; Robert E. Taylor, "Expected Choice to Head Civil Rights Unit Is Said to Have Little Experience in Field," *Wall Street Journal*, May 12, 1981; Robert Pear, "Former U.S. Aide Proposed for Federal Rights Job," *New York Times*, May 13, 1981.

41. Kaiser and Lieberman, *Later Life*, 359.

42. Robert Pear, "Reagan's Choice for Civil Rights Post," *New York Times*, June 8, 1981.

43. Wolters, *Right Turn*, 72.

44. Ibid., 363–65; "Federal Rights Chief Favors Moderate Tack," *New York Times*, August 21, 1981; Charles R. Babcock, "U.S. to Shift Stand on Seattle Busing," *Washington Post*, September 6, 1981.

45. Howell Raines, "Blacks Shift to Sharper Criticism on Civil Rights," *New York Times*, July 26, 1981; "New U.S. Policy on Job Bias Draws Anger in House Panel," *New York Times*, September 27, 1981; "Affirmative Action," editorial, *Washington Post*, October 10, 1981.

46. "Affirmative Action vs. None at All," editorial, *New York Times*, October 10, 1981. A subsequent assessment of the Reagan administration's civil rights policies reiterated the Justice Department's strong record in challenging voting rights violations, but raised concerns about Reynolds's positions on affirmative action and busing, citing as troubling Reynolds's determination to be sensitive to local opinion on busing and especially his statement, "We are not going to compel children who don't choose to have an integrated education to have one." Robert Pear, "Rights Policy: New Outlook," *New York Times*, December 14, 1981. A subsequent and equally critical report in the *Wall Street Journal*, "Putting the Brakes on School Desegregation," by Joe Davidson, October 22, 1985, cited the same Reynolds statement.

47. The controversy involving Bob Jones University, which reached back to the Nixon administration and drew the attention of Reynolds early in his appointment to the Justice Department, is described in detail in Wolters, *Right Turn*, 465–86.

48. Stuart Taylor Jr., "Justice Dept. Says Dissidents 'Are Welcome to Leave Jobs,'" *New York Times*, February 4, 1982; Stuart Taylor Jr., "Rights Chief Holds 'Tense' Meeting with Lawyers," *New York Times*, February 18, 1982; "Ruling Sought on Tax Exemptions for Schools Practicing Racial Bias," *New York Times*, February 25, 1982.

49. Lee Lescaze, "Rights Group Seeking Exemptions Injunction," *Washington Post*, January 14, 1982; Charles R. Babcock, "Justice Dept. Defends Civil Rights Policies," *Washington Post*, April 4, 1982.

50. Mary Thornton, "Justice's Rights Division Assailed on Racism," *Washington Post*, April 6, 1982. A *Wall Street Journal* editorial, "A False Alarm," October 4, 1982, by contrast, chastened civil rights organizations for attempting to privilege people of color while still defending their position as a fight against discrimination.

51. A staunch defender of civil rights, Maryland Republican senator Charles Mathias was one of three members of the House Judiciary Committee who submitted the first civil rights bill to integrate public accommodations, in 1963. Challenged for his seat in the Republican primary in 1964 by L. Brent Bozell, William Buckley's brother-in-law and staunch conservative ally, Mathias survived what

Geoffrey Kabaservice describes as the first New Right challenge to a Republican moderate. Kabaservice also reminds us that Republicans were more staunchly supportive of civil rights legislation in the 1960s than Democrats were. Geoffrey Kabaservice, *Rule and Ruin: The Downfall of Moderation and the Destruction of the Republican Party, from Eisenhower to the Tea Party* (New York: Oxford University Press, 2012), 80–81, 98–101.

52. Phil Gailey, "Reagan Reaffirms Civil Rights Stand," *New York Times*, December 18, 1981; John Herbers, "Reagan's Changes on Rights Are Starting to Have Impact," *New York Times*, January 24, 1982.

53. Robert Pear, "Justice Dept. Aide Warns Senators on Passing the Voting Rights Bill," *New York Times*, March 2, 1982; William Bradford Reynolds, letter, *Washington Post*, February 11, 1982; "Mr. Reynolds' Letter," editorial, *Washington Post*, February 11, 1982; Wolters, *Right Turn*, 63–66.

54. Wolters, *Right Turn*, 116–19.

55. Mary Thornton, "Top Justice Aide Calls Race Quotas 'Morally Wrong,'" *Washington Post*, April 30, 1983; Dorothy Gilliam, "Mean Message," *Washington Post*, May 7, 1983; Carl Rowan, "Going Colorblind," *Washington Post*, May 24, 1983; letter from Peggy Anne Hansen, "Give It a Try, Mr. Reynolds," *Washington Post*, May 2, 1983.

56. *Wall Street Journal* editorial, "The Colorblind Vision," March 11, 1985; Anthony Lewis, "White Man's Lawyer," *New York Times*, June 6, 1985; Mary Thornton, "Assistant Attorney General Defends Record on Rights," *Washington Post*, May 10, 1985; "Don't Promote Civil Rights Wrongs," editorial, *New York Times*, June 5, 1985. Among those testifying against Reynolds's promotion was Frank R. Parker, who served as a civil rights lawyer for the Mississippi office of the Lawyers' Committee for Civil Rights Under Law, writing in his book, *Black Votes Count*: "Although Reynolds did object to a number of discriminatory voting-law changes, he also to an unprecedented degree failed to object to changes that subsequently were struck down by federal courts as racially discriminatory, overruled staff recommendations to object to discriminatory changes, and sided with covered jurisdictions in litigation aimed at enforcing the Voting Rights Act" (188). For Parker's obituary see the *New York Times*, July 14, 1997.

57. Reynolds interview, February 16, 2012.

58. William Bradford Reynolds, "The Reagan Administration's Civil Rights Policy: The Challenge for the Future," *Vanderbilt Law Review* 42 (1989): 993–94, 995. Reynolds uses similar language in his contribution to a decidedly pro–affirmative action collection: see "An Experiment Gone Awry," in *The Affirmative Action Debate*, ed. George E. Curry (Reading, MA: Addison-Wesley, 1996), 130–36. In his February 16, 2012, interview with me, Reynolds affirmed his earlier positions, noting, "If I was to say what was the biggest success story of those eight years, it was turning the affirmative action agenda to something that makes sense."

59. Detlefsen, *Civil Rights under Reagan*, ix, 9; Collier and Horowitz, *Deconstructing the Left*, 149, 153. Clint Bolick provides perhaps the most complete advocacy position for a conservative "color-blind" approach to civil rights, building on the Reynolds record, most notably in *Unfinished Business: A Civil Rights Strategy for America's Third Century* (San Francisco: Pacific Research Institute for Public Policy, 1990), and *Changing Course: Civil Rights at the Crossroads* (New Brunswick, NJ: Transaction Publishers, 1988). Subsequently based at the Goldwater Institute in Phoenix, Bolick is profiled in Marc Lacey, "A Watchdog for Conservative Ideals," *New York Times*, December 26, 2011.

60. Steven M. Teles, *The Rise of the Conservative Legal Movement: The Battle for Control of the Law* (Princeton, NJ: Princeton University Press, 2008); "Prop 8 Trial Defense Attorney: Charles Cooper," *San Jose Mercury News*, January 11, 2010. Cooper was also actively engaged in pressing for a tax exemption for Bob Jones University, according to Anthony Lewis, "The Court Says No," *New York Times*, May 26, 1983.

61. James J. Duderstadt, *A University for the 21st Century* (Ann Arbor: University of Michigan Press, 2000), 201–8; Barbara A. Perry, *The Michigan Affirmative Action Cases* (Lawrence: University Press of Kansas, 2007), 53.

62. Formed in 1989, the Center for Individual Rights drew heavily on Reagan administration alumni, including Theodore Olson, who had served as assistant attorney general for the Office of Legal Counsel before being succeeded by Charles Cooper.

63. Perry, *Michigan Affirmative Action Cases*, 135–56; King and Smith, *Still a House Divided*, 109.

64. Reynolds, "The Reagan Administration's Civil Rights Policy," 994. Columnist Paul Gigot echoed Reynolds's confidence in the court's new direction: "Lone Wolf's Work: A Constitution More Color-Blind," *Wall Street Journal*, June 16, 1989.

65. For Thomas's position on voting cases, most notably decisions in *Shaw v. Reno* (1993) and *Miller v. Johnson* (1995), which allowed whites to sue under the Fourteenth Amendment if race was considered the "predominant factor" in shaping election districts, see J. Morgan Kousser, *Colorblind Injustice: Minority Voting Rights and the Undoing of the Second Reconstruction* (Chapel Hill: University

of North Carolina Press, 1999), 58–66. For Thomas's growing influence on the court see Jeffrey Toobin, "Partners: Will Clarence and Virginia Thomas Succeed in Killing Obama's Health-Care Plan?," *New Yorker*, August 29, 2011, 41–51.

66. Telephone interview with Jon Van Dyke, August 30, 2011; Jon Van Dyke, "*Bakke v. the Regents of the University of California*," *Hastings Constitutional Law Quarterly* 3 (1976): 891–98; *Who Owns the Crown Lands of Hawai'i?* (Honolulu: University of Hawai'i Press, 2008).

67. Gary Saxonhouse interview with Jodi Lynne Wilgoren, February 23, 1992, Wilgoren Collection, Yale University Archives.

68. Interview with Joseph Rich, Washington, DC, December 13, 2010; Dan Eggen, "Politics Alleged in Voting Cases," *Washington Post*, January 23, 2006; Alex Kingsbury, "Why Eric Holder Sees Civil Rights as the Top Priority after the Bush Years," *U.S. News & World Report*, March 12, 2009. See also Rich's contribution, "The Attack on Professionalism in the Civil Rights Division," in *The Erosion of Rights: Declining Civil Rights Enforcement under the Bush Administration*, ed. William L. Taylor, Dianne M. Piche, Crystal Rosario, and Joseph D. Rich (Citizens' Commission on Civil Rights / Center for American Progress, 2007), 13–17.

69. Telephone interview with Stephen Bingham, January 13, 2013.

70. Chip Nielsen, consistent with his participation in Aaron Henry's 1963 Mississippi gubernatorial campaign, for instance, remained active in politics in California. A Republican, he nonetheless worked with two prominent Democrats, George Moscone and Art Agnos, both of whom were elected mayor of San Francisco, and he retained a commitment to federal intervention for civil rights. John Hollister Stein joined with his brother to organize a law student civil rights research council while they studied together at George Washington University Law School in the mid-1960s. While his brother Adam directly extended that commitment in forming a firm with the prominent black civil rights attorney Julius Chambers, John indirectly fostered those early concerns by establishing over time his own practice to defend the rights of victims. As head of the Chicago Legal Foundation's Disability Law Project, Wallace Winter counted among his achievements the successful relocation to group homes of three thousand disabled persons who had been neglected through casual placement in nursing homes not suited to their needs. William Roth, whose commitment to civil rights extended especially to the disabled, wrote an important early book, under the auspices of the Carnegie Council on Children, on the rights of handicapped children, and he advanced the use of computers for the disabled while serving as a professor at the University at Albany.

71. William M. Drennen Jr. and Kojo (William T.) Jones Jr., *Red, White, Black, and Blue: A Dual Memoir of Race and Class in Appalachia* (Athens: Ohio University Press, 2004), 89–90.

72. Ibid., 73.

73. Ibid.

74. Ibid., 147–54, 160, 199.

75. Writing in Curry, *Affirmative Action Debate*, 134, Reynolds asserted, "It is, of course, neither necessary nor proper to embrace policies of reverse discrimination in order to repudiate the segregated practices that so stained our past. Ours is an equal opportunity society. The promise is that all racial, ethnic, and gender barriers to access to work or educational opportunities will be removed. But how one runs the race—indeed, if one even chooses to run the race—is in every case an individual decision. Nor is the order of finish to be manipulated by considerations of skin color, national origin, or sex. Just as the starting gate must be open to all, so, too, can there be no artificial adjustments at the finish, whether in the name of diversity, racial norming, or otherwise. Those who, by reason of perseverance, hard work, and maximizing their raw talent cross the line ahead of others must not be denied their hard-won victory in a wrongheaded attempt to achieve a 'more balanced' student enrollment, a 'more diverse' workplace, or a 'more representative' contracting force." Even George Will, however, writing in the early years of the Reagan administration, discounted the favored conservative metaphor of the footrace, writing, "All citizens should be roughly equal at the starting line of the race of life. But much of what we have learned and continue to learn . . . suggests that 'equality of opportunity' is a much more complicated matter than most conservatives can comfortably acknowledge. . . . There is, of course, vast scope for intelligent disagreement as to what can and should be done to make 'equality of opportunity' more than an airy abstraction. But surely it is indisputable that 'equality of opportunity' can be enhanced by various forms of state action." George F. Will, *Statecraft as Soulcraft: What Government Does* (New York: Simon & Schuster, 1983), 130–31.

76. Michael B. Katz, Mark J. Stern, and Jamie J. Fader, "The New African American Inequality," *Journal of American History* 92 (June 2005): 75–76, 107. Katz builds on these findings in *Why Don't American Cities Burn?* (Philadelphia: University of Pennsylvania Press, 2012), describing what he calls

"limited ladders of social mobility" aimed at the selective incorporation of minorities into social and economic opportunity structures. While not dismissing the importance of even limited paths to mobility, he concludes that such effort "cools out insurgencies; it does not resolve the problems that underlie them" (87). Douglas Massey and his colleagues arrive at a similar conclusion, answering critics of affirmative action in higher education by pointing to historically grounded deficiencies—most fully manifest in African Americans among minorities—of human and financial capital. Douglas S. Massy, Camille Z. Charles, Garvey F. Lundy, and Mary J. Fischer, *The Source of the River: The Social Origins of Freshmen at America's Selective Colleges and Universities* (Princeton, NJ: Princeton University Press, 2003). Their study builds on Bowen and Bok's *Shape of the River*, by examining the background of minority candidates for select colleges and universities.

77. Michael K. Brown, Martin Carnoy, Elliott Currie, Troy Duster, David B. Oppenheimer, Marmorie M. Shultz, and David Wellman, *Whitewashing Race: The Myth of a Color-Blind Society* (Berkeley: University of California Press, 2003), 4. Countering arguments by what they call "racial realists," among them notably Abigail and Stephen Thernstrom, the authors concur with the University of Pennsylvania authors that durable and persistent inequalities accumulated over time and continue to divide African Americans from whites. A series of articles assessing the long-term effect of *Brown v. Board of Education* published at the fiftieth anniversary of the court's decision generally criticizes the court for presuming that elimination of past obstacles to African Americans could be assured simply by removing barriers to access to schools. As Kevin Gaines puts it in the introduction to the collection, "*Brown* fell considerably short of the structural vision of equality and redistributive justice sought by African American litigants and many black parents. Instead, what triumphed through *Brown*'s interpersonal logic of eliminating separateness by placing black and white students in proximity to one another was an attenuated formal equality that failed to address the inequitable distribution of resources and opportunities." "Whose Integration Was It? An Introduction," *Journal of American History* 95 (June 2004): 21.

78. Graham, *Civil Rights Era*, 472; *Regents of the University of California v. Bakke* (No. 7811) 18 Cal.3d 34, 553 P.2d 1152, online at Cornell University Legal Information Institute at http://www.law.cornell.edu/supct/html/historics/USSC_CR_0438_0265_ZX3.html.

79. Adam Liptak, "Justices Step Up Scrutiny of Race in College Entry," *New York Times*, June 25, 2013. In the same issue of the paper, Lee Bollinger, the named defendant in the 2003 University of Michigan admissions case, in reiterating the need for affirmative action in light of "nearly four centuries of racial subjugation and subordination," nonetheless recognized the ongoing challenge, noting, "While a strong majority has affirmed the status quo on affirmative action, for now, advocates of racial justice have much work ahead of us before the next time this issue reaches the high court." See also Adam Liptak, "Roberts Plays a Long Game," *New York Times*, June 28, 2013. Tanzina Vega, "'Colorblind' Notion Aside, Colleges Grapple with Racial Tension," *New York Times*, February 25, 2014, cites James Duderstadt on a number of factors contributing to contemporary racial tensions on the Michigan campus, where the percentage of black students had fallen from 6.2 to 4.6 percent between 2009 and 2013.

80. Adam Liptak, "Justices Back Ban on Race as Factor in College Entry," *New York Times*, April 23, 2014; Maggie Sterns, "The Woman Who Killed Affirmative Action. Twice," *Politico*, April 22, 2014. Citing her admission to Princeton and Yale Law School, Justice Sonia Sotomayor, in an impassioned dissent, returned to themes Justice Blackmun introduced in *Bakke*, while fellow Yale Law School graduate Justice Thomas denounced any program that included race as a factor in decision making.

81. Adam Liptak, "Justices Void Oversight of States, Issue at Heart of Voting Rights Act," *New York Times*, June 26, 2013; telephone interview with William Bradford Reynolds, June 27, 2013.

4. War and Peace

1. Thomas Powers, *Intelligence Wars: American Secret History from Hitler to al-Qaeda* (New York: New York Review Books, 2002), 105–6.

2. *Yale Daily News*, November 13, 15, 18, 1963.

3. Andrew J. Bacevich, *Washington Rules: America's Path to Permanent War* (New York: Henry Holt, 2010), 14.

4. Myra MacPherson, *Long Time Passing: Vietnam and the Haunted Generation* (New York: Doubleday, 1984), 11.

5. Bill Drennen, "Miscarriage: Reflections on a War," in Robert G. Kaiser and Jethro K. Lieberman, eds., *Later Life: The 25th Reunion Classbook; The Class of 1964* (New Haven, CT: Yale University, 1989), 504.

6. *Yale Daily News*, April 27, 1962, April 27, 1964. Faced with a jeering crowd, '64's Shannon Ferguson complained to campus police about the lack of security for the event. The following day, John Bruce Wilkinson, 1965, defended the crowd's unruly behavior, citing the inflammatory nature of the film.

7. John S. Wilbur Jr., *Split/Vision* (New York: Iuniverse, 2004), 7. Like Powers, Wilbur recounted a childhood memory drawn from the deep well of Cold War experience. Reacting to headlines that the "valiant" French Foreign Legion was in a fight to the finish at Dien Bien Phu, his imagination ignited as "the news of it came incomprehensively to me like a thunderbolt from a black sky. I remember running down the classroom corridors shouting out the terrible news until my teacher, unable to equate the enormity of this doom with my hysteria, grabbed me to calm me down" (ibid., 54). Wilbur's observations about the place of military service at the time he graduated from Yale is reflected in a collection of veterans' memories compiled from members of Dartmouth's class of 1964, *Dartmouth Veterans: Vietnam Perspectives*, ed. Philip C. Schaefer (Hanover, NH: Dartmouth College Press, 2014).

8. Robert Self, *All in the Family: The Realignment of American Democracy since the 1960s* (New York: Hill & Wang, 2012), 50. Self reports that of the thirty million draft-age men during the war years, only 10 percent actually served (p. 56).

9. Telephone interview with Tyler Smith, February 9, 2011; Mimo Robinson, "Bruce," in Kaiser and Lieberman, *Later Life*, 515. The first to die was John Phinny Works. A graduate of Hinsdale High School in Illinois, Works was one of those leaving Yale early to enlist, inspired, according to his brother, by President Kennedy's call to service. After being commissioned as an army officer and being promoted to first lieutenant, he was serving during his second tour of duty, as a Green Beret, with the Fifth Special Forces Group (Airborne) when he was killed in an accident at Hai Yen Camp, Chau Doc Province, Vietnam, on January 28, 1966. *Yale 1964: The Class at 50* (Hagerstown, MD: Reunion Press, 2014), 859.

10. Telephone interview with Gill Cochran, November 30, 2011.

11. That battle, and Kapica's role in it, are described in Michael O. Gregory, *Shiny Bayonet* (Victoria, BC: Trafford, 2005).

12. "City Lieutenant Is Hero as Beleaguered Calvary Battles Encircling Reds," *New Britain (CT) Herald*, March 31, 1966; *Yale Alumni Magazine*, December 1965, copy supplied by Daniel Kapica; telephone interview with Daniel Kapica, September 14, 2011. Kapica's maneuvers against superior odds were sufficiently impressive to become a model for subsequent training, according to his classmate James Bowers, who encountered the lesson through a recorded session about the battle as he entered army training for service in Vietnam following completion of his law school degree. Telephone interview with James Bowers, October 16, 2011.

13. Kaiser and Lieberman, *Later Life*, 540; interview with Gill Cochran, November 11, 2011; telephone interview with Daniel Kapica, September 19, 2011; Dan Kapica, *The Way of the Mangrove Seed: Living a Balanced Lifestyle* (Sarasota, FL: Mangrove Seed Expressions, 2010).

14. Drennen, "Reflections on a War," 504.

15. Interview with Robert Musil, Washington, DC, June 16, 2010.

16. On leaving the campus McNamara was surrounded by students who shouted antiwar slogans and rocked his car back and forth. Such tactics were sufficiently unpopular in 1966 to generate a letter of apology signed by twenty-seven hundred students. Roger Rosenblatt, *Coming Apart: A Memoir of the Harvard Wars of 1969* (Boston: Little, Brown, 1997), 23.

17. Jon M. Van Dyke, *North Vietnam's Strategy for Survival* (Palo Alto, CA: Pacific Books, 1972), 13; telephone interview with Jon Van Dyke, August 30, 2011. Edward P. Morgan reports that the United States dropped on Vietnam four times the tonnage of bombs that was dropped everywhere during all of World War II. *The '60s Experience: Hard Lessons about Modern America* (Philadelphia: Temple University Press, 1991), 141.

18. Wilbur, *Split/Vision*, 34–35.

19. Telephone interview with Thomas McAdams Deford, June 4, 2011; Mac Deford, "McNamara and Afghanistan: When Will We Ever Learn?" *Free Press*, July 16, 2009. Written as part of a series of weekly columns for the Maine paper, Deford's essay revisited his Vietnam experience on the occasion of former secretary of defense Robert McNamara's death.

20. Robert G. Kaiser, "Reflections on Vietnam: Very Ugly, Very Mean, Very Stupid," in Kaiser and Lieberman, *Later Life*, 497.

21. Ward Just, "The Heart-Mind Gap in Vietnam War," *Washington Post*, November 19, 1967; Robert G. Kaiser, "Negative Gains in Vietnam," *Washington Post*, August 23, 1970.

22. Kaiser, "Reflections on Vietnam," 497.

23. Thomas Powers, *Vietnam: The War at Home* (New York: Grossman, 1973), 314, xix.

24. Thomas Powers, *The Man Who Kept the Secrets: Richard Helms and the CIA* (New York: Alfred A. Knopf, 1979), 173–75, 186–90; Albin Krebs, "Samuel Adams, Ex-C.I.A. Officer and Libel Case Figure, Dies at 54," *New York Times*, October 11, 1988.

25. Telephone interview with George Pickett, February 28, 2012. Mac Deford, while in the field, also recognized the overcounting of enemy dead in Vietnam. In his July 16, 2009, *Free Press* essay he cited this practice, which struck him early in his assignment, as one of the factors indicating that the United States could not win the war.

26. Musil interview, June 16, 2010.

27. Telephone interview with Andrew Harris, February 17, 2011.

28. Telephone interview with Robert Lamson, May 21, 2012.

29. Steven M. Gelber and Martin L. Cook, *Saving the Earth: The History of a Middle-Class Millenarian Movement* (Berkeley: University of California Press, 1990); http://www.globalcommunity.org/history.shtml; and http://www.beyondwar.org/history-of-beyond-war.

30. Interview with Anthony Lee, New Haven, CT, February 5, 2011. Gelber and Cook report that Creative Initiative started with studies of the Bible that emphasized Jesus as a model for life. In the early 1960s it shifted to becoming a nondenominational sect, a condition it maintained until it completely secularized as it devoted its energies entirely to nuclear disarmament, changing its name to Beyond War. It formed a relationship with Physicians for Social Responsibility in the early 1980s through that organization's president, Helen Caldicott, who, like the Lees, credited Creative Initiative with saving her marriage. See Gelber and Cook, *Saving the Earth*, 276.

31. From a collection of Jack Cirie's poems compiled by Patrick Caviness, April 2009.

32. Personal communication from Keith Bentz, dated June 10, 2009, and shared by Patrick Caviness through e-mail, December 11, 2011. Esalen created a sports center in 1973 as part of the effort to address what its leaders considered an artificial mind-body split in America's value system. The Esalen catalog promoted athletics as "one vehicle for the comprehensive development of the whole person." Linda Sargent Wood, *A More Perfect Union: Holistic Worldviews and the Transformation of American Culture after World War II* (New York: Oxford University Press, 2010), 192.

33. George B. Leonard, *Education and Ecstasy* (New York: Delacorte Press, 1968), esp. chap. 2; Jeffrey J. Kripal, *Esalen: America and the Religion of No Religion* (Chicago: University of Chicago Press, 2007), 204–10. Not incidentally, Leonard cites Synanon as a primary example of the effectiveness of educational immersion in a whole environment, *Education and Ecstasy*, 182–87.

34. George Leonard, "The Warrior," *Esquire*, July 1986, http://yale64.org/remembrances/cirie.pdf.

35. Ibid. Leonard describes his close and affectionate relationship with Cirie in *The Way of Aikido* (New York: Plume, 1999), 123–31.

36. Patrick G. Caviness, "Remembrance of Jack Cirie," Yale 1964 website, at http://alumninet.yale.edu/classes/yc1964/remembrances/cirie.htm.

37. Joseph R. Svinth, "Martial Arts Meet the New Age: Combatives in the Early 21st Century American Military," in *Martial Arts in the New World*, ed. Thomas R. Green and Joseph R. Svinth (Westport, CT: Praeger, 2003), 262; Paul Heelas, *The New Age Movement: The Celebration of the Self and the Sacralization of Modernity* (Oxford: Blackwell, 1996), 97–98. For the background of aikido as "the way to reconcile the world and make human beings one family" see *Aikido and the New Warrior*, ed. Richard Strozzi-Heckler (Berkeley: North Atlantic Books, 1985), esp. Bob Aubrey, "Aikido and the New Warrior," 51–64. George Leonard is also a contributor to this volume.

38. Telephone interview with George Pickett, March 1, 2012. After leaving the army to serve as the budget expert for the newly formed Senate Intelligence Committee for several years, Pickett spent the last twenty years of his career working for defense contractor Northrop Grumman. Thomas Powers, *Intelligence Wars*, 342.

39. Interview with Chas Freeman, Washington, DC, June 16, 2010. These and other details of Freeman's family background and expansive diplomatic career are captured in an April 14, 1995, interview conducted by Charles Stuart Kennedy deposited at the Library of Congress and maintained online as part of the Foreign Affairs Oral History Collection of the Association for Diplomatic Studies and Training, at http://memory.loc.gov/cgi-bin/query/r?ammem/mfdip:@field%28DOCID+mfdip2004fre01%29.

40. Chas Freeman, "An Empire Decomposed: American Foreign Relations in the Early 21st Century," Remarks for the Foreign Affairs Retirees of Northern Virginia, Arlington, Virginia, March 24, 2010, online at http://chasfreeman.net/an-empire-decomposed-american-foreign-relations-in-the-early-21st-century-2/.

41. Chas W. Freeman Jr., *America's Misadventures in the Middle East* (Charlottesville, VA: Just World Books, 2010), 21–28.

42. Robert G. Kaiser, "A Foreign Policy, Falling Apart," *Washington Post*, May 23, 2004.

43. Thomas McAdams Deford, *Eight Lost Years* (Rockland, ME: Free Press, 2009), 33, 42, 25, 30, 36, 39.

44. Thomas Powers, "The Vanishing Case for War," *New York Review of Books*, December 4, 2003, 12, 17, 15; Thomas Powers, "The CIA and WMDs: The Damning Evidence," *New York Review of Books*, August 19, 2010, 54.

45. Thomas Powers, "Secret Intelligence and the War on Terror," originally published in the *New York Review of Books*, December 16, 2004, reprinted in Powers, *The Military Error: Baghdad and Beyond in America's War of Choice* (New York: New York Review Books, 2008), 45. See also his review of Paul Pillar, *Intelligence and U.S. Intelligence Policy*, in the *New York Times*, October 2, 2011.

46. Interview with Thomas Powers, South Royalton, VT, July 20, 2010.

47. John Ashcroft, *Never Again: Securing America and Restoring Justice* (New York: Center Street, 2006), 130. According to a profile in the *New Yorker*, Ashcroft often repeated Bush's charge to him. Jeffrey Toobin, "Ashcroft's Ascent," *New Yorker*, April 15, 2002, 53.

48. Ashcroft, *Never Again*, 51, 59, 48. Ashcroft, on page 45, recounts a distinctly more cordial exchange with Lieberman. Sensing Lieberman's resistance to providing early support, he acknowledged that a vote for him might harm any future run for president the Connecticut Democrat might have had in mind. Nancy V. Baker, *General Ashcroft: Attorney at War* (Lawrence: University Press of Kansas, 2006), 38–39, reports that while Ashcroft described his opposition to White as based on a record that was soft on crime, the two men had clashed some years earlier over abortion legislation when White was in the legislature and Ashcroft was governor.

49. Baker, *General Ashcroft*, 73–74, 109, 124; David Cole, *Enemy Aliens: Double Standards and Constitutional Freedoms in the War on Terrorism* (New York: New Press, 2003), 22; Ashcroft, *Never Again*, 280–81. For Ashcroft's full defense of the Patriot Act see the reprint of his August 25, 2003, speech before law enforcement officers in Boise, Idaho, "Preserving Life and Liberty," in *At War with Civil Rights and Civil Liberties*, ed. Thomas E. Baker and John F. Stack Jr. (Lanham, MD: Rowman & Littlefield, 2006), 17–23.

50. Baker, *General Ashcroft*, 113–19; Kate Martin, "Secret Arrests and Preventative Detention," in *Lost Liberties: Ashcroft and the Assault on Personal Freedom*, ed. Cynthia Brown (New York: New Press, 2003), 75–90. Stephan Salisbury, *Mohamed's Ghosts: An American Story of Love and Fear in the Homeland* (New York: Nation Books, 2010). Salisbury further reported the chilling effect of suspicions directed at Muslims in America at the time of the tenth anniversary of the 9/11 attacks, in "U.S. Muslims' Fears after 9/11," *Philadelphia Inquirer*, September 11, 2011. David Cole provides additional details of the federal crackdown, and its implications for civil liberties, in "In Case of Emergency," *New York Review of Books*, July 13, 2006, and "The Grand Inquisitors," *New York Review of Books*, July 19, 2007.

51. Ashcroft, *Never Again*, 285.

52. Ibid., 186–87, 193–94.

53. See, for instance, Frank Rich, "Confessions of a Traitor," *New York Times*, December 8, 2001.

54. Baker, *General Ashcroft*, 159–62. She reports that Ashcroft aggressively used emergency warrants, issuing more than 170 the first eighteen months after 9/11, compared to 47 over the two preceding decades.

55. Jack Goldsmith, *The Terror Presidency: Law and Judgment inside the Bush Administration* (New York: W. W. Norton, 2007), 144–60, 181–84; Jane Mayer, *The Dark Side: The Inside Story of How the War on Terror Turned into a War on American Ideals* (New York: Doubleday, 2008), 289–91. See also Thomas Powers's essay "The Biggest Secret" in *Military Error*, 85–100

56. Barton Gellman, "In New Memoir, Dick Cheney Tries to Rewrite History," *Time* Swampland, August 29, 2011, at http://swampland.time.com/2011/08/29/in-new-memoir-dick-cheney-tries-to-rewrite-history/; Jack Goldsmith, "Wrong Mission Accomplished: How Dick Cheney Reined In Presidential Power," *New York Times Magazine*, September 18, 2011, 15–16.

57. John Ashcroft interview on National Public Radio, September 11, 2011, at http://www.npr.org/2011/09/11/140360443/ashcroft-war-on-terror-won-one-day-at-a-time.

58. David Stout, "Ashcroft Faults Clinton Era at 9/11 Panel," *New York Times*, April 13, 2004; Andrew C. McCarthy, "*Post* Rallies to Gorelick's Defense and Gets It Wrong," *National Review*, April 21, 2004. For Ashcroft's own reaction to the 9/11 hearings, and his account of how it took the Patriot Act to remove the obstacles to intelligence sharing between agencies, see Ashcroft, *Never Again*, 231–49, 147–56.

59. Frederick A. O. Schwarz Jr. and Aziz Z. Huq, *Checked and Unbalanced: Presidential Power in a Time of Terror* (New York: New Press, 2007). Schwarz served as legal counsel to Congress's Church Committee in 1975 and 1976.

60. Gerald Shea, "The Question of Torture: The Legal and Ethical Implications of the Torture Opinion of Jay S. Bybee and John C. Yoo," August 27, 2006, copy in the author's possession. Baker, *General Ashcroft*, 28–29, details Bybee's advice to President Bush on interrogation while Bybee was head of the Office of Legal Counsel.

61. Mac Deford, "Afghanistan Reset," *Free Press*, August 5, 2010. A Vietnam veteran who earned a PhD in history from Princeton while in the military, Bacevich wrote as a professor of history and international relations at Boston University.

62. Mac Deford, "American Decline: Sure That Used to Be Us, but There's a Reason," *Free Press*, October 13, 2011.

63. Chas Freeman, "America's Faltering Search for Peace in the Middle East: Openings for Others?," remarks to the staff of the Royal Norwegian Ministry of Foreign Affairs, Oslo, Norway, September 1, 2010.

64. See Deford's postscript to his *Eight Lost Years*, 131–33, originally published November 13, 2008, under the title "Obama and Abraham En Route to the Promised Land."

65. Mac Deford, "Obama's Hamlet Meets Netanyahu's Fortinbras," *Free Press*, May 26, 2011; "Obama in the Middle East: Discredited, En Route to Irrelevant," *Free Press*, August 18, 2011; "Obama (and US Strategic Interests) vs. the Israel Lobby," *Free Press*, September 21, 2011.

66. Jodi Rudoren, "Israeli Settlement Plan Would Split West Bank," *New York Times*, December 2, 2012; Mac Deford, "Israel and Palestine; When Military Strength Is Not Enough," *Free Press*, December 5, 2012; Trudy Rubin, "Grim Death of Two States," *Philadelphia Inquirer*, December 6, 2012.

67. Philip Weiss, "The Israel Lobby Gets Its Man—and Tips Its Hand," *American Conservative*, September 23, 2009, at http://www.theamericanconservative.com/article/2009/mar/23/00006/. For a critical evaluation of how the American Israel Public Affairs Committee uses its influence in Washington to the detriment, in particular, of a negotiated Middle East settlement see Michael Massing, "The Storm over the Israel Lobby," *New York Review of Books*, June 8, 2006, 64–73.

68. In a chapter entitled "The Good Fight: Israel after Vietnam," Melani McAlister details the way Israel's tough Middle East stance appealed to policy makers, especially men, in the aftermath of America's failure in Vietnam. Noting that Israel's influence on the United States could not be explained simply by the work of a Jewish lobby or the influence of American Jews, she posits that "Israel played a rhetorical role in an argument about U.S. foreign policy and American identity. That argument itself was also connected to problems of gender: as feminism and women's political activism shook American culture to its core in the 1970s the fascination with military power served to reassert a certain kind of masculinity." *Epic Encounters: Culture, Media, and U.S. Interests in the Middle East, 1945–2000* (Berkeley: University of California Press, 2001), 158.

69. For a thorough and much more critical view of the effect of expanded settlements on preempting prospects for a negotiated peace see Gershom Gorenberg, *The Unmaking of Israel* (New York: HarperCollins, 2011). In contrast to his classmates Freeman and Deford, Lieberman did not see the U.S. role in the Mideast as that of an honest broker. Rather, as he said in criticizing his opponents in the Democratic primary race for president in 2003, "We do not gain strength as a negotiator if we compromise our support of Israel." Adam Nagourney and Jodi Wilgoren, "At Debate, Democrats Clash over Mideast," *New York Times*, September 10, 2003.

70. "Joe Lieberman Helping Palin with Foreign Policy," *Huffington Post*, September 5, 2008, http://www.huffingtonpost.com/2008/09/05/joe-lieberman-helping-pal_n_124190.html.

71. See, for instance, Mac Deford, "Dreams and Nightmares in the Middle East of the Future," *Free Press*, December 21, 2011, "Obama vs. Netanyahu, 2012: And the Winner Is …," *Free Press*, March 14, 2012; Thomas Powers, "The Options on the Table," introduction to *Military Error*, ix–xxi. To these testimonials could be added yet another critical review of the reliance on military threat behind American foreign policy, this one from '64's Leon Sigal, who writes of the U.S. effort to rein in North Korea, "The American foreign policy establishment proved remarkably resistant to trying cooperative threat reduction. Instead, it reflexively favored coercion—economic sanctions and air strikes—that brought the United States to the brink of war." Leon V. Sigal, *Disarming Strangers: Nuclear Diplomacy with North Korea* (Princeton, NJ: Princeton University Press, 1998), 251. As North Korea again appeared to be threatening South Korea in the spring of 2013, Sigal reiterated the importance of diplomatic efforts: "Path to Peace in Korea: Sustained Diplomacy with China Will Ease Tensions in Asia," *Boston Globe*, April 12, 2013.

72. Wilbur, *Split/Vision*, 4, 103–19; telephone conversation with Beverly Wilbur, January 7, 2014. Wilbur's book was self-published. His death in 2013 from complications associated with dementia could have stemmed from shrapnel lodged in his brain, according to one medical judgment, thus making him a possible late victim of the war.

73. Telephone interview with John Boardman, May 7, 2012. Boardman's sense of the diversity of issues facing the United States was deepened by his assignment to the U.S. mission to the United Nations, where he concentrated on issues taken up by the Security Council.

74. Mac Deford, "Israel, Iran, and the US; Succumbing to Blackmail," *Free Press*, August 22, 2012.

75. Chas Freeman, "Nobody's Century: The American Prospect in Post-Imperial Times," National Press Club, September 4, 2012, http://www.yale64.org/news/freeman.htm.

76. Chas Freeman, "Snowden and Snooping," remarks at the MIT Center for International Studies, December 12, 2013, http://chasfreeman.net/snowden-and-snooping/. Freeman's position was largely reflected in a January 2, 2014, *New York Times* editorial, "Edward Snowden, Whistle-Blower," calling for an offer of clemency or a plea bargain in place of the criminal charges lodged against him.

77. E-mail communication from Thomas Powers, January 8, 2013.

5. The Greening of '64

1. Lead-in to Eugene Linden, "Books: Storm Warnings Ahead," *Time*, April 5, 2004; James Gustave Speth, *The Bridge at the Edge of the World: Capitalism, the Environment, and Crossing from Crisis to Sustainability* (New Haven, CT: Yale University Press, 2008), xi. For a sample of the broad range of reactions Reich's book generated see Philip Nobile, ed., *The Con III Controversy: The Critics Look at "The Greening of America"* (New York: Pocket Books, 1971).

2. Speth, *Bridge at the Edge of the World*, 2008, xi.

3. Ibid., 204. In *Red Sky at Morning: America and the Crisis of the Global Environment* (New Haven, CT: Yale University Press, 2004), 82–83, Speth cited Reich's belief that a new generation's determination to throw off the control of the corporate state was a primary factor energizing the environmental movement.

4. James Gustave Speth, "A New American Environmentalism and the New Economy," Tenth Annual John H. Chafee Memorial Lecture, National Council for Science and the Environment, Washington, DC, January 21, 2010.

5. After receiving his PhD in architectural science in 1972 from the University of Edinburgh, Arens headed the Architectural Research Section at the National Bureau of Standards, where he concentrated on energy conservation, before taking a position at the University of California, Berkeley. There he served for a number of years as director of the Center for Environmental Design Research. Telephone interview with Edward Arens, October 7, 2010.

6. Interview with Sherman Kent, Woodstock, VT, July 27, 2011. A history major at Yale, Kent became interested in the environment through his grandfather, William Kent, 1887, who named the redwoods area Muir Woods after the nation's premier conservationist. His gift prompted a letter of praise from President Theodore Roosevelt that Sherman Kent displays in his Vermont home to this day.

7. Telephone interview with G. Gordon Davis, January 20, 2012; Richard A. Liroff and G. Gordon Davis, *Protecting Open Space: Land Use Control in the Adirondack Park* (Cambridge, MA: Ballinger, 1981).

8. Adam Rome, "'Give Earth a Chance': The Environmental Movement and the Sixties," *Journal of American History* 90 (September 2003): 549–50; Robert Gottlieb, *Forcing the Spring: The Transformation of the American Environmental Movement* (Washington, DC: Island Press, 2005), 137–39; Philip Shabecoff, *Fierce Green Fire: The American Environmental Movement*, rev. ed. (Washington, DC: Island Press, 2003), 105; Nicholas Lemann, "When the Earth Moved," *New Yorker*, April 15, 2013, 73. Adam Rome, *The Genius of Earth Day: How a 1970 Teach-In Unexpectedly Made the First Green Generation* (New York: Hill & Wang, 2013), 57, makes the connection between the antiwar and environmental movements overt when he quotes Senator Gaylord Nelson, who is broadly recognized as the man who conceived Earth Day, proclaiming, "I am convinced that the same concern the youth of this nation took in changing this nation's priorities on the war in Vietnam and on civil rights can be shown for the problems of the environment."

9. Interview with Gus Speth, South Royalton, VT, July 20, 2010.

10. See Laura Kalman, *Yale Law School in the Sixties: Revolt and Reverberations* (Chapel Hill: University of North Carolina Press, 2005).

11. Divya Subrahmanyam, "Speth: Saving the Environment Requires Overhauling Capitalism," *Yale Daily News*, May 1, 2008; Speth interview, July 20, 2010.

12. Robert D. Citron, "Charles Reich's Journey from the *Yale Law Journal* to the *New York Times* Best Seller List: The Personal History of *The Greening of America*," *New York Journal of Law* 52 (2007/8):

402; Speth interview, July 20, 2010. Citron details Reich's career before and after the publication of *Greening*, pointing to his hostility as a practicing lawyer, then as a law professor at Yale, to constraints on individualism from the state as well as corporate culture. That bias extended to environmental issues, in *Greening* as well as in Reich's journal article, "The Public and the Nation's Forests," *California Law Review* 50, no. 3 (1962): 381–407.

13. John H. and Patricia Adams, *A Force for Nature: The Story of NRDC and the Fight to Save Our Planet* (San Francisco: Chronicle Books, 2010), 23.

14. Richard Ayres, interviewed by Philip Shabecoff, in Shabecoff, *Fierce Green Fire*, 107; Steven M. Teles, *The Rise of the Conservative Legal Movement: The Battle for Control of the Law* (Princeton, NJ: Princeton University Press, 2008), 49–50, 43.

15. Rome, "'Give Earth a Chance,'" 531–34.

16. E. W. Kenworthy, "G.A.O. Says Insufficient Funds Peril Deadlines for Water Pollution Control," *New York Times*, February 2, 1974; E. W. Kenworthy, "Proposed E.P.A. Rule on Chemical Spills Is Denounced as a 'Cave-in' to Industry," *New York Times*, January 13, 1976; "Court Rejects Plea for U.S. to Clarify Perils of Reactors," *New York Times*, March 25, 1972; Speth, *Red Sky at Morning*, x, 79.

17. Richard Halloran, "Optimism on Fuel Efficiency," *New York Times*, February 21, 1979; Philip Shabecoff, "Carter Sees a Marriage of Environment and Economy," *New York Times*, May 29, 1977.

18. Philip Shabecoff, "President Pledges Energy Crisis Won't Alter Environment Goals," *New York Times*, August 3, 1979.

19. Interview with Angus Macbeth, Washington, DC, December 13, 2010. Macbeth's role at the NRDC is described more fully by his former Yale classmate and colleague at the council, David Schoenbrod, in *Saving Our Environment from Washington: How Congress Grabs Power, Shirks Responsibility, and Shortchanges the People* (New Haven, CT: Yale University Press, 2005), chap. 10.

20. Although he did not study with him at Yale Law School, Bradford nonetheless found it appropriate to draw on Reich's consciousness typology, describing Washington County in Maine, where the refinery would have been located, as characteristic of a Consciousness I, as Reich described it, in believing that "nature is beautiful but must be conquered and put to use. Competition is the law of nature and man." See Peter Bradford, *Fragile Structures: A Story of Oil Refineries, National Security, and the Coast of Maine* (New York: Harper's Magazine Press, 1975), 54.

21. Interview with Peter Bradford, Peru, VT, July 10, 2012.

22. Telephone interview with Michael Sherwood, January 12, 2011. For a full account of the case and its implications see Jack R. Nelson, "*Palila v. Hawaii Department of Land and Natural Resources*: State Governments Fall Prey to the Endangered Species Act," *Ecology Law Quarterly* 10 (1982–83): 281–310.

23. Steiger's controversial career is detailed in the obituary that appeared for him in the *New York Times*, October 6, 2012.

24. Telephone interview with Bruce Driver, September 2, 2010. For a summary of Reagan's efforts to roll back environmental regulation, including rejection of recommendations from mainstream Republicans with environmental experience, William Ruckelshaus, Russell Train, and Dan Lufkin, Yale 1962, see Shabecoff, *Fierce Green Fire*, 199–224.

25. Once out of his position with the Nuclear Regulatory Commission, Bradford defended himself against charges from Reagan officials that he was "antinuclear," retorting, "I always considered myself pronuclear but on my own more limited and, I hope, realistic terms than those that are normally implicit in that word." Peter Bradford, "The Man/Machine Interface," remarks before the Public Citizen Forum, Washington, DC, March 8, 1982. Unafraid to charge leaders in the industry with self-delusion and advancing misleading claims, he grounded his opposition to costly projects that failed to serve consumers, both as commissioner of public utilities in Maine, from 1982 to 1987, and subsequently as Mario Cuomo's choice as chair of the New York Public Service Commission, from 1987 to 1995. He also objected to the Reagan administration's determination to heavily subsidize nuclear power, while starving government investment in renewable resources, notably wind and sun. Bradford interview, July 10, 2012.

26. Speth, *Red Sky at Morning*, 2; Philip Shabecoff, "Scientists Warn U.S. of Carbon Dioxide Peril," *New York Times*, July 11, 1979.

27. U.S. Council on Environmental Quality and U.S. Department of State, *The Global 2000 Report to the President—Entering the Twenty-First Century*, 2 vols. (Washington, DC: Government Printing Office, 1980), quoted in Speth, *Red Sky at Morning*, 4–5.

28. Gus Speth, "Environmental Regulation: The ImmMOBILization of Truth," *Vital Speeches of the Day*, April 15, 1980, 388; Speth, *Red Sky at Morning*, 7. The critical response to *Global 2000* was quick

and extensive. While much of the attention was favorable, objections also arose, which continued to stall action in ensuing years. See the comments of a range of critics gathered in Julian L. Simon and Herman Kahn, eds., *The Resourceful Earth: A Response to Global 2000* (New York: Basil Blackwell, 2004). A founder of "free market environmentalism," Simon remained until his death in 1998 among those conservatives who have continued to question claims that human activity has caused global environmental damage. He institutionalized support for his position by founding the Science and Environmental Policy Project in 1990 to campaign against the idea that the earth faced a serious threat from global warming and ozone depletion. See his obituary in the *New York Times*, February 12, 1998.

29. Telephone interview with Thomas Lovejoy, December 1, 2010; Bruce Fellman, "The Place Where Ecology Was Born," *Yale Alumni Magazine*, July/August 2004. For conservative criticism of Lovejoy's work see, for instance, Dixie Lee Ray, *Environmental Overkill: Whatever Happened to Common Sense?* (Washington, DC: Regnery Gateway, 1993), 81–82; Thomas Gale Moore, *Climate of Fear: Why We Shouldn't Worry about Global Warming* (Washington, DC: Cato Institute, 1998), 98–99; David Horowitz, "From Red to Green," article originally published in *National Review*, March 19, 1990, reprinted in Peter Collier and David Horowitz, *Deconstructing the Left: From Vietnam to the Persian Gulf* (Lanham, MD: Second Thoughts Books, 1991), 182. The worst of Lovejoy's predictions was subsequently reaffirmed in a 2013 report issued by the National Research Council. Justin Gillis, "Panel Says Global Warming Risks Sudden, Deep Changes," *New York Times*, December 4, 2013.

30. Robert L. Peters and Thomas E. Lovejoy, *Global Warming and Biological Diversity* (New Haven, CT: Yale University Press, 1992), xviii; Thomas E. Lovejoy and Lee Hannah, eds., *Climate Change and Biodiversity* (New Haven, CT: Yale University Press, 2005). The aptness of Lovejoy's concern for the potential loss of species was subsequently confirmed by Elizabeth Kolbert, *The Sixth Extinction: An Unnatural History* (New York: Henry Holt, 2014).

31. William Tucker, "Environmentalism and the Leisure Class," *Harper's* 255 (1977), 49–56, 73–80; *Progress and Privilege: America in the Age of Environmentalism* (Garden City, NY: Anchor Press, 1982), xvi, 284. For a thorough critique of Tucker's book see William J. Bennetta, "Progress and Privilege: A Book about Environmentalism Meets the Press," *Environmental Management* 8, no. 6 (1984): 455–62.

32. Driver interview, September 2, 2010.

33. John N. Culliney, *The Forests of the Sea: Life and Death on the Continental Shelf* (San Francisco: Sierra Club Books, 1976); John N. Culliney, *Islands in a Far Sea: The Fate of Nature in Hawai'i*, rev ed. (Honolulu: University of Hawai'i Press, 2006), viii, 345; telephone interview with John Culliney, December 21, 2010.

34. John F. Stacks, *Stripping* (New York: Sierra Club, 1972), 135, 66, 118, 78. As ghostwriter for Judge John Sirica's 1979 memoir, *To Set the Record Straight*, and his own book on Watergate, among other publications, Stacks was described at the time of his death in a *Boston Globe* obituary of October 8, 2012, "as part of an ambitious generation of Ivy League–educated journalists who had entered the field expecting to wield influence with powerful figures and instead played a role in toppling them." Stacks's classmate and fellow *Yale Daily News* alumnus Paul Steiger carried the tradition of crusading journalism into the twenty-first century. Following a distinguished career at the *Wall Street Journal*, serving for fifteen years as its managing editor, Steiger founded ProPublica, the investigative journalism center launched with a multimillion dollar investment by Herb and Marion Sadler in 2008. The environment ranked high on the list of topics selected for in-depth examination to help make up for the erosion of investigative sources at daily papers. As of early 2013, ProPublica had, for example, posted 145 stories on fracking as an environmental threat; see http://www.propublica.org/series/fracking. Richard Pérez-Peña, "Group Plans to Provide Investigative Journalism," *New York Times*, October 15, 2007; Joe Nocera, "Self-Made Philanthropists," *New York Times Magazine*, March 9, 2008; "Paul Steiger—Setting the Truth Free," *Independent.co.uk*, June 17, 2010.

35. Telephone interview with Daniel Berman, August 24, 2010; Daniel Berman, *Death on the Job: Occupational Health and Safety Struggles in the United States* (New York: Monthly Review Press, 1978). Rome, *Genius of Earth Day*, 20–22, nicely summarizes Commoner's importance as a transition figure to the environmental movement.

36. Daniel M. Berman and John T. O'Connor, *Who Owns the Sun? People, Politics, and the Struggle for a Solar Economy* (White River Junction, VT: Chelsea Green Publishing Co., 1996), chap. 5. Acting on his own prescription, while working as an analyst for the California Public Utilities Commission in the early twenty-first century, Berman helped start on his own time the Coalition for Local Power in Davis and Yolo County in efforts to find an alternative to Pacific Gas & Electric, which he described as "our bankrupt local utility conglomerate." A campaign to get a portion of PG&E's territory annexed by the publicly held Sacramento Municipal Utility District failed when PG&E poured more than $11 million

into opposing the change proposed through public referendum. Berman could still take some pride a few years later, however, in helping defeat California's statewide Proposition 16, pressed by PG&E, which would have prevented local communities from being able to create their own electricity systems. *Yale 1964 Class Directory: 40th Reunion* (2004), 16.

37. Speth, *Red Sky at Morning*, xi.

38. World Resources Institute website, http://www.wri.org/, accessed September 20, 2010.

39. James Gustave Speth, foreword to Irving M. Mintzer, "A Mater of Degrees: The Potential for Controlling the Greenhouse Effect," World Resources Institute, Research Report no. 5 (April 1987).

40. Gus Speth, "Can the World Be Saved?" *Ecological Economics* 1 (1989): 296, 301.

41. Berman and O'Conner, *Who Owns the Sun?*, 42–43.

42. Thomas E. Lovejoy, "Applying Third-World Debt to the Environment," *New York Times*, December 26, 1990; Dana R. Visser and Guillermo A. Mendoza, "Debt-for-Nature Swaps in Latin America," *Journal of Forestry* 92 (June 1994): 13–16.

43. Speth, *Red Sky at Morning*, 69.

44. For thorough accounts of the politics that killed cap-and-trade legislation see Ryan Lizza, "As the World Burns," *New Yorker*, October 11, 2010, 70–83, and Theda Skocpol, "Naming the Problem: What It Will Take to Counter Extremism and Engage Americans in the Fight against Global Warming," on the Scholars Strategy Network, at http://www.scholarsstrategynetwork.org/sites/default/files/skocpol_captrade_report_january_2013y.pdf. Skocpol's account reinforces Daniel Berman's judgment that environmental groups had put too much faith in cooperating with polluters at the expense of building their own grassroots efforts to bring pressure on Congress, a point reiterated by Joshua Green, "The Wrath of a Green Billionaire," *Bloomberg Businessweek*, April 29–May 5, 2013, 24.

45. Carl Hulse and David M. Herszenhorn, "Democrats Call Off Effort for Climate Bill in Senate," *New York Times*, July 23, 2010; Thomas L. Friedman, "What 7 Republicans Could Do," *New York Times*, July 21, 2010; Ross Douthat, "The Right and the Climate," *New York Times*, July 26, 2010. See also Paul Krugman, "Who Cooked the Planet?" *New York Times*, July 26, 2010. Douthat's wait-it-out approach is fully consistent with Thomas Gale Moore's assertion in *Climate of Fear* that "even if significant warming were to occur, public policymakers could, at the time it became evident, launch programs to adapt to the change, such as building dikes, increasing air conditioning, and aiding farmers and ecosystems to adjust to the new weather . . . what is often overlooked is the strong possibility that global warming would turn out to be beneficial." "History teaches us," he adds, "that warmer is better, colder is worse. The optimal way to deal with potential climate change is not strive to prevent it (a useless activity in any case, as we shall see) but to promote growth and prosperity so that people will have the resources to deal with any shift, whether toward a warmer or a colder climate." *Climate of Fear*, 3, 68.

46. Ronald D. Brunner and Amanda H. Lynch, *Adaptive Governance and Climate Change* (American Meteorological Society, 2010), vii–viii; Ronald D. Brunner, "Adaptive Governance as a Reform Strategy," *Policy Science* 43 (2010): 301–4.

47. Bary G. Rabe, *Statehouse and Greenhouse: The Emerging Politics of American Climate Policy* (Washington, DC: Brookings Institution Press, 2004); Felicity Barringer, "Massachusetts Sets Targets to Slash Carbon Emissions," *New York Times*, December 30, 2010; Bruce Usher, "On Global Warming, Start Small," *New York Times*, November 28, 2010. Brunner's approach stemmed directly from his Yale experience, where as a graduate student he was introduced to Harold Lasswell, the chief innovator and integrator in the field of policy sciences.

48. Interview with William Duesing, New Haven, CT, September 7, 2010; Bill Duesing, *Living on the Earth: Eclectic Essays for a Sustainable and Joyful Future* (Stevenson, CT: LongRiver Books, 1993), 37; *Yale 1964: The Class at 50*, 267.

49. Bruce Wood, interview with John Jeavons, *Mother Earth News*, March/April 1980, http://www.motherearthnews.com/organic-gardening/john-jeavons-zmaz80mazraw.aspx. Among Jeavons's publications was the immensely popular *How to Grow More Vegetables, Fruits, Nuts, Berries, Grains, and Other Crops Than You Ever Thought Possible on Less Land Than You Can Imagine*, 8th ed. (Berkeley, CA: Ten Speed Press, 2012).

50. Grow Biointensive, http://www.growbiointensive.org/. John Jeavons, "Meeting the Challenge of Feeding the World," in Robert G. Kaiser and Jethro K. Lieberman, eds., *Later Life: The 25th Reunion Classbook; The Class of 1964*, (New Haven, CT: Yale University, 1989), 522–25. See also Jeavons's blog, "World of Hope," at http://www.johnjeavons.info/worldofhope_Home.html.

51. Kaiser and Lieberman, *Later Life*, 120–21; telephone interview with Vivian Donnelley, January 20, 2013.

52. At the end of *The Bridge at the Edge of the World* Speth relates a pilgrimage he took to the rural Wisconsin home of Aldo Leopold, widely recognized as the father of environmental ethics. There, Speth recounted, was the shack where the classic *Sand County Almanac* was written "and environmental ethics was born." These stemmed from "an appreciation that humans and nature are ecological equals." Speth, *Bridge at the Edge of the World*, 235; *Red Sky at Morning*, 24. Shabecoff, *Fierce Green Fire*, 107, reports that Senator Gaylord Nelson, the son of a Wisconsin country doctor and who is widely credited for launching the first Earth Day, had been influenced by Aldo Leopold's *A Sand County Almanac* as well.

53. Strachan Donnelley, "Minding Nature, Minding Ourselves," *Minding Nature*, journal of the Center for Humans and Nature, vol. 2 (April 2009): 6. The article was adopted from an essay Donnelley wrote in 2003 but was never published before his death on July 12, 2008.

54. *Environment Yale*, journal of the Yale School of Forestry and Environmental Issues, Fall 2008: 21, 43. Donnelley reiterated his position in another context in terms that again related closely to Speth's viewpoint, writing, "Our technological triumphs and our economically good lives (for some of us) become seriously suspect. They tend to make us forget our origins, neglect our worldly home, and threaten the biotic future of the land community. Herein lies the human and ethical importance of Leopold's cosmogonic account, world view, and moral landscape." "Leopold's Wildness: Can Humans and Wolves Be at Home in the Adirondacks?," in *Wolves and Human Communities: Biology, Politics, and Ethics*, ed. Virginia A. Sharpe, Bryan G. Norton, and Strachan Donnelley (Washington, DC: Island Press, 2001), 195.

55. Strachan Donnelley, "Civic Responsibility and the Future of the Chicago Region," *Hastings Center Report* 28, no. 6 (November-December 1998): S2–S5.

56. Robert K. Musil, *Hope for a Heated Planet: How Americans Are Fighting Global Warming and Building a Better Future* (New Brunswick, NJ: Rutgers University Press, 2009), 153. Musil served as executive director and CEO of Physicians for Social Responsibility and its director of policy and programs from 1992 to 2006, subsequently becoming scholar in residence and adjunct professor in the School of International Studies at American University, where he taught in the Nuclear Studies Institute and the Program on Global Environmental Politics. Active politically on behalf of liberal candidates, he served on the governing boards of the Council for a Livable World, PeacePac, and Population Connection. Returning to the roots of the environmental movement, he published *Rachel Carson and Her Sisters: Extraordinary Women Who Shaped America's Environment* (New Brunswick, NJ: Rutgers University Press, 2014).

57. James Gustave Speth, "Off the Pedestal: Creating a New Vision of Economic Growth," *Environment 360*, the online publication of the Yale School of Forestry and Environmental Studies, posted May 31, 2011.

58. Katarzyna Klimasinska, "Opponents to TransCanada Pipeline Protest by the Thousands at White House," Reuters, November 7, 2011.

59. Ross Douthat, "The Decadent Left," *New York Times*, December 4, 2011. Released on Earth Day 2012, the antienvironmental video blamed bureaucrats and draconian regulations for curtailing freedom and preventing energy independence; accessed at http://now.msn.com/anti-environmentalism-video-goes-viral-on-earth-day.

60. John Fullerton, "The Freedom of Martin Luther King, Jr.," *Huffington Post*, August 30, 2011; Kirk Johnson and Dan Frosch, "A Pipeline Divides along Old Lines: Jobs versus the Environment," *New York Times*, September 29, 2011; e-mail from Wallace Winter, September 6, 2011.

61. James Gustave Speth, *America the Possible: Manifesto for a New Economy* (New Haven, CT: Yale University Press, 2012), 9, 137, 196.

62. Speth, *America the Possible*, 126; Jason DeParle, "Harder for Americans to Rise from Lower Rungs," *New York Times*, January 4, 2012. See also Hedrick Smith, *Who Stole the American Dream?* (New York: Random House, 2012); Donald L. Barlett and James B. Steele, *The Betrayal of the American Dream* (New York: Public Affairs, 2012) and associated website, http://americawhatwentwrong.org/.

63. Schoenbrod was a graduate of New Trier High School in Winnetka, Illinois. His grandfather was a declared socialist. Family political conversations in his household were sometimes heated but nearly always on the left, he reported in an October 1, 2013, interview, to the point that he was scarcely aware in his early maturity of what was happening within the Republican Party.

64. Dennis Hevesi, "Rhonda Copelon, Lawyer in Groundbreaking Rights Cases, Dies at 65," *New York Times*, May 8, 2010.

65. Telephone interviews with David Schoenbrod, October 1, November 5, 2013; Schoenbrod, *Saving Our Environment from Washington*, 19–22.

66. Adams, *Force for Nature*, 165–67.

67. David Schoenbrod, *Power without Responsibility: How Congress Abuses the People through Delegation* (New Haven, CT: Yale University Press, 1993); Ross Sandler and David Schoenbrod, *Democracy by Decree: What Happens When Courts Run Government* (New Haven, CT: Yale University Press, 2003), 9.

68. Schoenbrod, *Saving Our Environment from Washington*, 230, 229.

69. David Schoenbrod and Richard B. Stewart, "The Cap-and-Trade Bait and Switch," *Wall Street Journal*, August 24, 2009; Schoenbrod, *Saving our Environment from Washington*, 193. A 1961 graduate of Yale College and a Rhodes Scholar, Stewart inspired Schoenbrod's decision to accelerate his degree program at Yale in order to apply for a prestigious postgraduate fellowship in England. A longtime trustee of the Environmental Defense Fund in New York City, Stewart helped craft the cap-and-trade approach to combating greenhouse gases while serving President George H. W. Bush as assistant attorney general for environment and natural resources in the Department of Justice.

70. When Gus Speth assumed the position of dean of the School of Forestry and Environmental Studies, the class of 1964 adopted the school, providing in the process considerable financial support. Most notably, Richard Kroon's gift made possible the construction of a new home for the school, the environmentally advanced Kroon Hall. In addition, Owsley Brown and his mother donated the funds to endow a professorship, which Speth filled while he was dean. In 2010 the Association of Yale Alumni presented the class of 1964 the university's outstanding class volunteer engagement and leadership award, based in large part on its role in environmental affairs, on and off the campus.

71. The U.S. record in meeting that challenge, Speth charged in a letter to the *New York Times* that appeared May 15, 2014, was "pathetic." Citing once again the climate change report that the Council on Environmental Quality had issued in 1980, he called the failure to act effectively "probably the greatest dereliction of civic responsibility in the history of the Republic."

6. God and Man

1. Driven from First Presbyterian after rousing the ire of fundamentalists, Fosdick was provided another pulpit by his allies, most notably John D. Rockefeller, with the construction of the new Riverside Church at the edge of the Columbia University and Union Theological Seminary campuses. It was Riverside that William Sloane Coffin moved to following his tenure as chaplain at Yale. Charles H. Lippy, *Pluralism Comes of Age: American Religious Culture in the Twentieth Century* (Armonk, NY: M. E. Sharpe, 2000), 21–22.

2. Telephone interview with Douglas Grandgeorge, November 20, 2012; *Yale 1964 Class Directory: 40th Reunion* (2004), 81.

3. John B. Judis, *William F. Buckley, Jr., Patron Saint of the Conservatives* (New York: Simon & Schuster, 1988), 77.

4. *Ten Years Out: The Tenth Reunion Classbook, Yale 1964* (June 1974), 144; Robert G. Kaiser and Jethro K. Lieberman, eds., *In Later Life: The 25th Reunion Classbook; The Class of 1964* (New Haven, CT: Yale University, 1989), 535.

5. James Turchik, "The Spiritual Journey of James B. Turchik M.D.," August 24, 2013; Roger Thompson, "My Spiritual Journey," September 13, 2013, both at http://yale64.org/soundoff.php.

6. Nate Jessup, "An Urgent Philosophical Journey," September 15, 2013; Frank Hotchkiss, "Being a Buddhist," July 23, 2013, both at http://yale64.org/soundoff.php. This declaration followed a letter Hotchkiss addressed to his classmates, dated April 4, 2000, http://yale64.org/news/hotchkiss.htm.

7. Telephone interview with Van Lanckton, October 4, 2010; "My Spiritual Journey," posted on the Yale '64 website July 23, 2013, http://yale64.org/soundoff.php.

8. Born Alan Richard Griffiths and also known by the end of his life as Swami Dayananda ("bliss of compassion"), Griffiths became a noted yogi while living in ashrams in South India. Among his publications are *Christ in India: Essays towards a Hindu-Christian Dialogue* (1967) and *The New Creation in Christ: Christian Meditation and Community* (1994).

9. Telephone interview with Peaslee DuMont, August 24, 2012. Matthew Fox, once a member of the Dominican Order within the Roman Catholic Church, is known as the founder of Creation Spirituality, a radically inclusive tradition that embraces spiritual traditions around the world, including Buddhism, Judaism, Sufism, and Native American spirituality. DuMont cited Fox's book, *Original Blessing*, published initially in 1983, as an influence on him.

10. For an explanation of the practice see Chungliang Al Huang, with a foreword by Alan Watts, *Embrace Tiger, Return to Mountain: The Essence of Tai Ji* (Berkeley, CA: Celestial Arts, 1987).

11. Interview with Jonathan McBride, Washington, DC, December 13, 2010; Kaiser and Lieberman, *Later Life*, 282.

12. Produced by Helen Schucman in association with William Thetford, *A Course in Miracles* professed to be the message of Christ channeled through Schucman, who said she transcribed the words she had received through an inner voice. It subsequently became a favorite in New Age circles, selling more than half a million copies. Richard Kyle, *The New Age Movement in American Culture* (Lanham, MD: University Press of America, 1995), 67.

13. Interview with Jon McBride, December 13, 2010; Kaiser and Lieberman, *Later Life*, 202. As a naval public information officer, McBride had some preferred assignments, including one to Hollywood. That did not mean that he was not affected by the loss of men he knew while assigned to the USS *Kitty Hawk* during the Vietnam War.

14. *Ten Years Out*, 76.

15. Christopher Schaefer, "Why I Am Here: Reflections on the Occupy Wall Street Movement," December 7, 2011, copy in the author's possession. Schaefer provides further reflection on his lifework in Christopher Schaefer and Tyno Voors, *Vision in Action: Working with Soul and Spirit in Small Organizations* (Hudson, NY: Lindisfarne Press, 1986).

16. Telephone interview with Alexander McKleroy, May 24, 2012; Kaiser and Lieberman, *Later Life*, 264; *Thirty-fifth Reunion Classbook* (1999), 362.

17. Such Whole Life Expos, Catherine Albanese suggests, form a vital part of New Age networks, which while they can be quite loose nonetheless share much in common with a tradition of metaphysical religion. Catherine L. Albanese, *A Republic of Mind and Spirit: A Cultural History of American Metaphysical Religion* (New Haven, CT: Yale University Press, 2007), 510.

18. The Teachings of Bruno Groening, http://www.bruno-groening.org/english/lehre/default-lehre.htm. J. Gordon Melton identifies such emphasis on universal as opposed to more recognized forms of energy such as heat and light with New Age beliefs, writing, "This energy goes by many names—prana, mana, odic force, orgone energy, holy spirit, the ch'i, the healing force. It is the force believed to cause psychic healing to occur. It is the force released in various forms of meditation and body therapies which energize the individual mentally and physically. It is the force passed between individuals in the expressions of love." Melton, *Encyclopedic Handbook of Cults in America* (New York: Garland, 1986), 113.

19. Telephone interview with Alexander McKleroy, May 16, 2012. In turning from social to personal redemption, McKleroy was acting very much in line with the human potential movement, as Donald Stone describes it: "Rather than taking direct action to change the political structures or setting up an exemplary countersociety, members of these groups seek to transcend the oppressiveness of culture by transforming themselves as individuals. They see that, if society is to realize its potential, they must first realize theirs. This potential includes greater insight, body awareness, and communication with others. It refers increasingly to heightened spiritual awareness and the possibility of feeling at home in and at one with the universe." "The Human Potential Movement," in *The New Religious Consciousness*, ed. Charles Y. Glock and Robert N. Bellah (Berkeley: University of California Press, 1976), 93.

20. William W. Everett and T. J. Bachmeyer, *Disciplines in Transformation: A Guide to Theology and the Behavioral Sciences* (Washington, DC: University Press of America, 1979). For more on Maslow and Rogers's influence on belief in the 1960s see Linda Sargent Wood, *A More Perfect Union: Holistic Worldviews and the Transformation of American Culture after World War II* (New York: Oxford University Press, 2010), chap. 5. For Rogers's influence on pastoral counseling, a subject of considerable concern to Bachmeyer, see Jessica Grogan, *Encountering America: Humanistic Psychology, Sixties Culture, and the Shaping of the Modern Self* (New York: Harper Perennial, 2013), 154, 311.

21. Muriel James and Dorothy Jongeward, *Born To Win: Transactional Analysis with Gestalt Experiments*, 25th anniversary ed. (New York: Da Capo Press, 1996).

22. Telephone interviews with Thomas Bachmeyer, March 3, 2011, November 6, 2013.

23. Interview with Franklin C. Basler, Bridgeport, CT, February 4, 2011; *Ten Years Out*, 11. Basler's views related both to the democratic thrust of early 1960s egalitarian movements and to subsequent New Age philosophy about work. See Paul Heelas, *The New Age Movement: The Celebration of the Self and the Sacralization of Modernity* (Oxford: Blackwell, 1996), 90–92. Robert S. Ellwood, *Sixties Spiritual Awakening: American Religion Moving from Modern to Postmodern* (New Brunswick, NJ: Rutgers University Press, 1994), 26, describes a more general attack in the era on hierarchical structures as part of "the breakdown of the modern bureaucratic ideal."

24. Basler interview, February 4, 2011.

25. In the aftermath of deindustrialization in the 1970s and 1980s, Youngstown became a touchstone for policy critics, including Ronald Reagan, who selected Youngstown Sheet and Tube as a background for a stop in his 1980 campaign for president to claim the company (which fully shut down some seven years after Miner's arrival in the city) would have remained open had his deregulatory policies and supply-side economic theories been in place. John Russ and Sherry Lee Linkon, "Collateral Damage: Deindustrialization and the Uses of Youngstown," in *Beyond the Ruins: The Meanings of Deindustrialization*, ed. Jefferson Cowie and Joseph Heathcott (Ithaca, NY: Cornell University Press, 2003), 204.

26. A full account of Burt's life can be found in the October 20, 2009, obituary posted by the Episcopal News Service at http://archive.episcopalchurch.org/81831_115715_ENG_HTM.htm.

27. Ross Douthat, "Can Liberal Christianity Be Saved?" *New York Times*, July 15, 2012. See also the letters in rejoinder from Mark Beckwith, bishop of the Episcopal Diocese of Newark, and Rev. Bruce Shipman, *New York Times*, July 19, 2012.

28. Ellwood, *Sixties Spiritual Awakening*, 11–12; e-mail communication from James Miner, August 2, 2012.

29. Joseph I. Lieberman, *The Gift of Rest: Rediscovering the Beauty of the Sabbath* (New York: Howard Books, 2011); Joseph I. Lieberman with Michael D'Orso, *In Praise of Public Life* (New York: Simon & Schuster, 2000), 63, 67; Kaiser and Lieberman, *Later Life*, 260.

30. Lieberman's ability to attract evangelical support, despite his positions on abortion and gay rights, is taken up in an article written during the 2000 election: David Firestone, "What Hath God Wrought? Lieberman and the Right," *New York Times*, September 3, 2000. Firestone concludes that Lieberman's ability to draw on a generalized morality, a civil religion once quite central to American political life, allowed him to navigate this religious thicket.

31. Glenn Gohr, "J. Robert Ashcroft: A Man of Prayer and Faith," *Assemblies of God Heritage* 16, nos. 2–3 (Summer/Fall 1996): 19–23; John Ashcroft, *Lessons from a Father to His Son* (Nashville: Thomas Nelson Publishers, 1998), 7.

32. John Ashcroft, with Gary Thomas, *On My Honor: The Beliefs That Shape My Life* (Nashville: Thomas Nelson Publishers, 1998), 13; Jeffrey Rosen, "John Ashcroft's Permanent Campaign," *Atlantic*, March 2004, http://www.theatlantic.com/magazine/archive/2004/04/john-ashcroft rsquo-s-permanent-campaign/2926/.

33. Easha Anand, "Ashcroft '64 Kept Views Constant," *Yale Daily News*, December 7, 2005; Jeffrey Toobin, "Ashcroft's Ascent," *New Yorker*, April 15, 2002, 54, 58.

34. Leslie Wayne, "Same Washington, Different Office," *New York Times*, March 17, 2006.

35. Telephone interview with Ashcroft's college roommate, Thomas Bachmeyer, November 6, 2013. Ashcroft's approach is well illustrated in the online video of his role in the service marking the Assemblies of God 2013 General Council meetings, at http://new.livestream.com/agusa/events/2223430/videos/26756121.

36. Interview with Joseph Lieberman, Stamford, CT, May 18, 2012.

37. Telephone interview with James Miner, June 28, 2012.

7. Sex and Marriage

1. Mark Lilla, "A Tale of Two Reactions," *New York Review of Books*, May 14, 1998, 7. For commentary on Clinton's place in the history of sexual politics in the office see Julie Berebitsky, *Sex and the Office: A History of Gender, Power, and Desire* (New Haven, CT: Yale University Press, 2012), 287–94.

2. The issue of Gingrich's sexual history surfaced again during his 2012 campaign for president when his second wife, Marianne, revealed that during the Clinton impeachment Gingrich had asked her for an "open marriage"—shorthand for the extreme permissiveness associated with the early 1970s—in order to maintain the relationship he had with Callista Bisek, whom he ultimately married. For the larger context see Alex Williams, "Open Marriage's New 15 Minutes," *New York Times*, February 5, 2012.

3. Among the many examples of the continued debate over the feminist agenda that derived from the late 1960s and early 1970s are two essays included in *Reassessing the Sixties: Debating the Political and Cultural Legacy*, ed. Stephen Macedo (New York: W. W. Norton, 1997). In "Women in the Sixties," the University of Chicago's Martha Nussbaum offers a measured defense of that agenda; while in "Feminism: Where the Spirit of the Sixties Lives On," one cannot help but be struck by the strident language of the author, Jeremy Rabkin, a law professor at George Mason University and an adviser

to the American Enterprise Institute. He writes: "The extraordinary self-indulgence of contemporary feminism does not, however, represent a degeneration of a movement that once held high ideals and made tough demands on itself. It should have been expected from the tone of the original women's liberation movement of the sixties. Starting from the premise of women as a class oppressed by men as a class, feminism was launched amid self-dramatizing narcissism. It was the most natural thing for women of this character to throw tantrums, not to notice how selfish they were being, to aggrandize more and more. Succeeding in aggrandizement, they indulged totalitarian or coercive impulses" (*Reassessing the Sixties*, 69).

4. *Yale Daily News*, February 19, March 4, 9, 1964. In a February 26, 1964, editorial, striving for balance, the *News* said of McLaughlin, "Probably few students vowed immediately never to indulge before marriage. But because of these lectures, many individuals gained a sense of moral responsibility which will remain long after specific arguments against premarital relations have been forgotten." Sex also made the *News*'s front page on February 18, 1964, in a story under the headline "Former President of Barnard Warns of Promiscuity's Effect on Stability."

5. News of the availability of the pill arrived precisely at the time of this class's admission to college. Buried on page 75 of the May 10, 1960, issue of the *New York Times* that reported the statistics relating to admission to Ivy League colleges was the headline "U.S. Approves Pill for Birth Control." "Approval was based on the question of safety," the associate commissioner of the Food and Drug Administration, John L. Harvey, reported. "We had no choice as to the morality that might be involved."

6. John W. Johnson, *Griswold v. Connecticut: Birth Control and the Constitutional Right of Privacy* (Lawrence: University Press of Kansas, 2005). Only a few months after the decision, Brown University attracted unwanted critical publicity when the student newspaper revealed that a university physician had prescribed birth control pills to two unmarried students. To mark the sea change in attitude, a Yale dean asserted, "We are not interested in the private lives of students as long as they remain private," a position that by 1966 was widely accepted in university circles. By 1970, 60 percent of all married and unmarried women were using the birth control pill, an intrauterine device, or had been sterilized. David Allyn, *Make Love Not War; The Sexual Revolution: An Unfettered History* (Boston: Little Brown, 2000), 38, 51; Stephanie Coontz, *Marriage, A History: How Love Conquered Marriage* (New York: Viking, 2005), 254.

7. For a succinct summary of what women of this age group faced when seeking an abortion see Ruth Rosen, *The World Split Open: How the Modern Women's Movement Changed America*, paperback ed. (New York: Penguin, 2001), 52–55. For a more complete account of conditions under which pregnancies were terminated before abortion was legalized see Leslie J. Reagan, *When Abortion Was a Crime: Women, Medicine, and the Law in the United States, 1967–1973* (Berkeley: University of California Press, 1999).

8. Elaine Tyler May reminds us that the nuclear family so celebrated as the locus of virtually all its members' personal needs through an energized and expressive personal life was less the norm for the twentieth century than a particular postwar construction, quite in contrast to families formed before, in the early part of the century. In between baby boomers and their grandparents, it is this generation, she argues, "with its strong domestic ideology, pervasive consensus politics, and peculiar demographic behavior—that stands out as different." May, *Homeward Bound: American Families in the Cold War Era* (New York: Basic Books, 1988), 9.

9. Telephone interviews with Frederick Buell, February 16, 2012, and Sydney Lea, September 10, 2012.

10. Obituary, *Daily Hampshire Gazette*, Northampton, MA, September 5, 2012.

11. Margaret Marsh, "Suburban Men and Masculine Domesticity, 1870–1915," *American Quarterly* 40 (June 1988): 165–86.

12. Coontz, *Marriage, A History*, 238, 281.

13. Peter Filene, *Him/Her/Self: Sex Roles in Modern America* (Baltimore: Johns Hopkins University Press, 1974), 205.

14. *Yale Daily News*, May 18, 1962.

15. David Steigerwald, *The Sixties and the End of Modern America* (New York: St. Martin's Press, 1995), 248.

16. Betty Friedan, *The Feminine Mystique* (New York: W. W. Norton, 1963), 305–18, devotes pages to psychologist Abraham Maslow's views of self-actualization that later became so central to New Age belief. For an evaluation of the book's wide influence see Stephanie Coontz, *A Strange Stirring: "The Feminine Mystique" and American Women at the Dawn of the 1960s* (New York: Basic Books, 2011). Although there is some temptation to credit the origins of feminism to the 1960s, Coontz is not

alone in tracking its stirrings to the 1950s and earlier. In a book that mixes personal with sociological observation, Wini Breines, born like the majority of Yale's class of 1964 in 1942 and an activist in the women's and civil rights movements of the 1960s, argues that for women her age, growing up in the 1950s, there was enough cultural space, largely introduced through popular culture, to escape the tight restrictions that served as normative and sexually constraining. Wini Breines, *Young, White, and Miserable: Growing Up Female in the 1950s* (Chicago: University of Chicago Press, 1992).

17. Coontz, *Marriage, A History*, 247.

18. David Brooks, *Bobos in Paradise: The New Upper Class and How They Got There* (New York: Simon & Schuster, 2000), 18–20, identifies the *Times* wedding announcements, complete with clubs and prep school affiliations, as true markers of the dominant white Anglo-Saxon culture, one that dominated into the early 1960s. For examples from this class see both the engagement and marriage announcements for William Bradford Reynolds to Lynn Morgan, a junior at Sweet Briar College, appearing in the *New York Times*, January 3 and June 28, 1964. Ward Cates's engagement to Joan Roberts appeared in the *Times* on January 2, 1967. Thomas Lovejoy's marriage to Charlotte "Mopsy" Seymour, the granddaughter of Yale's fifteenth president, Charles Seymour, appeared in the *Times* January 29, 1966. The announcement of my own engagement to Jane Brown appeared in the *Times* May 30, 1968.

19. Telephone interview with Michelle Mead Armor, January 25, 2012.

20. The landmark U.S. Supreme Court case *Loving v. Virginia*, decided in 1967, overturned a Virginia statue that read in part, "If any white person intermarry with a colored person, or any colored person intermarry with a white person, he shall be guilty of a felony and shall be punished by confinement in the penitentiary for not less than one nor more than five years." Posted at http://www.law.cornell.edu/supct/html/historics/USSC_CR_0388_0001_ZO.html.

21. Telephone conversation with Henry Putzel, November 8, 2012; Skype interview with James Rogers, December 21, 2011. For evidence for how rare it was to marry outside one's own ethnic group before the sexual revolution of the 1960s see David T. Courtwright, *No Right Turn: Conservative Politics in a Liberal America* (Cambridge, MA: Harvard University Press, 2010), 25.

22. G. Gordon Davis, *Everything Has a Life*, e-book, posted at Amazon.com, September 2012.

23. Interview with Michael Arons, August 23, 2012; Robert G. Kaiser and Jethro K. Lieberman, eds., *Later Life: The 25th Reunion Classbook; The Class of 1964* (New Haven, CT: Yale University, 1989), 23. Engaged in hospital administration when she met him, Arons's first wife, he reported, bridled at his control of the family budget. That the male head of household might insist on such control was not surprising, given the fact that it was not until 1975 that it became illegal to require a married woman to have her husband's written permission in order to get a loan or even a credit card. Coontz, *Marriage, A History*, 310.

24. Steigerwald, *Sixties*, 255.

25. The national divorce rate doubled between 1960 and 1970, rising to a peak in 1980, when half of married persons could be expected to divorce at some point in their lives. The rate subsequently declined, dropping in 1998 by 26 percent to the rate of 1979. Hugh Carter and Paul C. Glick, *Marriage and Divorce: A Social and Economic Study*, rev. ed. (Cambridge, MA: Harvard University Press, 1976), 393; Coontz, *Marriage, A History*, 263–64.

26. Kaiser and Lieberman, *Later Life*, 534.

27. Such was the expectation coming into the 1960s, Elaine Tyler May reports: "To achieve this secure, stable, and materially comfortable life, women had to adapt. The adaptation took two forms: adapting to their husband's needs and adapting their own goals and aspirations to fit the marriages they had created. Both husbands and wives recognized that marriage required more adjustments for women than for men." May, *Homeward Bound*, 202–3. More broadly, Robert Self, *All in the Family: The Realignment of American Democracy since the 1960s* (New York: Hill & Wang, 2012), places the concept of the male breadwinner and his defense at the heart of the political contest that has witnessed a partial if not complete realignment of the two major political parties over the past half century.

28. While it is clear that not all women reporting worked full time, this was the period that the percentage of two-parent households with children where both parents worked increased significantly, from 30 percent in 1975 to 47 percent in 1988. By 1994 the proportion of women working between the ages of twenty-five and fifty-four had reached 75 percent. Robert L. Griswold, *Fatherhood in America: A History* (New York: Basic Books, 1993), 220; Self, *All in the Family*, 314. A subsequent poll prepared for its fiftieth reunion reported that 75 percent of Yale '64 wives had worked full time, while only 13.6 percent had not worked at all. Another 40 percent questioned reported part time work, reflecting, no doubt, transitional employment during their childbearing years.

29. Kaiser and Lieberman, *Later Life*, 129; interview with Donald Edwards, Bordentown, NJ, September 12, 2012. Although the evidence of concern about changing marital roles is sketchy in '64's tenth-reunion book, Lawrence Chapman, an architect who married in 1967, voiced his view explicitly, writing, "The biggest and most unexpected challenge I have found has been my marriage. The responsibilities are awesome; the demands on my whole being are much greater than I ever imagined." *Ten Years Out: The Tenth Reunion Classbook, Yale 1964* (June 1974), 18. Sociologist Andrew Hacker captured the sense of transition at the time, writing in 1970, "For all the injustice in marriages of the past, at least they were governed by rules that both partners acknowledged. But the growing reluctance of more and more American wives to accept the double standard imposed by outside authorities has forced married couples to devise guidelines for themselves. Unfortunately, most adults lack the capacity for so bewildering an enterprise. This does not imply that husbands and wives showed more intelligence or intuition in earlier eras. Marital success now calls for unselfishness and sensitivity that the average person simply does not have." Andrew Hacker, *The End of the American Era* (New York: Atheneum, 1970), 174.

30. Lucy Moore, *Into the Canyon: Seven Years in Navajo Country* (Albuquerque: University of New Mexico Press, 2004), 5–6.

31. Ibid., 26, 35, 22.

32. Telephone interview with Lucy Moore, November 15, 2011.

33. Ibid.; http://www.lucymoore.com/.

34. Miriam Horn, *Rebels in White Gloves: Coming of Age with Hillary's Class—Wellesley '69* (New York: Times Books, 1999), xi–xii, xvi. As affirmation of the hinge moment Hillary Clinton's remarks represented, Stephanie Coontz reports that as late as 1968 two-thirds of women in their teens and mid-twenties still expected to become full-time homemakers. *Marriage, A History*, 249.

35. Moore interview, November 15, 2011.

36. Born from the realization that there were political dimensions to private lives and that power relations shaped life in marriage, in the kitchen, the bedroom, and the nursery, as well as work, consciousness-raising groups proliferated rapidly in the late 1960s. As historian Ruth Rosen reports, these experiences helped women question "the natural order of things": "When enough women had told their stories, enough such meetings had taken place, the 'personal' no longer seemed a purely individual problem, but the result of deep cultural, social, and economic forces and assumptions." Rosen, *The World Split Open*, 196–97. Some feminists, including Betty Friedan, hoped men's groups would help men raise their consciousness as well as be part of an enriching process that could help men identify a more sensitive self entombed within the hard shell of masculinity. Griswold, *Fatherhood in America*, 250.

37. Telephone interview with Owen O'Donnell, February 12, 2012. The timing as well as the nature of the men's group was not unusual, according to Todd Gitlin, who comments on the movement to self-examination in the 1970s: "The sea change from politics to personal salvation and the cultivation of personal relations also gave movement men, at the turn of the decade, a way to cope with women's liberation. Sulking, they organized 'men's groups.' Political subjects came up, but it was the therapeutic spirit that rode highest." Gitlin, *The Sixties: Years of Hope, Days of Rage*, rev. ed. (New York: Bantam Books, 1989), 427. R. W. Connell provides a more nuanced academic view of the emergence of men's groups in the period, describing them as initially a potentially complementary movement to women's liberation by helping men break out of the traditional male role to become more sensitive and emotionally expressive. R. W. Connell, *Masculinities* (Berkeley: University of California Press, 1995), 206–7.

38. Kaiser and Lieberman, *Later Life*, 105–7. The author of two books bemoaning the loss of male authority to feminist demands, *Sexual Suicide* (New York: Quadrangle, 1973) and *Wealth and Poverty* (New York: Basic Books, 1981), George Gilder argued that women and their families served as a necessary check on men's natural antisocial behavior. "The liberationists have no idea where their program would take us," Gilder proclaimed in *Sexual Suicide*, 7. "They are promoting in the United States an epidemic of erotic and social disorders." Gilder was editor of the *Ripon Forum*, the journal of the liberal Republican policy and advocacy organization I was president of in the early 1970s. He and I went our separate ways politically as he, and the Republican Party, turned sharply to the right.

39. Interview with Nicholas Danforth, Weston, MA, December 5, 2011; e-mail communication with Nicholas Danforth, February 4, 2013. Among the problems Danforth was introduced to through this relationship were common gender-based traditions—some still prevalent in many African areas, including "dry sex," when male partners, apparently in an effort to discourage female sexual pleasure, will not allow their partners to use vaginal secretions or lubricants; the beating, even murdering, of women found using birth control by jealous partners suspecting infidelity; and induced, septic

abortion, manifested in averages of 20–30 percent of beds in maternity wards in sub-Saharan Africa occupied by women with dangerous hemorrhage or infection. Such traditions, she explained, were all very dangerous for women's gynecological and obstetric health—especially "dry sex," which is especially painful for women and often leads to HIV/AIDS and other sexually transmitted infections.

40. David J. Garrow, *Liberty and Sexuality: The Right to Privacy and the Making of Roe v. Wade* (New York: Macmillan, 1994), 498, 493–94, 514–17; Sarah Weddington, *A Question of Choice* (New York: G. P. Putnam's Sons, 1992), 85.

41. *New York Times*, August 31, 1975.

42. Judith Walzer Leavitt provides a larger context for the shift in mores that brought men increasingly into the birthing process, in *Make Room for Daddy: The Journey from Waiting Room to Birthing Room* (Chapel Hill: University of North Carolina Press, 2009).

43. Danforth interview, December 5, 2011; Cheryl W. Thompson, "Businesswoman, Man Shot to Death in Kalorama Home," *Washington Post*, October 16, 1997.

44. Danforth interview, December 5, 2011.

45. Kaiser and Lieberman, *Later Life*, 30.

46. Gay "conversion therapy," as it has come to be called, has hardly been abandoned in the twenty-first century—witness the publicized occupation of 2012 Republican presidential contender Michelle Bachman's husband—but as gay rights have advanced, the practice has been challenged in the courts. See Sheryl Gay Stolberg, "For Bachmann, Gay Rights Stand Reflects Mix of Issues and Faith," "Christian Counseling by Hopeful's Spouse Prompts Questions," *New York Times*, July 16, 2011; Erik Eckholm, "Gay 'Conversion Therapy' Faces Test in Courts," *New York Times*, November 27, 2012.

47. Telephone interview with Robert Ball, October 20, 2010; *Yale 1964: The Class at 50* (Hagerstown, MD: Reunion Press, 2014), 144.

48. *Ten Years Out*, 94; In Memoriam: Colston Young, at http://www.yale64.org/remembrances/young.htm.

49. '64 Class Notes, *Yale Alumni Magazine*, October 1998, 78.

50. Jim Rogers, *Investment Biker: Around the World with Jim Rogers* (New York: Random House, 1994); Skype interview with Jim Rogers, December 21, 2011.

51. Telephone interview with Brooks Carder, June 19, 2012. As bizarre as Dederich's October 1977 directive to change marriage partners was, the way for his policy was paved by broader societal patterns, including liberalization of California's statutes in 1976 to allow legal cohabitation. That prompted Synanon to establish a three-year trial period for couples to live together without marrying, after which they could undergo a "rite of separation." Rod Janzen, *The Rise and Fall of Synanon: A California Utopia* (Baltimore: Johns Hopkins University Press, 2001), 145–47.

52. *Ten Years Out*, 37; telephone interview with Peter Harding, November 15, 2012.

53. See Charles M. Blow's column "Santorum and the Sexual Revolution," *New York Times*, March 3, 2012.

54. "Vows: Michelle Mead and John Armor," *New York Times*, June 22, 2008; telephone interview with Michelle Mead Armor, January 25, 2012.

55. First published in 1953, *Playboy* may have been liberating in terms of publishing standards, but it did everything it could to preserve existing sex-role dichotomies along traditional lines. If David Allyn is right in his assessment that "hippies did not need lessons in creative copulation but their parents and older siblings did," then *The Joy of Sex* may have been the perfect handbook for this transitional generational cohort. Allyn, *Make Love, Not War*, 230.

56. Telephone interview with Michelle Mead Armor, January 31, 2012.

57. Ibid.

58. R. W. Connell, *Gender* (Cambridge, MA: Polity Press, 2002), 142.

59. John Charles Armor, *Six O'Clock Man* (Birmingham, AL: Southern University Press, 1988).

60. Later known as Democratic Socialists of America, the committee formed in 1977. Harrington's 1962 book, *The Other America: Poverty in the United States*, remains a classic 1960s volume.

61. Telephone interview with Thomas Roderick, October 17, 2012. Maxine Phillips ultimately became executive editor of *Dissent* before retiring in 2013 after twenty-eight years with the magazine.

62. Jessica Weiss, *To Have and to Hold: Marriage, the Baby Boom, and Social Change* (Chicago: University of Chicago Press, 2000). *Ten Years Out*, 37; telephone interview with John Hanold, November 27, 2012.

63. Weiss, *To Have and to Hold*, 226, 228.

64. William H. Chafe, *Women and Equality: Changing Patterns in American Culture* (New York: Oxford University Press, 1977), 149–52, 157–58, 148. Like Chafe, Robert Self, *All in the Family*, 11, uses

the contrast between negative and positive rights to address the central challenge in achieving gender equity, writing, "As Americans demanded new rights they tugged the state in two directions. In one direction, the state simply acknowledged new liberties and allowed citizens to pursue them unhindered. In the other, the state actively assisted citizens in fully exercising their newfound rights. This distinction has often been rendered as the difference between negative liberty, the right to be left alone, and positive liberty, the rights guaranteed by state action."

65. Stephanie Coontz, "Why Gender Equality Stalled," *New York Times*, February 17, 2013. On the critical question whether it was "much better for everyone involved if the man is the achiever outside the home and the woman takes care of the home and family," Coontz reports a shift from two-thirds in agreement in 1977 to two-thirds in disagreement in 1994, only to see that number in disagreement drop again before leveling off again at 65 percent in 2010. Feminists pressing for greater flexibility in the workforce have been disappointed in a lack of results, confirmed by a recent report, Tara Siegel Bernard, "In Paid Family Leave, U.S. Trails Most of the Globe," *New York Times*, February 23, 2013. That men too suffer from the lack of family-friendly policies at work is the thrust of Sheelah Kolhatkar's essay "Men Are People Too," *Bloomberg Businessweek*, June 3–9, 2013, 58–63.

8. Culture Wars and the University

1. *Ten Years Out: The Tenth Reunion Classbook, Yale 1964* (June 1974), 17.

2. The validity of the term "culture war" has evoked its own debate among scholars, captured nicely in the volume edited by E. J. Dionne Jr. and Michael Cromartie, *Is There a Culture War? A Dialogue on Values and American Public Life* (Washington, DC: Pew Research Center and the Brookings Institution, 2006). Undoubtedly rooted in the cultural divide that emerged in the 1960s, the "war" that heated up in the 1990s, as indicated in Edward Morgan's book cited in the introduction, *What Really Happened in the 1960s?*, was largely politically manufactured. It would be hard to suggest, however, that it did not have consequences reaching well beyond university campuses, even to the premier agents of national cultural philanthropy, the National Endowment for the Humanities and the National Endowment for the Arts. For prime examples of those consequences see Edward T. Linenthal and Thomas Engelhardt, eds., *History Wars: The Enola Gay and Other Battles for the American Past* (New York: Henry Holt, 1996), and Steven B. Dubin, *Displays of Power: Controversy in the American Museum from the Enola Gay to Sensation!* (New York: NYU Press, 2001).

3. David Horowitz and Jacob Laksin, *One-Party Classroom: How Radical Professors at America's Top Colleges Indoctrinate Students and Undermine Our Democracy* (New York: Crown Forum, 2009); Dinesh D'Souza, *Illiberal Education : The Politics of Race and Sex on Campus* (New York: Free Press, 1991); Roger Kimball, *Tenured Radicals: How Politics Has Corrupted Our Higher Education*, 3rd ed. (Chicago: Ivan Dee, 2008); Roger Kimball, *The Long March: How the Culture Revolution of the 1960s Changed America* (San Francisco: Encounter Books, 2000). Bruce Bawer brings the conservative cultural critique of the university up to date in *The Victims' Revolution: The Rise of Identity Studies and the Closing of the Liberal Mind* (New York: Broadside, 2012). In promoting the "Contract with America" that propelled Republicans into control of both houses of Congress in 1994, Newt Gingrich reiterated the belief that university faculties were dominated by tenured radicals who "have now become the comfortable, all-purpose 'deconstructionists' of American culture." As a primary example of the egregious effects of such domination, Gingrich cited Yale's decision to return a $20 million gift to oilman Lee Bass because "after several years the university could not get the faculty to agree to teach Western Civilization." Newt Gingrich, *To Renew America* (New York: HarperCollins, 1995), 220. George Will helps account for the timing of this phenomenon, writing, "Bloom and other conservative critics gave voice to a set of cultural anxieties that the Reagan revolution barely addressed, anxieties that no amount of economic growth or military might could really salve. Conservatives increasingly warned of the threats to our moderate commercial democracy posed by the permissiveness and easy self-indulgence that were undermining the (sometimes) hard disciplines of family life and sexual restraint. It seems doubtful that such anxieties were ever far from the surface of the popular mind, even if some intellectuals have been apt to forget them." Foreword to *Reassessing the Sixties: Debating the Political and Cultural Legacy*, ed. Stephen Macedo (New York: W.W. Norton, 1997), 11.

4. Brook Thomas, *The New Historicism and Other Old-Fashioned Topics* (Princeton, NJ: Princeton University Press, 1991), vii. The reference to opening the American mind is to Allan Bloom's widely circulated and commented-upon book, *The Closing of the American Mind* (New York: Simon & Schuster, 1987).

5.   Alvin Kernan, *The Death of Literature* (New Haven, CT: Yale University Press, 1990), 8. If there were ever any doubts that Kernan blamed the changes he decried from the 1960s, especially as they radiated out from universities, he put them to rest in a subsequent essay, bemoaning the time when "the sweet smell of marijuana floated through the dormitories, and the sound of gunfire crackled in the groves of academe. . . . Free-speech movements coarsened the vocabulary of higher education, and student protests, strikes, and sit-ins were only the most visible of many continuing challenges to *in loco parentis* authority." Alvin Kernan, "Change in the Humanities and Higher Education," in *What's Happened to the Humanities?*, ed. Kernan (Princeton, NJ: Princeton University Press, 1997), 14–15.

6.   Alvin Kernan, *In Plato's Cave* (New Haven, CT: Yale University Press), xvi.

7.   Interview with Stephen Greenblatt, Cambridge, MA, December 6, 2011; quoted in Mitchell Stephens, "The Professor of Disenchantment," *West* magazine (*San Jose Mercury*), March 1, 1992, http://www.nyu.edu/classes/stephens/Greenblatt%20page.htm.

8.   Greenblatt interview, December 6, 2011. Alvin Kernan was convinced enough that this was the case to write a four-page lament of how he perceived Greenblatt had broken with him as both friend and mentor: "I was . . . startled when, some years later, without naming me, Steve, who by then was a professor at Berkeley and had progressed mightily in the academic world, wrote a piece in a prominent journal in which he expounded an oedipal theory of intellectual development, making it clear that it was very important for him to feel that he was entirely the author of his own achievements." Too bad, he concluded, "but a brilliant student inevitably adds to a master's sense that the world has passed him by, a bit before he thought it was his time to leave the stage." *In Plato's Cave*, 283, 286.

9.   Thomas, *New Historicism*, 20.

10.   E-mail communication with Stephen Greenblatt, January 8, 2013; Greenblatt, quoted in Jeffrey J. Williams, "Critical Self-Fashioning: An Interview with Stephen J. Greenblatt," *Minnesota Review* (Winter/Spring 2009), www.theminnesotareview.org/journal/ns7172/interview_greenblatt.shtml.

11.   Kernan, *Death of Literature*, 7.

12.   Stephens, "Professor of Disenchantment"; Williams, "Critical Self-Fashioning." Greenblatt provides a thorough summary of the early influences on his academic career in *Learning to Curse: Essays in Early Modern Culture* (New York: Routledge, 1990), 1–3.

13.   Stephen Greenblatt, *Renaissance Self-Fashioning: From More to Shakespeare* (Chicago: University of Chicago Press, 1980), 3, 5.

14.   Stephens, "Professor of Disenchantment."

15.   Stephen Greenblatt, "Towards a Poetics of Culture," in *The Greenblatt Reader*, ed. Michael Payne (Malden, MA: Blackwell, 2005), 18–19.

16.   Catherine Gallagher and Stephen Greenblatt, *Practicing the New Historicism* (Chicago: University of Chicago Press, 2000), 4. See especially Greenblatt's discussion of Raymond Williams's antagonism to Marxist literary criticism, 60–66.

17.   Adam Begley, "The Tempest around Stephen Greenblatt," *New York Times Magazine*, March 28, 1993; Kernan, *In Plato's Cave*, 285.

18.   Williams, "Critical Self-Fashioning."

19.   The *Washington Post* book columnist Michael Dirda pointed out Greenblatt's failure to acknowledge Bloom's embrace of "the swerve," a concept he labeled "clinamen," as derived from Lucretius's extended poem *On the Nature of Things* at the heart of Greenblatt's book. True to form, Greenblatt differed markedly in his use of the analogy drawn from Lucretius, referring to atoms as they occasionally swerve from their otherwise straight fall in the void. While Bloom used the concept to suggest the nature of influence within a confined literary space, Greenblatt's concept, in the spirit of his era, was much more dynamic and comprehensive in epitomizing a startling shift in culture manifest in the Renaissance, about which he has written so significantly. Michael Dirda, review of *The Swerve*, *Washington Post*, September 21, 2011; Robert Pogue Harrison, "The Faith of Harold Bloom," *New York Review of Books*, October 13, 2011, 42.

20.   Greenblatt confirmed the story he originally shared with classmates Thomas Trowbridge and Henry Putzel in his December 6, 2011, interview with me.

21.   See Jeffrey J. Williams, "Prodigal Critics," *Chronicle of Higher Education*, December 6, 2009.

22.   Frank Lentricchia, *After the New Criticism* (Chicago: University of Chicago Press, 1980), 342, 345.

23.   Harold Bloom, *The Anatomy of Influence: Literature as a Way of Life* (New Haven, CT: Yale University Press, 2011), 5.

24.   Harold Bloom, *The Western Canon: The Books and School of the Ages* (New York: Harcourt Brace & Co., 1994), 23, 29. Elsewhere, Bloom labels contemporary critics "gender and power freaks,"

responsible for "arbitrary and imposed contextualization, the staple of our bad time." Harold Bloom, *Shakespeare: The Invention of the Human* (New York: Riverhead Books, 1998), 10, 9. Similarly, the former Cornell University professor Walter Berns claims that the new historicism reduces Shakespeare's plays to "simply reflect the prejudices of his day. They are said to be worthy of study only because in them can be found the seeds of racism, sexism, capitalism, classism, all the evils that are said to characterize bourgeois society." "The Assault on the Universities: Then and Now," in Macedo, *Reassessing the Sixties*, 180–81.

25. George Will, "Literary Politics," *Newsweek*, April 22, 1991; Stephen Greenblatt, "The Best Way to Kill Our Literary Inheritance Is to Turn It into a Decorous Celebration of the New World Order," *Chronicle of Higher Education*, June 12, 1991, reprinted in *Public Culture* 4 (Fall 1991): 144–48. The exchange is further taken up and Greenblatt defended in Gerald Graff, *Beyond the Culture Wars: How Teaching the Conflicts Can Revitalize American Education* (New York: W. W. Norton, 1992), 160–63. Responding directly to Bloom's characterization of his work as part of a School of Resentment, Greenblatt used similar language in a more academic defense of the new historicism, noting that while he and his colleagues tended to be more skeptical, wary, critical, and even adversarial, "we have never given up or turned our backs on the deep gratification that draws us in the first place to the study of literature and art. Our project has never been about diminishing or belittling the power of artistic representations, even those with the most problematic entailments, but we never believe that our appreciation of this power necessitates either ignoring the cultural matrix out of which the representations emerge or uncritically endorsing the fantasies that the representations articulate." Gallagher and Greenblatt, *Practicing the New Historicism*, 8–9.

26. Kimball quoted in Stephens, "Professor of Disenchantment"; Kernan, *Death of Literature*, 76. Kernan's comments conform closely to the charge, made in 1992 by the National Endowment for the Humanities chair Lynne Cheney, that "an increasingly influential view is that there is no truth to tell: What we think of as truth is merely a cultural construct, serving to empower some and oppress others. Since power and politics are part of every quest for knowledge—so it is argued—professors are perfectly justified in using the classroom to advance political agendas." Lynne Cheney, *Telling the Truth: A Report on the State of the Humanities in Higher Education* (Washington, DC: National Endowment for the Humanities, 1992), 7, cited in Lawrence W. Levine: *The Opening of the American Mind: Canons, Culture, and History* (Boston: Beacon Press, 1996), 158.

27. Greenblatt, *Renaissance Self-Fashioning*, 256–57.

28. Kernan receives some support for his dark view of campus life in Paul Bass and Douglas W. Rae, *Murder in the Model City: The Black Panthers, Yale, and the Redemption of a Killer* (New York: Basic Books, 2006). At the same time, Bass and Rae identify Vice President Agnew's call for Kingman Brewster's ouster at the height of the controversy as a new front in what would later come to be known as America's culture war (142). While Geoffrey Kabaservice, in *The Guardians: Kingman Brewster, His Circle, and the Rise of the Liberal Establishment* (New York: Henry Holt, 2004), 401–12, generally credits Brewster with managing the crisis, Roger Kimball, *The Long March*, 120–26, joins Kernan in blaming the Yale administration for a "liberal capitulation." Kimball (111–20) links the Yale protests with the black student takeover at Cornell the same year. A more balanced account of the events at Cornell can be found in Donald Alexander Downs, *Cornell '69: Liberalism and the Crisis of the American University* (Ithaca, NY: Cornell University Press, 1999).

29. Kernan, *In Plato's Cave*, 161. Kernan had plenty of support for his criticism among academics in his generation, including Columbia University historian Richard Hofstadter and Yale Law School professor Ralph Winter. Dennis Deslippe, *Protesting Affirmative Action: The Struggle over Equality after the Civil Rights Revolution* (Baltimore: Johns Hopkins University Press, 2012), 72, 77.

30. Robert Bork, *Slouching towards Gomorrah: Modern Liberalism and American Decline* (New York: HarperCollins, 1996), 36, 53, 2. In his comments Bork echoes William Bradford Reynolds's similar assertion in defending the Reagan civil rights record when he complained, "We suffer today from a wholesale breakdown of societal values. Respect is flagging for the individual, the family, and the community. Large segments of our population now hold in contempt moral standards that once mattered. . . . Having cleared the road to equal opportunity of much of that debris, we find still standing in the way impediments of another sort, stemming principally from a breakdown in both our educational and our moral systems." William Bradford Reynolds, "The Reagan Administration's Civil Rights Policy: The Challenge for the Future," *Vanderbilt Law Review* 42 (1989): 1000–1001.

31. William Roth, *The Assault on Social Policy* (New York: Columbia University Press, 2002), 5; William Roth and Katharine Briar-Lawson, eds., *Globalization, Social Justice, and the Helping Professions* (Albany: SUNY Press, 2011), 232, 87.

32. William Roth, "Handicap as a Social Construct," *Society* 20 (March/April 1983): 57, opens with the declaration, "Although there is clearly a biological difference between the disabled and the able-bodied, this is not the decisive difference between the two groups. Handicap is a social construction. There is a biological substratum, but what it means to be handicapped to others and to oneself is overwhelmingly social and decisively political."

33. Although Reich was not a significant presence among undergraduates in the first part of the 1960s, a speech he gave to Young Democrats in the spring of 1964 was distinctive in that he extended his criticism well beyond racial discrimination to attack a recent stop-and-frisk law enacted in New York and called for higher taxes on the rich. *Yale Daily News*, March 5, 1964.

34. Kimball, *Long March*, 111–26; Berns, "Assault on the Universities," 157–69.

35. Telephone interview with Frederick Buell, February 16, 2012. Buell elaborates his argument that Thoreau's "Walking" involves a change of consciousness, in *From Apocalypse to Way of Life: Environmental Crisis in the American Century* (New York: Routledge, 2003), 205.

36. Frederick Buell, *W. H. Auden as a Social Poet* (Ithaca, NY: Cornell University Press, 1973), 2.

37. Frederick Buell, *National Culture and the New Global System* (Baltimore: Johns Hopkins University Press, 1994); *From Apocalypse to Way of Life*, 16; Buell interview, February 16, 2012; e-mail January 1, 2013.

38. E-mail communication with T. H. Breen, January 15, 2013.

39. T. H. Breen and Stephen Innes, *"Myne Owne Ground": Race and Freedom on Virginia's Eastern Shore, 1640–1676* (New York: Oxford University Press, 1980), 20, 113–14.

40. T. H. Breen, *The Marketplace of Revolution: How Consumer Politics Shaped American Independence* (New York: Oxford University Press, 2004), 331.

41. T. H. Breen, *American Insurgents, American Patriots: The Revolution of the People* (New York: Hill & Wang, 2010); Jan Ellen Lewis, *Washington Post*, August 8, 2010; T. H. Breen, "Whose Revolution Is This?" *Washington Post*, March 31, 2010.

42. T. H. Breen, *Imagining the Past: East Hampton Histories* (Reading, MA: Addison-Wesley, 1989), 14–15.

43. Stephen Greenblatt, *Will in the World: How Shakespeare Became Shakespeare* (New York: W. W. Norton, 2004), 173, 113.

44. Ibid., 314–17.

45. Ibid., 311, 321, 318.

46. Stephen Greenblatt, *Hamlet in Purgatory* (Princeton, NJ: Princeton University Press, 2001), 4–7.

47. Stephen Greenblatt, *Shakespeare's Freedom* (Chicago: University of Chicago Press, 2010), 1.

48. Stephen Greenblatt, *Shakespearean Negotiations* (Berkeley: University of California Press, 1988), 3, 5. The contrast with Bloom on Shakespeare is stark, as Bloom writes, "Though professional resenters insist that the aesthetic stance is itself an ideology, I scarcely agree, and I bring nothing but the aesthetic . . . to Shakespeare in this book. . . . Even now, when our education has faltered, and Shakespeare is battered and truncated by our fashionable ideologues, the ideologues themselves are caricatures of Shakespearean energies." Bloom, *Shakespeare*, 9, 13.

49. Adam Gopnik, "Will Power," *New Yorker*, September 13, 2004.

50. Greenblatt, *Will in the World*, 286.

51. Stephen Greenblatt, "Shakespeare and Shylock," *New York Review of Books*, September 30, 2010, 91.

52. Stephen Greenblatt, "Story-Telling," *Threepenny Review* 11 (1990): 23, reprinted in Payne, *Greenblatt Reader*, 306.

53. Sydney Lea, *A Hundred Himalayas: Essays on Life and Literature* (Ann Arbor: University of Michigan Press, 2012), 41, 44; Lea, "Dirge for My Brother," in *To the Bone: New and Selected Poems* (Urbana: University of Illinois Press, 1996), 84.

54. Sydney Lea, "Fourth of July," in *To the Bone*, 25.

55. Lea, *Hundred Himalayas*, 9, 13.

56. Robert G. Kaiser and Jethro K. Lieberman, eds., *Later Life: The 25th Reunion Classbook; The Class of 1964* (New Haven, CT: Yale University, 1989), 249.

57. Lea, *Hundred Himalayas*, xi.

58. Telephone interview with Sydney Lea, September 10, 2012; Kaiser and Lieberman, *Later Life*, 249.

59. Sally Pollak, "In Frost's Footsteps: Vermont Poet Laureate Sydney Lea," *Burlington Free Press*, October 9, 2011.

60. Lea interview, September 10, 2012. The weak poet, Bloom argued in *The Anxiety of Influence*, is one who is unable to transcend the influence of his predecessors in order to assure his own survival into posterity.

61. Lea, *Hundred Himalayas*, 73–74, 78.

62. In his 1991 exchange with George Will, Greenblatt retorted, "The columnist George F. Will recently declared that Lynne V. Cheney, the chairman of the National Endowment for the Humanities, is 'secretary of domestic defense.' 'The foreign adversaries her husband, Dick, must keep at bay,' Mr. Will wrote, 'are less dangerous, in the long run, than the domestic forces with which she must deal.' Who are these homegrown enemies, more dangerous even than Saddam Hussein with his arsenal of chemical weapons? The answer: professors of literature. You know, the kind of people who belong to that noted terrorist organization, the Modern Language Association." Greenblatt, "Best Way to Kill Our Literary Inheritance," 146.

63. Lea, *Hundred Himalayas*, xiii.

64. Self employs language very close to that used by Greenblatt in describing his own approach to literature, when he writes of rights activists, "They argued that men, male and female, sex and sexuality are in the end socially constituted, made by human society. As such, they can be remade." Robert Self, *All in the Family: The Realignment of American Democracy since the 1960s* (New York: Hill & Wang, 2012), 13–14. In an earlier affirmation of the family's central role in a hardening political divide based in cultural difference, Rosalind Pollack Petchesky writes, "Far more than an opportunistic appeal to the 'irrational,' the New Right represents a highly conscious conservative response to those broad and changing social conditions. . . . This backlash is aimed primarily at those organizations and ideas that have most directly confronted patriarchal traditions regarding the place of women in society and the dominant norms of heterosexual love and marriage. But it is also a reaction to the New Left and the counterculture generally, which many white middle-class parents experienced as having robbed them of their children, either literally or spiritually." "Antiabortion, Antifeminism, and the Rise of the New Right," *Feminist Studies* 7 (Summer 1981): 234–35.

Conclusion

1. David Brooks, *Bobos in Paradise: The New Upper Class and How They Got There* (New York: Simon & Schuster, 2000), 41, 45, 43. Jack Whalen and Richard Flacks provide another way of viewing the accommodation Brooks describes, calling it a trade-off between settling for "alienating" jobs while still revealing "an eager willingness to express self and seek pleasure through an unprecedented elaboration of leisure-time consumption." *Beyond the Barricades: The Sixties Generation Grows Up* (Philadelphia: Temple University Press, 1989), 268.

2. Charles Murray, *Coming Apart: The State of White America, 1960–2010* (New York: Crown Forum, 2012); Christopher Hayes, *Twilight of the Elites: America after Meritocracy* (New York: Crown, 2012), 22.

3. Before the election of Barak Obama in 2008, Joseph Soares notes, a Yale degree holder had been sitting as president for twenty successive years, and the presence of at least one Yale man in national presidential elections had gone all the way back to 1968. Joseph A. Soares, *The Power of Privilege: Yale and America's Elite Colleges* (Stanford, CA: Stanford University Press, 2007), 5.

4. Nedra Pickler, Associated Press, "Obama Nominating 3 to US Appeals Court," *Philadelphia Inquirer*, June 5, 2013.

5. Yale director of admissions Jeremiah Quinlan confirmed as much when he told an interviewer, "In America, institutions of higher education are meant to promote social mobility, and right now, Yale and other leading universities aren't serving that function. For the most part they are replicating existing inequalities." A chart accompanying the article ranked Yale, at 14 percent, ahead of only Princeton among Ivy League peers in the number of its undergraduates receiving Pell grants, federally funded scholarships that provide a good measure of success in enrolling low-income students. Twenty percent of Harvard students receive Pell grants. David Zax, "Wanted: Smart Students from Poor Families," *Yale Alumni Magazine*, January/February 2014.

6. Brooks, *Bobos in Paradise*, 25, 30. It should be noted that Ivy League institutions in the 1960s were doing exactly what sociologist E. Digby Baltzell, who famously popularized the term WASP (White Anglo-Saxon Protestant), hoped for when he wrote, "In a free society, while an establishment will always be dominated by upper-class members, it also must be constantly rejuvenated by new members of the elite who are in the process of acquiring upper-class status." That this process owed much

to shifting admissions policies at elite schools Baltzell had no doubt, writing, "This indeed represents a systematic policy of aristocratic assimilation, as caste on the campus has steadily retreated before the modern admissions policies which stress individual accomplishment rather than family background." *The Protestant Establishment: Aristocracy and Class in America* (New York: Random House, 1964), 8, 341.

7. Interview with Angus Macbeth, Washington, DC, December 13, 2010.

8. Robert G. Kaiser and Jethro K. Lieberman, eds., *Later Life: The 25th Reunion Classbook; The Class of 1964* (New Haven, CT: Yale University, 1989), 399.

9. "Breaking the Logjam: Environmental Reform for the New Congress and Administration," http://www.breakingthelogjam.org/CMS/index.php?cID=80; David Schoenbrod, Richard B. Stewart, and Katrina M. Wyman, *Breaking the Logjam: Environmental Protection That Will Work* (New Haven, CT: Yale University Press, 2010). Not finding members of Congress initially responsive to the project proposals, Schoenbrod determined to further press his case through another book that was nearing completion at the end of 2014, "Congress without Tricks." Laying out the elements of an "Honest Deal," Schoenbrod made the hopeful pronouncement in a November 5, 2013, telephone interview that there were enough incentives for members of Congress to change direction that his program could actually take effect.

10. E-mail communication with Stephen Greenblatt, January 8, 2013.

11. Robert Self, *All in the Family: The Realignment of American Democracy since the 1960s* (New York: Hill & Wang, 2012), 50.

12. Gail Collins, "Political Page Turners," *New York Times*, August 18, 2012. In his own assessment of the retiring senator, *Washington Post* columnist Michael Gerson quoted Lieberman as saying, "I don't know how much Democrats want to hear my advice," and added in his own words, "It is an indictment of both main parties that a supporter of civil rights, economic justice, strong defense, economic opportunity and religious values should end his service as a party of one." Michael Gerson, "Joe Lieberman, Party of One," *Washington Post*, September 3, 2012. No doubt Gerson, who headed George W. Bush's speechwriting team at the time that the United States invaded Iraq, viewed Lieberman's political exile sympathetically.

13. Lieberman provided a summary of his position in a 2003 statement: "The Democratic Party is the party of the American Dream. We believe that every person born on our soil or arriving at our shores who works hard and plays by the rules should be able to go as far as their God-given talent takes them. We believe that each one of us has a responsibility to one another and to our nation. We believe in a national community, rich in diversity and united around our shared values and aspirations. We believe in an America that is an arsenal for democracy and a beacon for freedom the world over." "The Dream Scenario," in *Crossroads: The Future of American Politics*, ed. Andrew Cuomo (New York: Random House, 2003), 167.

14. Interview with Joseph Lieberman, Stamford, CT, May 18, 2012.

15. Cited in Daniel T. Rodgers, *Age of Fracture* (Cambridge, MA: Belknap Press of Harvard University Press, 2011), 16.

16. Joseph I. Lieberman, "Turn the Tide against Bashar al-Assad," *Washington Post*, May 17, 2012. In this, Lieberman was embracing George W. Bush's "freedom agenda" as spelled out especially in Bush's 2005 inaugural and actively promoted especially in his second term.

17. In describing the way liberals crafted the war in Vietnam over time, David Burner makes the domestic and foreign policy connections overt, writing that the American presence abroad "was supposed to bring the effusion of expert knowledge and democratic progressivism that had characterized domestic liberalism at least since the New Deal." *Making Peace with the 60s* (Princeton, NJ: Princeton University Press, 1996), 195.

18. Byron Tau, "Joe Lieberman to Join Conservative Think Tank," *Politico*, March 11, 2013. Zack Beauchamp, writing on the ThinkProgress website the same day, pointed out that Lieberman would be joining former Bush administration officials and advocates for the invasion of Iraq John Bolton and Richard Perle. Additionally, in November 2013 Lieberman joined the advisory board of United against Nuclear Iran, where he promptly cautioned against diplomatic efforts to negotiate a halt to Iran's nuclear program development. See *Politico*, November 14, 2013, and the *Washington Post*, November 21, 2013.

19. John A. Andrew III, *The Other Side of the Sixties: Young Americans for Freedom and the Rise of Conservative Politics* (New Brunswick, NJ: Rutgers University Press, 1997), 5. See also Rebecca Klatch, *A Generation Divided: The New Left, the New Right, and the 1960s* (Berkeley: University of California Press, 1999).

20. An adviser to Nixon campaign manager John Mitchell (Mitchell subsequently became Nixon's polarizing attorney general), Phillips assured Republicans that they could profit from at least one aspect of the civil rights campaign, the Voting Rights Act of 1965. The purpose was not to secure the support of African American voters but quite the opposite, as he advised, "Maintenance of Negro voting rights in Dixie, far from being contrary to GOP interests, is essential if southern conservatives are to be pressured into switching to the Republican Party—for Negroes are beginning to seize control of the national Democratic Party in some Black Belt areas." Kevin P. Phillips, *The Emerging Republican Majority* (New Rochelle, NY: Arlington House, 1969), 464. Not shy about his ambitions to drive political realignment, Phillips rejected the idea that increased support for Democrats among African Americans would more than compensate for the loss of support among whites. "No," he told Gary Wills, "white Democrats will desert their party in droves the minute it becomes a black party." Gary Wills, *Nixon Agonistes: The Crisis of the Self-Made Man* (Boston: Houghton Mifflin, 1970), 267. Nate Cohn, "Why a Democratic Majority Has Yet to Materialize," *New York Times*, April 24, 2014, credits the GOP success among white males in the South in particular in remaking the party and its identity.

21. Tanya Melich, *The Republican War against Women: An Insider's Report from behind the Lines*, updated paperback ed. (New York: Bantam, 1998), 31–32; Self, *All in the Family*, 3.

22. Ripon emerged publicly in the form of a thirty-six-hundred-word manifesto issued by *Advance*, then being coedited for liberal Republicans by George Gilder, Harvard 1962, calling for a presidential candidate with "those qualities of vision, intellectual force, humaneness and courage that America saw and admired in John F. Kennedy, not in a specious effort to fall heir to his mantle, but because our times demand no lesser greatness." Quoted in Rick Pearlstein, *Before the Storm: Barry Goldwater and the Unmaking of the American Consensus* (New York: Hill & Wang, 2001), 285–86.

23. Geoffrey Kabaservice, *Rule and Ruin: The Downfall of Moderation and the Destruction of the Republican Party* (New York: Oxford University Press, 2012), 333; Gail Collins, "The State of the 4-Year-Olds," *New York Times*, February 13, 2013; Nancy L. Cohen, "Why America Never Had Universal Child Care," *New Republic*, April 24, 2013. Melich, *Republican War against Women*, 31–32, recounts how Republican feminists objected to Nixon's claim that provisions of the Comprehensive Child Development Bill sponsored by senators Javits and Mondale would weaken the family. "Republican feminists were startled," she recounts. "We were in the process of formulating our 'wish list' of women's issues to submit to the president's campaign, and here was the president opposing the right of women to choose whether they would work."

24. E-mails from George Gilder, December 13, 2012, and Tanya Melich, December 12, 2012.

25. This was the argument I made in assessing Nixon's first term in *Jaws of Victory: The Game-Plan Politics of 1972, the Crisis of the Republican Party, and the Future of the Constitution*, ed. Clifford Brown Jr. (Boston: Little, Brown, 1973), 26–48. Agnew tied together this polarizing strategy with his courtship of the South in addressing a GOP dinner in Jackson, Mississippi, only days after launching his offensive. There he declared that "for too long the South has been the punching bag for those who characterize themselves as liberal intellectuals.... This group may consider itself liberal, but it is undeniable that it is more comfortable with radicals. These are the ideas of the men who are taking control of the Democratic Party." That there was little doubt that Nixon sanctioned Agnew's attack was subsequently confirmed in entries to his chief of staff Bob Haldeman's diary: "Now have to take the offensive. Tag those involved with left-wing—and take the heat." Quoted in Rick Pearlstein, *Nixonland: The Rise of a President and the Fracturing of America* (New York: Scribner, 2008), 431.

26. David T. Courtwright, *No Right Turn: Conservative Politics in a Liberal America* (Cambridge, MA: Harvard University Press, 2010), 89.

27. Liddy cited in Pearlstein, *Nixonland*, 667.

28. Bernard von Bothmer, *Framing the Sixties: The Use and Abuse of a Decade from Ronald Reagan to George W. Bush* (Amherst: University of Massachusetts Press, 2010), 127, captures the way Buchanan managed to succinctly tie the Clintons to a period when "radicals and liberals dressed up as moderates and centrists" by charging, "There is a religious war going on in our country for the soul of America. It is a cultural war, as critical to the kind of nation we will one day be as was the Cold War itself. And in that struggle for the soul of America, [Bill] Clinton and [Hillary] Clinton are on the other side, and George Bush is on our side." Gingrich, von Bothmer notes (167), chose to mark the triumph of the 1994 Republican campaign to take control of both branches of Congress by declaring the Clintons "countercultural McGovernicks" representative of a "quaint period of Bohemianism brought to the national elite." Credited with inventing the term "silent majority," it was Buchanan whose speeches for Vice President Agnew established the theme of demonizing the 1960s, a theme he later revived in his 1992 convention address.

29. James Davison Hunter, *Culture Wars: The Struggle to Define America* (New York: Basic Books, 1991), 34, 42. While Hunter's stark evaluation of the nation's political divide is contested, not the least from Boston College's Alan Wolfe—whose book title, *One Nation, after All* (New York: Viking, 1998), itself conveys another view—both men agree that the country is more universally located at the moderate middle than contemporary discourse would suggest. It is institutions of disproportionate influence and the elites who manage them, political and intellectual, however, that keep the culture war alive. Suggesting why the cultural divide has been so persistent, Davidson later amplified his understanding, writing, "Underneath the push and pull of these institutional conflicts were competing moral ideals as to how public life ought to be ordered and maintained. These are not mere political ideologies, reducible to party platforms or political scorecards, but moral visions from which the policy discussions and political disputes derived their passion. Embedded within institutions, these ideals were articulated in innumerable ways with every conceivable nuance and shade of variation. As they were translated into the signs and symbols of public discourse, however, they lost their complexity and nuance and thus divided into sharply antagonistic tendencies." See "The Enduring Culture War," in *Is There a Culture War? A Dialogue on Values and American Public Life*, ed. E. J. Dionne Jr. and Michael Cromartie (Washington, DC: Pew Research Center and the Brookings Institution, 2006), 14.

30. The class poll commissioned for '64's fiftieth reunion proved somewhat contradictory itself. Of the 422 respondents, 83 percent affirmed that they were the product of an educational system that favors the privileged. At the same time, an even greater number, 93 percent, affirmed the belief that that same education "rewards the talented." Although 46.1 percent of those polled felt things had gone in a "totally unexpected direction" in their lives, only 14.9 percent felt they had tried to fulfill their dreams and failed. *Yale 1964: The Class at 50* (Hagerstown, MD: Reunion Press, 2014), 97, 99.

31. Ibid., 402. Kaiser spelled out his critical assessment of contemporary political life in two books: *So Damn Much Money: The Triumph of Lobbying and the Corrosion of American Government* (New York: Vintage, 2010), and *Act of Congress: How America's Essential Institution Works, and How It Doesn't* (New York: Alfred A. Knopf, 2013). He amplified the basis of his disillusion with Washington politics in an essay, "How Republicans Lost Their Minds, Democrats Lost Their Souls and Washington Lost Its Appeal," for the *Washington Post*, February 28, 2014. Although he pointed to a decline in intellectual as well as governing skills among Democrats, he reserved his harshest criticism for Republicans, noting that "the most consequential political development in my time has been the transformation of the Grand Old Party." The GOP shift to the right did not sit well with this class. While only 28 percent identified as Democrats in 1964 and 41 percent in 1989, 53 percent identified as such in 2014. Republican affiliation, on the other hand, dropped from 63 percent to 22 percent over the half century. More than 65 percent reported being more liberal than they had been in college, while 34.6 percent had become more conservative. *Yale 1964: The Class at 50*, 96, 103.

32. *Yale 1964: The Class at 50*, 378, 372; Gordon Davis, "Closing the Books on Global Climate Change," July 23, 2013, http://yale64.org/soundoff.php.

33. *Yale 1964: The Class at 50*, 709, 386, 708, 520. The interest in problem solving among 1964 graduates was not confined to Yale. At Amherst College, the class of 1964 titled its reunion "The World We Inherited and the World We Will Bequeath." In an effort not just to remember the past, reunion organizers invited classmates and their spouses to join a problem-solving team "to provide a forum for engaging with class members (and their family members) prior to, during and, perhaps, following the reunion."

34. Doug McAdam, *Freedom Summer* (New York: Oxford University Press, 1988), 13.

Acknowledgments

This book built from more than one hundred interviews of my Yale classmates. Some conversations lasted less than an hour. Others carried over several days. In every instance, I was gratified by the cooperation and interest I received. Where I have drawn directly from those interviews, I have included a footnote. On other occasions, I have drawn on the information in a more general sense, and for that reason not every classmate I interviewed appears directly in the text. I am equally grateful for this help each classmate provided. Readers interested in knowing more about these men can visit the Yale 1964 website at http://yale64.org/index.htm. Ably maintained by 1964's Sam Francis, this public site is a rich source of information about publications, issues, and activities related to this class. It also lists obituaries and testimonials to those class members who have died. A number of other people outside this class spoke to me: members of other Yale classes, spouses, and, in one instance, the surviving son of a deceased member. I want to thank especially Michelle Mead Armor and Lucy Moore for bringing the female perspective to their lives with Yale men.

My wife, Margaret Marsh, read an early version of the manuscript and made many valuable suggestions for shaping the argument. I am deeply grateful for her steadfast belief in and support for this project. My Ripon Society colleague and friend Tanya Melich read the conclusion and offered helpful suggestions for contextualizing the forces that marked the transformation of the Republican Party over the past half century. Jane Freundel Levey proved a masterly editorial coach as I entered the final stage of writing. I am grateful to her for jumping in with grace and intelligence, not the least when I was working under a tight deadline. Finally, I want to thank my editor at Cornell University Press, Michael McGandy, who took a chance on an unorthodox project, for me as well as for him, and continued to offer encouragement as we navigated the various checkpoints for securing final approval for publication.

Among the many things I agree with Gus Speth about is the importance educators have in steering succeeding generations to a better understanding of the world we live in. With that in mind, I have dedicated this book to my two sons, their wives, and their children. It's my hope that they will not just witness but help bring about some of changes my generation hoped for when we were young.

Index

Note: Italic page numbers refer to illustrations.